WORLD REGIONAL STUDIES

In recent years the teaching of history has reflected two trends: (1) a growing appreciation of the fact that the past of "Western man" constitutes only a small part of the history of the human race, and (2) recognition that discovery and analysis, interpretive thinking, and use of the inductive method provide important roads to learning. The first calls for the use of instructional materials that deal in depth with the lands, peoples, and cultures of the great world regions. The second is facilitated by the introduction of materials that encourage extensive reading and provide the necessary basis for analysis and inductive learning. The World Regional Studies series has been planned with both of these trends in mind.

Basal Texts. The World Regional Studies series includes a number of texts dealing in depth with important regions or leading nations of the world. Each of these regional volumes develops concepts that are derived from many fields of study — not only history but also the other social sciences and the humanities. Political and economic systems, geography, methods of communication, social organization, human values, the fine arts, and religion have all received attention.

Selected Readings. For each of the regional study texts there is a companion volume of selected readings. These books illuminate the evolution of ways of life which have been and continue to be different from our own. They include primary sources, selections from literary and religious works, and excerpts from readable books written by scholars. These readings provide opportunity not only for developing deeper understanding but also for further analysis and inductive learning. They may also be used advantageously to supplement other "area books" as well as any of the standard textbooks in world history.

The goal of the World Regional Studies series is to provide a well-rounded treatment of human experience in important areas around the globe. Without knowledge of traditions and ways of life different from our own, there can be no adequate understanding of the present-day world.

WORLD REGIONAL STUDIES

Hyman Kublin, General Editor

HOUGHTON MIFFLIN COMPANY ✓ **BOSTON**

Atlanta / Dallas / Geneva, Illinois / Hopewell, New Jersey / Palo Alto

AFRICA

Fred Burke

Editorial Consultant: Howard R. Anderson

Fred Burke

Commissioner of Education for the state of Rhode Island, Dr. Burke has written numerous books and articles on Africa. He received his Ph.D. from Princeton University and until 1971 was Dean of International Studies and World Affairs at the State University of New York at Buffalo. He was also the Director of the Program of Eastern African Studies at Syracuse University. Concerned primarily with problems of political change, Dr. Burke has spent a number of years working and living in Africa.

Hyman Kublin

Dr. Kublin, general editor for the World Regional Studies series, received his Ph.D. from Harvard University. At present he is Professor of History at Brooklyn College. Dr. Kublin has also taught at the University of California (Berkeley), the University of Delaware, and the University of Hawaii.

Howard R. Anderson

Dr. Anderson, consulting editor, taught social studies in the secondary schools of Michigan, Iowa, and New York. He also taught at the University of Iowa and at Cornell University, and has served as Provost of the University of Rochester and as President of the National Council for the Social Studies.

The author wishes to offer a special word of appreciation to Eva P. Ingle, who reviewed the manuscript and made many important contributions.

Title page: Headpiece, shaped in the form of an antelope's head and neck by the Bambara people of Mali.

Printed in the U.S.A.
Library of Congress Catalog Card Number: 73–8436
ISBN: 0–395–17716–2

CONTENTS

1. THE LANDS AND PEOPLES OF AFRICA   1

1. Seeing Africa as it is. 2. Africa is a vast continent. 3. Africa's climate and vegetation pose special problems. 4. Geography and climate have affected African ways of living. 5. Who are "Africans" and where did they come from? 6. African society is close-knit.

2. EARLY AFRICAN CIVILIZATIONS NORTH OF THE SUDAN   43

1. Egyptian civilization develops along the northern reaches of the Nile. 2. A rival center of power emerges in Ethiopia. 3. Mediterranean and Saharan cultures shape early North Africa. 4. Islamic civilization flourishes on African soil.

3. EARLY WEST AFRICAN CIVILIZATIONS SOUTH OF THE SAHARA   81

1. Ghana emerges at the crossroads of the gold trade. 2 The Mandingo people establish Mali as a great empire. 3. Songhai replaces Mali as West Africa's foremost power. 4. Other states continue the tradition of empire.

4. PATTERNS OF CHANGE IN CENTRAL AFRICA   119

1. Bantu peoples expand into central and eastern Africa. 2. Bantu kingdoms are established in the Great Lakes region. 3. Kingdoms rise and fall in Zimbabwe. 4. New Bantu states evolve in the Congo Basin.

5. THE ERA OF AFRICAN SLAVE TRADE   168

1. Europeans and Asians become interested in trade with Africa. 2. Portugal establishes an empire in Africa. 3. The slave trade cripples Africa's progress. 4. Several factors lead to direct European involvement in Africa.

6. CONQUEST AND COLONIAL RULE   198

1. European explorers and adventurers turn to Africa. 2. Renewed search for the sources of the Nile leads Europeans to the Great Lakes. 3. Missionaries become involved in the scramble for Africa. 4. Rivalry develops over control of Africa's resources. 5. African nationalism emerges during the post-World War I period.

7. TOWARD LIBERATION   242

1. The spirit of independence catches fire throughout Africa. 2. British colonies in West Africa win independence. 3. France's colonial empire in Africa opts for independence. 4. Independence comes slowly in areas with large numbers of European settlers. 5. African liberation is not complete.

8. PROBLEMS OF NATION-BUILDING IN AFRICA   289

1. Emerging countries must overcome many economic and social barriers to achieve a viable nationhood. 2. The fabric of traditional life is threatened by many changes. 3. Africans strive to preserve their cultural and political integrity.

BIBLIOGRAPHY   319

ACKNOWLEDGMENTS   321

INDEX   323

MAPS

The Land   6

The People   7

Ancient Africa   70

The Thrust of Islam   84

Bantu on the Move   149

Colonial Footholds — 1885   232

Colonial Empires — 1914   233

Africa Today   255

CHARTS

A Time Chart of African History:
3000 B.C.–1500 A.D.   viii

A Time Chart of African History: 1500–1970   ix

African Waterpower — An Undeveloped Resource   9

Africa's Largest Cities   16

Manpower Lost in the Slave Trade   190

Former Colonies Trade with France   261

"Single-Export" Economies   300

Sisal Production in Tanzania   301

1. A TIME CHART OF AFRICAN HISTORY: 3000 B.C. - 1500 A.D.

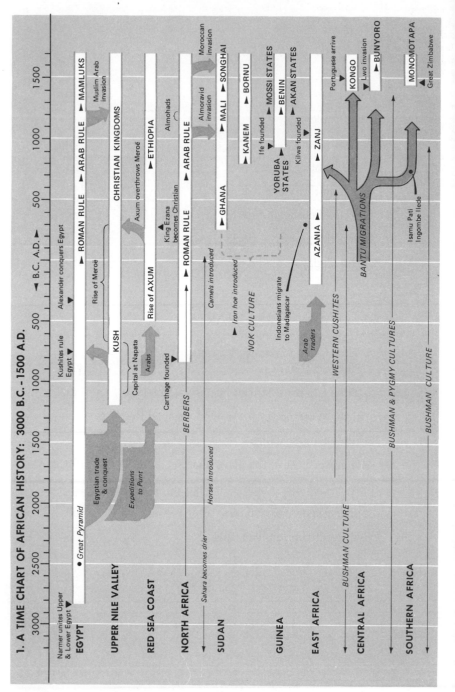

2. A TIME CHART OF AFRICAN HISTORY: 1500 - 1970

Time scale: 1500 · 1550 · 1600 · 1650 · 1700 · 1750 · 1800 · 1850 · 1900 · 1950

🏳 = INDEPENDENCE

EGYPT
MAMLUKS ► TURKISH RULE · Suez Canal opened · FR. & BR. INFLUENCE · Br. Protectorate · ► Br. leave Suez

UPPER NILE VALLEY
Egyptian conquest · Rule of the Mahdi · ANGLO-EGYPTIAN RULE

RED SEA COAST
Portuguese missions · Bruce at Gondar · Italians in Eritrea · Battle of Adowa · Italian conquest

ETHIOPIA

NORTH AFRICA
► TURKISH RULE over semi-indep. BARBARY STATES · Moroccan conquest · Fr. conquest of Algeria · Fr. Protectorates: ▼ Tunisia ▼ Morocco

SUDAN
SONGHAI · Mungo Park on Niger R. · Caillié at Timbuktu · ► FR. RULE · ► BR. RULE (Nigeria)

Rise of HAUSA STATES · ► FULANI EMIRS

KANEM-BORNU at its peak: *Mai Idriss*

GUINEA
YORUBA STATES · *Oyo at its peak* · SLAVE TRADE AT PEAK · ▼ Outlawed by Br. · • Liberia founded
► DAHOMEY
AKAN STATES form ASHANTI UNION · ► FR. RULE · ► BR. & FR. RULE · ► BR. RULE (Ghana)

EAST AFRICA
► PORTUGUESE RULE · Mombasa taken · ► OMANI ARABS · Capital at Zanzibar · Livingstone explores · Speke - Grant - Baker ▼ · *King Mutesa* · *Stanley's travels* · ► BR. RULE

CENTRAL AFRICA
KONGO ► Rise of LUBA & LUNDA KINGDOMS · ► CONGO (Belg.)

BUNYORO at peak · ► Rise of BUGANDA · ► BR. RULE

SOUTHERN AFRICA
Dutch land at Cape Town · Br. occupy Cape Town · Great Trek · Boer War · ► BR. RULE

MONOMOTAPA & CHANGAMIRE · BRITISH INFLUENCE · ◄ Zulu Empire

1

THE LANDS AND PEOPLES OF AFRICA

A learned scholar once wrote that "the study of landscapes is a good beginning for the study of societies of men because men must live on and off the land as a first condition of their survival."

How realistically do Americans see and understand Africa today? What are its major geographical features, its major climatic characteristics? How have geography and climate affected settlement, migration, and ways of living? Who are the Africans? How do they live? This chapter seeks to answer these important questions.

1. Seeing Africa As It Is

Herodotus, the ancient Greek historian, wrote more than two thousand years ago that Africa was

> the tract in which the huge serpents are found, and the lions, the elephants, bears, and the horned asses. Here, too, are the dog-faced creatures, and the creatures without heads, whom the Libyans declare to have their eyes in their breasts; and also the wild men and wild women and many other less fabulous beasts.

Surely more is known about Africa today; but many Americans still keep company with Herodotus and think of Africa primarily as a land of wild animals, naked savages, and dense, steaming jungles.

Lack of information has led to misunderstanding of Africa. Although Herodotus, more than 20 centuries ago, knew vaguely of the mysterious lands of the south, it was only about one century ago that the outside world came to know about the interior of the world's

1

second largest continent. But it does not follow from this general ignorance of African history and culture that Africa contained no societies and cultures and that no important events transpired there. Africa was not a "dark continent" to the Africans themselves.

Americans must try to see Africa through Africans' eyes. Imagine an African student studying history at a high school on the slopes of Mount Kilimanjaro (kil-ih-mahn-*jah'*roh) in Tanzania (tan-zah-*nee'*uh). Possibly he is daydreaming, gazing at the clouds drifting above the shining snows of magnificent Kilimanjaro. His eyes return to the history textbook. Written by Englishmen who ruled before 1960, it states that Mount Kilimanjaro was discovered in 1847 by Rebmann (*rayb'*mahn), a German missionary and explorer. But as a young Chagga (*chah'*guh), the student knows from the songs and traditions of his people that his ancestors lived on that mountain's fertile slopes and gazed at the beauty of Kilimanjaro centuries before Rebmann arrived. To this student, Africa is not a continent discovered and explored by Europeans but rather a land in which you have enormous pride; an ancient land rich in tradition, history, and promise for the future.

Therefore, if Americans are truly to understand Africa they must try to see it as the African does; for it is he who is shaping its destiny.

• CHECK-UP

1. What false conclusions about Africa have long been widely accepted in Western lands? Why?
2. Why is it important for Western peoples to try to see Africa through the eyes of Africans?

2. Africa Is a Vast Continent

The second largest continent has the shortest coastline. Africa accounts for a fifth of the earth's land surface. The United States could be fitted easily within the northern third of Africa. The distance from Anchorage, Alaska, to Panama City in Central America is about equal to the the distance between Tangier (tan-*jeer'*) in North Africa to Cape Town in the south. From east to west at its widest points the distance is equivalent to that separating Moscow from New York.

Geography is largely responsible for the fact that for centuries African contact with Europe and Asia was limited. Because it has a

"NO ADMITTANCE!" Natural barriers helped to cut off Africa from the rest of the world in past centuries. African rivers frequently are blocked to navigation by angry rapids, like those shown above, which trouble the lower Congo River for a 230-mile stretch below Brazzaville. The coastline of West Africa is relatively unbroken, with few deep harbors, but many dangerous sand bars. In the past, goods had to be brought ashore in smaller boats (*right*) from ocean-going vessels which remained at anchor several miles offshore. Goods for export made the same trip out through the surf. To avoid this slow and costly method of cargo-handling, West African nations have tried to improve their ports and even built artificial harbors. Below, at Dakar in Senegal, concrete piers and breakwaters have been extended far out from shore to provide shelter and berths for ocean-going ships.

relatively unbroken coastline, Africa has very few natural harbors that would provide anchorage for curious seafarers from Europe and Asia. As if this were not enough to discourage would-be explorers, Africa has an extremely narrow coastal plain, averaging only twenty miles wide.[1] Africa's rivers tend to have falls or rapids where they drop down from the interior plateau on their way to the sea. These rapids were yet another major obstacle to the exploration of the interior.

The high African plateau dominates the continent. The elevation of Africa is considerably higher than that of the other continents. On the average, the earth's land masses do not rise very far above the level of the sea. Whereas only about half of Europe is 500 feet or more above sea level, nearly 90 per cent of Africa is that high. In the eastern half of the continent the average elevation of the plateau is 5000 to 6000 feet. The plateau does not level off gradually to sea level, but drops off sharply. As one moves westward, however, the high elevation declines more gradually to sea level.

This plateau is not a smooth expanse, of course, but is broken by mountains and by five large river basins. The largest of these, the Congo Basin, is located in the very heart of Africa. Far to the south of the Congo Basin lies the Kalahari (kah-lah-*hah′*ree) depression. To the north of the Congo Basin running from east to west and spanning the entire continent are the Nile, the Chad, and the Niger basins. The history of Africa, in many respects, is the story of the rise, spread, and fall of civilizations along the river systems which drain or bypass these enormous basins. (See map, page 6.) It is also the story of the attempts of men from other continents to ascend and to dominate the African plateau.

Geographically, Africa looks inward, rather than towards the sea and her would-be invaders. The major basins are much like enormous inland seas; indeed at one time these basins contained huge inland lakes. Lake Tumba (*tum′*bah) in the center of the Congo Basin is all that remains of what was once an enormous expanse of water.

The Congo Basin lies astride the equator. In contrast to most of Africa, the Congo Basin is hot and moist and heavily forested. The Congo River (also called the Zaire) and its major tributaries, the Ubangi (oo-*bahng′*gih) and the Kasai (kah-*sye′*), drain this enormous basin, gathering its waters and channeling them over the falls at Kinshasa (kin-*shah′*suh). Below the falls the Congo cuts through

[1] There are a few exceptions to this pattern, notably the Niger Delta and the Mozambique coastal plain.

hills to the Atlantic. Ocean-going ships can navigate the Congo, the world's fifth longest river, only to Matadi, less than 100 miles from the sea. But from Kinshasa, capital of the Republic of Zaire (zah-*eer'*) (formerly the Congo Republic), river steamers can travel nearly 1100 miles to Kisangani (kis-an-*gah'*nih). The Congo River system is the most extensive and useful in Africa, covering approximately 8000 miles of navigable waterways. Many sizable passenger and freight ships are engaged in this inland traffic.

Two of the continent's major depressed basins — the Kalahari and, in the north, the Chad — are not connected by rivers to the sea. The Kalahari Basin is little more than a huge desert, the home of the nomadic Bushmen. The Chad Basin is also isolated, since it lies in the southern portion of the desolate Sahara Desert. At the center of this depression is Lake Chad, once an enormous body of water, but now only a shallow and swampy lake, fed by several rivers. Although Lake Chad is navigable, its waters are so choked with weeds as to make travel difficult, particularly during the dry season when the water level is low.

The Nile and the Niger are two of the earth's longest rivers. The Nile and Niger rivers, as well as the Congo, drain their huge depressed basins and provide outlets to the sea. The Nile is probably the most famous of rivers. Its 4150 miles make it the world's longest river, but more important is the link that the Nile has provided between the Mediterranean world and the interior of Africa. Unfortunately, there are six cataracts, or stretches of rapids, in the river. For centuries, the Nile cataracts and the Sahara Desert combined to make communication between African and Mediterranean civilizations difficult. The Nile has two branches. One, the White Nile, flows languidly northward from the great lakes of East Africa, at times nearly choked by masses of floating vegetation, or *sudd*. The other branch, called the Blue Nile, winds its course from Lake Tana (*tah'*nuh) in the mountains of Ethiopia to meet the White Nile at Khartoum (kar-*toom'*), capital of the Sudan Republic.

Because the Niger Basin includes the arid western region of the Sahara Desert, it has a small population. The Niger River, at its source in the Loma (*loh'*muh) Mountains on the Sierra Leone-Guinea (sih-*er'*uh lih-*oh'*nih *gin'*ih) border, is less than 200 miles from the Atlantic. But before the waters of the Niger reach the sea they flow northeastward into the arid basin. Then, near Timbuktu (tim-buk-*too'*), the Niger bends southward, flowing through Nigeria

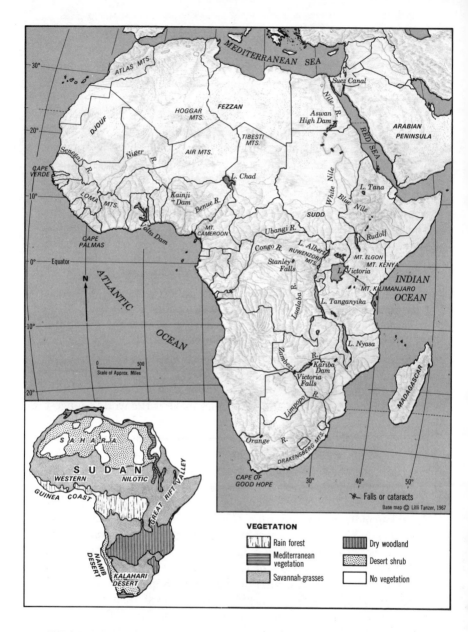

VEGETATION

	Rain forest		Dry woodland
	Mediterranean vegetation		Desert shrub
	Savannah-grasses		No vegetation

Falls or cataracts

Base map © Lilli Tanzer, 1967

THE LAND: Africa is the world's second largest continent and its vast land mass is not broken by arms of the sea. Great rivers flow for thousands of miles, but their descent from the high interior plateau creates cataracts and waterfalls that are barriers to navigation. The small map of vegetation zones shows that large areas of Africa are desert, which affects the distribution of population (see small map on facing page).

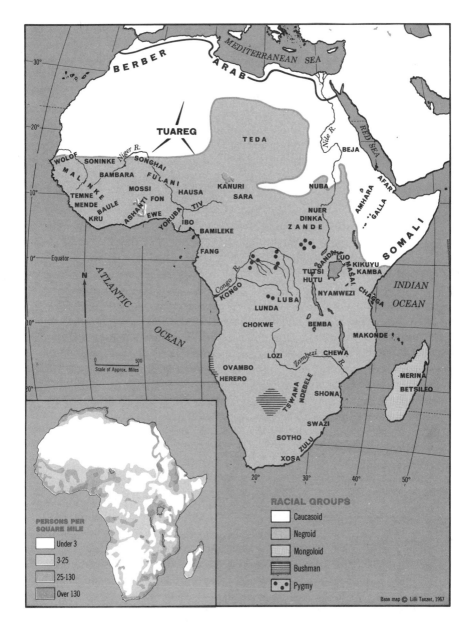

THE PEOPLE: Africans can be divided into two major racial groups, Negroid and Caucasoid. The earliest inhabitants of Africa probably were the Pygmies and Bushmen, small numbers of whom still survive among the Negroid peoples. The island of Madagascar has been influenced by immigrants from Southeast Asia. The names on the map indicate the approximate homelands of some important African ethnic groups.

and finally into the Atlantic — a total distance of 2600 miles, or 300 miles longer than the Mississippi.

The Rift Valley could be seen from the moon. Along a line running from the Red Sea in the north to South Africa, the great African plateau is split by an enormous rift formed thousands of years ago. This rift extends a distance equivalent to about one-fifth of the way around the world. Portions of this narrow but deep depression have filled with water, and are today some of the world's largest and deepest lakes.

The widest section in this major fracture of the earth's surface is the Red Sea, which separates the Arabian peninsula from Africa. The rift then runs southward through Lake Tana in Ethiopia, and into Lake Rudolf on the border of Kenya. There the rift divides into a western section which includes lakes Albert and Edward, separating Uganda from the Republic of Zaire. The western Rift Valley then continues southward through Lake Kivu (*kee'*voo) into Lake Tanganyika, which forms the boundary between Tanzania, Zaire, and Zambia (*zam'*bih-ah). How far the earth's surface must have fallen to create this rift is revealed by the fact that at its deepest point Lake Tanganyika is more than 2000 feet below sea level. The eastern Rift Valley runs through central Kenya and Tanzania. A number of smaller lakes such as Lake Naivasha (nye-*vah'*shuh) in Kenya mark its course southward. The two sections of the rift seem to rejoin at the northern end of Lake Nyasa (nih-*yah'*suh) which forms the boundary between Malawi (mah-*lah'*wee), Zambia, Mozambique (moh-zam-*beek'*), and Tanzania.

Some geologists think that Lake Victoria — next to Lake Superior the world's largest fresh-water lake — may also be a product of the enormous rift system. A glance at the map on page 6 will show that this huge but relatively shallow lake lies cradled between the eastern and western arms of the rift. The three great African lakes — Victoria, Tanganyika, and Nyasa — are among the world's ten largest bodies of fresh water, and play an important part in the life of the peoples of Africa.

The Sahara separates tropical Africa from North Africa. The Sahara, the world's largest desert, occupies more than 3.5 million square miles, an area larger than the United States. It extends from the Red Sea in the east to the Atlantic Ocean in the west, and at its widest extends a greater distance than that from New York to San Francisco. Contrary to popular belief, the Sahara is more rocky than

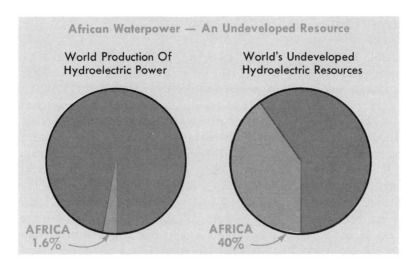

World Production Of
Hydroelectric Power

World's Undeveloped
Hydroelectric Resources

AFRICA
1.6%

AFRICA
40%

Two graphs reveal a case of underdevelopment: (left) Africa has far less than its share of the electric power essential to modern civilization, but (right) has the greatest hydroelectric potential of any continent. For example, in the Congo Basin there are many possible hydroelectric sites (below, left), but under Belgian rule only a few dams were built (right) to generate power for the mines in Katanga province.

sandy. Because the United States enjoys a highly developed technology and abundant rainfall, Americans are inclined to think of the land as a link uniting countries and peoples. The Sahara, however, has long been an obstacle to north-south travel and to the exchange of ideas between the heartland of Africa and the Mediterranean coastlands. During the early centuries of the Christian era, however, camel caravans made their appearance, linking the north with tropical Africa.

Only the mighty Nile River, rising in the interior, pierces the Sahara. Were it not for the Nile's six cataracts, the civilization of the Mediterranean world might well have moved southward into Africa rather than northward into Europe. And had the Sahara not become a desert, but remained a well-watered and fertile region as it was during the Ice Ages, Africa might have been one of the world's most highly developed regions.

The Guinea tropics have adequate rainfall and are heavily populated. One other geographical region of Africa needs to be described. The plateau region of West Africa is neither as high nor does it rise as sharply from the sea as is the case in East Africa. In fact, along the vast expanse of West Africa's inner curve, the land often slopes very gradually to the sea, and the continuation of this gradual slope in many cases forms shoals and reefs off the coast. The low-lying Guinea tropics are well watered and support large populations. It is from this region that European and American merchants obtained the slaves that they transported across the Atlantic. This part of the world, therefore, is the land inhabited by the ancestors of most of the Western Hemisphere's black population.

Geography is only a part of the setting within which Africa's varied people play their roles. Of equal importance is the climate, for it is this factor which goes far to determine the limits of what man can and cannot do with the land. This is particularly true in Africa, where more than 80 per cent of the people depend for survival upon the food which they themselves grow.

● CHECK-UP

1. What and where in Africa are: (a) the African plateau? (b) The five chief basins? (c) The two longest rivers? (d) The Rift Valley? (e) The Sahara Desert? (f) The Guinea tropics?

2. How have geographic factors and conditions influenced: (a) Africa's relations with the outside world? (b) Travel and transportation between various parts of Africa?

3. Africa's Climate and Vegetation Pose Special Problems

It is important to remember that 90 per cent of Africa lies within the tropics. The equator lies almost exactly mid-way between Cairo and Cape Town. The major climatic regions of this vast continent, insofar as they are affected by latitude, are generally the same whether one moves north or south towards the equator. Both the extreme northern and southern parts of the continent lie in the temperate zone and have a Mediterranean climate. Winters in the Republic of South Africa, for example, are usually mild, but can be cold, and occasionally there is snowfall. Traveling towards the center of the continent from north or south, one encounters first dry plains and then desert regions. The Sahara occupies more than half of the northern portion of the continent and is larger than the desert regions of the south (including Kalahari). Closer to the equator, the desert gives way to savannah grasslands and to scattered forests. Along the equator — and especially in the Congo Basin, the Guinea coast, and on the lower slopes of the higher mountains — are to be found the tropical rain forests.

Africa has a great variety of climate and vegetation. Not all regions along the equator are hot and damp, because altitude as well as latitude determines climate. The Kenya Highlands, for example, straddle the equator, but there the winds often are bitterly cold, and hailstorms are not rare. The Kenyan who can afford it may spend his vacation on the East African coast, only a day's drive from the highlands. There he finds relief from the heat of the tropical sun in the balmy waters of the Indian Ocean.

The combination of high plateaus, low-lying coastal regions, great basins, prevailing winds, and the effect of the ocean currents provide Africa with an extremely varied climate. An African student going to college in the northeastern United States is likely to find the winters cold and uncomfortable. But, depending on what part of Africa he comes from, he may find the summer temperatures equally unexpected. For it is all but impossible to find a place in Africa, except of course in the Sahara or another desert, where the highest thermometer reading during the year equals that of Washington, D.C.

Few regions receive enough rain at the right time. Water, or rather lack of it, is possibly Africa's greatest problem. About 60 per cent of the continent does not receive enough rain to support an agricultural population. Indeed it has been estimated that about a third of the world's arid lands are in Africa.

Except for the subtropical climates of South Africa and the regions north of the Sahara, the four seasons as we know them in the United States do not exist in Africa. Nearly everywhere on that continent, however, there are distinct rainy and dry seasons. A casual visitor to East Africa during July, for example, might think that most of the country was a lush green paradise. But if he returned in October, the once green fields would be brown and dry, and some areas that earlier looked like green meadows would resemble a desert.

The great fear of the African farmer is that the rains may fail. When this happens, the earth is barren for the entire year and famine stalks the land. On the other hand, if the rains are overabundant, they may wash away the newly-planted seed and cause streams and rivers to flood.

William A. Hance, a well-known American geographer who spent many years studying Africa, concludes pessimistically that "about 92 per cent of the continent may be said to suffer from one or another climatic disability. . . . As far as water is concerned, [there is] plenty where it cannot be used and . . . [too little] where it is most needed."

Ivory Coast workers build an earth dam to store rainwater so it will be available for animals and crops during the dry season. More efficient use of scanty rainfall is necessary to feed Africa's growing population.

African soils are generally poor. Not only does the frequency and the amount of rainfall directly affect the farmer's chances of growing sufficient food, the rain also affects the *quality* of the soil. Most African soil is *tropical laterite*. This type of earth, usually reddish in color, is damaged by heavy rains which tend to leach the soil — that is, wash away, its nutritive minerals. Unfortunately, much of Africa has sporadic torrential rains which leach the laterite soil. Consequently most African lands are not very fertile, and even when modern agricultural practices are used, the crop yields per acre are low.

The most productive agricultural areas are located in the higher plateau regions, many of which have volcanic soils. The river valleys covered with alluvial soils are also fertile.

Savannah grasslands cover large areas. The savannah grasslands which cover nearly a fourth of Africa are much like parts of Utah and Texas. During the rainy season the grass grows tall and green and the wild flowers are in magnificent bloom. But during the dry season the countryside is best described as "bush," a term often used to identify the sparsely settled savannah regions. Here one sees small, crooked, flat-topped trees and thorn bushes, with red laterite earth showing between clumps of tall dry grass.

Rain forests are found in the Congo Basin and along the Guinea coast. Rain forests cover only about 10 per cent of the entire continent. The term "rain forest" is not very precise. Where the rainfall is very heavy and regular, huge trees tend to grow so close together that their tops shade the earth and little undergrowth survives. Here one walks quietly in a mysterious twilight under a high green canopy. Where the rains are less torrential, the undergrowth is often so thick that it is impossible to penetrate. Finally, where the rains are still less frequent and more seasonal, trees are scattered and frequently stunted. It is here that the rain forest merges into the savannah.

The most favorable climates are in the highlands. Most white farmers live in the cool fertile highlands of East, Central, and South Africa. Africa's best soils and climates are found in these regions at an elevation of 5000 feet or more. Among the highlands are the high Ethiopian plateau, the water slopes of the East African mountains, and the high veld (prairie) regions of Kenya, Zambia, and Rhodesia. In the Kenya Highlands (which before independence were largely reserved for Europeans and called the White Highlands), the roads run through lush green meadows and large stands of coniferous trees. A Wisconsin dairy farmer would feel at home in this invigorating climate and would gaze with pleasure upon cattle feeding on the green slopes. He would also approve of the neatly furrowed fields extending as far as the eye can see.

These regions are among the most heavily settled in Africa. Because there is only a limited amount of land in the fertile highlands, it is valued highly. It is not surprising that the African farmer and the white settler have clashed over its ownership. In Kenya conflict between the white settlers and the Kikuyu people over control of the good land was one cause of the Mau Mau (*mow' mow'*) rebellion. In Zambia it was a major issue in the struggle for independence. In Rhodesia and South Africa, competition for scarce, well-watered, and fertile lands is a major cause of tension and unrest between whites and blacks.

Nearly two thirds of Africa is semi-arid or desert. Except for Australia, Africa has the largest proportion of arid land of any continent. The Sahara Desert has already been mentioned (pages 8–10). The Kalahari Desert, which takes up much of Botswana, is larger than all of Italy. There are also deserts in Somalia, Ethiopia, Namibia (formerly South-West Africa), and northeastern Kenya.

Africa's great deserts are bordered by semi-arid regions where rainfall is rare and the dry season lasts about nine months of the year. There are two huge semi-arid belts — one running east and west, the other north and south. South of the Sahara, a semi-arid belt extending from Dakar (duh-*kar'*) in West Africa to the Red Sea is used almost solely for nomadic cattle herding. Another large semi-arid region extends from southwestern Zaire through Angola, Namibia, and Botswana.

● CHECK-UP

1. What factors contribute to Africa's varied climate? Give examples.
2. What natural conditions pose problems for African farmers? Explain.
3. What is a savannah? Rain forest? Highland? Semi-arid region?

4. Geography and Climate Have Affected African Ways of Living

Over thousands of years, those men who have proved best able to cope with their environment have tended to persist; the others have gradually disappeared. Modern man has persisted largely because of the evolutionary development of his intellect. And it is intelligence that in our time has given man a near mastery of the environment. Indeed, civilization is a measure of how well men control their environment and regulate their own behavior in human societies. **Most of Africa is inhabited by dark-skinned people.** There is a wide range of skin color among Africans, but by far the largest number are dark-skinned. It is likely that man's various skin colors evolved in response to environmental differences. Biologists tell us, for example, that ultra-violet sunlight is a basic source of vitamin D, without which man cannot survive, but too much of which may be injurious. It is conceivable that natural selection favored lighter-skinned people in the temperate colder climates and darker pigmentation in the tropics. The factor of skin color, according to this theory, was nature's way of regulating the penetration of ultra-violet rays. The important point is that different races of man have evolved and have tended to settle in certain parts of the globe. But since man has never stopped moving about, there are no "pure" racial types. As a matter of fact, in any discussion of racial differences, one should make clear what period of time is involved, for the races are constantly blending and changing.

A developing country is greatly dependent on its environment. Except for the Republic of South Africa, all African states may be considered *developing* countries. This means that the majority of the people produce for themselves the greater part of their food and shelter. This type of living is called a "subsistence economy." People living in a subsistence economy are greatly dependent upon the environment, for they lack the technical means or the resources (or both) with which to control nature. For example, in much of Africa when the soil fails to grow crops, the farmer and his family move to a more fertile area. The less developed the region, the greater is the necessity for man to conform to his environment. We have already pointed out that Africa is not a rich continent; its soils are poor and its rainfall is often sparse and seasonal.

According to a recent United Nations estimate, about 375 million people live in Africa. Though Africa is the second largest continent, it has only 10 per cent of the world's population. Can we conclude, then, that Africa is underpopulated and could support additional millions of people? Actually the capacity of a country or continent to support people depends upon the natural environment (rainfall, water, soil) and man's capacity to manipulate and control

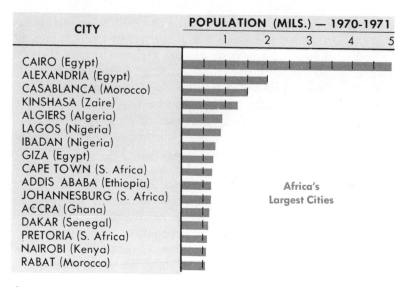

CITY	POPULATION (MILS.) — 1970-1971
	1 2 3 4 5
CAIRO (Egypt)	
ALEXANDRIA (Egypt)	
CASABLANCA (Morocco)	
KINSHASA (Zaire)	
ALGIERS (Algeria)	
LAGOS (Nigeria)	
IBADAN (Nigeria)	
GIZA (Egypt)	
CAPE TOWN (S. Africa)	
ADDIS ABABA (Ethiopia)	
JOHANNESBURG (S. Africa)	
ACCRA (Ghana)	
DAKAR (Senegal)	
PRETORIA (S. Africa)	
NAIROBI (Kenya)	
RABAT (Morocco)	

Africa's Largest Cities

that environment. Some of the most sparsely settled areas of Africa may actually be overpopulated; for example, such an arid region as Chad yields but a poor living to its scattered inhabitants. Most of Africa cannot support a dense population; but as the capacity of the people to control the environment increases, the continent will be able to support an expanding population. Modern science and medicine have lowered the death rate in Africa whereas the birth rate has continued to be high. Thus the African population, like that in other developing regions, is increasing rapidly. It is estimated that by the year 2000 about three-quarters of a billion people will be living in Africa.

Africa is predominantly rural. Some authorities think that much of Africa is already overpopulated and that too large a part of the population is clustered in certain areas. Among the most densely populated parts of Africa are the Mediterranean coastal regions, the Nile Valley, the Guinea coastal regions of West Africa, and the highland lake regions of eastern Africa.

Despite the fact that some areas of the continent are densely populated, most Africans live a rural life. In fact, about 80 per cent of the African people live in towns of fewer than 20,000 inhabitants. This is the highest such percentage for all the continents. Only 9 per cent of all Africans live in cities of 100,000 or more. In recent years, however, Africans have been moving to the big cities at a rapid rate. With few exceptions, large cities did not

CITIES: African cities with more than 500,000 inhabitants are listed in the chart on the facing page. Other African cities are growing fast, especially capitals of new nations, such as Abidjan (*above*) in Ivory Coast, with its high-rise office buildings and hotels. Kano (*right*), in northern Nigeria, represents an older style of city found in the sudan region which has been influenced by Islam. Kano has been a center of caravan trade since the 12th century. Here, clay walls and inner courtyards provide both coolness and privacy in a close-set neighborhood.

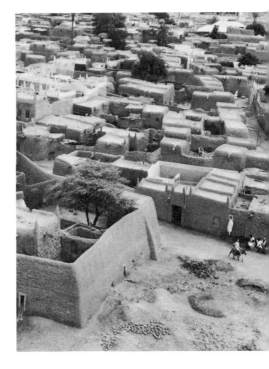

exist in Africa before the arrival of the Europeans. It is not surprising, therefore, that most of Africa's larger cities are along the coast where Europeans and Asians first established bases for trading purposes.

Most Africans are food growers or nomadic herders. Most African families grow the food they eat. Where the rainfall permits at least one good crop each year, the people usually farm the same fields, sometimes in rotation, year after year. Usually it is the wives and mothers who cultivate the family gardens while older unmarried daughters look after the small children. Today many families have enough good land to grow a "cash crop" such as cotton, coffee, or peanuts. To market such a crop the family needs to live near a road, railroad, or river so that the "cash crop" can be shipped to market. Often it is a lack of transport rather than a shortage of land or a deficiency of climate which discourages commercial agriculture.

Except for tilling the soil, the most common occupation is cattle herding. Although agriculture and cattle herding sometimes are combined, cattle herding is usually found in the drier regions.

Two main types of rural culture have emerged. How a people procures its livelihood determines its culture. In Africa, as elsewhere, the habits, clothing, and languages of cattle-herding people are quite different from those of subsistence farmers. Before the coming of European rule, warfare between farmers and herders was quite common. A major concern of many new African states is the problem of accommodating two such radically different life styles.

In most cattle cultures the men are responsible for the herds. It is not uncommon for a young boy of eleven to be able to identify as many as 200 cows and call each one by name. The herding of cattle requires a different kind of community organization from that appropriate to a village of subsistence farmers. In addition to being organized in extended families (which include grandparents, uncles, and wives of married sons, as well as parents and their children), the nomadic herding group often is also divided in terms of age. Young men of approximately the same age are initiated into manhood together and forever after are linked as closely as if they were members of the same family. Each age group has its special responsibilities. The boys often herd the cattle, the young men are warriors and hunters, while the older men are the civil officials and judges.

When grass and water are plentiful, the cattle-herding people remain in one place and live in semi-permanent houses. But when the dry season arrives, they must move in search of the water and grass without which their cattle cannot survive. Whereas most subsistence farmers are found in the moderate rain forests and the well-watered savannahs, the cattle herders live along the fringes of the desert and in the drier portions of the savannah.

Economies based on food-gathering and hunting are disappearing from Africa. A rapidly diminishing part of the African population is composed of people who live by hunting wild game, fishing, and gathering berries, roots, and other natural foodstuffs. Of course, many cattle herders live in areas where wild life is plentiful, and they supplement their food supply by hunting. But the number of nomadic people who move about in search of wild game and other natural foods is decreasing rapidly. Some have given up a nomadic life for cattle herding or agriculture. Others, such as the Bushmen of the Kalahari Desert and the Pygmies of the Congo rain forest, are either being absorbed by neighboring agricultural peoples or are failing to reproduce themselves.

Geography and climate have largely determined where Europeans and Asians settled. The first major settlement of non-African people in Africa was made along the East African coast by Asian merchants and Arabs who wished to establish commercial ports. The Dutch established a way station at the Cape of Good Hope in 1652 to provide food and fresh water for ships bound to and from the East Indies. Soon thereafter European settlers from Holland, Germany, and France were attracted to South Africa by the temperate climate and fertile soil. During the eighteenth and nineteenth centuries, descendents of those early settlers moved inland, occupying much of what is now the Republic of South Africa. More recently, white settlers from England and South Africa have moved into the cool and fertile highland regions of present-day Kenya, Tanzania, and Rhodesia.

Beginning in the last part of the nineteenth century, thousands of Asians from what is now India and Pakistan crossed the Indian Ocean to settle in the major East African cities and towns where their commercial skill soon gave them a monopoly of trade and storekeeping. One of the major problems of present-day Africa is relations between the large African majority and the white and Asian minorities.

• CHECK-UP

1. Why are most African states "developing countries"? Is Africa underpopulated?

2. How does the culture of subsistence farmers differ from that of cattle herders in Africa?
3. Where in Africa have Europeans tended to settle? Asians? Why?

5. Who Are "Africans" and Where Did They Come From?

Africa is widely regarded as the birthplace of the human race.
Recent evidence suggests that man's ancestors existed first in Africa.
In 1948, Dr. Louis Leakey, an English anthropologist,[2] discovered a
fossil [3] on a small island in Lake Victoria. Some authorities believed
it to be the oldest evidence of the existence of humanlike creatures.
The earth stratum in which Dr. Leakey found the fossil — labeled
"Proconsul" — was estimated to be approximately 25 million years
old. Proconsul does not qualify as a human, however, for there is no
evidence that he used tools of any kind. (Anthropologists consider
the use of tools an important distinguishing hallmark of human beings which set them apart from their primate cousins — such as apes,
monkeys, and lemurs.) In 1959, Dr. and Mrs. Leakey again startled
the world with their discovery in Tanzania of a skull 1,750,000 years
old. More important, they found near this skull simple implements
or "pebble tools." Their son, Richard Leakey, announced in 1972
that a skull strikingly resembling that of modern man had been
found in a layer of material 2.6 million years old. This site, in Kenya,
has also yielded many stone tools, thought to be the oldest known
artifacts made by human beings.

Thousands of generations passed before our early ancestors emerged
as modern man — *Homo sapiens* (*hoe'*moh *say'*pee-enz), as anthropologists refer to him. During the hundreds of thousands of years
before that time, Africa was probably the center of human evolution.
It was about 300,000 years ago that early man evolved to the point
of using a general-purpose hand axe rather than the less efficient
pebble tools. Although other examples of the hand axe have been
found in Europe and Asia, the majority have been uncovered in
Africa. Some 30,000 years ago — and after he had already acquired
the use of fire — early man moved from the open savannah to the

[2] **anthropologist:** a scientist who studies the origin, development, and cultures
of mankind.
[3] **fossil:** a remain or impression (or trace) of a remain, of any plant or animal
life, preserved from past ages in the earth's crust, such as a skeleton or a footprint
that has been hardened in a rock.

forests of the Congo and the Guinea coast. Here we find evidence of more sophisticated tools used in gathering grubs and possibly in cultivating the soil.

Professor Paul Bohannan, a respected American anthropologist who has spent many years studying this subject, states that "Africa seems to have been the home not merely of mankind but also of . . . human culture. It is not until the Neolithic period and the agricultural

ROCK PAINTINGS. Postage stamps of new African nations feature prehistoric art found in the Sahara Desert. At right is a silhouette of an ancient Saharan warrior; below, two archers crouch as they stalk each other. Below, right, another archer takes aim at an antelope. Hunting scenes show that thousands of years ago the Sahara was fertile enough to support big game, such as the elephant (*bottom*).

revolution that we must look outside of Africa for major contributions. . . ."[4]

The definition of race lacks precision. Because the term "race" has been used in so many different ways, it has taken on a wide range of meanings. Anthropologists, who classify mankind into many varieties or groups according to whatever particular set of traits or characteristics they may be studying, do not agree on any fixed system of classification. In general, however, they describe all men as belonging to three great racial stocks. They do this for the sake of study and convenience only. These stocks are: (1) the Mongoloid (*mahn'*guh-loyd) or "yellow-skinned" peoples; (2) the Caucasoid (*kaw'*kuh-soyd) or "white-skinned" peoples; and (3) the Negroid (*nee'*groyd) or "black-skinned" peoples. In a literal sense, of course, none of these categories is accurate, for there does not exist any people with a true white, yellow, or black skin color. There is a wide range of physical traits — including many shades of skin color — within each of the great racial stocks. And there are in addition many combinations of these three stocks. Hence there is no absolute way of determining whether a person is primarily Negroid, Mongoloid, or Caucasoid. Race is not a fixed difference, for types of *Homo sapiens* are constantly in the process of change.

Europeans treated African Negroes as inferiors. Before 1950, only Egypt, Liberia, and Ethiopia among the African states were independent. The vast majority of Africans until recently had long been living under European colonial governments. In the last 25 years the situation has changed drastically. Today, European governments rule over African majorities only in the Portuguese and Spanish colonies and in France's small foothold in East Africa — the French Territory of the Afars (ah-*farz'*) and the Issas (*ees'*sahs). Settlers of European descent maintain a similar domination in Rhodesia and in the Republic of South Africa.

But despite the fact that most African nations finally have acquired their independence, the memory of being governed and exploited for years by Europeans cannot be erased. Even though there is no evidence of the innate superiority of any one race, during the long years of colonial rule Africans were treated by white Europeans as inferior. African institutions and cultures were often regarded as evil and degraded. Africans were forced to speak an alien language and to defer to the white invaders.

[4] Paul Bohannan, *Africa and the Africans* (New York: Doubleday, Natural History Press, 1964), pp. 58–59.

The struggle for independence which finally bore fruit during the 1950's and 1960's was an expression of the African's desire to win his freedom from white European domination. But many Europeans still live in Africa. Because of the very limited education permitted them under colonial rule, few Africans were prepared to take over the more important jobs in the government and in the economy of their newly-independent countries. The memory of years of humiliation is reinforced by the continuing need to retain Europeans in important positions.

Most Africans are sensitive about race. Doubtless because of the experience of living under colonial rule, Africans are very sensitive about the issue of race. This is reflected in the economic and political policies of the newly-independent African states, and in the relations of African nations with the rest of the world. It is reflected also in African writing, in which *négritude* (nay-grih-*tüd'*), literally "Negroness," is a prominent theme. Négritude is a conscious effort to glorify the African Negro and his African way of life. It is the African's response to the white man's assumptions of superiority, a reaction against the idea of inferiority.

Black Africans are proud of their race — of their customs and traditions. Because Africans are proud and because they are mindful of centuries of European domination and humiliation, they are quick to demand that they be treated with dignity. And they insist that their new nations be respected and regarded as the equal of other nations. The extraordinary energy of the new African nations is a reflection of how deeply their leaders feel the need to disprove the idea that European civilization is superior to African cultures.

It is important that Americans understand the intensity of this feeling. It is a feeling which is not limited to Africa. Indeed, it is present wherever one people dominates, humiliates, and degrades another people. Because 23 million Americans are descendants of Africans, African leaders are also concerned about race relations in the United States.

Many people continue to use the term "race" inaccurately. Many people still find it difficult to talk dispassionately about "race," which is not surprising in view of the way the word is used. On the one hand, it is a concept used in the biological sciences; on the other hand, it represents a social and cultural idea. The term has been used so carelessly that these two sets of meanings tend to become mixed. In Nazi Germany, race as a *cultural* idea was equated with the *biological* concept of race — with catastrophic results. The Nazis preached that non-Jewish Germans were Aryans (*ayr'*ee-unz) and were a "master race" whose blood was being contaminated by Jewish genes. Actually, both Jews and Germans belong to the Caucasoid race. But a religious-cultural difference was interpreted as racial and biological, and six million Jews were murdered by the Nazis to "purify the Aryan race." (Aryans were actually prehistoric peoples who settled in India and parts of Europe and spoke Indo-European languages.)

To the scientist, the word "race" refers to a group of people within the human species which, in contrast to other groups, shares a pattern of genes. Variations between members of different races are not due to the fact that one race has genes that the other does not have. The difference results from a variation in the frequency with which certain genes occur in the races. Genes determine, among other things, our physical appearance. Therefore, representatives of the different races may look different, even though all have the same genes. For example, although many Caucasoid and Negroid people have wavy hair, some do not. Most Mongoloid people, on the other hand, have straight hair, although some do not. Blue-eyed persons are found most frequently among Caucasions, but there are blue-eyed people among the other great racial stocks as well.

No race is "better" or "worse" than another. Social concepts of racial inferiority have no basis in science. Yet, in our country the false idea of racial inferiority has been used by some individuals to deny American Negroes equal rights and opportunities for jobs and education. In the Republic of South Africa, a racist white government has adopted a policy termed *apartheid* (uh-*pahr'*tayt), or "apartness," which calls for complete separation of the races. This confusion of scientific concept and cultural idea has led to the mistaken belief — still held by some people — that Europeans are biologically different from Africans, and that Caucasian Europeans have reached the highest stage of biological and cultural development. It is argued that for this reason Europeans have the right to determine the government of any country where they happen to live — even if Europeans are but a small minority of the population.

That there are visible differences between men of different races and regions cannot be denied. But there are no significant biological differences between them. People must understand this emotionally-loaded concept if they are to deal intelligently with the problems of race. We need to do more than simply point out racial differences if we are to know much about the people of Africa. Important cultural and physical differences exist within any given race. There are, for example, as great cultural and physical differences among various Negroid peoples of Africa as there are between Norwegians and Italians, or Spaniards and Persians.

Anthropologists disagree about the precise origins of Africa's dark-skinned peoples. There is little agreement among African experts about how the various peoples of Africa should be classified. Although the predominantly Negroid peoples of modern Africa are related to the original inhabitants, they are themselves a mixture of Caucasian and possibly other races. A few scholars believe that the Negroid peoples of modern Africa are a relatively "new" racial stock, perhaps only ten thousand years old.

The Bushmen are probably the oldest, if not the original, inhabitants of Africa. It is also possible, although there is no conclusive evidence, that the modern Negroid race is a product of the interbreeding of Caucasian peoples, who migrated to Africa from the Arabian peninsula ten or twelve thousand years ago, with the original Bushmen.

Anthropologists have classified the peoples of Africa on the basis of language. The best known attempt to classify the African people according to language is that of Professor Joseph Greenberg.[5] He maintains that there are four major language groups: (1) Niger-Congo, (2) Sudanic, (3) Afro-Asiatic, and (4) Khoisan (*koy'*sahn), or Click languages. (The simpler term — Click — is used in referring to this fourth group.)

1. *Niger-Congo.* The Niger-Congo family of languages is the largest. Geographically it extends over an area from Dakar in the west to Kenya in the east, and southward from this east-west line to the Cape region of South Africa. However, within this enormous area are to be found small pockets of Click-speaking Bushmen and Hottentots. The largest language group in the Niger-Congo category is called *Bantu* (ban-*too'*). Many people think that the term Bantu refers to a tribe or an ethnic group. Actually the Bantu people living in Central and South Africa are less alike in terms of race than in terms of language.

2. *Sudanic.* The second largest family of languages is the Sudanic. People speaking Sudanic languages live in the region of the upper Nile, the vast semi-arid areas of the sudan, and along the mid-section of the Niger River Basin.

[5] Joseph H. Greenberg, *The Languages of Africa* (Bloomington, Ind.: Indiana University, 1963).

AFRICANS ALL. Three "typical" Africans reflect the variety of ethnic and cultural groups on the continent: the turbaned Arab (*above*) farms cotton in Sudan; left, a Nigerian college student carries English books to class, but wears the flowing robes of his people; below, a young Masai mother in Kenya wears traditional jewelry and carries her baby comfortably on her back.

3. *Afro-Asiatic.* Professor Greenberg has applied the title "Afro-Asiatic" to the languages spoken in the north of Africa. Included in this category is Arabic, which originated in the Middle East. Also included are other Semitic languages, such as those spoken by the Somali and Ethiopian peoples in northeastern Africa.

4. *Khoisan or Click.* The fourth major language category is the Click group spoken by the rapidly disappearing Bushmen and Hottentots of southern and central Africa. Two small tribes — the Hadza (*hahd'*zuh) and the Sandawe (sahn-*dah'*wee) — in Tanzania, also employ a Click sound in their speech.

The language barrier is a serious obstacle to progress. In only three or four of Africa's 42 countries do most of the people speak the same language. The difficulties of communication, due to the existence of many languages as well as to cultural differences, pose severe problems for the new nations of Africa. European languages — especially French and English — were introduced by the colonial powers and have been widely adopted as the official languages for government, business, and education. Arabic is spoken by a large number of

---

African Word Imports

Here is a sampling of words used by English-speaking peoples which originated in Africa. The African language of origin is enclosed in parentheses.

gumbo (Umbundu) — soup

voodoo (Ewe) — cult worship involving incantation and sorcery

zombie (Kongo) — person in a trancelike or drugged state suggestive of a "walking corpse"

banjo (Kimbundu) — a musical instrument akin to the guitar

erg (Amharic)—a desert area of shifting sands

oasis (Egyptian)—fertile spot in a desert

goober (Kongo) — peanut

cola (Temne or Mandingo) — from kola tree, whose nuts are used in making many soft drinks

yam (Fulani) — a kind of sweet potato

juke (Wolof) — originally "disorderly," "noisy"; a "juke box" is a coin-operated record-player

Africans, especially in North Africa and in the predominantly Muslim regions of the Sahara.

Only two African languages — Swahili (swah-*hee'*lee) and Hausa (*how'*sah) — are spoken by as many as ten million people. Swahili, a Bantu language which has incorporated many Arabic words, is the mother tongue on the East African coast. It is also the second language of nearly all Tanzanians, most Kenyans and many Ugandans, as well as of many people in the eastern Congo, southern sudan, and northern Zambia and Mozambique. In West Africa, Hausa, which is spoken by people living in the western sudan — the savanah region extending from northern Nigeria to northern Senegal — is probably the most widely spoken African language.

Most people of European and Asian descent live in southern and eastern Africa. About six million people of European descent live in Africa. In the Republic of South Africa, immigrants or descendants of immigrants from Europe make up about one-sixth of the population. Most of the other countries of Africa south of the Sahara, however, have only a tiny European minority. Most of the Europeans living and working in West Africa regard themselves as temporary residents who intend to return home to England, France, or Belgium in the not-too-distant future. By way of contrast, nearly all Europeans in southern Africa have made their permanent homes on the continent. Indeed, most of them were born in Africa. Although few in number, the European farmers in Tanzania and Kenya also regard Africa as their home, and many have no intention of leaving, even though the country is now governed by Africans.

People from the Asian mainland first settled along the East African coast many centuries ago. However, the major influx of Asians came early in this century when the British imported large numbers of Indian workers to build port facilities and railways and to work on the plantations. Today there are about one million Asians, or people of Asian descent, living in Africa.

Through the years the Asian community within Africa has prospered. Most of the skilled jobs and small businesses in the cities and towns of eastern and central Africa are held by Asians. Many have been highly successful, and a few Asians are wealthy. However, the Asian community has been as little inclined as the Europeans to intermarry with other races. They have retained their language and culture almost completely intact. A major problem in present-day East Africa is the impatience of Africans with the Indian minorities who refuse to become "Africanized" and yet continue to dominate Africa's commercial life.

- **CHECK-UP**
  1. What light, if any, have the Leakeys' discoveries shed on the origins of human beings?
  2. How has the unscientific use of the word "race" created problems? Give examples.
  3. What are the four major language groups in Africa? How has language proved to be an obstacle to progress?

6. African Society Is Close-Knit

There is great variety in the way African peoples live and work together. In parts of Africa people live very much today as they did a thousand years ago. In most regions, however, ways of living are undergoing rapid change from traditional life to what one may call modernity. In a few places, and especially in the capital cities, wealthy and well-educated Africans lead a life very similar to that of their counterparts in the United States. Perhaps the best way to study these various ways of living is to begin with a description of traditional cultures.

The tribe is the major form of social organization. Men have always lived together in a community of one type or another. The interrelationships of people living in close association obviously require that they develop some form of organization to regulate their communal life. The types of societies that exist in any given place and time reflect the nature of the community. In Africa until very recently, the tribe as a form of social organization was characteristic of nearly the entire continent south of the Sahara. The term "tribe," however, is itself controversial. There is a tendency for Americans to use it only in talking about Africans or American Indians, but it could apply to European peoples as well. In general, however, "tribe" refers to a group of people who share a common language and culture, and usually also a common territory. Frequently the feeling of oneness is strengthened by a mythical belief that in the distant past all members of the tribe had a common ancestor. It was doubtless with these elements in mind that a few years ago the Nigerian delegate to the United Nations, Chief S. O. Adebo (uh-*dee'*boh), suggested that "tribe" really meant "ethnic group" or "nation." Often the word "people" is to be preferred.

Western society — American and European — tends to emphasize the importance of individual rights and privileges. Tribal society, on the other hand, stresses the responsibilities of the individual toward his community, or tribe. A sense of "we-ness" makes the individual feel that his life has meaning only in relation to the other members of the community to which he belongs. An African who has spent all or most of his life in a tribal environment might have some difficulty even in conceiving of himself as living outside this closely-knit community.

Because anthropologists do not agree on the criteria for defining the separate tribe, it is not possible to say with any accuracy how many distinct language and cultural groups there are in Africa. There are between 600 and 800 languages and dialects in Africa, however. This fact alone is an indicator of the very large number of tribes.

Rapid change is making the tribe less important. Although still an important form of social organization, the tribe nearly everywhere in Africa is losing ground to forms of social organization more characteristic of the modern world. For example, the family of mother, father, and children, as we know it, is becoming more important, as are religious and occupational associations. More significant, however, is the increasing importance of the nation. Twenty years ago, if an African were asked who he was, he would most likely give the name of his tribe or clan. Today he is more likely to say proudly that he is a Kenyan, a Ghanaian, or a Somali.

National boundaries often ignore tribal residence. Almost every African country includes a large number of different tribes. The tribes of Tanzania, for example, number more than one hundred. Nigeria has some fifty tribes, and each of these has its own distinctive culture, language, and religion. Sometimes the boundaries which these young African nations have inherited from their European colonizers cut across the lands of important tribes, dividing people who share a common language and customs. Some of the current tensions between African countries are caused by the efforts of "divided" tribes to come together within a single national territory. Some tribes are very large; the Ibo (*ee′boh*) in eastern Nigeria, for example, number more than five million. Others are very small and include only a few thousand persons. Some tribes have developed elaborate systems of government, much like those with which we are familiar. Others have very little formal government outside the authority of the father of the immediate family, or the eldest member of an extended family.

Possibly the best way to come to understand how Africans lead their daily lives is to consider again their three major traditional occupations. Each of these determines not only the way in which people obtain their food and shelter, but also their form of government, religion, relations with outside groups, and other aspects of their culture.

Few Africans still follow hunting and gathering life styles. The two principal population groups which still pursue hunting and gathering for their subsistence are the Bushmen and the Pygmies. The 50,000 remaining Bushmen live in the inhospitable Kalahari Desert. Here they roam in small bands of a few families over their allocated regions in search of game, roots, berries, and other edible wild foods. To us their life may seem difficult and uncomfortable. But these remarkable golden brown people are fiercely independent and prefer to live hidden in the arid Kalahari Desert. The Pygmies, many of whom inhabit the Ituri (ee-*too*′ree) forest of Zaire, are seldom over four feet tall. Like the Bushmen, the Pygmies live in small hunting bands, each made up of a few families. But in some respects the Pygmies' environment is a friendlier one than the harsh desert homeland of the Bushmen, for the forest provides a plentiful supply of game, roots, berries, and fruits.

Unlike the Bushmen, the Pygmies have established close relations with neighboring farming peoples. They trade surplus meat and other forest food for agricultural products. Some Pygmy women have married into the farming tribes and have left the forest. Most Africans prefer to avoid the dense tropical rain forest, parts of which are almost impenetrable. But the Pygmy sees the forest as his friend and as his home. His whole culture revolves about life in the forest. The Pygmy's language is very rich in words used to describe the forest, and he may even be heard referring to it as though it were his mother.

In parts of Africa, cattle herding is both an occupation and a way of life. What is important in a people's culture is often revealed by the richness of their language in describing it. Americans, for example, have many words for motor vehicle: automobile, car, convertible, truck, sedan, hot rod, pick-up, and so on. The cattle-herding Masai (muh-*sye*′), on the other hand, have one word for automobile, but at least a hundred words referring to the cow.

The major pastoral peoples of Africa south of the Sahara include the Nilotic peoples of southeastern Sudan, the Fulani (foo-*lah*′nee) of West Africa, the Masai of Tanzania and Kenya, and the Tutsi of

Tending the cattle is the first responsibility of a youth who grows up among one of Africa's many pastoral peoples. Alone, he needs his spear to protect the herd against wild animals and raiders from other tribes.

Rwanda (ruh-*wahn'*duh)and Burundi (boo-*run'*dee).[6] These proud herders lead a nomadic or semi-nomadic life. When grass and water are plentiful they establish more or less permanent homes, but when the dry season arrives it is necessary to move constantly to obtain food and water for the cattle. Wealth is determined by the size of a man's herd. Birth, marriage, and death ceremonies involve the exchange of cattle. Education is focused on learning the skills of herding cattle and on building the courage needed to protect them from marauding animals and the raids of neighboring tribes. It is not unusual for a lone Masai boy to fight off a lion to protect the cattle in his custody. Cattle are rarely killed for meat, and if a favorite bull should die, there is great sorrow. The major food consists of milk mixed with blood which is obtained by periodically tapping a vein in the neck of a cow.

Some pastoral peoples organize herding responsibilities around age groups. Raiding the cattle of a neighboring tribe is commonplace among many pastoral people. Because caring for cattle, fighting,

[6] Sometimes the Tutsi (*toot'*see) are called Batusi or Watusi. The prefixes *Ba-* and *Wa-* indicate particular grammatical inflections of the words to which they are attached. Wherever possible, this text uses only the stems of tribal names.

Age Groups Among Masai Males

Age	Status	Duties
Up to 14	Boys ("Ol Ayoni")	At about age 12 or 13, the boys of a village form an age-set and prepare for initiation. They learn how to hunt and to tend herds of cattle.
14–18	Junior Warriors ("Ol Aibertani")	After initiation, young men roam the country, learning to fight and visiting various other Masai groups.
18–32	Guardians or Warriors ("Ol Morrani") (a) Warriors of the Left Hand (age 18 to 25) (b) Warriors of the Right Hand (age 25 to 32)	Men in this age group live in barracks called the *manyatta*. They are organized into regiments for war, hunting, or guarding the herds. Senior warriors are married.
35 and over	Elders ("Ol Nesher") (a) Councilmen ("Ol Piron") (b) Priests ("Ol Aibon")	The elders hold the positions of authority. (a) The "Ol Piron" — literally, "firesticks" — sit on the tribal council and help to elect the chief. (b) The priests are rainmakers, medicine men, and prophets. The head priest pronounces blessings on warriors and supervises age-group initiations.

and leadership are major responsibilities of a pastoral tribe, members are frequently organized on the basis of age groups. (See fact panel on page 33.) Young boys are entrusted with responsibility for tending the cattle. When they are about fifteen years of age, the boys take part in an elaborate initiation ceremony during which they are required to undergo extreme pain to demonstrate their manly qualities. The group of young men initiated at the same time live together and become as close as brothers. Among the Masai, a mature warrior (aged 18 to 32) is called *ol morrani* — meaning "protector of the cattle." When a man's son is initiated into the warrior age group, the father in turn is likely to be moving into an elder age group where his main task will be to make decisions and to settle disputes.

Tillers of the soil have developed relatively complex societies. Because farmers tend to live a settled life in comparatively densely populated communities, agriculture has led to the development of societies which are more complex than the relatively simple societies of the herders. Contrary to widespread belief, African people were not all ruled by "chiefs." A system whereby the elders of extended families met in council to make major decisions and settle disputes was much more common.

Farmers share a concept of land ownership different from that held by Westerners. To the farmers, land was as sacred and important as was cattle to the pastoralists. The herders associated life with cattle, whereas the agriculturalists viewed the land as life itself. Thus it was inconceivable that one would sell his land to another, for like the air one breathes, the land was necessary for life. Among the Kikuyu (kee-*koo'*yoo) of Kenya, for example, land might be *held*, or occupied, by the individual, but it *belonged* to the tribe. The tribe, in turn, was an association made up of one's departed ancestors, one's living relatives, and relatives yet to be born. A man's most important inheritance was his right to cultivate the common possession of his people — the land.

This attitude toward land differs sharply from the Western concept of land as real estate that may be bought and sold. When the British came to Kenya, they gave money and other valuables to Kikuyu elders for land which was not then occupied. The English settler believed that he had purchased the land. But the Kikuyu farmer understood that he had accepted a gift in exchange for which he would allow the Englishman to *cultivate* the land. It was inconceivable to a Kikuyu that he could have sold his land. How could he sell the graves and

Like many other African farmers, the Somba people of northern Dahomey depend on simple hoes. They rotate their crops, shifting from one field to another, but gain only a bare living by their long toil. In gratitude, however, the Somba revere the earth as the source of life.

spirits of his ancestors or the birthright of his children and his children's children?

Among the Kikuyu, each extended family cultivated its own fields and was generally self-sufficient. Disputes were heard and decisions made by the family elders. Neighboring families were likely to belong to the same clan, and disputes between families were settled by a council of elders. When threatened by their traditional enemies (the Masai), or on special ceremonial occasions, the Kikuyu leaders of the various clans would meet in a tribal council.

The Baganda and Ashanti developed elaborate social and political systems. Although the extended family and the clan were important, the Baganda people of Uganda went farther than the Kikuyu in developing the tribe as a highly centralized organization. In contrast to the Kikuyu, they had a king called the *kabaka* (kuh-*bah'*kuh), who ruled the people through major and minor chiefs, each in charge of a division of the kingdom.

35

A still different system existed among the Ashanti cultivators in present-day Ghana. Whereas the Baganda and the Kikuyu, as *patrilineal societies,* inherited rights to land through the father's side of the family, the Ashanti, as a *matrilineal* society, traced their descent through the female line. When an Ashanti boy reached puberty he would leave his father's home to live with his mother's brother's family.

Government existed on several levels. The social and political system of the Ashanti was complex. The family elders met together as a village council. In each village, however, one extended family was especially important, for it was believed to be directly descended from the founder of the village. A man from this elite family was selected as a village chief. A meeting of all the village chiefs from one district constituted a district council. Each district council, in turn, would elect its own chief. Then, in turn, the chiefs of the district councils would sit together to constitute a divisional council, headed by the paramount chief — the *asantehene.* At each level, chiefs were regarded not only as leaders but as priests in charge of ceremonies venerating the ancestors. The Ashanti believed that their ancestors lived in a spirit world which to them was just as real as the physical world. There they watched over the living chiefs to see how well they were doing.

The symbol of the unity of the Ashanti at every level was a sacred stool, or throne. The chief was the caretaker of the stool. The most important of these seats was the fabled "Golden Stool" entrusted to the care of the paramount chief of all the Ashanti.

Kinship patterns are more extensive in Africa than in the United States. In the United States, family life centers about the husband, wife, and their children. Grandparents, uncles, aunts, and cousins are important, but they usually do not play a part in the daily life of the family. Most African societies, however, have more extensive kinship patterns, in part because many are polygamous. Since a husband may have two or more wives, it is necessary not only to think of mother and father but of the wife-of-my-father, the child of the wife-of-my-father, and so on. This seems strange and confusing to us, but to the African it is commonplace.

American women cannot easily imagine a marriage in which the husband has two or more wives. In part this reflects American culture, where romantic love between two individuals is so important. In African societies, however, polygamous marriage is considered desirable because it provides security and ensures the propagation of the group. Each wife has her own house and garden, and knows her obligations to the head of the family. The wives usually become close friends for they have much in common. They help one another in the fields and assist in rearing the children. They share each other's sorrow and happiness.

Some Americans erroneously believe that Africans buy their wives. In reality, marriage in Africa — as everywhere — involves an exchange of vows. As a symbol that he will keep the marriage contract and be able to support his wife, the groom's family gives the family of the bride a form of dowry. If the marriage is dissolved or if no children are born to the couple, this dowry generally is returned to the groom's family. Usually cattle or other livestock make up the dowry.

African societies are based upon a series of descent (or relative) groups. The "descent groups," in order of increasing size, are the immediate family, the extended family, the lineage, the clan, the tribe, and today, the nation. The extended family is perhaps best described as all the people descended from the oldest living male ancestor. The close bonds of respect, mutual affection, and obligation which are inherent in the relationships of mother, father, and children in our society, apply to the entire extended family in most African societies. When an African speaks of his brother and sister, he often is referring to his cousins. An extended family which traces its ancestry to a particular person, even though he may no longer be alive, is called a *lineage*. Associations of lineages which share belief in a common origin are termed *clans*. The Ashanti of Ghana, for example, are divided into eight clans. Fellow clansmen feel a special sense of obligation and loyalty to each other.

This system, though it may be inappropriate in some ways in the modern world, worked very well in traditional Africa. The extended family provided security and love; it ensured that everyone would be cared for. A member of the extended family could return home at any time and stay as long as he liked. The family felt a deep obligation to all its members, and each member was expected to do his share of the work. There were no orphanages, insane asylums, or nursing homes in traditional Africa. The aged and infirm had a home in the family and the comfort of knowing that there would always be a place where they would be welcomed and cared for.

Loyalty to the kinship group is paramount. To Africans, the kinship unit is more important than the individual, and everybody has an obligation to work for its perpetuation. The dead are important for they are spirits who watch over the living, rewarding them for doing what is proper and punishing them for failure to do whatever is necessary to continue the life of the family. The newly born are important for they testify to the health of the family and to the fact that there always will be someone to look after the parents when they grow old. The birth of a child is a sign of the continuation of the family, and a woman is not accepted into her husband's family until she has given birth to a child. To the grandparents, this means that their spirits will live on.

Most African religions recognize a Supreme Being. The belief that in the distant past a God created the earth, all life, and a social order, is shared by nearly all African religions. It usually is believed, however, that lesser deities and the ancestor spirits stand between the individual and this creator God. Although a majority of Africans today regard themselves as Christians or as Muslims, the traditional African religions are still important. In part this is because these earlier religions are an inseparable part of traditional culture. The elder members of an African community served as its rulers, priests, and allocators of land, and they did not make clear-cut distinctions between their political, religious, and economic functions. The various aspects of traditional African life were so closely interwoven that a change in one facet of life was bound to affect all other areas of activity. A change in the principles of land ownership, for example, would alter African religious practices, occupations, politics, and economics.

To regard all African religion as necessarily primitive, or as based largely on magic or voodoo would be a grave error. Prayers and offerings are common, as they are in most religions. Animals are sacrificed because they symbolize life and, therefore, are considered the most valuable offering one can make to God. Usually the meat is eaten by those who participate in the offering ceremony. African religions are comparable to Judaism or Christianity in their complexity. They teach not so much about God as about the nature of his relationship to man.

The African peasant and herdsman live close to nature. If rains fail or the crops are flooded or eaten by pests, the African may be threatened with starvation. Thus, ritual ceremonies associated with all life — human, animal, and plant alike — are most important. Births, deaths, christenings, initiation ceremonies, and celebrations to mark the seasons are taken very seriously. Their purpose is to im-

An African diviner carries his various amulets and charms in skin pouches slung from his neck. If misfortune occurs, he uses these sacred objects in ceremonies to discover, or "divine," the cause. A successful diviner must have keen insight into the habits and personalities of his people. Such knowledge makes him a person of great authority.

plore the gods to continue to make the world function as it has in the past so that man may live without constant threat of danger from the elements.

When nature does not behave according to man's expectation — when streams dry up, crops fail, or children are stillborn — the African seeks the advice of a diviner. Europeans frequently refer to the African diviner as a "sorcerer" or "witch doctor." It is true that the African diviner invokes supernatural powers, and that the ways in which he does this seem strange to Europeans (and Americans), even as European rituals and symbols may seem strange to an African. More important is the awe with which many Africans regard the diviner and his claim to supernatural power. This can give a diviner great influence over his community — an influence which he may use to pay off grudges or to benefit himself and his relatives. Diviners, however, often are intelligent and responsible men who have undergone extensive training in their art. Like modern psychoanalysts, they possess extraordinary insight into the ways that people think and act. Their task is not an easy one, for they must bring harmony to a distracted and disturbed community. Sometimes this requires them to help an individual to see clearly the conflicts, inadequacies, and peculiarities underlying his own life.

39

Some of the newly-independent countries have undertaken systematic study of their ancient religions. It seems likely that in the future such religions as Christianity and Islam will absorb more of the ideas and spiritual values of the traditional African religions.

- **CHECK-UP**

    1. Define the word "tribe." What present problems in Africa stem in part from arbitrary boundaries established by colonial powers?
    2. Compare these ways of living: hunting and gathering, cattle herding, tilling the soil. Contrast the conception of land ownership held by African and American farmers.
    3. Contrast kinship patterns in Africa and in this country. How would an African trace his "descent groups"?
    4. What is the place of religion and ritual ceremonies in African life? What is the role of the diviner?

Summing Up

Variety and contrast characterize the landscape and peoples of Africa. To develop a useful understanding of either, the non-African must strive to view the continent through African eyes.

Perhaps Africa's most conspicuous single topographic feature is the generally high elevation of this land — 90 per cent of it is 500 feet or more above sea level. This vast "plateau" is broken up by mountains, rivers, and basins. The principal river systems are those of the Nile, Congo, Niger, Volta, Zambezi, Limpopo, Orange, and Vaal. The Chad and Congo basins in northern and central Africa, and the Kalahari Basin in the south comprise Africa's chief basins. Running through much of eastern Africa is another kind of depression — the Rift Valley, a land fault formed thousands of years ago by a fracture in the earth's crust. The Rift includes deep canyons, and a series of long, narrow, and deep lakes.

The Sahara Desert occupies most of the northern third of the continent. Although it separates the Mediterranean coast from the interior, the desert was never an impassable barrier, for it was crossed by many well-traveled caravan routes from time immemorial. The introduction by Romans (about 300 A.D.) of the Arabian camel greatly facilitated and expanded trans-Saharan transport.

South of the Sahara extends a broad stretch of savanna called the sudan. Its grassy plains merge to the south with a belt of dense vegetation and rain forest. The more heavily populated western coast of this forest belt provided by far the greatest number of blacks sold into slavery in the Western Hemisphere. Much of the eastern and southern part of the continent is covered by dry woodland and savanna, and in the west, by the Namib and Kalahari deserts.

Evidence suggests that Africa was the home of the first humans. Climate and genetic patterns may have been the main factors which led to the continent's present racial differentiation, but scientists disagree on the exact origins of Africa's dark-skinned peoples. Some 600 to 800 distinct languages and dialects are spoken — a serious obstacle to African unity. Among the occupations, cattle-herding ranks second only to farming. But productive farming is made difficult by Africa's distinct rainy and dry seasons. Torrential rains leach the soil, which is mainly a tropical laterite. The much-coveted highland areas, on the other hand, have better soil and a more temperate climate.

African cultures and life-styles are molded in large part by the dominant occupations. Farming, food-gathering, and cattle-herding economies engender their own distinctive forms of political and social organization. Nearly all Africans, however, attach great value to family ties — extended to include in-laws and cousins. The clan and tribe, once simply extensions of the family, derived much of their cohesiveness from the belief that all members were descended from a common ancestor. The frequently-misused term "tribe" is applied here to any group of people who share a common language, culture, and, usually, territory. But rapid changes, including the emergence of new African nations with boundaries which cut across tribal lines, are tending to weaken traditional forms of social organization. Nevertheless, loyalty to one's kinship group still is regarded as a paramount social virtue. This feeling is strengthened by African religious traditions and rituals, in which the spirits of ancestors figure prominently. Rituals also remind men of their dependence on the forces of nature. Persons thought to possess special knowledge and insight into such forces — the diviners (whom Europeans called "witch-doctors") — often occupy positions of great influence in their communities. Today's educated Africans are trying to preserve within a modern framework the best elements of their ancient traditions.

CHAPTER REVIEW

Can You Identify?

great African lakes	age-groups	basin
Kalahari Desert	negritude	Nile
homo sapiens	Swahili	Niger
subsistence economy	Bushmen	Congo
extended family	laterite	Sahara
Guinea tropics	"we-ness"	Bantu
fossil	diviner	Click
Rift Valley	culture	Hausa

What Do You Think?

1. Why does Africa, the second largest continent, have only a tenth of the world's population?

2. Why are most of Africa's large cities near the coast?

3. Why have Africans and Europeans clashed over land ownership in the Kenya highlands?

4. What conclusions about Masai society can be inferred from the status and duties of each age group among Masai males?

5. Why have some African states, even after independence, continued to use such foreign languages as English and French in business, education, and government?

6. What advantages were provided by the extended family in traditional African societies?

Extending and Applying Your Knowledge

1. Selections in Burke, *Africa: Selected Readings* (Houghton Mifflin) contain vivid descriptions of the African landscape — highlands, rain forest, and desert. See pages 10–19.

2. For an understanding of the significance of sacrifice in African religions, see *Africa: Selected Readings*, pages 27–36.

3. The reason some Africans have been reluctant to introduce cash-crop farming is suggested on pages 20–23, *Africa: Selected Readings*.

4. You will find some African folk tales on pages 40–44, *Africa: Selected Readings*. Peggy Rutherford has edited an anthology of contemporary African writings, *African Voices* (Vanguard), 1959.

2

EARLY AFRICAN CIVILIZATIONS NORTH OF THE SUDAN

The last chapter discussed the continent of Africa from the standpoint of its geography and people. This and succeeding chapters will deal with the main strands of African history. Even though the focus will be on separate regions of the continent, relationships which existed between them will not be neglected. North, south, east, and west interacted, giving to African history great cultural variety. Archaeological and anthropological discoveries are steadily adding to knowledge of the African past. Nevertheless, enough is already known about the history of Africa to make it an essential part of the history of mankind.

1. Egyptian Civilization Develops Along the Northern Reaches of the Nile

Some 4500 years ago, people in the lower (i.e., northern) Nile Valley began to build huge pyramids and temples and to develop an elaborate government. They also devised a system of writing which greatly facilitated the progress of their society — its religion, commerce, and political structure. Egyptian civilization — "the gift of the Nile," as Herodotus called it — was destined to play an important role in the history of Africa generally. What circumstances are responsible for the early emergence of this civilization? To answer this question, archaeologists go back to a period of history which antedated by at least a thousand years the building of Egypt's Great Pyramid.

Ancient Egyptians rejoiced when the Nile River flooded, since they needed its water and silt to grow crops in a desert region. This flood, however, is caused by the high dam recently built at Aswan, and is undermining the 2200-year-old temple of Isis at Philae. Plans have been made to dismantle the temple and relocate it above the new water level.

A revolution in food production makes possible a larger population along the Nile. The silt deposited by the regular overflowing of the Nile provided fertile soil especially favorable for farming in the plain along its banks. The people of that region, therefore, gradually abandoned hunting and food-gathering in favor of agriculture and herding as primary sources of food. They adopted agriculture much earlier than the rest of Africa's inhabitants. Thus, we find by about 5000 B.C. a settled and fairly dense population in the lower Nile Valley. South of the Sahara this change began to take place in the third millennium B.C. (between 3000 and 2000 B.C.), whereas in other parts of Africa south of the equator the switch to the settled life of an agricultural economy did not begin until the Christian era. Indeed there are now only a few isolated parts of Africa where hunting still provides the main source of food.

Climatic changes helped determine the location of the earliest civilization. Thousands of years ago — beginning around 4000 B.C. — long periods of drought changed a large part of Egypt's arable land into desert. The shifting sands of the desert drove the earliest farmers of Middle Egypt from their cultivated hillsides to the bottom of the valley. They cleared the Nile valley — which was then swamp and dense forest — and made it suitable for growing crops. Using the tools which they seem to have acquired earlier from Asia and had improved, these people successfully cultivated wheat, barley, flax, and various vegetables and forage plants. At some point during this period they also learned how to domesticate goats, sheep, pigs, and cattle. Their most important crops were wheat and barley, for the production of these two cereal grains in large quantity made possible a rapidly expanding population.

The food-producing revolution could not spread to the rest of Africa until the discovery of grain cereals and other foods suited to the more tropical climate and conditions of rainfall in those areas. Sorghum was one such cereal crop, but it appears not to have been cultivated in sub-Saharan Africa before 1000 B.C. The Nile Valley was thus especially favored with the soil and climate necessary for the development of a settled and civilized society.

The idea of kingship takes root in Egypt. The people who moved into the flood plain of Middle Egypt early in the fourth millennium B.C. quickly formed themselves into permanent village settlements fortified against invasion from other villages. By about 3500 B.C. the larger of these villages were expanding into towns. These towns had rectangular houses made from sun-baked mud bricks with wood doors and windows, not unlike some of the buildings still found in towns in the Middle East. Paintings reveal that these townsmen had built large boats and that they carried on trade with other centers of civilization which were then emerging. From the Aegean (ee-*jee'*un), for example, silver and lead were imported, and from Nubia (*noo'*bih-uh), south of Egypt, came shipments of gold. Lebanon was a source of timber, while copper was obtained from the Sinai Peninsula. Excavations of cemeteries show that great differences in wealth were developing. Such differences led to the emergence of classes, and to what today is called a power structure. In the past, some historians have held that Egypt derived its earliest ideas of kingship from Mesopotamia. More recent evidence, however, shows that the first royal dynasties, or ruling houses, of Mesopotamia dated from about the same time as the fifth royal dynasty of Egypt (or about 2500 to 2300 B.C.). It is reasonable, therefore, to assume that a form of kingship was developed by the Egyptians themselves.

Ancient Egyptian tombs reflect the development of the kingship idea. The oldest Egyptian tombs date back to nearly 4000 B.C. But the tombs bear little resemblance, if any, to the imposing royal tombs which were built a thousand years later. They all do have one thing in common, however. Both the early and the later tombs contain utensils and other articles belonging to the dead person. This shows

The Egyptian pyramids look down on the reconstruction of an ancient Nile River boat, woven of papyrus reeds by men from Lake Chad who still build boats by this method. One of them later made a trans-Atlantic voyage in the boat with archaeologist Thor Heyerdahl to test the possibility that ancient Egyptians might have come to America.

that the Egyptians from earliest times had a strong interest in the hereafter. This belief in a future life was a prominent feature of Egyptian culture throughout its long history.

The concern of the people for the hereafter was not expressed on a really grand scale, however, until the time of the ruler Narmer. His tomb at Abydos (uh-*bye'*dahs), built sometime around 2800 B.C., was much more elaborate than any which preceded it, both in its size and in the provisions made for his comfort in the next life. Narmer's body was accompanied by those of others buried with their master to serve him in the hereafter. An examination of the tombs of later rulers (who came to be called *pharaohs* [*fair'*ohs] from an Egyptian word meaning "palace of the ruler") shows that they became progressively larger and more elaborate, reaching their peak of grandeur in the Great Pyramid, built for Pharaoh Khufu (*koo'*foo). The tomb of Khufu, who lived several centuries after the reign of Narmer, attained a height of 481 feet — an incredible engineering feat for those times.

According to Herodotus the construction of this pyramid required the labor of some 100,000 people, who worked without let-up for approximately 20 years.

Unification goes hand in hand with the expansion of Egyptian power. At first, northern, or Lower Egypt (the Delta) and southern, or Upper Egypt seem to have been organized as distinct kingdoms. The earliest ruling families of the village settlements in Egypt were undoubtedly those who made the most skillful use of the Nile's flood waters in producing a surplus supply of food. This surplus then became a growing source of wealth. Some authorities have estimated that Egyptian peasants could produce as much as three times their own domestic requirements of food, once their labor had been organized by a powerful overlord.[1] Increasing travel by boat along the Nile facilitated the exchange of goods and ideas. Certain towns acquired a reputation for producing special types of goods, and this also helped to increase trade. A rivalry between districts sometimes led to friction, and over a long period, to wars, conquests, defeats, and alliances.

Eventually Upper Egypt gained the ascendancy and conquered the cities of the Delta. Tradition ascribed to Narmer (probably another name for Menes, a warrior king of Upper Egypt) the conquest which resulted in the establishment of Egypt's First Dynasty, around 2850 B.C. The story of Egypt's unification is summarized by Walter A. Fairservis, Jr., in *The Ancient Kingdoms of the Nile:*

> A . . . slate [tablet] of this king [Narmer] is in the Cairo Museum, and as the first conquest document of its kind it is of considerable interest. It is a . . . document recording the conquest of a portion of the Delta. . . . [It] indicates that the Upper Egyptians wanted something the Lower Egyptians had: perhaps ease of passage to the copper of Sinai, the possession of their cattle and fields, or the shores of the Mediterranean. . . . [Added to] these desires [were] grievances for earlier conquests and raids, . . . personal ambition and the like. . . . The Egypt that first appears on the stage of history is a nation united by war. It was a rich agricultural nation but woefully short in certain metals, semi-precious stones, [and] ivory. . . . Egypt, as one of the world's first civilizations, provides an

[1] Roland Oliver and John D. Fage, *A Short History of Africa* (Baltimore: Penguin Books, second edition, 1966), p. 37.

illustration for all civilizations. Rich in some things, poor in others, its economy and social order labored to stay in balance.[2]

The picture we get of the process of unification is somewhat confused. But once the ruling power became consolidated under a single head, Egypt remained a stable land for centuries.

A slate tablet 5000 years old may record the unifying of Egypt by Narmer. Wearing the tall crown of Upper Egypt, Narmer is shown clubbing a defeated foe, probably a king of Lower Egypt. The hawk in the upper right corner was an emblem of Upper Egypt and of the god Horus, protector of the Egyptian pharaohs.

Religion reinforces the idea of kingship. Popular belief in the pharaoh's greatness and majesty was fostered by a variety of religious trappings and ceremonies. People came to believe that the pharaoh possessed superhuman qualities. The priests encouraged people to believe that their pharaoh was a god. As a matter of fact, the pharaoh was associated with a number of different gods. Most often, he was linked with Re (ray), god of the sun. Or, like Osiris (oh-*sye'*ris) — a god first worshipped by the peasants — the pharaoh was thought to be reborn after death. In battle, the pharaoh's troops carried the

[2] Walter A. Fairservis, Jr., *The Ancient Kingdoms of the Nile* (New York: Thomas Y. Crowell Company, 1962). Quote is from Mentor paperback edition, p. 81.

standard of the falcon-god Horus — who in Egyptian mythology had fought for his father, Osiris. Thus the authority of the pharaoh was reinforced by religious ritual. And by exercising his growing military power, the pharaoh was able to extend his personal authority over a vast area. At its peak, around 1470 B.C., the empire of Egypt extended from the river Euphrates (yoo-*fray′*teez) in southwestern Asia into most of Nubia — a distance of more than two thousand miles (see map on page 70). During periods of peace, Egyptian culture as we have come to know it developed into maturity.

Egypt's administrative system proves to be a source of weakness as well as strength. The Egyptian Empire was subdivided into a number of provinces, called *nomes* (*nohms*), which were governed by officials responsible to the pharaoh. This system worked well as long as these officials had close personal and economic ties with the pharaoh and depended on him for protection. But as the number of officials increased and the distance between them and the pharaoh widened, the ties of loyalty which linked the pharaoh with his administrative officials grew weaker. Even more important, positions in the government came to be passed on from father to son. The inheritance of offices often prevented men of talent and ambition, but without family connections, from advancing in government service. During the Sixth Dynasty (2315–2175 B.C.), Egypt's administrative machinery began to fall apart. Local officials became increasingly independent of the pharaoh. The state religion which had been one of the chief unifying forces during this period, known as the "Old Kingdom," was all but lost sight of in the worship of more popular local deities. Thus the first great age of Egypt — a period of high intellectual and moral achievements — ended in a gradual decline.

The center of power moves southward. An "Intermediate Period" of some 150 years followed the reign of Pepi (*pay′*pee) II, last of the outstanding rulers of the "Old Kingdom." It was a period of disorder, of rivalry among the local rulers, and of war with foreign powers. According to an Egyptian writer of the time, "Great and humble men say, 'Would that I might die!' and little children cry out, 'I never should have been born!' "

Out of this upheaval there emerged once again a strong line of kings, who restored a single authority in Egypt. But by now the center of power had been moved three hundred miles to the south—from Memphis to Thebes, the modern Luxor (see map on page 70). During this period of the Middle Kingdom — from about 2100 to 1800

B.C. — the pharaohs turned their attention increasingly southward toward the land beyond the cataracts of the Nile. From its earliest days, Egypt had imported supplies of gold from Nubia, and there are records of large expeditions to Nubia and lands still farther south. A stone inscription dating from about 2275 B.C., for example, tells of four expeditions led by a servant of Pharaoh Merenra (me-*ren*'rah) into the south country. He is described as having returned from his last journey — which took him to the Congo forest — with 300 asses laden with incense, ebony, skins, and boomerangs, and with a Pygmy for the pharaoh's court. Scholars have interpreted this as evidence that even in early times Egypt had established contacts with lands as far south as the rain forest of the Congo.

Nubia is brought into the Egyptian Empire. During the period of the Middle Kingdom, the pharaohs attempted to conquer the territory of the Nubians, perhaps to gain control of the southern trade. They therefore made frequent raids on Nubian lands during the Eleventh and Twelfth Dynasties. By the end of the Middle Kingdom (about 1785 B.C.), the pharaohs had completed their conquest of Lower Nubia as far as the Second Cataract of the Nile.

A "Second Intermediate Period" followed, during which powerful conquerors from Asia known as the *Hyksos* (*hik*'sohs) invaded Egypt and even gained control of the whole empire for a time. They were aided in their victories by their use of horse-drawn chariots. The Hyksos were ultimately overthrown, however, and during the Eighteenth Dynasty they were expelled from the empire. The shakeup of the administrative machinery brought on by the Hyksos invasion seems to have restored some of the efficiency and drive that characterized the Egyptians in earlier times. For this age, known as the New Kingdom, was one of expansion and imperial glory. It lasted more than five centuries (from about 1580 to 1050 B.C.). Insofar as Nubia is concerned, the powerful Ahmose (*ah*'mohs) I (1580–1558 B.C.) began, and later Thutmose (thoot-*moh*'seh) I (c. 1525–1512 B.C.) completed, Egyptian conquest of that territory as far as the Fourth Cataract. Thutmose, a great general, fought off the Libyans in the west as well as Asian peoples in the east, and expanded his empire to include the land from the Euphrates to Napata (*nap*'uh-tuh) in Kush[3]

[3] Note that the spelling "Kush" refers here to the ancient kingdom and its civilization. The spelling "Cush" occurs in subsequent chapters when referring to certain peoples, mainly those in northeastern Africa, who speak a related class of languages — Cushitic. (Cushitic is a subdivision of the Afro-Asiatic branch of languages. See pages 25–27.)

An ancient Egyptian tomb painting shows (*top*) dark-skinned Nubians on the deck of a boat in the Nile River, and (*bottom*) other Nubians bringing gifts to the Egyptian viceroy. The sculptured head of a Nubian princess (*right*) was found at Gizeh and identified as the wife of a noble at the court of Khufu, the pharaoh who built the Great Pyramid.

and beyond. The enterprising Queen Hatshepsut, who followed him, was famous for her great trading expeditions by water down the Red Sea to Somalia (or "Punt"). Egypt's New Kingdom flourished until about 1050 B.C., by which time Egyptian civilization once more began to stagnate.

Egyptian civilization moves closer to Black Africa. Rameses (ram′-uh-seez) XI, the last pharaoh of the 20th Dynasty, ruled during a period of internal unrest and division. Lower (or northern) Egypt became a constant prey to Libyan princes, who established a series of short-lived dynasties in the Delta (22nd–24th Dynasties). As Egypt declined, the power of Kush, centered in the city of Napata, grew in the south. The rulers of the Napata area had gradually unified the whole region from the Second to the Fifth Cataract. Meroë (*mer′*oh-ee), south of the Fifth Cataract, became a kind of second capital ruled by members of the Napatan royal family, and the whole realm was called the "Kingdom of Kush."

Kushite rulers aspire to conquer Egypt. Kush was blessed with excellent troops, cavalry experienced in patrolling the bordering desert areas, and rich economic resources. Egyptians residing in Kush seemed to have urged a takeover of the lands to the north, and the Kush rulers listened to them. One of them, Kashta, who reigned just before 751 B.C., finally invaded Upper (or southern) Egypt. His son Piankhi (*pyang′*kih), whose reign lasted from about 751 to 716 B.C., carried the war northward into the Delta, breaking up the various coalitions formed against him, and conquering Memphis. His brother later consolidated these conquests and moved the capital to Thebes. He and his successors restored many of the temples in Egypt and Nubia, and began the building of new ones also. For about a hundred years Kush was a great power.

Egypt succumbs to new foreign invasions. Egypt might have continued under Kushite rule but for a blunder in foreign policy which brought the wrath of the Assyrian armies down on her. Phoenicia (fih-*nee′*shuh), a small kingdom of traders on the eastern Mediterranean shores, had rebelled against its Assyrian overlord, who dominated much of southwestern Asia, and the Kushite leaders came to its defense. But Kushite forces could not match the iron weapons of Assyria. In 671 B.C. King Esarhaddon (ee-sar-*had′*un) of Assyria defeated the Kushites and expelled them from Memphis. The Kushites made a brief comeback, but in 661 Esarhaddon's son, the mighty Ashurbanipal (ah-shoor-*bah′*nih-pahl), inflicted a crushing defeat upon them. Forced to withdraw to their ancestral land, the Kushites never again invaded Egypt.

Egypt was ruled, after the withdrawal of the Assyrians and Kushites, by the royal family of Sais (*say′*is), a city on the Delta, until 525 B.C. The Persians were the next to invade Egypt, holding it under their sway until Alexander the Great drove them out. Then there was a long period of Greek rule under the Ptolemies (*tahl'*uh-meez). The Romans made Egypt part of their empire in 30 B.C., and it remained under their rule (including Byzantine, or East Roman, rule) more or less uninterruptedly until the Muslim conquest in the seventh century A.D. The great empire of the pharaohs had become only a memory, but the achievements and the cultural inheritance of the Egyptians gave inspiration to many other civilizations in Europe, Asia, and Africa.

- **CHECK-UP**
  1. Why did a great civilization develop in the lower Nile Valley? How were Upper and Lower Egypt united? How did the pharaohs become increasingly powerful?
  2. With what countries did Egypt trade? How was Egyptian civilization extended southward? What were the relations of Kush to Egypt?

2. A Rival Center of Power Emerges in Ethiopia

According to an ancient Greek legend, the gods spent twelve days each year feasting in the land of the "blameless Ethiopians." It was to these peoples — to "Africa beyond Egypt" — that the Greeks gave the highest rank and dignity in their estimate of Africans. The great Greek historian and traveler, Herodotus, for example, made this observation about Ethiopia after his visit to southern Egypt around 450 B.C.: "The furthest inhabited country [south of Egypt] . . . is Ethiopia. Here gold is found in great abundance, and huge elephants, and ebony, and all sorts of trees growing wild. The men, too, are the tallest in the world, the best-looking, and the longest-lived."

The Greeks used the term "Ethiopian" very broadly, applying it in general to any of the dark-skinned peoples found in larger numbers in the lands *south* of Egypt rather than in Egypt itself. (The word *Ethiopia* comes from two Greek words meaning "[sun]burned face.") The term "Ethiopian" was used by Greeks and other ancient peoples with the same lack of precision that the term "Negro" is used by Americans today. It is well-known that dark-skinned peoples — people who if they were living in the United States today would be considered Negroes — played an important role in the development of imperial Egypt. They served as laborers, officials, and occasionally as kings. But south of Egypt there was an area where dark-skinned Africans were in the majority and where a distinctive civilization had developed.

Kush develops independently of Egypt. We have seen how Egypt, during the New Kingdom, brought most of Nubia — including the two provinces of Wawat (*wah'*waht) and Kush — into its sphere of influence and, at times, under direct rule. It is natural, therefore, that Kush would be greatly influenced by Egyptian culture. Yet, despite obvious similarities with Egypt, the people of Kush managed to retain many of their own ideas and customs. One evidence of this is found in the tombs of the Kushite pharaohs of the Twenty-Fifth Egyptian Dynasty, which show in their style and arrangement of burial objects a return to ancient Kushite practices.

Meroë becomes the dominant Kushite city. The first phase of Kushite power, then, was the period when Kushite rulers at Napata had accumulated sufficient wealth and power — based on their control of the Nubian gold supply — to invade and conquer Egypt. As already noted, the Assyrians drove the Kushites out of Egypt in the seventh century B.C. The court at Napata — which was greatly influenced by Egyptian culture — remained the dominant seat of authority in Kush for about another century; but simultaneously another Kushite town, Meroë, was gaining importance. Moreover, Meroë was exhibiting a more self-conscious and deliberate cultural independence of Egypt than was its sister city to the north. Meroë eventually displaced Napata as the center of Kushite civilization. Although the reasons for this southward shift are not entirely clear, two factors undoubtedly weighed heavily: (1) the continuing desiccation (drying up) of the land around Napata with the resulting shortage of pasturage and timber and (2) a destructive raid on Napata by a Persian army in 591 B.C.

Meroë benefits from its iron industry. At the time when Kushites fought the Assyrians, the Assyrian superiority in weaponry was brought home to Africans. The Kushites, however, were determined to profit from their defeat. Having acquired from the Assyrians the knowledge of how to smelt iron, they set themselves the task of forging iron weapons and tools. Taking advantage of the natural resources which were available in the southern region of Kush,[3] they eventually became

---

[3] Egypt had neither iron ore nor fuel for smelting; northern Kush had ore but not fuel; southern Kush around Meroë had both ore and fuel in abundance.

KING OF KUSH. A statue found in the ruins of a temple near Napata shows King Aspalta of Kush as a powerful figure, striding forward in Egyptian style. The temple was built to honor the great Egyptian sun-god, Amun-Re. Aspalta reigned in the 6th century B.C. after the Kushites had lost control of Egypt. The monarchs who followed Aspalta shifted the capital of Kush to the city of Meroë, farther south in the Nile Valley. There they built new temples, such as the one at Musawarat shown in the photograph above. Its heavy stone columns reflect the style of Egyptian temples, but it was dedicated to the old lion-god Apedemak, whom the Kushites worshipped before they came under Egyptian influence.

masters of the metalworkers' craft. In time, Meroë became one of the major iron-founding centers of the ancient world, comparable in modern times to Birmingham (England) or Pittsburgh. The iron-working slag-heaps of Meroë are visible even today; in fact one of its most important temples was built on the top of a slag-hill.

While the Ptolemies were ruling Egypt, the people of Meroë were carrying on a highly profitable trade. Caravan routes extended to Kushite ports on the Red Sea, to Egypt and the Mediterranean, and southward. Much farther to the southwest, at Koro Toro (*kohr'*oh *tohr'*oh) near Lake Chad, archaeologists have uncovered what some authorities assert are positive evidences of a Meroitic presence. The trade carried on by Meroë consisted not only of the traditional African luxury products — ivory, rare skins, ostrich feathers, ebony, gold — but also products of the Meroitic ironworking industry. With the aid of iron spears, the people of Meroë pushed the frontiers of Kush far to the south. Meanwhile, the introduction of the iron hoe benefited Meroitic agriculture. Meroë's prosperity, therefore, was based on its success in trade, mining, metalworking, and agriculture.

Cultural ferment accompanies Meroë's rise. Meroitic Kush covers eight or nine centuries of history, but its period of greatness lasted from about 250 B.C. until the first centuries of the Christian era. Of interest is the racial composition of Kush. Blacks were prominent throughout Kush from the beginning, but in Meroë they apparently were in the majority. But though whites (as that term is used today in the United States) were a minority, the racial factor apparently went unnoticed or was unimportant to the people of Meroë.

Meroitic Kush developed a sophisticated culture. For temple inscriptions, the people of Meroë used Egyptian hieroglyphs. The priests and tradesmen, however, devised an alphabetical writing — a script which presumably facilitated bookkeeping. Artistic expression flourished and took on a distinctively Meroitic style. The rise of Meroë was also accompanied by a return to the worship of Kushite gods. Prominent among them was the lion-god Apedemak (ah-*ped'*-uh-mahk). Under King Arnekhamani (ahr-nek-ah-*mah'*nee), of the late third century B.C., the great Lion Temple was built at Musawarat (moo-zuh-*wah'*raht), southwest of Meroë; another temple farther south at Naga (*nah'*gah) boasted a large and particularly fine stone engraving of a python — a frequent symbol of spiritual power in Africa. Stone ruins at Musawarat are decorated with relief sculpture depicting trained elephants in ceremonial processions.

Like all great trading centers, Meroë owed much to outside influences. Its temples and palaces were most obviously affected by Egyptian examples. But fragments of cotton cloth in the tombs, the use of tanks for water storage, and sculptured reliefs of Kushite kings riding on elephants all point to eastern influences from at least as far off as southern Arabia and perhaps even India. Some scholars see traces of Chinese styles in many of their copper vessels. All these elements were adapted to Meroitic tastes and needs.

Axum emerges as Meroë's competitor for power. Some 400 miles southeast of Meroë, in what is now northern Ethiopia, the second of the two outstanding civilizations of the land "beyond Egypt" arose. Like the civilization of Kush, Axum (*ahk'*soom) was a blend of several different cultures; unlike Kush, its principal early influence stemmed not from Egypt but from southern Arabia, across the Red Sea. The history of Axum is not yet well known, for it is only in recent years that archaeologists have begun to investigate it in a systematic way. They have been able to reconstruct the general development of the Axumite Kingdom, however.

It is now known, for example, that by the fifth century B.C., trade centers were flourishing along the coast and in the interior of northeastern Ethiopia. Altars have been unearthed which are engraved in the Sabaean (suh-*bee'*un) script of southern Arabia; and the gods depicted in Axumite art are likewise traceable to this source. Even so, objects uncovered in excavations of the 1950's reveal that Axumite culture also had its own distinctive qualities. This local originality increased with time.

By the fourth century B.C., Axum began to reflect greater Greek influence. Trading vessels which sailed between Ptolemaic Egypt and the East frequently stopped at the Ethiopian port of Adulis (ah-*doo'*-lis), north of Axum. The effects of the trade carried on through Adulis were felt in the city of Axum. An Alexandrian sailor, whose identity is unknown, published a mariner's guide in the late first century A.D. called the *Periplus* (*pair'*uh-plus) *of the Erythraean* (*er'*uh-*three'*un) *Sea,* or in modern English, "Sailing Directions for the Indian Ocean." This work, which apparently was used for centuries after its original publication, informs us that by the beginning of the Christian era Axum had become the most important ivory market in northeastern Africa.

By the time the *Periplus* made its appearance, Axum already had become the seat of a new line of kings. It had made a complete cultural break with Arabia, although the worship of certain old Arabian deities lingered on. The Sabaean language was displaced by Ge'ez (gee-*ez'*) — the popular tongue of the Axumites and parent of the modern Ethiopian language — and by Greek. Axum became a city of splendid palaces, temples, and carved stone "obelisks" or stelae (stone slabs). Imported iron weapons were used by Axumite hunters and traders. Such weapons, in turn, encouraged Axumite traders to penetrate farther south in search of new markets and new sources of wealth.

Axum subdues Kush and develops its own civilization. As Axumite power and wealth grew, that of Meroë diminished. Not only did Axum outdo its rival in trade, but other forces were contributing to the downfall of Kush. During the early fourth century A.D., new peoples, such as the Noba (*noh'*bah), were filtering into Kush from the north and west — people who had been forced off lands that were becoming too dry and arid to cultivate. We are told in one famous inscription that the Noba kept provoking the Ethiopians (Axumites) to fight. Finally, King Ezana (ee-*zah'*nah) of Axum met the Noba in battle and pursued them into the heart of Meroitic Kush. The con-

In comic-strip style, an Ethiopian painting (*top row*) first shows the Biblical King Solomon; next, dark-skinned Ethiopians tell him about their beautiful Queen of Sheba. Bottom row shows a messenger first, then the Queen on her way to visit Solomon, traveling on horseback and by boat.

In the ruins of ancient Axum, Ethiopian boys play on a fallen obelisk. The tallest obelisk in the background is 70 feet high. It was carved from a single block of granite with decorations representing windows.

flict which followed resulted in the final destruction of Meroë and its allied "towns of masonry" and "towns of straw." Ancient Kush never recovered from this crushing blow.

It was probably not long after the fall of Meroë that King Ezana of Axum accepted Christianity. Coins dating from this period suggest that at first Christianity existed side by side with pagan religions. But in time, Axum developed a strong Christian tradition — so strong that it resisted the rising tide of the Islamic faith which during the seventh century and later swept over most of Axum's neighbors.

Ethiopian culture develops in a kind of cultural isolation. Ethiopia's separation from other African cultures became more marked as the Axumite civilization merged into the Amharic (am-*har'*ik) civilization of medieval Ethiopia. Historians doubt that Ethiopia's isolation was total, however. Ethiopian traders and hunters probably maintained some contacts with the cultures of East Africa, which were also coming to use iron. There was an important copper-producing center at Katanga (in modern Zaire) which had trade connections with the East African coast, with the cities of the north, and probably with Axum. So far, however, the evidence is too scanty to enable historians to reconstruct these intercultural ties between various parts of early Africa.

● CHECK-UP

1. Why was the development of an iron industry important to Meroitic Kush? What cultural advances were made by this country?
2. Why did Axum become a rival of Kush and conquer it?

3. Mediterranean and Saharan Cultures Shape Early North Africa

According to legend, the city of Carthage in North Africa was founded in 814 B.C. by Dido (*dye'*doh), a Phoenician refugee princess of Tyre. Dido and her followers landed at a peninsula on the North African coast, where they decided to plant a colony. The native inhabitants — the Berbers — did not take kindly to the presence of these foreigners, however. In the discussions which followed, the Berbers consented to turn over to Dido only as much land as could be contained by the skin of an ox. Dido agreed; and to the chagrin of the Berbers she proceeded to cut up the hide into a long and narrow strip. With this strip she then enclosed enough land for a small town. From the small town grew the mighty Carthaginian Empire, for centuries Rome's chief rival in the Mediterranean.

The favorable location of Carthage at the crossroads of the Mediterranean trade routes facilitated contacts with Berber caravans from the Sahara and the African interior, and gave that city an advantage over other Phoenician towns which had been established as trading posts along the northern coast of Africa.[4] Carthage is perhaps the best-known of the ancient kingdoms of North Africa, but it was not the only one.

Who were the Berbers? Scattered across northwestern Africa today are a large number of tombs — stone monuments of varying heights and shapes — which date from before the Christian era. They testify to the presence of people who from about 1500 B.C. on had become an important part of the African scene. It is possible that the name Berber came from a Greek word meaning foreigner or barbarian. From the

---

[4] The North African trading posts had been established at short intervals because the Phoenicians sailed only by day and within sight of land. They were interested in obtaining rare metals of the Iberian Peninsula. Although Carthage became the most important of these Phoenician settlements and eventually gained control of the copper and tin mines of Spain, its real trading strength, by the fifth century B.C., was drawn not from Spain, but from the African interior with its gold, ivory, and other African goods.

Berbers the Greeks learned how to harness four horses to a chariot. In fact, Berber horsemanship spread the fame of these peoples throughout the ancient world. Herodotus, the "father of history," mentions a religious festival celebrated by the Auses (*aw'*seez), a Berber people who inhabited the southern part of modern Tunisia. The festival, or one like it, still continues to be celebrated by people of that area. The Berber script continues to be used by the Tuareg (*twah'*reg) Berbers of the Sahara, but the Berber inscriptions which the ancient Berbers left us have shed very little light on the nature of the old Berber culture.

The Berbers become an important link between North Africa and the African interior. Herodotus in the fifth century B.C. spoke of several branches of the Berbers, of which perhaps the best known are the Garamantes (gar-uh-*mahn'*teez). These branches corresponded to cultural and political divisions which had already come into existence, and which are reflected in the present-day divisions of North Africa: Morocco, Algeria, Tunisia, Libya. Differences between these peoples became blurred when Arabs mixed with them beginning in the seventh century A.D. But the persistence of the divisions suggests that the Berbers never overcame their differences sufficiently to unite into a single nation. The Greek name of one North African kingdom, Numidia (new-*mid'*ee-uh), reflects the unsettled character of the early Berbers. It comes from a Greek verb meaning "to wander," and our own word "nomad" is derived from it.

Once the Phoenicians were established along the coast of North Africa, they were quick to welcome these "wanderers" as carriers of goods to and from the African hinterland. Since the Phoenicians were skilled in farming as well as in business, the Berbers benefited from the example of more settled communities, first in producing food and second in organizing trading expeditions. In and around Tunisia, the Berbers became "Punicized," that is, they began to adopt Punic (the language of the Carthaginians) and to establish more settled agricultural kingdoms. They also adopted elements of Carthaginian and Semitic religious beliefs.

In the course of their wanderings, the Berbers penetrated far into Black Africa. The rock drawings which Berbers left behind testify to the existence of two major trade routes, both of which met at the great bend of the Niger River. Evidently there were regular contacts between the Mediterranean civilizations and the peoples of the African interior, such as those who later founded the empires of Kanem-

Modern-day horsemen in North Africa show the same spirit that character-ized their ancient Berber forbears. Fiercely independent, the Berbers had a taste for adventure and a skill in horsemanship which qualified them to be the middlemen between North Africa and the desert interior.

Bornu (*kah'*nem-*bor'*new), and Songhai (sahn-*gye'*). The Berbers were the middlemen in these contacts.

The growing commercial power of Carthage leads to war with Rome. Carthage at her peak of power was an empire to be reckoned with, having ports as far north as Britain, Spain, and Gaul (France). In the fifth century B.C., Hanno, a Carthaginian navigator, led one of the most daring expeditions of ancient times, sailing into the Atlantic and then along the African coast as far south as Cape Palmas (Liberia). According to one ancient source, he had a fleet of 60 light ships, each equipped with 50 oars. The expedition is said to have established six trading stations along the coast of western Africa. Whether or not this account is exaggerated, it suggests that the Carthaginians were sufficiently interested in continental African trade to wish to carry it on directly, rather than through middlemen.

As its trade expanded, Carthage came into conflict with Rome, a rising commercial power directly across the Mediterranean. Rome fought three major wars with Carthage (the Punic Wars), during which some of history's most spectacular military engagements took place. In the Second Punic War, for example, the Carthaginian general, Hannibal, led an expedition of soldiers, horses, and elephants northward in Spain into Gaul, and then across the Alps southward into Italy. Carthage had as an ally the Berber king of Numidia, Masinissa (*mas'*uh-*nis'*uh), who later sided with Rome.

North Africa becomes part of the Roman Empire. Finally, in 146 b.c., Rome defeated and utterly destroyed Carthage. Carthaginian North Africa became a Roman province. The Berbers regarded this development with some misgivings, for they wished to retain their independence. They were willing to trade with the Romans, as they had been willing to trade with the Phoenicians, provided that the exchanges were profitable. But they were proud and unwilling to surrender their independence.

Not until the Roman Empire was firmly established as the great power in the Mediterranean world did areas that are now known as Tunisia, Algeria, and Morocco come under strong Roman influence. There followed several centuries of comparative peace and prosperity, during which many new cities were founded, North Africa (especially Egypt) became the "granary" of the Roman Empire, and the Berbers of coastal North Africa became Roman citizens.

Roman rule transforms the culture of North Africa. Historians often use the term "synthesis" — literally, the "putting together" of two quite different elements — to describe the fusion or blending of different cultures into a new civilization. This process is illustrated again and again in the course of African history — for example, in the history of North Africa following Rome's victory over Carthage in the Third Punic War.

Carthage itself was completely destroyed by the Roman army. But the other Phoenician cities along the North African coast were left intact, and in these cities interaction between the Phoenician and Berber peoples had been going on for a long time. Now the government and traditions of Rome were superimposed on this Phoenician-Berber culture. Now, too, vast possibilities for trade with the far-flung cities of the Roman Empire were opened up. Basil Davidson is of the opinion that these cities — Timgad (tim-*gad'*), Tipaza (tee-*pah'*zah), Dougga (*doo'*guh), and others — "grew into cities that were among the finest in the world; but they were Roman with a big difference, and the difference was African."

ROMAN RUINS. Stone pillars (*left*) in Libya once supported a trip-hammer used to crush olives. Oil collected in the circular groove and flowed into a sunken reservoir. North African ports grew rich on the olive oil and grain trade in Roman times. Below, Leptis Magna had a theater decorated with statues and columns like those in Rome.

Rome promotes trans-Saharan trade. The history of North Africa under Roman rule is reflected in the ruins which dot the North African landscape. References to Africa in the writings of authors of the period add to our information. From these sources it may be inferred that in the second century A.D. a new expansion of trade between Black Africa and the Mediterranean world began. As the camel became more widely used in desert travel and as Roman troops maintained law and order along the trade routes of the empire, the groundwork was laid for increased trade with Africa south of the Sahara. The Berbers were still the principal carriers of this trade — much of it in gold and ivory. There is evidence, too, that this trade provided regular contact with the Africans of the western sudan. These were the same peoples whose descendants were to form the great kingdoms of West Africa which will be discussed in the next chapter.

Christianity becomes an important cultural force in North Africa. Once North Africa had become an integral part of the Roman Empire this region shared in the empire's cultural life. By the second century A.D., Christian churches had been established in the major cities, including Rome. By the end of the third century it had become a widely-respected faith, and in the fourth century it was sufficiently powerful to win the support of the Roman Emperor Constantine himself. Thus from a small, persecuted sect, Christianity grew to become the official religion of the Roman Empire.

Two cities in North Africa became centers of the new religion — Alexandria and Carthage.[5] Alexandria was the native city of two of the most controversial leaders of the early Christian church — Athanasius (*ath'*uh-*nay'*shus) and Arius (*ayr'*ee-us) — whose sharp doctrinal differences led to the calling in 325 A.D. of a church council at Nicaea (nye-*see'*uh) in Asia Minor. This council issued the still-widely-used Nicene Creed.

North Africa nurtures conflicting views about Christianity. The most famous of the early church fathers was a Libyan Berber, St. Augustine of Hippo, who grew up in Carthage. His writings, particularly his *Confessions* and *The City of God*, are classics of Christian literature. The first of these describes Augustine's long search for faith, which led him to forsake Rome's "pagan" religions and to join the Christian church. From his highly personal account we learn that numerous "heretical" Christian sects were competing for followers in North Africa. One such heresy, Donatism (*dahn'*uh-tiz-um),[6] had gained an especially wide following among the Berbers. Their acceptance of Donatism is thought to have been one way of showing their long-standing dislike for Rome.

---

[5] This Carthage was a Roman colony established near the site of the old city by Julius Caesar. It became, under the Emperor Augustus (31 B.C.–14 A.D.), an important administrative center.

[6] Donatism gets its name from a dissenting bishop of Numidia, Donatus (doh-*nay'*tus), who lived in the early fourth century.

Other parts of Africa adopted forms of Christianity which also differed markedly in doctrine from that of the official state church. For example, the "Coptic" church became the dominant form of Christianity in Egypt. After its introduction into Ethiopia by missionaries from Egypt and Syria, Coptic Christianity also became the state religion of Ethiopia.

Roman power in Africa begins to disintegrate. By the fifth century A.D., Roman power in Africa had greatly declined and the area under Roman administration became steadily smaller. The growing use of camels favored the nomad's way of life. Increasing numbers of Berbers formed themselves into robber bands to raid the towns of Roman provinces. Known as the Zenata (zah-*nah'*tah), these bands were influenced by ideas of political unity thought to be derived from Judaism. Such unity and strength as they achieved were won at the expense of the settled agricultural civilization of North Africa.

Roman rule in Africa was dealt another blow when the Vandals descended on the African coast. The Vandals were Germanic tribes which had embraced Arian Christianity, a heresy outlawed by the Council of Nicaea in 325. At first they were welcomed by the Berbers as a people who had delivered them from the Roman yoke. But the Vandals initiated a rule that was at least as cruel and oppressive as anything the Berbers experienced under Rome. A period of civil disorder and religious persecution followed, which the camel-riding nomads used to their own advantage by making further raids on the towns. This state of confusion and lawlessness continued into the sixth century, and did not end even when North Africa was reconquered by Belisarius (bel-ih-*sayr'*ee-us), the general of Emperor Justinian of the East Roman (or Byzantine) Empire.

The "Mediterranean period" of North African history comes to a close. The Vandal conquest and the subsequent breakup of Roman power in the west signaled the end of the "Mediterranean period" of North African history. During this period, North African civilization had been largely influenced by Carthage and Rome. It was followed by the "Muslim period," an era which ushered in profound changes in the cultural and political life of northern and western Africa. A "cultural vacuum" existed which now had to be filled.

● CHECK-UP

1. Who were the Berbers? What was their role in African trade?

2. Why did rivalry develop between Carthage and Rome? What was the outcome?

3. What changes resulted from Roman rule in North Africa? What forces led to the overthrow of Roman rule there?

4. Islamic Civilization Flourishes on African Soil

Is it accurate to speak of Islam as in any sense African? Some African scholars would answer emphatically in the negative, and would argue that Islamic culture in Africa was nothing more than the logical extension of Middle Eastern influences into Africa. The religion of Mohammed (moh-*hah'*med) was, after all, born in Arabia; the language of the Koran is Old Arabic; and the religious and cultural centers of the Islamic faith are in the Middle East — Mecca, Medina, Jerusalem, Damascus, and Baghdad.

Nevertheless, Islamic culture acquired a distinctive style in Africa. The Muslim faith proved attractive to African peoples first in North Africa and the sudan, but later, through trade and missionary activity, in Central Africa as well. The Muslim faith continues to be a strong competitor to Christianity. In fact, during the last 150 years it has won twice as many converts in Africa as has Christianity. To understand the reasons for the great success of Islam, we must know something about that religion.

The basic teachings of Islam were easily understood. The founder of Islam — an Arabic word meaning "submission to the will of God (Allah)"[7] — was a native of the Arabian city of Mecca. Mohammed was born about 570 A.D. to a poor but respected family. At about the age of 40 he underwent a series of profound religious experiences, arriving at a belief in one God which was not unlike that held by Jews. This led him to denounce the polytheism (belief in many gods) which prevailed among his fellow Arabs and to preach his own new revelations. He proclaimed that he was ordained by God as the last in a line of prophets sent to make known to man the will of God. In earlier times, Allah had sent Abraham, Moses, Jesus, and others to disclose the divine will to men. Now, according to Mohammed, it was again time to call men to God.

---

[7] A "Muslim" is "one who submits," that is, one who accepts Islam. Muslims find fault with the term "Mohammedan," which suggests that one is a follower of the man, Mohammed. (Mohammed is honored but not worshipped by Muslims.)

"There is only one God, Allah, and his prophet is Mohammed." This statement was at the core of Mohammed's new faith. The *Koran* (koh-*rahn'*), a book of religious verse which followers believed had been communicated to Mohammed by heavenly messengers, elaborated on this central idea. The Koran is written in forceful yet simple Arabic rhyming couplets, much of the beauty of which is lost in English translations. But the power of this great book was not and is not lost on the millions of Arabic-speaking Muslims who have committed it to memory during the centuries since their prophet walked the earth.

Mohammed lived to see his religion grow powerful. Mohammed had a forceful personality. He set his people an example of simplicity and religious devotion which they could understand and follow. Known to his followers as "The Prophet," Mohammed envisioned a brotherhood of all believers. He proclaimed the equality of all Muslims before God. A man's color, geographical origin, wealth, or social status did not affect his standing in the sight of Allah. According to Mohammed, Allah had no need of temples, sacrifices, or priests. This bold assertion at first made the priests of the prevailing Arabic religions[8] hostile to Mohammed. The government officials and the merchants of Mecca also opposed Mohammed's radical teachings, because they thought his ideas would breed dissatisfaction and unrest among the people.

Opposition to the new religion was so great that Mohammed and his closest followers were obliged to flee to Medina (meh-*dee'*nuh), an oasis town some 300 miles to the north of Mecca. This flight, referred to as the *Hegira* (heh-*jeye'*ruh), occurred in 622, which became the Year One of the Muslim faith. At Medina the religion prospered. After seven years (629 A.D.), Mohammed returned to Mecca with a large band of followers, this time as the city's master. There he spent his remaining years strengthening his religion and clarifying its doctrines. In a short time his teachings had spread throughout Arabia and his fame throughout much of the world.

---

[8] "Mecca was at that time the center of a pagan cult famous throughout Arabia. This cult centered upon the worship of a wonderful black stone (El Ka'aba [*kah'*uh-buh]) — the remains of an immense meteorite. Side by side with the worship of this stone was the worship of a goddess named Allat. Allat was to become the origin of the name Allah applied by [Muslims] . . . to the Supreme God. Allah acquired a masculine sense, although in its original form the word was feminine." — J. D. de Graft-Johnson, *African Glory: The Story of Vanished Negro Civilizations* (New York: Walker and Company, 1954), pp. 61–62.

Islam gives Arabs a sense of unity. The Muslim religion changed the course of world history and transformed the Arabs' way of life. Until the introduction of Islam, Arabs had been divided into hundreds of warring tribes. But the teachings and the example of Mohammed inspired the Arabs to join together, and soon their boundless energy spilled over beyond the borders of the Arabian peninsula. The more fanatical Arabs joined forces to wage "holy war" (the *jihad* [jih-*hahd'*]) against the infidel, and thus carry the faith into lands bordering Arabia. Within eighty years after the death of Mohammed (632 A.D.), his followers had conquered a greater territory than did ancient Rome in four centuries. Most of the Middle East, Central Asia, North Africa, and Spain came under Muslim control. Not since the days of Alexander the Great had armies made such swift advances.

North Africa comes under Muslim rule. The first Muslim Arabs entered Egypt in 639 A.D. In that year, the caliph ([*kay'*lif] the title given to the men who succeeded Mohammed as head of the Muslim empire) sent one of his commanders, Amir (ah-*meer'*), on an expedition to Egypt with a few thousand men. The Byzantine rulers of the country were defeated in 642, partly because the majority of Egyptians were glad to be rid of them. In the same year, the Arabs gained control of Cyrenaica (seer-ih-*nay'*ih-kuh), a province of North Africa first settled by Greeks in the seventh century B.C.; five years later, new Arab forces invaded Tripoli and defeated the local Byzantine governor. They pushed their conquests into Tunisia and Algeria, and in Tunisia founded what later became the fourth holy city of the Muslims, Kairouan (kair-*wahn'*). By 683 Muslim pioneers could see the Atlantic Ocean. Early in the eighth century they continued their advance, this time into Spain and France. They were finally stopped by Charles Martel at the decisive battle of Poitiers (732) near Tours in France.

Why were the Arabs successful? It may seem strange that the Arabs, in this comparatively short period of time, were able to establish their rule over the diverse populations of North Africa. Their success did not result wholly from the force of arms. In parts of North Africa, the people adopted Islam during a period of social and political turmoil within their own borders. Dissatisfaction among many North Africans with the existing system of government and with their rulers — men not of their own choosing — made easier the acceptance of Islam. North Africa had known earlier invaders such as the Vandals and the Goths. But unlike the Muslims, these had succeeded

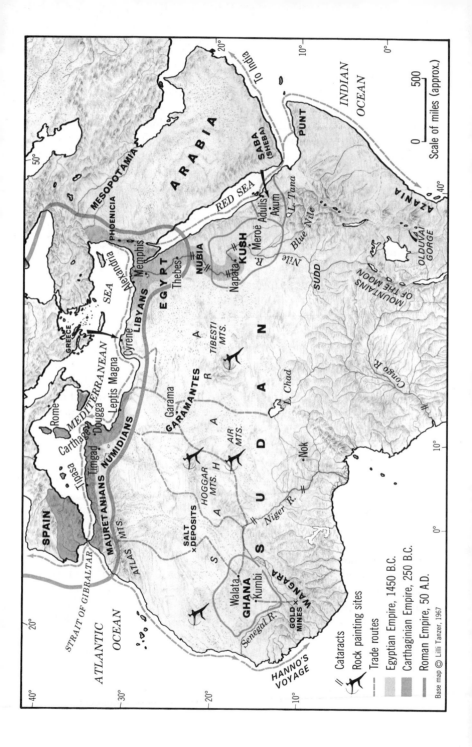

Base map © Lilli Tanzer, 1967

only in destroying, plundering, and overthrowing the existing provincial governments. They failed to adapt themselves to the Roman system of administration or to create a workable system of their own.

Where other invaders had failed, the Muslims succeeded. First, the Muslim philosophy of brotherhood and the doctrine of the equality of all believers before Allah appealed to the Africans as to many other peoples. Second, Muslim local government, centering around small groups of Arabs, managed to win the support of local populations. Muslim government officials were persons of diverse origin, skin color, and customs — though they all were required to learn Arabic, the official language of Islam. Men of ability made their way up the ladder of government service. In time, however, strong differences did arise within the Muslim ruling class.

Rival factions mar the unity of the Muslim world. After the death of Mohammed, Islam was governed successively by four caliphs who had been among the Prophet's original companions. The third of these, Othman (*ahth'*man), widely disliked because of his political policies, was murdered in 656. The fourth caliph, Ali, based his claim to succession on the fact that he was married to Mohammed's daughter, Fatima (*fat'*ih-mah). Despite this, he failed to win complete acceptance. The governor of Syria, Mu'awiyah (muh-*ah'*wih-yah), was especially opposed to Ali's caliphate. Engaging in a bitter dispute, the two opposing camps were, however, reluctant to fight each other in open combat. The dispute was ended in 661 when Ali was assassinated, leaving Mu'awiya sole claimant to the office of caliph. He established himself as the first in the Umayyad (oo-*my'*yad) dynasty which ruled Islam from Damascus until 750.

The orthodox (or "pure") Muslims, the *Sunnis* (*suhn'*eez), accepted the Umayyad succession, but two major groups — the Shi'ites (*shee'*ites) and the Kharijites (*kah'*rih-jites) — did not. The Shi'ites went underground and became a mystical sect within Islam. The Kharijites, on the other hand, became a brotherhood of religious

ANCIENT AFRICA. This map shows the empires which overlapped each other at the beginning of African history. First, Egypt was born in the Nile Valley, then the kingdoms of Kush. In North Africa the Berber nomads were influenced by Carthage, Greece, and Rome, but never lost their independence as the blazers of caravan trails across the Sahara.

fanatics who denounced the corruptions of town and city life. Islam as a whole has rejected the Kharijite form of the Muslim faith, but many Berber tribes along the borders of the settled areas of the North African Maghreb [(*muh′*grib), Arabic for "west," (see map, page 84)] became Kharijites.

New ruling families compete for power. In the middle of the eighth century the center of Muslim power shifted from Damascus to Baghdad, a new city built in the rich Syrian province of Mesopotamia. The office of caliph was now in the possession of a new ruling family called the Abbasids (*ab′*uh-sids). Under the Abbasids, the Muslim empire reached its peak of cultural splendor, but it gradually ceased to be a predominantly Arab empire. Its major source of wealth was no longer conquest but the exploitation of lands already conquered. The Abbasid rulers wished to turn to their own advantage the wealth of their subjects. This meant heavy taxation and a much more elaborate administrative system than that of the Umayyads. Under the new regime, professional soldiers and officials usually were chosen from among the caliph's Turkish slaves.

In the Middle East, the Abbasid system was efficient — despite the outbreak of occasional revolts — but it was never accepted in Islamic Spain, where the Umayyads remained in power, or in the African Maghreb, where groups of Berbers were setting up independent Muslim states. For example, the Berbers carved out a sizable kingdom in the western Maghreb after having recognized Idris (*ee′-*dris), a great-grandson of Caliph Ali (see page 71), as their ruler. The forty years of Idrisid rule resulted in the establishment of Fez — Morocco's first native capital city. Two other Berber ruling houses which were to influence the course of African history were the Almoravids (*al′*muh-*rah′*vids) and the Almohads (*al′*muh-*hahds′*).

The Aghlabids create an empire of their own in Tunisia. Arab governors subject to Baghdad had continued to rule in Tunisia. But in 800 a new governor, Ibrahim ibn Aghlab (ee-brah-*heem′ ib′*un *ahg′*lub), obtained the office permanently for his family, the Aghlabids (*ahg′-*luh-bids). The Aghlabid dynasty was built on the agricultural and economic foundation laid by the Roman Empire, and in 827 undertook the conquest of Sicily, Malta, and Sardinia, and even invaded southern Italy. But early in the tenth century the Aghlabids were overthrown by a newly-emerging Shi'ite power. During the next two centuries the Shi'ites expanded eastward into Egypt and established Africa's great Fatimid Empire.

Egypt becomes the center of a new Muslim empire. In theory, at least, ninth-century Egypt was subject to the authority of the Abbasid court in Baghdad. The administrators of Egypt were Baghdad appointees, recruited from among the caliph's Turkish subjects — descendants of the tribes who were pushing south into the Middle East from Central Asia. In time these governors of Egypt tired of turning over to Baghdad the tax money collected in Egypt. Retaining this money for their own use, they built splendid palaces, and outfitted an army of Turkish and Black African slaves. By 935 Egypt was no longer under Abbasid domination. But this fact did not improve the lot of the Egyptian people, who became increasingly weary of being ruled by foreigners.

Outside Egypt, meanwhile, a powerful Berber clan, upholding a new Shi'ite gospel, overthrew the Aghlabids in 909. Although at first unsuccessful, they finally conquered Egypt in 968. Thus was established the powerful Fatimid dynasty which claimed descent from Ali and Fatima, the daughter of Mohammed. The Fatimid Empire reached its greatest extent in the last quarter of the tenth century, when the empire extended from the Euphrates to the Atlantic. But early in the eleventh century Fatimid power began to decline. The caliphs withdrew into the luxury of their palaces in Cairo, and left the business of government to viziers (vih-*zeers'*), or ministers, and to generals appointed from among their Asian subjects. In time the downfall of the Fatimids was brought about by viziers who had taken over more and more power.

Under Ayyubid and Mamluk rule, Egypt shields Africa from invaders. In 1174, one of the most outstanding of these viziers, known in European history as Saladin (*sal'*uh-din), took the title of Sultan of Egypt. Having established the Ayyubids (eye-*yoo'*bids) as the ruling family of Egypt, he subdued Syria and defeated the Crusaders led by King Richard of England. Under about two centuries of Ayyubid rule, Islamic culture in Egypt achieved an even greater height than under the Fatimids. Perhaps even more important for the later history of Africa was Egypt's role as a shield against invaders. For another 250 years after the decline of the Ayyubids, this role was assumed by the Mamluks (*mam'*looks) — a military aristocracy recruited originally from among Turkish and Circassian (sur-*kash'*yun) slaves captured in the region of the Caucasus Mountains.

The Mamluks expelled the Crusaders from the Middle East and halted the onrush of fresh invaders from Central Asia — the Mongols.

But the Mamluks' concern for military affairs also caused the Egyptian government to neglect foreign trade, agriculture, and irrigation. Thus the real bases for Egypt's prosperity were allowed to decay. Despite her military might, Egypt became weaker, and in 1517, fell to new Muslim invaders — the Ottoman Turks. During three centuries of Ottoman rule, Egypt was of little political importance. But this situation changed in the late eighteenth and early nineteenth centuries when France and Britain became interested in a more direct route to India via the Isthmus of Suez. During the later nineteenth century and the first four decades of the present century, Egypt became a pawn of the European powers.

The Almoravids form an empire in the Maghreb. Fatimid control over Africa's western provinces — the Maghreb — was never very strong. There, Muslim Berbers had established their own versions of the Islamic ideal of *umma* or "community." One of them began to be preached about 1000 A.D. by a fanatical Muslim leader, Abdullah ibn Yasin (ahb-*doo*'luh *ib*'un yah-*seen*'), but the Tuaregs of the Maghreb at first did not welcome his strict teachings. According to tradition, he then withdrew far south to an island (probably in the Senegal River) and established himself in a *ribat* (ruh-*baht*'), a fortified monastery. There he gave religious and military training to a

Fez, a large commercial city in Morocco, was founded in 793 by the Arabs and became one of the holy cities of Islam. Ornate decoration of the archway shows the influence of Arab styles. In the background, the square minarets typical of North Africa mark the location of mosques. For many years Fez was a capital of the Almohad empire.

small band of his followers. When these men returned to their tribes, they made a tremendous impression. Gradually, they succeeded in uniting the Tuaregs and other Berbers of the desert. Known as the Almoravids, from the Arabic word *al-Murabitum* — "the people of the *ribat*" — they swept across the Maghreb. By 1103 they controlled all of Morocco, western Algeria, and Muslim Spain. At the same time, a second wing of the Almoravids led by Abu Bekr (*ah'*boo *bek'*er) marched southward, determined to wrest control of the Saharan trade routes from the West African kingdom of Ghana. After a long siege, the Almoravids captured the capital of Ghana in 1067. But they were unable to hold this kingdom for long. Meanwhile, another movement was forming among the Berbers which eventually pushed aside the Almoravids.

The Almoravids are challenged by the Almohads. The Almoravids had begun as a purifying and liberating movement. But early in the twelfth century, their enthusiasm and drive began to wane, and resentment mounted against Almoravid rule among many Moroccan tribes. It was time for a change, they said.

In response to this need, a new reformer appeared — this time in the person of Ibn Tumart (*ib'*un too-*mart'*). Like Ibn Yasin earlier, he attacked various abuses. He criticized the new taxes imposed by the Almoravids, charged them with corruption, and urged a return to the pure teachings of the Koran. The importance of faith in the oneness, or unity, of God was especially emphasized. Thus Ibn Tumart and his followers came to be called the *Almohads* from an Arabic word meaning "believers in one God."

North Africa is united under Almohad rule. Surprisingly, the Almohads at first drew their support mainly from mountain tribes traditionally hostile to desert Berbers. But the influence of the Almohads soon spread to the towns and cities also, and in 1147 they installed a caliph in Marrakech, Morocco. The power of the new caliph was extended eastward until, by 1159, a single Berber government ruled the entire Maghreb — Morocco, Algeria, and Tunisia. Almohad rule also displaced that of the Almoravids in Spain. This new empire became an important force in the Mediterranean world.

Under Almohad rule, the Maghreb bloomed. Cities like Marrakech, Fez, Tlemcen (tlem-*sen'*), and Rabat (rah-*baht'*) became centers of culture and trade. They rivaled the chief European cities in beauty and learning. The Almohads created a professional civil service which attracted the best educated men in the empire.

Muslim Officialdom in Africa

Sheikh (or sheik): Arabic for "old man." The head man of a village or tribe.

Mufti: Arabic for "one who delivers judgment." A Muslim legal adviser; a civil official learned in Islamic law.

Pasha: Turkish for "head" or "chief." A title, placed after the name, of high military or civil officials in the Ottoman Empire. Later an honorary title in Egypt.

Bey: Turkish for nobleman or prince, and, later, any person of authority. In Tunisia it was used alternately with another Turkish word, "Dey" (maternal uncle), as the title of the ruler.

Emir (or Amir): originally Arabic for "commander" (as in *Amir al-Mu'minin,* "Commander of the Faithful"). Applied to rulers within the Arab empire.

Khedive: Turkish for "viceroy" or "deputy" — a title given to the Ottoman viceroy of Egypt.

Vizier: derived from Arabic *wazir,* "bearer of burdens." The vizier was a principal helper of the Muslim sovereign. The Abbasid caliphs had only one; but the Ottoman sultans had several, with the Grand Vizier as chairman. The council of viziers was called the Divan.

Caliph: Arabic for "successor" — meaning successor of Mohammed as the head of Islam. The caliph originally was the supreme religious and secular authority, but gradually secular power was assumed by the emirs, leaving the caliphs only a theoretical religious authority.

Sultan: Arabic for "he-with-authority." First used as a title in the tenth century. The Ottomans preferred it to the older term, caliph.

Almohad power goes into a decline. Despite its early promise, the Almohad empire began to crumble in less than a century. The reasons for this decline were internal as well as external. The Almohad rulers showed favoritism toward members of the original Almohad community and their families. This policy aroused resentment among other Berbers, and charges of laxity and corruption were heard once again. Clearly the Almohad caliphs had failed to inspire any deep feeling of loyalty to the empire among the many Berber tribes. The situation

A sign is lettered in both Arabic and English in Khartoum, capital of Sudan. Arabic has been a common language in Africa for 1200 years, especially in the northern part. It was introduced as the language of the Koran, the sacred book of the Islamic religion.

At Entebbe Airport in Uganda, Muslim pilgrims gather to board a plane for the Arabian city of Mecca. African Muslims save money for years to make a pilgrimage to the holy city of their religion. In the past their journey was a hard one, first by desert caravan, and then by ship across the Red Sea. Today, African Muslims who can afford the fare make the trip swiftly by plane.

became crucial when the empire had to deal with two external threats to its existence — the renewed attacks of the Spanish Christians and Bedouin raids from the central Màghreb.

In 1212, Spanish Christians won an important victory over the Almohads, and year after year took over more of Muslim Spain. With the fall of Cadiz in 1262, the only part of Spain under Muslim (or "Moorish") rule was Granada, which held out until 1492. As for the Bedouins, they were brought under control only after the caliph had delegated major military authority to his subordinates. Thus the solution to the Bedouin problem diminished the power of the caliph. As a consequence, Tunisia under its Hafsid (hahf-*seed'*) governors broke away from the empire in 1229. The Hafsid monarchy in Tunisia lasted until the 1570's. In the western part of the Almohad empire, power similarly was taken over by the leading families of various Zenata clans. These rulers, who were themselves of nomad stock, proved unable to check the persistent raids of the Bedouins. In time Bedouin destruction of towns and, in fact, of all civilized society, became almost complete in this part of North Africa.

● CHECK-UP

1. What is Islam? How did it change the Arab way of life?

2. Why was Muslim rule quickly established in North Africa?

3. How did factions divide the Muslim world? What were the consequences in North Africa?

4. How did Egypt become the center of a new Muslim empire? What was Egypt's role in North Africa?

5. What was the role of the Almoravids in North Africa? The Almohads? Why did civilization tend to decline in North Africa after about 1200 A.D.?

Summing Up

African civilization was given a "head start" in Egypt, where a favorable climate and fertile soil, resulting from silt deposited by Nile floods, made possible greater production of food and thus a larger settled population. The need for organized effort to clear the Nile Valley and to provide and maintain an extensive irrigation system contributed to the emergence of strong rulers as early as 2500 B.C. Separate kingdoms were forged into a unified empire under the pharaohs. The Nile facilitated commercial and cultural exchanges between Upper and Lower Egypt and promoted the idea of empire. Egyptian power reached its zenith in the fifteenth century B.C. The extent of the empire, given limited means of communication, was a major factor in the decline of Egyptian power. Under the "New Kingdom," the seat of central authority alternated between north and south. Nubian and Kushite dynasties during this period helped to transmit elements of Egyptian culture to inhabitants along the southern fringes of the empire. An Assyrian invasion brought to an end the

Kushite period and introduced iron weaponry into Africa. Later, Egypt came under the domination of Persia, Greece, and Rome.

To the south, meanwhile, Egyptian and Ethiopian cultures were blended into a distinctive Kushite civilization, centering first at Meroë (famous for its iron production) and then at Axum. Axum's conversion to Christianity in the fourth century A.D. and its relatively protected position enabled it to resist Muslim conquest and to become a stronghold of the Christian religion.

For several centuries prior to its conquest by Rome in the second century B.C., Carthage had enjoyed commercial and political preëminence in North Africa west of Egypt. Even before Carthage's rise to power, however, the restless Berbers roamed over a broad expanse of North Africa, leaving everywhere the imprints of their culture, including a still-undeciphered script. For centuries the Berbers served as a link between the coastal region and the African interior.

The "Mediterranean period" of North African history came to an end with the Muslim Arab invasion of the mid-seventh century A.D. Fired by the new religion of Islam — meaning submission to the will of Allah as explained by his prophet, Mohammed — the Arabs moved across North Africa with surprising rapidity. In general the North Africans, weary of rule by corrupt Byzantine officials, welcomed the newcomers and adopted their religion.

Arab dynasties governed the Muslim world during its first centuries of expansion and consolidation, and this fact explains the impact of Arab culture upon it. But the unity of Islam was weakened by differences among Arabs and between Arab and non-Arab Muslims. Doctrinal differences led to the development of puritanical mystic sects within the Muslim faith. Gradually the caliphs ("successors") who ruled the Muslim empire from their capitals, first in Damascus and then in Baghdad, became puppets in the hands of their military commanders — mostly Turks. As a consequence, independent Arab dynasties came to power in Africa — the Fatimids in Egypt and the Idrisids in Morocco, for example. In the Maghreb, two Muslim splinter groups — the Almohads and the Almoravids — competed for control. In time the Almohads extended their rule across most of North Africa east of Tunisia, while the Almoravids carved out an empire reaching from Spain through Morocco and deep into West Africa. In the eleventh century, the Almoravids conquered Ghana, bringing with them a brand of Muslim culture that became part of the fabric of that West African kingdom, as well as of its neighbors to the south and east.

CHAPTER REVIEW

Can You Identify?

pharaoh	Meroë	Almohads
Ethiopia	Rome	Vandals
Periplus	Islam	*jihad*
Carthage	Lower Egypt	caliph
Berbers	Mohammed	vizier
Kush	Mamluks	Maghreb
Axum	Almoravids	Fatimids

What Do You Think?

1. Does a revolution in food production explain the rise of a great civilization in ancient Egypt?

2. What part did religion play in the expansion of Egypt? In the expansion of Muslim rule?

3. What part did an expanding commerce play in the rise of Kush and Axum to power?

4. Were the Muslims more successful than the Carthaginians and the Romans in unifying North Africa?

5. Why was the trans-Saharan trade important to North African seaports over the centuries?

Extending and Applying Your Knowledge

1. More information about "The Lands of Kush" is found on pages 56–63 of *Africa: Selected Readings.*

2. For a description of the glory that was Axum and reasons for Axum's decline, see *Africa: Selected Readings,* pages 64–67.

3. Garama, an important outpost for the trans-Saharan trade, is today a deserted site with a few ruins. Theories about what happened to it are presented in "The Mystery of Garama," pages 67–73, *Africa: Selected Readings.*

4. Selections from the Koran may be read in translation in Peretz, *The Middle East: Selected Readings* (Houghton Mifflin), pages 34–37.

3

EARLY WEST AFRICAN CIVILIZATIONS SOUTH OF THE SAHARA

The 100 million Black Africans who today inhabit the states of West Africa are the heirs of a glorious past. For in the vast region that today includes all or parts of a dozen modern African nations, there long ago were established several mighty empires. Their history spanned more than a thousand years. And in their culture and power these African empires rivaled contemporary European states. This chapter describes these empires, and suggests reasons for their rise to greatness as well as causes of their decline. Among the larger states were Ghana, Kanem-Bornu, Mali, Songhai, and the Mossi and Hausa states. Smaller kingdoms also developed along the Guinea coast.

1. Ghana Emerges at the Crossroads of the Gold Trade

About five thousand years ago, Africans living in the rich savannah belt of the western sudan (south of the Sahara) planted two new cereal crops — millet and rice. These cultivated grains freed the expanding population from dependence upon hunting game and gathering wild plants for food. Much later (after about 500 B.C.) farming became more efficient because of the introduction of iron implements. The groups which learned to make and use iron tools and weapons effectively soon emerged as the strongest. They then began to conquer their weaker neighbors. Conquests are made possible by skill in fighting and in the use of weapons. But to *hold* conquered land requires able administrators. Of the early West African societies, Ghana probably was the first to develop an efficient large-scale government. Ghana, having accumulated wealth through international trade, was for that reason more powerful than its neighbors. Let us trace briefly Ghana's rise to eminence.

People of the Nok culture use iron. Long before there was an empire of Ghana, the people living where the Niger and Benue rivers join (now northern Nigeria) displayed an unusual craftsmanship and talent for art. They fashioned pottery, figurines, and life-size heads, for example, from terra cotta (baked clay). Through barter these art objects circulated throughout the sudanic area of West Africa. Archaeologists refer to this era as the period of Nok (*nahk*) culture, because it was in the village of Nok (in 1931) that these terra cotta pieces were first unearthed.

It is not known exactly when this culture began, but it probably reached its full development during the last two or three centuries B.C. During this period Ghana benefited from the discovery of ironworking and from the agricultural advances made possible by using iron tools

Heads molded out of clay 2500 years ago are displayed in a museum near the Nigerian town of Nok where tin miners first discovered these remains of an ancient African civilization. West African sculptors used clay long before they learned how to cast their works in bronze.

such as the hoe. From Egypt and Meroë, Ghana may have learned principles of strong central government, particularly the idea of the divine king. According to some scholars, Ghana began to take shape as a state about 100 A.D.; others believe this happened about 300 A.D. But whichever is the date, Ghana in its development profited from the discoveries made by Africa's earliest cultures.

The exact boundaries of ancient Ghana are not known. The map on page 70 shows the approximate boundaries of ancient Ghana. But in those days no one thought it necessary to establish well-defined boundaries. We do know that its heartland was northeast of the Senegal River and northwest of the Niger. If a modern map of Africa were superimposed on one of ancient Ghana, parts of the present-day nations of Mauritania, Mali, Senegal, and Guinea would fall within the old empire.[1]

The Soninke people establish their rule over ancient Ghana. Among the peoples who inhabited the region between the Senegal and Niger rivers were the Soninkes (son-*in'*kays). They comprised a number of related tribes, and each, in turn, was made up of several clans. (A clan is a group of families descended from a common ancestor.) Apparently some clans specialized in metalworking; others acted as middlemen in trade. Still others would do the fishing, clothmaking, farming, and so on. From one of these clans — the Sisse (*see'*say) — came the kings and the administrative officials for the whole Soninke people.

When the first Arabs arrived in the western sudan in the eighth century, they found that the Soninkes governed a powerful state, with its capital near modern Walata (*wah'*lah-tah). The Soninkes informed the Arabs that the empire of Ghana had 22 kings even *before* the Hegira of Mohammed (622 A.D.). If this statement was true, Ghana would have been founded about 300 A.D. But what happened during the centuries in between? Traditions suggest that invaders from North Africa — probably Berber nomads — had invaded Ghana territory and established a dynasty of their own. Then, about 700 A.D., a Soninke warrior-leader led a successful revolt against the Berber overlords. Under Soninke leadership, Ghana entered a period of great

---

[1] Note that the *modern* state of Ghana is situated quite a long distance from the *ancient* empire of Ghana. The leaders of modern Ghana wished to celebrate their independence from Great Britain in 1957 by linking their country (formerly the Gold Coast) with the proud history of their ancient namesake. There is, indeed, a tradition that people of ancient Ghana moved southward to the region of the Ashanti people, which does lie within modern Ghana.

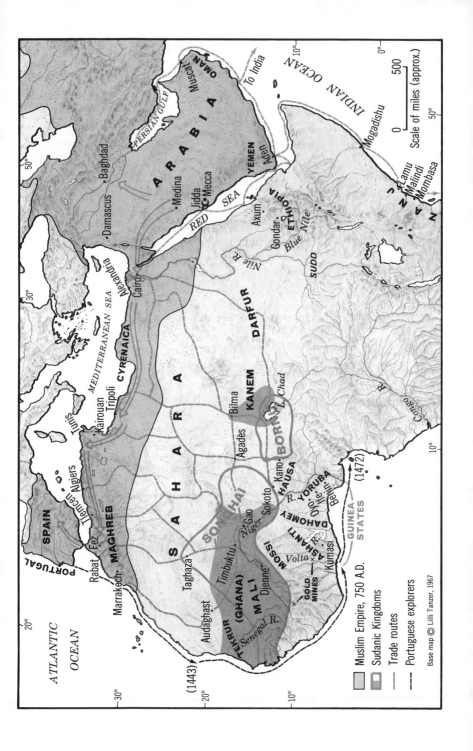

ATLANTIC OCEAN

PORTUGAL
SPAIN

MEDITERRANEAN SEA

Tlemcen
Algiers
Tunis
Kairouan
Tripoli
CYRENAICA

Rabat
Fez
Marrakech
MAGHREB

Taghaza

Audaghast

S A H A R A

Timbuktu
TEKRUR
(GHANA)
Senegal R.
MALI
Djenné
Niger
SONGHAI
Gao
Sokoto
MOSSI
Volta
GOLD MINES
ASHANTI
Kumasi
DAHOMEY
OYO
YORUBA
Ife
R.
Benin
GUINEA STATES (1472)

(1443)

Agadès
Bilma

KANEM
BORNU
L. Chad
HAUSA
Kano

DARFUR

Cairo
Alexandria

Damascus
Baghdad

ARABIA
Medina
Jidda
Mecca
RED SEA
YEMEN
Aden

OMAN
Muscat
PERSIAN GULF
To India

INDIAN OCEAN

Axum
ETHIOPIA
Gondar
Blue Nile
Nile R.
SUDD

Congo R.

Mogadishu
Lamu
Malindi
Mombasa
ZANJ

Scale of miles (approx.)
0   500
0   50

Muslim Empire, 750 A.D.
Sudanic Kingdoms
Trade routes
Portuguese explorers

Base map © Lilli Tanzer, 1967

development and expansion. Its army must have been powerful, for it successfully defended the country against the advancing Arab warriors. The Arabs then seemed to have settled down in the western Sahara and towns of the sudan and to have joined with the Berbers in what was to become a very profitable trade between the Muslim and Black African worlds.

Control of the gold trade made Ghana powerful. The name "Ghana" is actually a title. In the Mande (*man′*day) family of languages spoken by the Soninke people the word meant "warrior king." The Ghanaian people themselves called their country the kingdom of Wagadu (wah-gah-*doo′*). But as the fame and power of the Soninke kings grew, their title, Ghana, came to be applied to the kingdom. Another title given the king was Kaya Maghan (kay-yah *mah′*gahn), which means "king of gold." The significance of this title is borne out by a ninth-century Arab scholar, who wrote: "The king of Ghana is a great king. In his territory are mines of gold, and under him a number of kingdoms. . . . In all this country there is gold."

Ghana profited from its location about midway between the Sahara salt mines and the tropical gold mines. There are records of great caravans, including as many as a thousand camels, bringing cloth, copper, and salt to Ghana, and carrying gold dust northward. The peoples of the African interior were so eager to obtain salt that they are said to have traded equal weights of salt for gold. The gold actually was mined by the Wangara (wahn-*ga′*ruh) peoples who lived in a forest region south of the Senegal and Niger rivers. But the trade in gold was controlled by Ghana, and this trade made Ghana rich and powerful.

Ghana's capital included "twin cities." Ancient Arabic writers described Kumbi (*koom′*bee), the capital city of Ghana, as made up of two towns, each situated on a hill and spreading down into a wide valley. The towns, located six miles apart, were linked by a broad road. One of the two towns boasted twelve mosques, and many scholars and priests. Most of the Muslim citizens lived in it. The Arabs

THE THRUST OF ISLAM. Aflame with their new religion, Arabs swept across North Africa, but soon were forced to share power with Berbers whom they had converted. Muslim traders used the Sahara caravan routes, bringing Islam as well as wealth to the sudanic kingdoms. Other Muslims founded trade centers along the east coast in Zanj. Muslims met opposition from new kingdoms in Ethiopia and Guinea, and from the Mossi.

called the other of the "twin cities" al-Ghaba (al-*gah'*buh), which means "forest" or "grove." Within this town were mosques, a prison, and a merchants' trading center. Here, too, was the king's palace, a splendid building decorated with fine sculpture and paintings. The king's court was characterized by pomp and ceremony. The great Spanish-Arab geographer al-Bakri (al-*bahk'*ree) wrote the following description of the royal court, which he had pieced together from the reports of Muslim travelers of the early eleventh century:

> When the king gives audience to his people to listen to their complaints and to set them to rights, he sits in a pavillion around which stand ten pages holding shields and gold-mounted swords. On his right hand are the sons of the princes of his empire, splendidly clad and with gold plaited in their hair. The governor of the city is seated on the ground in front of the king, and all around him are his counsellors. . . . The gate of the chamber is guarded by dogs of an excellent breed. These dogs never leave their place of duty. They wear collars of gold and silver, ornamented with metals. The beginning of a royal audience is announced by the beating of a kind of drum they call *deba*. This drum is made of a long piece of hollowed wood. The people gather when they hear its sound. . . .[2]

Ghana develops a strong central government. Because the people believed their ruler a god, it has been suggested that the form of kingship practiced in Ghana originated with the people of the Nile Valley and the Nilotic sudan. Supposedly they migrated to West Africa and brought with them the conception of monarchy that developed in ancient Egypt. Since there is no proof that this was the case, one may assume with equal validity that the people of Ghana developed their own system of government. In doing so, they doubtless borrowed from other African systems of government whatever seemed useful for their purposes.

In Ghana, the chief ruler exercised power through many lesser rulers. Thus the system of government was more like that of an empire than a kingdom, and the chief ruler was really an emperor. The emperor's position was hereditary, but not in the sense that the oldest son inherited the throne of the father. When the emperor died, he was succeeded by the son of his sister. This is known as *matrilineal*

[2] Translated from the French version by Basil Davidson, in *A History of West Africa to the Nineteenth Century* (New York: Doubleday Anchor Books, 1966), pp. 42–43.

GOLD WEIGHTS. Shown at center is a balance scales, spoon, and box used in handling gold dust, which has been a medium of exchange in West Africa for centuries. Surrounding them is a museum display of brass weights for the scales. Some have been fashioned in the form of tools, weapons, and animals by Ashanti craftsmen.

succession — that is, succession through the mother's side of the family.

The principal sources of written information about Ghana's early history are in Arabic. They tell us that by the seventh century A.D., one of Ghana's emperors, Kinissai (kih-nees-*seye'*), was rich and powerful enough to own a thousand horses. Each horse, according to the Arab chronicler, "slept only on a carpet, with a silken rope for a halter." The same ruler was noted for his large and magnificent banquets. Actually Ghana reached its peak of power and influence under Emperor Tenkaminen (*ten'*kuh-*mee'*nen) around 1065 A.D. By that time the rulers of Ghana had expanded the empire to include such lesser neighboring states as Tekrur (*tek'*roor) in modern Senegal, and had forced the important Sahara trading center of Audaghast (*aw'*dah-gahst) to pay them tribute.

Ghana's economy prospers. Although the majority of Ghanaians were farmers, trade rather than agriculture was the main source of the country's great wealth. To the markets of Kumbi, merchants from far and near brought a great variety of goods. From North Africa came wheat, raisins, and dried fruits of various kinds; from Spain and Morocco came beautifully woven red and blue blouses and robes; and from the country south of Ghana came cattle, sheep, and honey. Leather goods were in demand then, as now, and African craftsmen produced them in considerable quantity. Ghanaian goldsmiths, coppersmiths, and ironsmiths contributed their handiwork in jewelry, utensils, tools, and weapons. At some time in Ghana's history, a slave market was established, and this too became a profitable — though ugly — business.

The government took advantage of the thriving trade and made it a major source of revenue. The gold-salt trade is the best example of how this was done. Before a merchant could bring a donkey-load of salt into Kumbi, he had to pay a tax in gold. He paid yet another tax in gold if he wished to take the same load of salt out of the country. In other words, the emperor of Ghana received two payments of gold every time a shipment of salt passed through his territory. Other merchandise was subject to similar taxation. Al-Bakri reported that five-eighths of an ounce of gold was levied for every shipment of copper; and other goods were taxed at the rate of one ounce of gold per load. These tariffs, or import and export taxes, were not so high that they discouraged merchants from selling and buying goods in Ghana; but they were high enough to provide an important source of income for the government.

The price of gold is regulated. By establishing a virtual monopoly over the gold mined in their empire, the rulers of ancient Ghana were able to maintain a fixed price for gold. Had this not been done, gold might have become so plentiful that its price would have declined. Our Arab informant, al-Bakri, tells us: "All pieces of native gold found in the mines of the empire belong to the sovereign, although he lets the public have the gold dust that everybody knows about; without this precaution, gold would become so abundant as practically to lose its value." In other words, all gold nuggets were turned over to the emperor. He would then release this gold to the market at intervals. Meantime those who needed gold had to buy gold dust already in circulation. Thus the emperor of Ghana was able to regulate its price and to sell it at a high price to other countries which wanted gold. For centuries, the gold of West Africa helped fill the needs of North Africa and Europe. The kings of France, Spain, and England made coins from gold mined in West Africa. And the rulers of Ghana and of the successor states to Ghana reaped great riches from their monopoly on the trade in gold in their territory.

Ghana's wealth attracts invaders. Ghana's less fortunate neighbors were jealous of her rise to power. During the first half of the eleventh century there were attempts both from inside and outside the empire to share Ghana's great wealth. In 1020, for example, Ghana was attacked by forces from North Africa. But Ghana's efficient army succeeded in driving back these invaders. Groups of Tuaregs to the northeast of Ghana, and Yoruba (*yoh'*roo-bah) tribesmen to the southeast launched similar attacks that failed. Many Ghanaians believed that they were protected by the spirit of a great holy serpent called Wagadu-Bida (*wah'*gah-doo-*bee'*duh). According to the legend, this serpent required an annual human sacrifice. The most beautiful maiden of Kumbi each year was offered to the serpent in its Sacred Grove. As long as the serpent-god was appeased, the people of Ghana would be protected. One year, Sea (*see'*uh), regarded as the most beautiful girl in Kumbi, who was to have been sacrificed, was rescued by a strong young warrior named Amadoo (ah-*mah'*doo), who slew the serpent after cutting off its seven heads. Thereafter, the people of Ghana could no longer count on protection from their serpent-god. From the middle of the eleventh century on, accordingly, Ghana was under increasing attack and was finally destroyed.

The Almoravids invade Ghana. In the last chapter mention was made that the Almoravids came into conflict with Ghana. Some historians believe that Africans dwelling along the Senegal River had

THE SAHARA. Desert landscape varies from rocky plains to high mountains. Even sand dunes (*left*) can shelter groves of date palms when they are near the springs of an oasis. Such oases serve desert dwellers as way stations and centers of trade.

The desert is home to nomads like the blue-veiled Tuareg (*right*). For centuries the Tuareg have led, or raided, caravans like the one shown below. The camels are loaded with bags of desert salt — a scarce commodity in the sudan — which was traded for the gold of ancient Ghana.

united to check the growing power of Ghana. When Ibn Yasin appeared with his disciplined troops and fiery religion, the Almoravids soon found themselves at the head of an army of some 30,000.

Ibn Yasin, religious fanatic that he was, had preached a *jihad* or holy war against all who opposed the Almoravids, including Ghana. When he died in 1059, Abu Bekr was left in control of the Almoravid forces. This leader had already shown his military prowess in 1054 when he captured Audaghast. Now he led an attack on the Soninke people of Ghana, whose ruler, Bassi (*bah'*see), had offended the Almoravids by refusing to embrace the Muslim faith. The Soninke ruler preferred the traditional African religion, even though he wished also to cultivate friendly relations with the Muslims. When Bassi died, his nephew Tenkaminen succeeded to the throne about 1062 A.D. and showed his determination to cling to his ancestral faith. Abu Bekr thereupon launched a full-scale invasion of Ghana. He captured and looted Kumbi, the capital city, in 1076 and made the Soninke emperor bow down to him. From that time Ghana's political fortunes declined rapidly.

Ghana experiences a "time of troubles." The fact that Ghana had successfully resisted the Almoravids for some fifteen years suggests the power of the empire. Even when Abu Bekr conquered Ghana, he was unable to win the loyalty and support of its people. Ghanaians doubtless regarded him as an aggressive "outsider." When the Almoravids started quarreling among themselves over dividing the spoils of conquest, Ghanaian patriots staged revolts. In 1087, Abu Bekr himself was killed in attempting to put down such an uprising.

For a time Ghana re-established its independence, but it never regained its former glory. The vital gold-salt trade routes had been disrupted by the Almoravid attacks. Furthermore, the Almoravid nomads had inflicted great damage on Ghana's agriculture. The dry land surrounding the capital never recovered from the damage done by the nomads and their flocks. Deprived of its chief sources of wealth, the economy of the empire was fatally weakened. Life for the common people — never easy — became harder. Local kings began to question the wisdom of remaining loyal to the emperor at Kumbi, and some of them tried to grab control of Ghana from the ruling Soninke. Others simply asserted their independence and broke away from the empire. In this way, the great empire of Ghana disintegrated. By the end of the thirteenth century it had ceased to exist in all but name.

- CHECK-UP
    1. What factors contributed to Ghana's rise to power?
    2. What were the chief sources of Ghana's wealth? How did the state regulate the price of gold?
    3. Why did the Ghanaian Empire break apart?

2. The Mandingo People Establish Mali as a Great Empire

Mali (*mah'*lee), one of the so-called successor states of Ghana, was formed by the Mandingo (man-*ding'*go) people. How this small kingdom rose from humble beginnings to become one of West Africa's most powerful empires is a fascinating story.

Mali emerges from the ruins of Ghana. About 1180 the Fulani people of Tekrur had become independent of Ghana. Some of them had moved eastward and established a kingdom of their own around the city of Susu (*soo'*soo). In time, the Susu kings felt strong enough to challenge Ghana, and in 1205, a strong king, Sumanguru (soo-man-*goo'*roo), captured the capital city. Like conquerors before him, Sumanguru imposed heavy taxes on the population. Legends tell of the ruthlessness and cruelty of his rule. In 1224, Sumanguru invaded the small Mandingo state of Kangaba (kahn-*gah'*buh) on the Niger River, some 250 miles south of Kumbi. According to legend, he killed anyone who might stand in his way.

But Sumanguru's efforts to build an empire on the ruins of Ghana did not succeed — any more than had Abu Bekr's earlier attempt. Sumanguru failed to win the loyalty of the Muslim traders, upon whom the prosperity of the country depended.[3] Furthermore, the Mandingo people of Kangaba were rallying to the support of their young prince, Sundiata (sun-dee-*ah'*tuh), who was opposed to Sumanguru's domination.

Sundiata leads the Mandingo people to victory. According to the legends, when Sumanguru first invaded Kangaba he put to death eleven brothers who were heirs to the Mali throne. But he failed to kill the twelfth child, Sundiata. Some legends say that Sundiata was sickly; others that he had been sent into exile for his own safety. At any rate, Sundiata in time grew to manhood and raised an army to oppose Sumanguru.

[3] The Muslim traders of Kumbi left the city and moved northward, where they founded a new trading center at Walata (*wah'*lah-tuh).

The legends describe the clash between Sundiata and Sumanguru in colorful language. They call to mind Homer's account of the Trojan War and the clash between Greeks and Trojans. In both cases, each side summoned certain gods and spirits to its aid. According to ancient legends, the two leaders resorted to witchcraft at the battle of Karina (kah-*ree'*nuh) in 1235. In the legend, Sundiata's witchcraft proved stronger: Sumanguru, struck by an arrow tipped with the spur of a white rooster, immediately disappeared. (Actually, he and his army withdrew to the mountains.) Although Sumanguru was killed shortly afterwards, his generals returned to Tekrur, where they and their successors continued to rule for many years. But "as for Sundiata," according to the legend, "he defeated the army of Sumanguru, ravaged the land of the Susu, and subjugated its people. Afterwards Sundiata became the ruler of an immense empire."

Sundiata lays the foundations for a great empire. Sundiata's victory left the Mandingo people in control of a much larger area than earlier had been theirs. The boundaries of the Mali Empire were extended still further by his generals. These generals became governors in the new territory, which in time was divided into provinces of the empire. Every year these governors would send gifts of farm produce, as well as weapons (arrows and lances), to their emperor.

Meanwhile, Sundiata moved the capital of Mali from Kangaba to the city of his birth, Niani (nee-*ah'*nee), near the common frontier of present-day Guinea and Mali.[4] Although the city of Niani has long since ceased to exist, a village of the same name occupies the site of the ancient capital. Sundiata encouraged former soldiers to become farmers, and some of them learned to raise livestock. Before long, Mali became one of the richest farming regions in West Africa.

Sundiata also attempted, without success, to convert his people to Islam. They not only refused to give up their traditional religion, but stopped working the gold mines until Sundiata promised them freedom of worship. In 1255 Sundiata died. One legend has it that he drowned; another that he was accidentally killed in an archery contest. Whatever the cause of his death, his memory still survives in the oral traditions of the people of West Africa.

Sundiata's successors strengthen Mali. During the half century between Sundiata's death and the accession to the throne of Mansa

---

[4] It was at this time that the empire of the Mandingo people came to be called Mali — a word meaning "where the king resides."

THE SUDANESE MARKET. In the sudan region, the center of town often is an open-air market (*above*) where merchants, many of them women, carry on a lively trade in foodstuffs and household goods. Sudanese markets thrived on the trans-Saharan trade which supported skilled craftsmen, such as the weaver (*left*) who produces colorful fabrics today in Bamako, Mali. Profits from trade enabled merchants to live in luxury and build ornate houses, like the one shown below in Zinder, a caravan terminal in Niger.

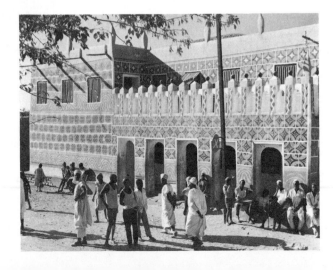

Musa, Mali had perhaps seven rulers. Though not of equal ability, each tried in his own way to strengthen the empire. The first of these was Mansa Uli (*man*'suh *oo*'lee), who reigned until 1270. Legend refers to him as "the Red King," because his skin was said to be of copperish hue. Following an ancient tradition, practiced by Sundiata, Mansa Uli made the *hajj* (hadj) or holy pilgrimage to Mecca, which every good Muslim is expected to make at least once in his lifetime.[5] Although Uli himself was religious and peaceloving, the generals he left behind him in Mali were not. They took it upon themselves during his absence to launch military expeditions in the course of which they annexed several neighboring states.

Uli's successors contributed little to the empire. But in 1285 a remarkable ex-slave of the royal household named Sakura (sah-*koo*'ruh) seized the throne and proclaimed himself emperor. He embarked on another series of conquests, in which he subdued Tekrur and Gao (*gah*'oh). During this emperor's fifteen-year reign, Mali achieved a high level of prosperity, and merchants from many different parts of Africa came to Niani and other towns in Mali to trade. Unfortunately, Sakura was assassinated in 1300 on his return from a pilgrimage to Mecca. The next four rulers apparently did little to strengthen the empire. When a struggle for power among rival "strong men" began, the fate of the empire for a time hung in the balance.

Mali reaches its peak under Mansa Musa's rule. About 1312, a grand-nephew of Sundiata ascended the imperial throne. This extraordinary young man was Mansa Musa.[6] During the quarter of a century of his rule, Mali's prestige increased immensely. According to some historians, his empire ranked second in size only to the Mongol Empire in Asia. Its wealth — at least when measured in gold — surpassed that of Egypt. Furthermore, Musa was an excellent "public relations" man. He saw to it that the pomp and majesty of his court became known far and wide. A noted fourteenth-century Arab scholar named al-Omari (al-oh-*mah*'ree) wrote that of all Muslim rulers of West Africa, Mansa Musa was "the most powerful, the richest, the

---

[5] The first of the Mandingo kings, Baramendana, who embraced the Muslim faith about 1050, made a pilgrimage to Mecca. This practice was followed faithfully by later rulers of Mali.

[6] His full name was Mansa Gonga (or Kankan) Musa — pronounced *man*'suh *gahn*'guh *moo*'sah. His formal title would be Musa I, Mansa of Mali. Mansa is a title which means "emperor." He is usually referred to, however, as "Mansa Musa."

most fortunate, the most feared by his enemies, and the most able to do good to those around him."[7] To understand why Mansa Musa achieved this reputation, it is necessary to look at developments which took place in Mali's economy and government during his reign.

1. *Mali was an unusually prosperous state.* The political and military strength of Musa's empire rested upon ample sources of revenue, the most important of which were taxes on trade. To insure that trade and commerce prospered, Mansa Musa encouraged the opening up of new trade routes and the exchange of a wider variety of goods. Trade with the Maghreb flourished, partly because Mansa Musa saw to it that travel over the caravan routes was safe and partly because he had established friendly relations with the sultan of Fez.

Mali also profited from the import and export of copper. It ranked second, however, to the gold-salt trade as a source of government income. Taxes collected on this latter doubtless surpassed those collected by the Ghanaian rulers (see page 88). Under Mansa Musa the boundaries of the Mali Empire were extended northward to include the salt-rich region near Taghaza (tah-*gah'*zuh). From the south, Mali received the gold output of Wangara. Mansa Musa traded copper, salt, grains, cowrie shells (used as money), livestock, and cloth for Wangara gold.

Even though Mali's revenues came chiefly from trade, its economy basically was one of food production. Most of the people of Mali were hunters and farmers. The chief food crops were sorghum, rice, taro, yams, beans, and onions. Poultry, cattle, sheep, and goats were raised for their meat, eggs, milk, and skins. In addition, Malian hunters killed hippopotamuses, wild buffaloes, elephants, and crocodiles, using spears and poisoned arrows for this purpose.

2. *Mali's government was efficient.* The Arab traveler and scholar Ibn Battuta, who journeyed through Mali in the middle of the fourteenth century, wrote: "Among the admirable qualities of these people are . . . the complete and general safety one enjoys throughout the land. The traveler has no more reason than the man who stays at home to fear brigands, thieves, or ravishers." The state of law and order maintained in this far-flung empire, as described by the Arab writers, suggests not only an efficient government but that people were not suffering want.

---

[7] Quoted in Basil Davidson, *The African Past* (New York: Grosset and Dunlap [Universal Library Edition], 1967) p. 77.

The sudanese girl from Chad (*left*) shows Muslim influence in her dress, while a Nigerian girl (*above*) wears the turbaned kerchief of Guinea.

The territory of the empire — about equal to that of western Europe — was divided into two categories. First, there were provinces administered by the emperor himself through his governors. For the more important towns or cities in these provinces the emperor himself appointed mayors or inspectors. Secondly, there were some fifteen provinces which owed allegiance to the emperor. Most of these provinces were ruled by local tribal leaders. Among the weaknesses of the government was the failure to create a civil service or to establish an effective court system. "Legal cases," a commentator noted, "go up to the sovereign who examines them himself." Such an arrangement placed a heavy burden on the ruler. It would yield poor results if a lazy or incompetent emperor came to the throne.

Mali maintained a large standing army. One of its functions was to prevent (or suppress) revolts in the semi-independent provinces ruled by the tribal leaders. Its other responsibility was to secure the empire against outside attacks. The army must have done its job well. Otherwise how would Mansa Musa and other Mali rulers have dared to absent themselves to make the long pilgrimage to Mecca?

Mansa Musa's pilgrimage enhances Mali's prestige. The most outstanding event of Mansa Musa's reign was his famous *hajj*, or pilgrimage, to Mecca. What stands out is not the fact of the journey but the grand style in which he traveled. Musa was accompanied by a great body of attendants. There were 12,000 slaves richly attired in silks and brocades. Of this number, 500 preceded Mansa Musa, each carrying a staff of gold weighing six pounds. Mansa Musa himself rode on horseback. Behind him trailed 80 camels, each weighed down by 300 pounds of gold dust. Such a display of wealth and pomp made a deep impression throughout Africa. There is a story that when the Mali emperor reached Cairo, the sultan of Egypt sent his representatives to greet Musa and to invite him to the royal palace in Cairo. At first Mansa Musa refused because he did not wish to pay the customary act of courtesy to the Egyptian ruler — either kissing the ground before the sultan or kissing the sultan's ring. When Mansa Musa finally agreed to visit the Egyptian ruler and was asked to kiss the ground, he refused, asserting that he would prostrate himself before no one but God (Allah). He then turned toward the East (Mecca) and bowed and touched his lips to the ground, thus honoring Allah. The Egyptian sultan, impressed by the mansa's dignified bearing, invited Mansa Musa to sit beside him and to tell him more about the fabulous empire to the south and west of Egypt. Later he presented Mansa Musa and his officers with many gifts.

Mansa Musa's generosity was fabulous. In Cairo, as well as in the holy cities of Medina and Mecca, the mansa distributed gifts of gold. In fact, he was so generous that he upset the price of gold on the Egyptian market. Because so much new gold was put into circulation, its value dropped sharply and did not recover, according to one Muslim writer, until twelve years later. Musa's generosity was reported far and wide. To quote a modern authority, "This journey of Mansa Musa placed the western sudan squarely on the map of the great states in the world of the time; quite literally, for Mali and its 'Lord of the Negroes' [Mansa Musa] appear on the very first map of West Africa ever drawn in Europe (in 1375)."[8]

Mansa Musa promotes cultural progress in Mali. Mansa Musa's pilgrimage to Mecca was not all show. It also contributed to the cultural enrichment of his empire. The emperor was quick to recognize the achievements of Muslim countries which he visited, and he determined that his own people should learn about them. During his

[8] Roland Oliver and J. D. Fage, *A Short History of Africa,* second edition (Baltimore: Penguin Books, 1966), p. 90. The map was drawn for King Charles V of France by the Majorcan cartographer Abraham Cresques, and is preserved in the Bibliotheque Nationale in Paris. It is decorated with a drawing of a Black African ruler in royal attire, holding a scepter in one hand and a nugget of gold in the other. The inscription accompanying the drawing reads: "This Negro lord is called Mousse Melly [i.e., Musa of Mali], Lord of the Negroes. . . ."

journey he had met a famous Arab scholar from Granada (Spain), es-Saheli (es sah-*hay′*lee), who was both a poet and an architect. Tradition ascribes to this gifted man the introduction into the western sudan of burnt-brick architecture. Es-Saheli is said to have designed a great mosque at Gao and a mosque and palace for Mansa Musa at Timbuktu (tim-buck-*too′*). The foundation of the mosque at Gao still survives. The learned Arab is also credited with the design of an auditorium in Niani, the capital. Timbuktu and Djenné (jen-*nay′*) at this time had begun to attract Muslim scholars as well as traders. These scholars were mainly theologians — men schooled in the law and philosophy of the Koran. By making the new mosque of Sankore (san-*koh′*ray) in Timbuktu their center of instruction, they laid the foundations for the University of Sankore. In later years, the fame of these towns as centers of learning spread throughout the Muslim world.

Mali begins to decline after Mansa Musa's death. After Mansa Musa died in 1332, the empire soon came under attack. Invaders from the south raided Timbuktu, routed the Mandingo garrison, and burnt down the city. Thereafter they continued to harass the empire. A still more ominous development, however, was taking place in the Songhai city of Gao, brought into the Mali Empire by Mansa Musa in 1325. The Songhai of Gao were never happy about their submission to Mali. Beginning in 1375, when they refused to pay the required tribute to Mali, they proved to be continuous troublemakers for the empire. In 1400 they rebelled. Mali's internal troubles doubtless encouraged the Tuareg Berbers of the southern Sahara to attack and plunder Mali towns along the empire's northern boundary. In 1431 the Tuaregs seized Timbuktu, as well as other key towns. In the following decades much of the rest of northern Mali fell to the Tuaregs. Along the western fringes of the empire other peoples also began to raid the empire.

Meanwhile Songhai (see page 104) was expanding at the expense of Mali. In the fifteenth and sixteenth centuries, the rulers of Mali, in an effort to meet the challenge of the Songhai Empire, sought help from Europeans. From 1434 on, Portuguese sea captains, encouraged by Prince Henry the Navigator, had been sailing along the western coast of Africa, establishing trading posts here and there. They had made contact with the Mandingo people, and had attempted to establish trade with the interior, without much success. In 1534 the emperor of Mali, in a last-ditch attempt to bolster his waning power, sent an ambassador to the king of Portugal to ask for help. The Portuguese king was unable to provide the aid requested. Consequently, by the middle of the seventeenth century, the Mandingo dynasty ruled only the petty state of Kangaba, the state which it held four hundred years earlier under Sundiata (page 92). Mali was back where it had started. But the idea of a unified West Africa was not dead. It would guide the efforts of other dynasties eager to build a great empire.

What is the significance of Mali's "decline and fall"? In surveying the early empires of the sudan, the focus has been on the towns which were centers of commercial and cultural activity. But we should not lose sight of the important fact that most of the people lived not in towns and cities but in the countryside. In many ways, these rural folk lived in a world different from that of the townspeople. Through commercial and other contacts, the religion of Islam had taken root in the towns. This was not true in the country, where peasants clung to traditional beliefs. Age-old mutual jealousy and suspicion tended to divide city-dwellers and country-dwellers, and this lack of unity helps to explain the instability of these empires. For a time, a powerful and magnetic leader would capture the loyalty of both the urban and the rural population. But after his death, men of lesser ability would come to power, rulers whose support would come mainly from merchants in the Muslim towns. Their reliance on this group would create ill-will in the countryside. Hence in time of crisis, their empires would fall apart. Having traced this pattern in the history of Mali, one might suspect that it also held true for Songhai.

• CHECK-UP

1. How did Sundiata build an empire? Why did Mali prosper during the reign of Mansa Musa? How was the empire governed?

2. What are our sources of information about Mali? How did Mansa Musa enrich Mali's culture? Why did Mali decline after his death?

3. Why were rural and urban folk often "out of step" with each other in the sudanese empires?

3. Songhai Replaces Mali as West Africa's Foremost Power

Knowledge of Songhai is based in part on tombstone inscriptions. In 1939, the tombstones in question were discovered by archaeologists in the village of Sané (sah-*nay'*) near the ancient city of Gao. Since then, historians have been able to piece together the main outlines of Songhai development by combining the oral and written traditions of the people with archaeological finds.

Gao forms the nucleus of the Songhai Empire. Songhai's beginnings seem to go back to the seventh century. It was then that the Songhai established themselves at Gao after pushing out the earlier inhabitants. In this early period, a small town named Kukya (*kook'-*yuh) — near the present-day northwest frontier of Nigeria — was their capital. But Berber nomads conquered Kukya and established a new ruling dynasty called the Dia (*dee'*ah). Led by the expansionist-minded Dia, the Songhai gradually extended their power over a sizable area around the bend of the Niger. In 1010 the king was converted to Islam. Soon afterwards, the capital of Songhai was moved to Gao, and that city entered upon a period of growth and prosperity.

Sunni Ali organizes and enlarges the empire. Songhai's expansion into a great empire during the fifteenth century owes much to the organizing genius of Sunni Ali (*soo'*nee *ah'*lee), who ruled Songhai from 1464 to 1492. During this long reign Ali was never defeated. He is often portrayed as a warlike and ruthless ruler who succeeded in establishing law and in creating a unified country. Ali beat back the Mossi, who were raiding Timbuktu, a city second in importance only to Gao. Ali next devoted himself to "cleaning up" Timbuktu, where the Tuaregs had been in control since 1433. During these years many of the city's leading citizens had collaborated with Tuareg rule. After ousting the Tuaregs, Ali put many of these pro-Tuareg citizens to death, an act which contributed to his reputation for cruelty. By 1476 Sunni Ali had brought the whole lake region of the middle Niger west of Timbuktu largely under his control. This area, to quote Basil Davidson, was "a vital segment of the whole commercial network of the central region of the sudan." Control of this area, with its resources and wealth, remained the keystone of Songhai imperial power.

The history of Sunni Ali's reign reads like a list of battles — but there was another side to his rule. From an administrative point of view, the Songhai Empire was an advance over Mali. Ali divided his empire into provinces, and placed governors in charge of each. In the central government at Gao, civil servants, in a descending order of rank, were appointed for longer terms of office. Consequently, Ali could be absent from his capital for extended periods of time, knowing that the business of government would be carried on efficiently.

Sunni Ali's military victories resulted in part from his belief that soldiering was a full-time occupation. He laid the foundation for a professional army, believing it more efficient than an army of drafted civilians. He also established a navy on the Niger. Men in the armed forces lived in barracks and military camps somewhat apart from the civilian population. His warriors were well-equipped with weapons of the time — bows and arrows, sabres, lances, and breastplates. Firearms had not yet been introduced into African warfare.

Estimates of Sunni Ali differ. Some of the Muslim chronicles describe Sunni Ali as a cruel tyrant. Since these writings originated in Timbuktu, they doubtless reflect the view that Ali had treated harshly the Muslim leaders who had collaborated with the city's Tuareg occupiers. These Muslims also resented the fact that Sunni Ali was not an orthodox Muslim like themselves. He seems to have favored the traditional religion of the countryside rather than the Muslim faith of the urban merchants and traders. However, Ali sought to gain the support of this latter group by going out of his way to show respect for Muslim scholarship. Once the emperor is said to have remarked that "without learned men, there would be no pleasure in life." But this lip-service failed to convince devout Muslims. They could not reconcile their belief in one God with traditional African beliefs in many gods and forms of worship. The Koran specifically denounced magic, sorcery, and witchcraft; yet Sunni Ali winked at such practices among non-Muslims.

A major source of friction was the fact that Muslim law and traditional African law often were in conflict. This was true, for example, in the matter of inheritance. This difference affected not only the inheritance of property but also the selection of kings and chiefs. The Islamic practice, increasingly, was based on *primogeniture* — which makes the first-born son the principal heir — whereas traditional African systems permitted choosing from a larger number. Sunni Ali tried to steer a middle course between the two systems, possibly in an attempt to blend the best elements of both. And in part he succeeded in doing so. Most of the Songhai people remembered Sunni Ali as a great hero and a brilliant soldier-king.

Askia Mohammed becomes Songhai's second great ruler. Sunni Ali died in 1492, having drowned in attempting to cross a large stream on his way back to Gao. Sunni Ali's son, Sunni Baru (*soo'nee bah'-roo*), named successor to the throne of Songhai, had a short reign. Early in 1493 he was overthrown by Mohammed Turé, one of his

ISLAM IN THE SUDAN. (*Above:*) Two Muslims in Niger study wooden tablets on which the sacred texts of the Koran have been engraved in Arabic letters. Behind them is the wall of their village mosque, a hut woven of straw. Other sudanese mosques are more imposing, such as the one in Mali shown at left. Its clay walls loom above the town like those of a European cathedral.

Modern mosque (*right*) with a cylindrical minaret is a showplace of the town of New Bussa in central Nigeria. New Bussa was built to house 10,000 people whose old homes in the Niger River Valley have been flooded by the recently completed Kainji Dam.

father's rebellious generals, who had the backing of the Muslim towns-men. Mohammed Turé took the name Askia Mohammed (*ahs'*kee-uh moh-*hah'*med) I. Becoming emperor at the age of 50, he reigned for 35 years and brought the empire to its peak of political and commer-cial power. If Sunni Ali was to Songhai what Sundiata had been to Mali, then Askia Mohammed was Songhai's Mansa Musa. Like his Mali counterpart, Askia Mohammed was a devout Muslim. His pil-grimage to Mecca in 1495–97 rivaled that of Mansa Musa in mag-nificence and generosity, and under his auspices Timbuktu regained its former eminence as a center of Islamic studies. Returning from Mecca with the spiritual authority to act as caliph for the entire western sudan, Askia played his part well.

Askia expands the Songhai Empire and tries to unify it. Askia was determined to extend his territories and bring them under the sway of Islam, to the greater glory of Allah. The Mandingoes, the Fulani in the west, the Tuareg Berbers in the north — all felt the force of his might. Only the Mossi states (see fact panel, page 105) could with-stand his armies. Askia reduced Mali to a shadow of its former self, and extended Songhai to the borders of Tekrur in the west. He wrested Taghaza and Agadès (ah-gah-*des'*) from the Berbers, and in the Aïr (*ah'*ir) region to the north of Agadès, the Tuareg were tem-porarily forced to make way for a group of Songhai settlers whose de-scendants may still be found there. The Hausa states in the east were overrun and forced to pay tribute. The eastward advance of Askia's armies was not halted until they reached the borders of Bornu — the western wing of the empire of Kanem-Bornu (see map, page 84). Once again the greater part of the western sudan's central region was brought under a single system of law and order.

Departing from the policy of Sunni Ali, Askia Mohammed sought to make all of the empire one big Muslim community. Although he did not succeed in converting the entire sudan to Islam, he remodeled his empire along Islamic lines as far as possible. Legal and social re-forms were introduced, Islamic judges were appointed in all the large districts of the empire, and justice was administered according to Muslim principles rather than traditional African laws. The court of Askia Mohammed was the highest court of the land, to which appeals from the lower courts could be brought.

Songhai power begins to decline after Askia Mohammed's death. Askia Mohammed's long reign ended in tragedy when he was over-thrown by his own sons. His eldest son, who seized the throne in

The Indomitable Mossi

The ways of the past are no longer the ways of many of the Mossi people in what is now the state of Upper Volta. From the thirteenth century the Mossi states of Wagadugu, Yatenga, Fada-n-Gurma, Mamprussi, and Dagomba had maintained their religion and their independence against the pressures of the Mali and Songhai empires and the Muslim faith, and for all that time they had been ruled by the same dynasties. By making skillful use of a tradition of divine kingship and of a form of ancestor worship, these rulers had succeeded in forging the varied groups over which they ruled into stable, unified nations. So effective was their method that the Mossi still regard themselves as a group apart, rarely forming ties outside the tribe.

But change has come even to the Mossi. The long years of colonial rule by the French and the influx of new political ideas weakened the institution of the chieftainship there as it did over much of Africa, and a new political elite emerged which was, to a great extent, the product of European education. The new constitution of Upper Volta has no provisions for the chiefs, and the present mogho naba, or king, of Wagadugu is now king in name only. An impressive two-hour ceremony is still held every Friday in the courtyard of his palace, in which his ministers and attendants kneel before him to renew their allegiance, but real political power has been wrested from him and transferred to the central government of Upper Volta. Only the older members of the Mossi community — and the most conservative of its young people — now revere the king in accordance with ancient traditions. The centuries-old dynasty of Wagadugu still clings to its time-honored ceremonies, however.

1528, was killed by his subjects after a reign of three years, probably because of his anti-Islamic policies. Then followed an eight-year struggle for power which involved generals and adventurers before order was restored. Unquestionably the internal struggles of the years following Askia Mohammed's overthrow seriously weakened the power of Songhai. These events, according to the historian J. D. Fage, revealed "the inherent weakness of a regime dependent on military power." In 1592 another series of quarrels over the succession broke out, hastening the downfall of the empire.

Al Mansur (ahl-mahn-*soor'*), the ambitious sultan of Morocco, saw an opportunity to profit from the internal weakness of the Songhai empire. Having won an important victory over Portuguese invaders at Kasr al-Kebir (*kah'*zer ahl-kuh-*beer'*), he raided Taghaza and its salt mines. Intrigued by reports of Songhai's wealth, he sent an army across the Sahara to conquer the gold lands of West Africa. The army which invaded Songhai in 1590–91 numbered only 4000 and was made up mostly of Europeans, Christian captives, and deserters armed with muskets. Their guns enabled them to put to rout a much larger army. Later their superior weapons enabled them to capture the cities of Gao, Timbuktu, and Djenné. When these cities fell, the power of Songhai was at an end.

Morocco fails to establish a lasting empire in the sudan. Al Mansur's bold thrust into the Songhai Empire was a military victory only. The Moroccans failed to get control of the gold of West Africa. As a matter of fact, Songhai's wealth did not stem from possession of the gold mines but from its control of the trade with gold-producing regions. This trade, in turn, had flourished because of the settled conditions which prevailed during the Songhai administration of the sudan. Songhai fighters, using guerrilla tactics against the Moroccans, saw to it that normal trade was disrupted. There simply were not enough Moroccan soldiers to cope with the Black Africans who were fighting in the bush and forest areas of their homeland. Furthermore, the troubles of the Moroccan invaders increased when Songhai's former enemies, the Fulani, the Tuaregs, and others, took advantage of the turmoil to plunder former Songhai lands. The Moroccans, however, continued to send reinforcements to the sudan, and not until 1618 was the invasion abandoned. In the meantime, the Songhai Empire had dwindled to the size of the original Songhai country. A great empire had been destroyed.

• CHECK-UP

1. How did Sunni Ali build the Songhai Empire? Govern it? Strengthen its armed forces?

2. What were the roots of the conflict between Muslim and non-Muslim Africans?

3. How did Askia expand his empire? Remodel it? Why was Morocco able to conquer Songhai? Unable to hold it?

4. Other States Continue the Tradition of Empire

The overthrow of Songhai did not put an end to the idea of an empire among the Africans of the sudan. East of Songhai was Kanem-Bornu. Between Kanem-Bornu and Songhai were the Hausa states, and south of Songhai were the Mossi, a people already mentioned in connection with Timbuktu (page 101). Other important West African kingdoms during the seventeenth and eighteenth centuries were Benin, the Akan state of Akwamu (ah-*kwah'*moo), Ashanti, Oyo, and Dahomey. Of all these, the one with by far the most extensive territory was Kanem-Bornu.

The Kanuri people establish themselves around Lake Chad. The empire of Kanem-Bornu may be said to have begun with the Kanuri (kah-*noo'*ree), just as the empire of Mali began with the Mandingo people. The Sefuwa (suh-*foo'*wah) family, the ruling dynasty of Kanem-Bornu, came to power about 850 A.D. By the end of the eleventh century, their kingdom — which was centered at Kanem, northeast of Lake Chad — had become strong enough to establish direct trade with Tripoli and Egypt. In 1086, the king of Kanem accepted Islam, and from that time on, all the rulers of Kanem-Bornu were Muslims. The conversion to Islam took place at the same time as two other important developments: (1) increased trade and (2) the establishment of a single system of law over the region. Through Kanem, the exports of Egypt and other northern lands — horses, metals, salt — came to West Africa, while West African wares such as ivory, cotton stuffs, and forest products were carried northward.

During the twelfth and thirteenth centuries Kanem succeeded in colonizing Bornu, southwest of Lake Chad, and in making its power felt across the desert as far north as the Fezzan. Eventually Kanem itself fell to a new group of invaders from the northeast, but the royal house had moved to Bornu, where it re-established its power.

The king of Bornu imports firearms. By the sixteenth century, the ruling dynasty was again a force to be reckoned with in the sudan. It dominated two major routes to North Africa: the one through Bilma (*bill'*muh) to Libya, and the other across the desert to the Nile. Control of these two routes made Bornu a more important center of trade than Kanem had been. Finally, in the early 1500's, Bornu succeeded in reasserting its power in old Kanem. This power was precarious, however, and probably would not have lasted long but for another factor of great significance for the future of Kanem-Bornu and of all Africa.

Firearms were introduced into Kanem-Bornu by that empire's most renowned ruler, *Mai* Idris Alooma (mye *ee'*drees al-*oh'*muh),[9] who reigned from about 1580 to 1610. Idris had come to the throne after a bitter struggle with several rival claimants. Doubtless this early experience taught him the importance of having modern arms. To this end he purchased muskets from Tripoli and brought in Turkish instructors to train his soldiers. Superior arms enabled Idris Alooma to maintain his authority in Kanem. Gradually, Bornu influence was extended into Hausaland (west of Kanem-Bornu) and southwards toward the Benue River. Idris had no compunctions about waging wars against people who refused to accept the Muslim religion. Once subdued, they were compelled to pay an annual tax, and some of them were enslaved.

Kanem-Bornu reaches its height during the early seventeenth century. The last decades of the sixteenth century and the first half of the seventeenth century were Kanem-Bornu's period of greatness. Although unrest buffeted other sudanese peoples, it was a time of relative peace and stability for Kanem-Bornu. Much of the credit for this condition must go to the empire's greatest mai, Idris Alooma, who by force of arms unified the country and established orderly rule over a vast area — from Darfur (dahr-*foor'*) in the east to the frontiers of Hausaland in the west. Kanem-Bornu did not possess the wealth in gold of Mali and Songhai, but like them it did benefit from a location at the crossroads of trade and travel between West Africa, the Fezzan (fez-*ahn'*),[10] Tripoli, and Egypt. It was the link between the peoples north of the Sahara and those in the western sudan. One of Kanem's noted writers, Ibn Fartua (*ib'*un *fahr'*too-ah), who served at the court of Idris Alooma, described with justifiable pride the pomp of the Bornu court. He tells of the visit of ambassadors from the Ottoman sultan of Istanbul, who brought gifts to the African ruler, and he exclaims:

> O, my wise friends and companions! Have you ever seen a king who is equal to our lord [Idris Alooma] at such a moment, when the lord of Stambul [Istanbul], the great sultan of Turkey, sends messages to him with favorable proposals?[11]

[9] *Mai* was the title used by the rulers of Bornu. It means "king."

[10] **Fezzan**: a region of desert and oases in southwestern Libya.

[11] Ahmed ibn Fartua, *The Kanem War of Idris Alooma*, translated by H. R. Palmer (Lagos, 1928); quoted in Basil Davidson, *A History of West Africa*, p. 140.

Idris Alooma died in 1617. During the next 40 years, the throne was occupied by four successive mais. It was during the reign of the last of these mais, Ali, that trouble began. Two circumstances combined to hasten Kanem-Bornu's decline: (1) attacks by the Tuaregs from the Aïr oases, which occurred at the same time as attacks from a small state in the southwest; and (2) a great famine in the later years of Ali's reign — precipitated, perhaps, by the destructive raids and the interruption in food shipments.

The Sefuwa dynasty lasts until 1846. The breakdown of the Kanem-Bornu Empire was very gradual. With each successive mai, the central government became weaker and less capable of dealing with differences among its subject peoples. As in the case of the earlier sudanese empires, revolts and secessions steadily diminished the domain of the mais. In 1808, the Fulani of Hausaland attacked Bornu and drove the mai from his capital. By this time, Kanem's ties with Bornu had been all but severed by the Fulani. Nevertheless, in response to the mai's appeal for help, the people of Kanem east of Lake Chad sent an army to his relief under an able soldier named Amin (*ah'*min). Amin was successful in driving back the Fulani, and after the death of the mai, he assumed leadership of the state of Bornu. A little later, in 1846, the last representative of the Sefuwa royal line quit the throne, bringing this thousand-year dynasty to an end.

The Hausa states lack a unifying central government. West of Bornu, as we have seen, lay a group of states — seven in number — which had come into existence by about the tenth century. The Hausa states came into their own after the decline of Songhai and even more so after Kanem-Bornu. Several of them entered a period of great prosperity in the seventeenth century, when they became the southern terminals of the trans-Saharan trade routes to Tunis and Tripoli. Hausa merchants became carriers of trade and of the Islamic religion from the Gold Coast eastward throughout West Africa.

These seven states never abandoned their separate existence in favor of becoming a federation of states or an empire. Not that the Hausa states were reluctant to expand. They had made themselves strong during the twelfth and thirteenth centuries. Each began as a strong walled village governed by its own king and council. A few developed into constitutional monarchies. By the late fourteenth century, Katsina (*kaht'*sih-nuh) and Kano (*kah'*noh) were the leading Hausa kingdoms. There were frequent wars, though not the long-drawn-out wars undertaken by Ghana, Mali, or Songhai. The great power exercised by some individual rulers — Mohammed Rumfa (*room'*fah) of Kano (1465–99), for example — suggests that the idea of divine kingship had gained some acceptance in the Hausa states. In time each state achieved a degree of stability and self-sufficiency unusual among the early kingdoms of West Africa. Not until the 1800's were these states united under a single ruler — the sultan of Sokoto (soh-*koh'*toh) — as part of a new Fulani empire. A century later, the British established colonial rule over most of the Fulani territory.

The kingship tradition is carried on by the peoples of Guinea. The region south of the sudan, along the great bend of Africa's Atlantic coast, is often referred to as "Guinea" (*gin'*ih).[12] As early as the thirteenth century, the Black Africans of this area had begun to develop small states and kingdoms. Later, in the fifteenth century, more advanced ideas of government filtered into the forest lands, as settlers arrived from the declining sudanese empires. At about this time also, improved agricultural skills made it possible to support an expanding population. This was true especially after the introduction of the banana and yam (from Indonesia, by way of East Africa), and corn and cassava (from tropical America). These new crops were necessary because the cereal grains of the sudan could not be grown successfully in the dense forests of Guinea.

The first of the Guinea states developed in the area between the lower Niger River and the Ivory Coast, where the forests were less dense and the land more suitable for farming and herding (see map, page 6). The principal states of Guinea were formed by two main groups of people, the Akan (*ah'*kahn) and the Yoruba (*yoh'*roo-bah). Probably as early as the thirteenth century, Bono and Banda, two Akan settlements to the north of the Gold Coast forest, grew to become important Akan towns. The Akan then expanded southward, avoiding the heavy forest by following the eastern sweep of the Volta River Valley and then moving into the coastal grasslands.

The Yoruba people of Guinea establish several important city-states. According to Yoruba tradition, the first Yoruba state was Ife (*ee'*fay), founded about 1000 A.D. From Ife, the Yoruba people

---

[12] The term "Guinea" was applied to this great area of the Atlantic coastline by Portuguese sailors in the fifteenth century. It is taken from the word for "Negroes" in the Berber language of Morocco. Smaller portions of the Guinea coast later were given names of their own as European traders and explorers increased their contacts with West Africa. Some of these names were: Grain Coast, Ivory Coast, Gold Coast, and Slave Coast. They suggest what these parts of Africa meant to European traders.

THE KING-CHIEF. An old bronze casting shows a Dahomey chief riding in a litter (*above*). He is preceded by the royal umbrella and followed by musicians, one of whom carries a drum on his head. The chiefs' courts remain a center for minstrels, like this Ivory Coast singer (*left*) who plays an African lute.

The umbrella (*right*) is still a sign of local royalty in Cameroon, where a veiled sultan rides forth in its shade. He is accompanied by trumpeters and guards whenever he leaves the peaked thatch huts of the royal compound. Most of the time he remains in seclusion and is rarely seen by his subjects.

fanned out into the surrounding area and established several "daughter cities." Two of the most important were Benin (beh-*neen'*), near the northern edge of the Nigerian forest, and Oyo (oh-*yoh'*), north of Ife. These "daughter cities" were politically independent of Ife, but the kings, or *oni* (*aw'*nee), of Ife did have a kind of spiritual supremacy over other Yoruba rulers. All the Yoruba dynasties were supposed to have descended from Oduduwa (*oh'*doo-*doo'*wah), a god said to have first settled at Ife.

Benin and Oyo develop new forms of kingship. Benin became the seat of an historic dynasty, where the kings, called *obas* (*oh'*buz), tried to introduce stronger central government. For perhaps two centuries, the king of Benin was elected by an influential group of nobles. But around 1500, this system underwent a change. The king was no longer elected, and royal succession in Benin from this time onwards was determined by primogeniture (see page 102). At the same time, two new classes of nobility were created — the palace chiefs, who were connected with the court, and the town chiefs, the "self-made men" who had excelled in business or in warfare.

In the Yoruba state of Oyo, however, the king, called the *alafin* (ah-*lahf'*in), continued to be elected from the governing council made up of Oyo nobles. The kingship was a position of honor rather than of power, for important decisions of state were made by the council. The head councilman, called the *bashorun* (buh-*show'*run), was the head of the civil administration and also performed a priestly function. His religious duty was the worship of the *orun* (*oh'*run) — the alafin's "spiritual double." If the rites connected with this worship ever revealed that the alafin was no longer acceptable to his "spiritual double," then it was the duty of the Oyo nobles to dethrone him. As a signal of his impending removal, the alafin would be sent a basket of parrot's eggs. (The alafin, however, could expect some protection from hostile forces through his worship of Shango [*shan'*goh] — who came to be regarded as the ruler's special protecting god.) Interesting as this system was, it seems to show that the kingship system in Oyo was not so strong as that of some of the other Guinea states — not to mention the empires of the western sudan.

New African empires are formed in Guinea during the seventeenth and eighteenth centuries. By the seventeenth and eighteenth centuries, Benin and Oyo had gained control over settlements within a radius of 100–200 miles. Oyo's expansion, furthermore, was the result of military conquests. Unsuccessful generals were expected to

BENIN BRONZES. The famous bronzesmiths of Benin worked for their all-powerful *oba*, or king. One of the ornaments which they fashioned for him was this hollow head (*left*), designed to fit over the base of an elephant tusk. Whenever an elephant was killed, the oba received one of the ivory tusks. His palace was adorned with bronze plaques, like the one below, which shows an animal being prepared for royal sacrifice.

commit suicide, or at any rate not to return home from battle. So ruthless did the alafin of Oyo become, that by the nineteenth century subject towns in desperation began to defy his authority and to assert their independence. One of the complaints of provincial chiefs against the alafin was that they were not receiving their share of the profits from the booming slave trade. According to historian J. D. Fage, the slave trade — and the cutthroat rivalry it engendered among empire officials — was a principal cause of the disintegration of these Yoruba kingdoms. "Once the process of disintegration and civil strife had begun," he writes, "the existence of the ready market provided by the European traders for the sale of slaves and the purchase of guns made it virtually impossible for the Yorubas to return to a more peaceable way of life. . . . The social canker which had beset [the Yoruba kingdoms] was only finally checked by the imposition of external authority and the introduction of new social doctrines in the form of British rule and Christian missions."[13] To a large extent the same was true of Benin (see Chapter 5, page 186).

Westward and somewhat northward along the coastline, the Akan-speaking peoples were forming their last, and most powerful, political system — that of the Ashanti (uh-*shahn*'tee) federation. After considerable rivalry and warfare among themselves, the Akan states finally agreed to form a confederation which became known as the Ashanti Union of Akan States. Each of the separate Akan peoples swore allegiance to the symbol of the confederation — the "Golden Stool," or throne, of Kumasi (kuh-*mah*'see). The occupant of the Golden Stool was recognized as the titular or symbolic head of the whole Ashanti people. Once the Ashanti Union was established, the resulting combined power of the Akan peoples enabled them to expand the boundaries of their empire. As they moved southward toward the coastline, they learned of the great European demand for slaves. The entry of the Ashanti kings into this trade set off a train of circumstances which eventually led to the collapse of Ashanti power.

In many respects the formation of Dahomey (duh-*hoh*'mih) parallels that of the Ashanti — with one important qualification. Unlike the Ashanti wars of expansion, the wars which preceded the expansion of Dahomey to the coast were prompted by the desire of

---

[13] J. D. Fage, *An Introduction to the History of West Africa* (Cambridge University Press, 1962), p. 91.

Dahomey's King Agaja (ah-*gah'*juh), who ruled in the early eighteenth century, to deal with the European slave traders directly rather than through the middlemen of the coast.

What was the legacy of the Guinea states to African history? The states of Guinea — Benin, Oyo, Ashanti, and Dahomey — had in common a great cultural tradition. Each of their cultures had a strong spiritual element. The tie which bound large ethnic units into the semblance of nations was in each case the worship of a common ancestral spirit. Their deep interest in spiritual matters was reflected in their arts — in music and the dance, and especially in sculpture. The peoples of Guinea attained a remarkable proficiency in the plastic arts — notably in the casting of figures and portrait heads in bronze and brass. These are the imperishable monuments of the genius of the Guinea peoples.

Politically, the Guinea states came close to achieving a nationhood based on common cultural traditions. During the twentieth century, when Africans asserted their independence from colonial rule, they became increasingly conscious of those elements of their culture which they shared, and which yet gave different African peoples their individual character. The Guinea states had arrived at this stage of cultural advance early, but they failed to achieve lasting political unity. The chief factor in this failure was the slave trade. To quote Professor Fage:

> It is of significance that the influence of the slave trade tended strongly towards the corruption and the ultimate decay of the political fabric of these states. The responsibility of their rulers and officials for the welfare of the people in their charge became subordinate to the lust for wealth and power which slave trading and aggressive wars could bring. The slave traders destroyed Benin as surely as its prosperity [came to be] based on it: the slave-traders fattened on the human booty of the civil wars which wrecked the Oyo state: the rapacious expansion of Ashanti and Dahomey eventually brought them into fatal conflict with European powers.[14]

• CHECK-UP

1. How did Kanem-Bornu rise to power? Why did this empire gradually decline? Why did the Hausa states prosper in the seventeenth century?
2. What developments in agriculture made possible a larger population

---

[14] J. D. Fage, *op. cit.*, p. 87.

in Guinea? What major city-states were established by the Yoruba? How did they expand? Why did they disintegrate?

3. Why did the Ashanti Union and Dahomey expand southward? Why did the slave trade bring misfortune to the Guinea states?

Summing Up

Of the early West African societies whose development was made possible by the introduction of new food crops and new techniques of farming, ancient Ghana was the first to develop a large-scale and efficient government. Under Soninke leadership, the kingdom increased in wealth and extent. Ghana's chief source of wealth was the gold trade. The king levied import and export taxes on gold and regulated the supply to maintain the price. Ghana reached the peak of its power under Tenkaminen in the eleventh century A.D. This king's refusal to embrace the Muslim religion provided a pretext for the Almoravids, led by Abu Bekr, to invade and conquer Ghana. Failing to win popular support for their rule, the Almoravids were driven out after ten years. But Ghana's resources were drained by the long wars, the occupation, and the disruption of the gold-salt trade. The country entered a period of steady decline and never regained its ancient glory.

During the thirteenth and fourteenth centuries, Mali expanded to include most of what had been ancient Ghana. To some extent, Mali evolved from the response of the Mandingo people to the invasion by the Fulani conqueror of Ghana. Rallying around their young prince Sundiata, they defeated Sumanguru in 1235. The Mandingo became the nucleus for a large empire which, like Ghana, owed its prosperity to control of the gold-salt trade. Mali prestige and power reached its high point under Sundiata's grand-nephew, Mansa Musa, who improved the empire's administrative and military structure and promoted its cultural development. His famed pilgrimage to Mecca gave Musa an opportunity to cement relations with other Muslim states and to impress them with Mali's great wealth. After Musa's death, Mali began to lose control of its subject states, and in consequence the empire began to decline. The growing animosity between Muslim townspeople and non-Muslim rural folk aggravated Mali's internal political weaknesses.

Although Songhai's beginnings have been traced back to the 600's A.D., it was not until Sunni Ali's reign in the fifteenth century that this state became a powerful empire. A succession of military victories enabled Sunni Ali to establish his country's supremacy over adjacent states and to get control of vital trade routes. The civil service system instituted by Sunni Ali and the creation of a professional standing army contributed to the efficiency and stability of the Songhai government. Askia Mohammed's reign, which began in 1493, was notable because of his reorganization of the government along the lines of Islamic principles. This included a judiciary in which the emperor's court became the highest court of appeal. Rivalry between members of the royal family culminated in the seizure of power by Askia Mohammed's eldest son in 1528. Continuing quarrels over the succession resulted in a steady weakening of the central authority. Other rulers took advantage of Songhai's internal weakness to plunder and conquer. In seeking to beat off these outside attacks, Songhai lost control of the trade routes. By the middle of the seventeenth century there was little left of the empire.

East of Songhai, Kanem-Bornu had come to dominate two important trade routes to northern Africa. Having early accepted Islam, Kanem-Bornu often used the pretext of a holy war to take over non-Muslim territory. Idris Alooma, the empire's most distinguished ruler, introduced firearms late in the sixteenth century, thereby assuring Kanem-Bornu's military superiority for a time. But continuing Tuareg attacks and prolonged famine not only arrested Kanem-Bornu's expansion but also contributed to that empire's decline. The royal Sefuwa dynasty, however, continued in power through much of the nineteenth century.

The kingship tradition was also upheld in the Hausa, Mossi, and Guinea states. Both the Hausa and the Mossi peoples organized politically into several small states or kingdoms, apparently resisting federation into large empires. Yet these states retained their separate identities and enjoyed remarkable stability for many centuries — which attests to their rulers' success in commanding the loyalty of the various kinship groups. New food crops, better suited to the climate and soil of that part of West Africa, sustained a growing population. The Guinea peoples experimented with elective and hereditary forms of kingship, and the Ashanti even formed a powerful confederation of states. Certain states, such as Ife and Oyo, excelled in the arts. The slave trade proved to be the biggest obstacle to progress in this region. The Guinea peoples, however, did approach a concept of nationhood based on common cultural traditions rather than on conquest.

CHAPTER REVIEW

Can You Identify?

sudan	Sundiata	Nok culture
Taureg	Timbuktu	Soninkes
Yoruba	Guinea	Ibn Battuta
Ghana	alafin	Askia Mohammed
Idris	Mali	Kanem-Bornu
Al Mansur	*hajj*	Ashanti Union
Sunni Ali	Gao	Abu Bekr
Mansa Musa	Oyo	Mandingo

What Do You Think?

1. What part did gold play in the economy of: (a) Ghana; (b) Mali; (c) Songhai?

2. How did differences between urban and rural dwellers contribute to the decline of African empires?

3. How was such an extravagant pilgrimage as that of Mansa Musa possible?

4. Why was Islam able to penetrate into Africa south of the Sahara?

5. What various types of sources provide our knowledge of the great African empires?

6. How could slave trade hurt African states which encouraged it as a source of revenue?

Extending and Applying Your Knowledge

1. For further information about Nok culture, see "The Art of the Forest Kingdoms," in *Africa: Selected Readings*, pages 76–82.

2. "Islam in Africa," pages 88–93 in *Africa: Selected Readings*, sheds light on why the Muslim faith has proved attractive to Africans.

3. Sir Richard Burton provides an interesting account of what Muslim pilgrims saw and did in Mecca. See *The Middle East: Selected Readings*, pages 37–45.

4. You will find descriptions of "fabled Timbuktu" in the early 1500's and three centuries later in *Africa: Selected Readings*, pages 136–140.

4

PATTERNS OF
CHANGE IN
CENTRAL AFRICA

There have been fewer archaeological discoveries in Central Africa — which includes parts of eastern and southern Africa — than in West Africa. But even the comparatively few finds which scholars have unearthed since 1960 make necessary a new look at Central African history.

For the early history of this region, scholars have been aided by a technique of dating known as radiocarbon analysis. This technique, a gift of atomic science, is based on the fact that carbon is present in all organic substances — plant or animal — and that the radioactive life of certain carbon atoms is fairly regular and may be used to establish the age of skeletal and other remains. Since 1960, more than 100 useful carbon dates have been established for the Iron Age in Africa — that is, for the period after about 500 B.C. About half of these new dates are related to the history of Zambia and Rhodesia. We now know conclusively that the knowledge of iron-working — regarded as a vital stage in the development of civilization — had reached northern Nigeria by the third century B.C. and was then carried southward to the Zambezi River during the succeeding 300 years. The great site of Zimbabwe (zeem-*bah'*bway) in Rhodesia (pages 143–146) has not yet been fully dated, but results so far obtained indicate that its builders were Iron Age Africans.

Another source of historical information is provided by old written records. According to Professor Roland Oliver, "Ge'ez and Amharic, the two written languages of Ethiopia, have records surviving from medieval times, and a small but growing band of trained Ethiopian historians are now joining in the study of these documents. Swahili, Hausa, and Malagasy peoples have all written chronicles dating from before the colonial period, and these, too, are receiving attention from scholars."[1]

There is also Africa's rich oral tradition — information memorized centuries ago and handed down by word of mouth from generation to generation. In recent years, African historians have increasingly tapped this "new" source of information. For example, an account of the settlement of western Kenya and eastern Uganda before 500 A.D. has been written, based almost entirely on taped interviews with persons living in those two areas. The "oral" evidence thus obtained was then compared with evidence from archaeology and other verifiable sources, and gradually a reliable picture of the history was pieced together. Oral tradition promises to yield a richer harvest of historical knowledge as scholars gain fluency in African languages and become accustomed to using the new information-gathering techniques. The work of Professor Joseph Greenberg and others in the field of African languages has also helped historians to reconstruct the movements of peoples in cases where direct historical records are lacking.

[1] Roland Oliver, *The Middle Age of African History* (London: Oxford University Press, 1967), p. 94.

Balanced rocks near Salisbury in Rhodesia are a landmark which local inhabitants compare with Stonehenge in England. Southern Africa is an ancient land whose history is only now being explored. Hills have been eroded into a jumble of boulders in this area which for thousands of years was a home of the Bushmen. No one is entirely sure whether the rocks were balanced by nature or man.

1. Bantu Peoples Expand Into Central and Eastern Africa

The term "Bantu" is applied to many Negroid peoples now found throughout much of central, eastern, and southern Africa. Indeed, they occupy approximately one-third of the African continent. Professor George Murdock has characterized the Bantu peoples as having "a capacity for explosive expansion paralleled, among all the other peoples of the world since the dawn of history, only by the Arabs after Mohammed, the Chinese, and the European nations since the Discoveries Period."[2] More than 2000 years ago the Bantu began to move from their original homeland in the Cameroon highlands southward and eastward across Africa. The process went on for hundreds of years — right down to the nineteenth century — as they continued to spread throughout much of what is now the Republic of South Africa. How do historians account for their phenomenal dispersion?

The Bantu peoples share a common linguistic tradition. The African word *bantu* simply means "people." And the term is almost as general and vague as its literal meaning suggests. As anthropologist Melville Herskovits has pointed out, we cannot think of the Bantu people as forming a separate racial group, since they are actually made up of a vast number of peoples with marked differences in physical type and culture. The one similarity shared by all Bantu peoples is their language background. "The Bantu languages as a group, despite their wide distribution, constitute but one of seven branches of the Macro-Bantu subdivision of the Bantoid subfamily of the [Niger-Congo] stock" of languages, according to Murdock. He and other scholars estimate that it took approximately 3000 years for the Bantu languages to reach their present state of differentiation, with the first thousand years being taken up with the major linguistic breakdowns. This first stage of differentiation is believed to have taken place within the Bantu homeland before the dispersion began.

One of the distinguishing marks of Bantu language structure is the frequent use of prefixes and suffixes. This may be illustrated by a sentence in Swahili, a language spoken widely in East Africa:

[2] George P. Murdock, *Africa: Its Peoples and Their Culture History* (New York: McGraw-Hill, 1959), page 271.

{*ki-su ki-kali ki-moja ki-me-potea*
knife sharp   one   has-been-lost = "One sharp knife has been lost."

In this sentence, *su* ("knife") has *ki-* ("one") as its class prefix, and this prefix is then repeated before every other word in the sentence agreeing with *su*. The plural form of this sentence would be:

{*vi-su   vi-kali   vi-nane   vi-me-potea*
knives sharp   eight   have-been-lost = "Eight sharp knives have been lost."

Note that the plural prefix corresponding to *ki-* is *vi-*. By comparing such linguistic characteristics in present-day Bantu languages, language scholars can trace some of the early movements of Bantu-speaking peoples.

Bantu-speaking peoples penetrate the tropical forest during the first five centuries A.D. Several developments facilitated the earliest migrations of Bantu-speaking peoples. One of these was the introduction of food plants from far-off Malaysia, carried to the African coast by traders. Two plants, the banana and the Asian yam, were especially important, because it was mainly due to these new food sources suitable for cultivation in hot, moist climates, that a population could settle the Congo Basin, the warmer regions of the east coast of Africa, the Zambezi River Valley, and the "great lakes" region.

Another important development which contributed to the expansion of the Bantu peoples was the introduction of iron. It will be recalled from Chapter 2 (page 54) that Meroë had been a center of iron-smelting even in pre-Christian times. When the kingdom of Meroë fell — about 350 A.D. — the Meroitic royal family fled westward to Darfur in modern Sudan and to Chad, and doubtless carried with them the precious knowledge of iron-smelting. From there, the iron-working craft was taken up by Bantu workmen. Other evidence suggests that the knowledge of iron-working was introduced to Nigeria at a much earlier period. At any rate, archaeologists have found the iron hoe in one form or another over a large part of the Bantu area. The hoe would facilitate the growing of certain staple food crops — such as sorghum — and make possible a more settled existence.

Bantu-speaking Africans, with these new discoveries, could move into more sparsely-settled areas and master an environment which they had once considered hostile. But what caused them to expand? One explanation has been that they moved because of the pressure of

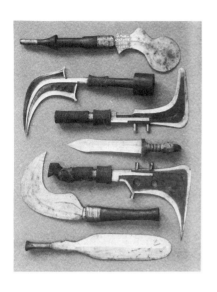

THE IRON AGE. The first iron implement adopted by the Bantu probably was the hoe. Below, cotton farmers of the modern Sudan are found swinging iron-bladed hoes in the region of Meroë, the ancient kingdom from which the use of iron may have spread southward to the Bantu. Bantu blacksmiths soon learned to fashion other iron tools and weapons. These efficient-looking hooked knives (*above, left*) were made in the northern Congo; the battle-axe at right comes from Kasai, farther south in the Congo Basin.

expanding population. The rise of the great sudanic empires, discussed in Chapter 3, and the coming of Islam to the sudan, may have increased the desire of some groups to strike out into new territory. Finally, it is not unreasonable to suppose that early Africans, like early Americans, were impelled to move simply by a love of adventure.

Stone Age peoples yield to the new settlers. One must not think of the Bantu expansion as a swiftly-advancing conquest. It was a slow process, lasting centuries. There were no wheeled vehicles to speed their progress, and at each stage the newcomers had to come to terms with their changing natural environment. This ranged from tropical rain forest to savannah, dry forest, and upland grasslands. The lands penetrated by the Bantu-speaking migrants frequently were already inhabited by other peoples — some more advanced in their culture than the Bantu, and others less so. Furthermore, the Bantu-speaking tribes were not the only people who were on the move. During much of its history, Central Africa was a land seething and moving with peoples of differing cultures who influenced each other.

In the earliest phase of their expansion, Bantu-speaking tillers from Cameroon got as far as the Congo Basin. There they occupied territory held by Pygmy hunters — a people of small physique who had not yet acquired an Iron Age culture. Although there seem not to have been serious hostilities between the two peoples, the Pygmy tribes eventually retreated to the heart of the forest, where they continued to do much of the hunting and fishing for both peoples. The Bantu people who established themselves in what are the northern

Pygmies and Bushmen are among Africa's most ancient peoples. Pygmies number some 170,000, the Twa of central Zaire being the most numerous. At left is a Pygmy elder tribesman from the Ituri Forest in eastern Zaire, where Pygmy culture is still comparatively free of other cultural influences.

When all southern Africa was the "preserve" of the Bushman hunter, he painted animals and hunting scenes on the rocks. Postage stamps show ancient paintings, an art which today's Bushmen no longer cultivate—perhaps because their hard life does not permit it.

provinces of the modern country of Zaire were the ancestors of the present-day Mongo peoples — which include some eleven tribal groups. They formed a society based on a tightly knit family and clan structure. Here in the tropical rain forest there could be no political states in the modern sense. But as new waves of Bantu-speaking peoples pressed on and settled in the savannah country adjacent to the rain forest, more elaborate political and social structures emerged, as will be shown later in this chapter.

Bushmen artists tell their story. In their slow but steady movement to the south and east, Bantu-speaking peoples came into contact with another Stone Age people, the Bushmen. The Bushmen's language classification is Khoisan, or Click. Having a less developed economic, political, and military structure than the Bantu-speaking groups, the Bushmen were forced by waves of Bantu peoples to move into more remote and inhospitable territories. Fortunately, these Bushmen left behind them a large number of striking rock paintings and engravings in limestone as mute witnesses to those earlier times when they, rather than the Bantu people, dominated most of Central Africa. These paintings reflect the Bushmen's nomadic existence and their primary means of subsistence, based on hunting and food gathering. The

125

drawings of buffaloes, rhinoceroses, lions, and cheetahs are particularly well executed in reds, browns, and ochers. Rock art probably began about 8000 years ago. Those paintings which date from the first millennium of the Christian era, however, show the influence of the Bantu newcomers, who at first lived side by side with the Bushmen, not destroying them, but nevertheless disturbing their way of life. There is an abundance of rock paintings in modern Rhodesia which show signs of this disturbance, and which provide additional evidence that the Bantu peoples had established their communities well south of the Zambezi River by 1000 A.D.

Some Bantu peoples encounter more advanced societies in East Africa. Thus, between 500 and 1000 A.D., waves of Bantu-speaking Africans were leaving the tropical rain forest of the Congo and entering Uganda, Rwanda, and Burundi, establishing settlements along the way. In this eastward push, many Bantu came into contact with the culture of another group, the western Cushites from Sidamo in modern Ethiopia. The latter had emigrated southwestward in an earlier period and established a state of their own in Uganda. The Cushites spoke a language strange to the ears of the Bantu-speakers, and communication was probably difficult at first. The Bantu people must have been impressed with the engineering achievements of the Cushites: great artificial reservoirs, one of which exceeded 300 feet in length; earth dams for impounding water to be used in irrigation; and fortifications that included extensive systems of trenches averaging 15 feet in width and 11 feet in depth. Archaeologists have found stone enclosures and stone monuments, as well as stone-faced terraces and graded roads, dating from 850 B.C. or even earlier. Pottery, agricultural and hunting implements, and even jewelry of semi-precious stones attest to the influence of Egypt and Nubia. The Bantu gradually infiltrated and took over this Uganda kingdom of the Cushites. They also adopted the Cushite dwelling, which is characteristically cone-cylinder in shape. But most important of all, these Bantu-speaking people obtained from the Cushites new cereals — eleusine and sorghum in particular — the first of which originated in Ethiopia and was especially suited to the soil and climate in which the Bantu now found themselves. These new food plants aided the Bantu of Central Africa in their penetration of the Bushmanoid territory to the south and east (modern Tanzania). Early in the second millennium the Bantu-speaking peoples of Tanzania adopted an important innovation which came to them through their Bantu neighbors in

Uganda — the herding of cattle, and the knowledge of how to milk them and how to make butter.

Contacts with other cultures lead to the development of new skills. The Bantu migrations followed different routes, but the classic pattern has already been described — through the Congo Basin to the savannah region bordering it on the south and east, thence to the Tanzanian plateau, crossing the region of the great lakes. Others went further eastward to Kenya and Somalia. Many settled along the low-lying plains bordering the Indian Ocean. From their northern cultural contacts, the new settlers in Central Africa brought with them the knowledge of mining and working gold and copper, the manufacture of pottery and human figurines, and the practice of dry stone building, believed to have originated in the highlands of Ethiopia. From the same source was acquired the technique of terracing steep slopes to make use of rich volcanic soils for growing crops. This would be especially useful when farmers had to retreat for defense to hilly areas.

The trade-empire of Zanj stimulates the growth of the new societies. During the tenth and eleventh centuries, the Bantu-speaking societies of Central Africa received a new impetus for growth from trade with coastal settlements on the Indian Ocean. A broad belt of black peoples existed along the coast of East Africa from Sofala to Mogadishu. The earliest Arab visitors to this area referred to it as "the empire of Zanj (or Zenj)" — meaning "empire of the blacks." During Greek and Roman times, most of this region was known as Azania. Much of it was inhabited by Cushites, who had migrated from the Kenya Highlands to the coast to engage in maritime pursuits. Trading posts were established, and their commercial activity was dominated by a succession of Persian, Arab, Indonesian, and Indian seamen. During the 600-year period from about 975 to 1498 (the year Vasco da Gama sailed to Mombasa), Muslim Arabs exerted the strongest outside influence on these coastal trading settlements, which grew into small states. Of these states, that of Kilwa (*keel'*wah), about a hundred miles south of modern Dar es Salaam, rose to a position of leadership. The other principal states were Sofala, Mozambique, Pemba,[3] Zanzibar, Vumba, Lamu, and Mogadishu. All of these trading states were in lively contact with the African peoples and rulers of the Zanj

---

[3] **Pemba:** the island Pemba, not the town in southern Zambia by the same name.

MILLET. At left, an Ethiopian farmer swings a flail over his head to scare birds away from his millet field. Millet is an important food grain throughout tropical Africa, as are the related grains, sorghum and eleusine.

Somalis (*right*) store millet heads in an underground pit. Forked sticks will support a roof of millet stalks covered with earth. The millet will be pounded into flour as needed. In the picture below, an Ethiopian couple lunch on a pancake baked of millet flour.

coastal region. Arab visitors to the area were under the impression that they had reached an important empire. One Arab scholar, al-Mas'udi (ahl mahs-*oo*'dee), who visited the "country of the Zanj" in the first half of the tenth century, wrote as follows:

The sea of the Zanj reaches down to the country of Sofala and of the Wak-Wak [probably present-day Natal in South Africa] which produces gold in abundance and other marvels. Its climate is warm and its soil fertile. It is there that the Zanj built their capital; then they elected a king whom they called Waklimi [wah-*klee*'mee]. This name . . . has always been that of their sovereigns. The Waklimi has under him all the other Zanj kings, and commands three hundred thousand men. The Zanj use the ox as a beast of burden, for their country has no horses or mules or camels. . . . Although constantly employed in hunting elephants and gathering ivory, the Zanj make no use of ivory for their own domestic purposes. They wear iron instead of gold and silver. . . .[4]

Later in his account, al-Mas'udi states that the Zanj overthrew their king whenever he became tyrannical. He also describes many Zanj political and religious customs and the Zanj diet.[5] Both al-Mas'udi and later Arab chroniclers have led modern scholars to believe that the extensive contacts of the Zanj with the outside world profoundly influenced not only the Zanj — which is believed to have become a predominantly Bantu society — but also the societies farther in the interior of Africa which were going through their formative stages.

• CHECK-UP

1. What did the Bantu peoples have in common? Why did they migrate? What discoveries enabled them to settle in hot, moist regions?

2. What Stone Age peoples were displaced by the Bantu in their southward migration? What evidences of their presence did these earlier settlers leave behind them? What can be inferred about how these earlier settlers lived?

3. What did the Bantu learn from the Cushites? What was the "empire of Zanj"? What Asian peoples traded with East Africa? How did the Asian trade influence Zanj and the interior?

[4] al-Mas'udi, "Meadows of Gold and Mines of Gems," quoted in Basil Davidson, *The African Past* (New York: Grosset and Dunlap [Universal Library Edition], 1967), p. 108.

[5] New food plants had been introduced as a result of Malaysian trade. See above, p. 110.

2. Bantu Kingdoms Are Established in the Great Lakes Region

The period from the thirteenth to the sixteenth centuries witnessed several important developments in Central Africa. First, the production of iron weapons and implements expanded southwards. Second, larger and stronger societies emerged, and urban settlements began. Thirdly, there was a growing demand on the East African coast for ivory, iron, gold, and other goods. The settled peoples of the interior became increasingly able to meet this demand. Increased trade contributed to the emergence of strong kingdoms at the end of this period, such as those of Monomotapa and Changamire in what is now Rhodesia. Before discussing these kingdoms, something should be said of developments in the lake region of East Africa and the territories adjacent to it.

Uganda becomes more thickly settled. The Bantu peoples who settled the country to the northwest of Lake Victoria, in what is now Uganda, were especially favored by climate and terrain. The climate is tempered by an altitude of approximately 3500 feet above sea level, and the 40 inches of average rainfall is a boon to farmers. It is a country of surpassing beauty, from the lush green landscape around the northern shores of Lake Victoria to the snow-covered peaks in the Ruwenzori mountain range. Small wonder that so many of the Bantu-speaking peoples who arrived here about 1000 A.D. decided to remain. There, in what is now Central Uganda, they developed a culture quite different from that of their Bantu neighbors living in the highlands of Kenya.

The settlers made effective use of the natural advantages of their surroundings. These advantages came to include a plant which provided an almost labor-free source of food, drink, and building material — the plantain (*plan'*tin). Its banana-like fruit is even today a food staple of the people in this area. As the population increased and the settled areas became more densely inhabited, the need for a more cohesive society and a more stable economy became apparent. Non-Bantu immigrants helped to meet both needs. The country's economy benefited from new crops and techniques of cattle-breeding introduced by the Cushites and settlers from the Upper Nile Valley. Some historians hold that the Cushite and Nilotic migrants also made im-

Navigational trade from the great lakes to the coast is interrupted by rapids and cataracts. But African fishermen, like these along Malawi's Shire River, have long found their inland waters profitable in other ways.

portant political contributions. A simple form of government by chiefs had been developed by the early Iron Age Bantu farmers in Uganda, probably no later than the thirteenth century. But the idea of a strong central kingship uniting clans of diverse origins was, in its early stages at least, a contribution of the Cushites. Once established, a strong hereditary monarchy flourished in southern Uganda down to modern times.

The Kitwara Kingdom is established by Hima nomads. For centuries, cattle-raising nomads drifted from the north and northeast into what is now Uganda, Rwanda, Burundi, and Tanzania, as well as western Kenya. Among the early pastoral (and nomadic) groups which migrated to Uganda was the Hima (*hee'*mah), a non-Bantu people with a long aristocratic tradition. By the fourteenth century the Hima had invaded Uganda and overwhelmed the Bairu (*bye'*roo), the Bantu-speaking people they found in possession of the land. The ruling clan of the Hima, the Chwezi (*kwee'*zee), initiated and ruled a political entity greater than the small extended family units of the Bairu. Traditions handed down for centuries tell of a hero named Kintu (*kin'*too), "the marvel," who came to central Uganda from beyond Mount Elgon in Kenya, and in time united the ancestral Bantu-speaking clans under his rule. He assigned to each clan certain ceremonial positions, thus establishing what became a kind of monarchical state — the Kitwara (kit-*wah'*ruh), or Kitara, Kingdom. The kings of Kitwara were drawn for many generations from the Chwezi clan, and the royal power was passed down from father to son (in this case, the youngest son). In consequence, the organization of the Bantu society in Uganda was in many respects similar to the feudal system of Europe during the Middle Ages.

A "caste system" is established. The Hima also brought with them a new economic order. The subjects of the Kitwara Kingdom were classified by occupation into seven or more "tradesman" categories, among which the blacksmiths or ironworkers were prominent. Other categories included the grain growers and the makers of pottery. All these craftsmen were required to pay tribute in food and labor to their new overlords, the Hima. The Hima did not permit intermarriage, and the Bairu were denied the privilege of owning productive cows or of holding high official positions. In effect, the Kitwara Kingdom was saddled with a "caste" system apparently designed to preserve the ruling-class privileges of the Hima. But the rigidity of the castes would be broken down — in Uganda, at least — by new incursions from outside.

The Nilotes adopt cattle-raising and move southward. At about the time of the rise of the Kitwara Kingdom, Nilotic groups in the Upper Nile region were also undergoing important economic and social change. The Nilotes, too, had mastered the art of cattle-raising and were becoming a full-fledged pastoral people. Thus they could combine cattle-raising with traditional agricultural pursuits, or abandon farming and become pastoral nomads. This freedom of choice became increasingly important whenever drought, invasion, or other emergencies forced them to move to new areas. According to Murdock, "once the Nilotes had learned to subsist primarily by pastoral nomadism, with only auxiliary dependence upon agriculture, they expanded with explosive force." They moved southward and attempted to take over the Bantu state of Kitwara, but it proved too powerful for them at this time. Consequently, they pushed toward the east and southeast, infiltrating Cushite territory. In southern Kenya, the Nilotes overcame certain Bantu settlements that were less organized than those in Uganda.

The Bito states are established. In time, the Nilotes became powerful enough to challenge the Chwezi rulers of Kitwara. One branch of Nilotes — the Lwo (*loo'*oh) — invaded Kitwara early in the fifteenth century[6] and replaced the Chwezi rulers with members of their own ruling clan, the Bito (*bee'*toh). During the sixteenth century, when Bito-ruled states were established throughout most of modern Uganda, the Hima aristocracy withdrew gradually to the south, going into what is today Rwanda.

Professor Roland Oliver has described the Lwo invasion as "the outstanding event that marked the beginning of a new age" for this part of Africa. Not that the Lwo brought a higher civilization with them. They were, in fact, more like the Anglo-Saxon conquerors of Roman Britain — barbarian conquerors of a more advanced culture. But like the Anglo-Saxons, the Lwo established new political, or ruling, units within the Bantu territory. Some of these units were to grow and become powerful, others were absorbed by more powerful neighbors, and still others moved away from Uganda.

Bunyoro becomes the dominant Bito state. Under the new Lwo dynasty of the Bito, the former kingdom of Kitwara became known to its neighbors as Bunyoro (bun-*nyor'*oh) — the country of the Nyoro. There seems to have been no ill feeling toward the ruling Lwo minority, largely because the Bito rulers had taken care to "legitimize" their rulership, to make it acceptable to the Bantu majority. How? By spreading elaborate — and probably mythical — stories of their intermarriage with the former Chwezi ruling houses.

King Rukidi (roo-*kee'*dee), the first Bito monarch,[7] built his capital on a hill just north of the modern town of Mubende (moo-*ben'* dee). Soon thereafter he sent members of his family into the former Chwezi provinces to establish subkingdoms which became tributary to the Bito kingdom of Bunyoro. These vassal kingdoms were allowed to pursue their own separate existences, however, and were not disturbed as long as they remained loyal. Meanwhile, the Lwo element of the population was becoming increasingly Bantuized, or assimilated into the mainstream of Bantu culture. The Lwo speech was replaced, for all practical purposes, by the language of the Bantu majority.

[6] The last capital of the Chwezi dynasty, according to tradition, was located in the entrenched earthwork site at *Bigo* (*bee'*goh) on the Katonga River, in western Uganda. It is the largest earthwork fortification in Africa — perhaps in the world — and bears certain resemblances to its stone counterpart, the Great Zimbabwe in Rhodesia. The site is still the object of archaeological study and may yield further clues to the history of this early African kingdom.

[7] **first Bito monarch:** His full name was Isingoma Mpuka Rukidi, which means "the father of the drums, the spotted one, from the land of the naked people." (The drum was a symbol of royal power.)

Buganda succeeds Bunyoro as the leading Bantu state. Buganda
(boo-*gahn'*duh) came into existence as a state in the early sixteenth
century, one of many subkingdoms bordering the Bito kingdom of
Bunyoro. According to tradition, King Rukidi assigned his twin
brother to rule over it. Buganda's royal house was thus a hereditary
sub-dynasty of the main Bito line. Had it remained this, it might
never have expanded beyond its original territory, the area within a
twenty-five-mile radius of Kampala (kahm-*pah'*luh), the capital of
modern Uganda. During the sixteenth century, Buganda remained
inconspicuous, whereas Bunyoro held the spotlight. Then, about
1600, Buganda began to assert itself. The Buganda king managed to
beat off a heavy attack from Bunyoro. After that, Bunyoro left
Buganda alone, but continued to wage aggressive wars against others
in the north. Meanwhile, Buganda, under King (or *Kabaka*) Katerega (kah-tuh-*ree'*guh), more than doubled its size through conquest and annexation. As Buganda expanded, it was careful to as-
similate the new elements into its population. Thus it developed a
more homogeneous society than Bunyoro ever achieved. During the
early 1700's, the kabakas increased the strength of the royal body-
guard, a force under their direct command. Gradually Buganda
completed its control of Lake Victoria's northwest coastline. There
was no longer any question about Buganda's supremacy.

NILOTIC WARRIORS

Before 1500, Sudanic-speaking Nilotes expanded southeastward into Kenya and Tanzania (see page 132). From Cushites they had adapted an age-group system which promoted military prowess and social cohesiveness (see pages 32–34), and partly offset their lack of complex political organization. The Nandi warrior (*right*) and the Samburu on the opposite page are descendants of the original invaders. The Samburu subsist entirely by animal husbandry (cattle, goats, chickens), while the Nandi raise a variety of grain crops.

Buganda's government undergoes important changes. During the early stages of Buganda's development, the king and the court were closely linked by bonds of marriage or of office with every clan in the country. The Lwo and Hima elements in the population had been completely absorbed, no longer existing as separate classes as in Bunyoro. The chieftainships within the "counties" of the kingdom were hereditary within particular clans, and until the eighteenth century, new chieftainships created by the expanding Buganda Kingdom were likewise hereditary. From the end of the eighteenth century onwards, however, Buganda moved from a feudal to a bureaucratic system, in which subordinate administrators held office by appointment from the king. All but the very oldest established posts were filled in this way. This, of course, helped to strengthen the central power of the king. This system worked well and made Buganda the most efficient and powerful of the Bantu states in Africa's "great lakes" region.

Trade strengthens the royal power. The power and wealth of the Buganda king was also increased by the establishment of long-distance trade over which the ruler exercised a monopoly. By the eighteenth century, plates, cups, glassware, and other manufactured items from overseas had reached the court of the kabaka. One of the late eighteenth-century kabakas, Semakokiro (sem-*ah'*ko-*keer'*oh), was an extremely wealthy man. He employed an army of hunters to obtain ivory, which was then traded through intermediaries south of Lake Victoria for imported articles such as cotton cloth. One result of the new trade was that the king could reward loyal subjects with gifts of goods as well as grants of land. The growth of commerce also provided a further incentive for territorial expansion. From the beginning of the nineteenth century, Buganda began to encroach on the territory of the smaller states in the "great lakes" region — Kiziba (kih-zee'bah), Koki (koh'kee), Kyamtwara (kyam-twah'ruh), Karagwe (kuh-rag'wee), and Ihangiro (ee-hahn-gee'roh). One by one, these states came under the control of Buganda. It was natural that the British should regard Buganda as the major African kingdom of the lake region and the foremost state to deal with in establishing the British "protectorate" of Uganda in the 1890's.

The idea of chieftainship spreads. The process of political change which has been traced in southern Uganda was repeated to the north, south, east, and west of that country. To the northwest of Uganda, the chiefs of Alur (ah'loor), another people of Lwo origin, extended their authority over neighboring peoples even during the period of colonial rule. Some of these had no central government of their own. Seeing definite advantages in the arbitrational role of chiefs, they accepted Alur rule without resistance. Some even requested it. South of Uganda, a somewhat different development had begun. There, the Hinda (hin'duh), a ruling clan which was probably an early offshoot of the Hima, had established ruling houses among the peasant population and introduced the knowledge of cattle-breeding. Many of the people among whom they established themselves had had no prior experience with chieftainship, but the Hinda demonstrated that this institution made economic as well as political sense. For example, they farmed out their cattle to the peasant inhabitants. This practice enabled the peasants to cultivate the banana on a larger scale, using the cattle manure as fertilizer. As a consequence, the banana became a staple food throughout much of the East African interior.

On the political side, the Hinda chiefdoms developed stronger ties between the chief and his subjects. Each of the subject clans was required to send some of its members to the chief's court to perform certain assigned duties. Some members of each clan were always at the court, since men were continuously rotated between the clan and the court to fulfill their special obligations. The chief benefited from this practice since it insured that a large number of his subjects were always at the court ready to defend him during times of crisis. Under

THE BANTU SCENE. A characteristic figure on the plains of Kenya is the Bantu herdsman with his cattle, humped like the zebu cattle of India. The Bantu probably learned to raise cattle from their neighbors, the Cushites and Nilotes. From the Cushites they also may have adopted the conical style of hut. The huts shown below are in eastern Zaire. Supported by posts, the thatch roofs overhang to shed rainwater. The round walls are plastered with clay and painted in geometrical designs.

this system the clans developed a stronger personal interest in their chief, whose well-being, to a great extent, was in their hands.

Many groups fail to develop states. As the Hinda dynasties divided, there was no apparent effort to preserve the seniority of the founder. This may account for the failure of the Hinda rulers to develop large, cohesive monarchical states such as those of the Bito to the north. Indeed some ethnic groups, such as the Kikuyu in Kenya, did not even progress to the stage of chiefdom. Their numerous village settlements remained separate entities, independent of each other, with each village choosing its own figurehead leader. In much of Tanzania and Kenya, the size of a political entity was determined simply by what a ruler could administer personally with the aid of his immediate family. Hence the size of the political units varied greatly.

In portions of western Tanzania the chief was widely known as Ntemi (muh-*tem'*ee), a title derived from the verb ku-*tema*, "to cut," and signifying "he who cuts short the discussion by giving judgment." A chief who ruled a thousand or even fewer subjects could still be referred to as a "divine king" if he possessed the special regal insignia, the "royal fire" from which all fire in his chiefdom was kindled, and if he was recognized by his subjects as the person most qualified to perform religious rituals. A chief's death and burial involved special rites — indeed, his death was often kept secret until a successor was chosen. These Bantu chiefdoms shared with many powerful states of modern times a concern for the preservation of social stability.

The persistence of old political and social structures has made nation-building difficult. Sometimes the process of nation-building in modern Africa has been hampered because centuries-old class (or clan) rivalries have persisted. In Africa as in other continents, established customs are not easily abandoned, even when they no longer serve their original, intended purpose. Rwanda and Burundi, the two small nations just south of Uganda, provide examples. There, the ruling families were drawn from a pastoral aristocracy which came to the country about the same time that the Hima pastoralists entered Uganda. The ruling clan, called the Tutsi (*toot'*see) — often collectively referred to as Batussi, Batutsi, or Watusi — are noticeably taller (many over six feet six inches) than the farmers whom they made their serfs. The latter are known as the Hutu (*hoo'*too), or collectively, as Bahutu. In both Rwanda and Burundi, the Hutu greatly outnumber the Tutsi. Much internal strife and bloodshed have resulted from the sharp class division which prevails, as well as from the

The main focus of the Tutsi aristocracy was the king (*right*). Above, the royal guard performs a ceremonial dance. Since independence, both the monarchy and Tutsi class privileges have ended in Rwanda and Burundi.

rivalry of Tutsi clans. The Tutsi have been determined to hold on to their centuries-old privileges in the face of majority opposition. The colonial powers profited from this rivalry, playing off one faction against the other. And yet the system made some sense when it was originally adopted, as did the feudal system in medieval Europe. Basil Davidson has put it this way:

> As with all other such processes of ripening, there were gains and losses for different groups. While Tutsi nobles gossiped among their equals, sipping honeydew and arguing the wisdom of the ages, or leaned upon their spears while composing verse in praise of their courage, virtue, and authority, the humble Hutu labored at their gates in producing food and bearing burdens. Yet the Hutu and their kind also had their benefits. The [system] . . . brought long periods when ordinary folk could feel free of the threat of invasion or warfare. For the Tutsi nobles and their like were under obligation to assume not only the responsibilities of government, but also those of defence. Just as the yeomen of medieval Europe preferred to bind themselves to strong masters, seeing in this their best assurance of safety and protection, so also did the farming peoples of these inland kingdoms think it wise to make themselves tribute-paying vassals of men for whom warfare and government were a professional duty, as well as a guarantee of privilege.[8]

[8] *Africa: History of a Continent* (New York: Macmillan, 1966), p. 171.

139

• CHECK-UP

1. What important developments took place in Central Africa after about 1200 A.D.? What advantages were enjoyed by Bantu farmers in what is present-day Uganda? What changes were introduced by the Hima?

2. Who were the Nilotes? On what was *h*eir economy based? What were their relations with Kitwara? How did Buganda achieve supremacy in the region?

3. Why did the king become increasingly powerful in Buganda? How did the Hinda chiefs develop stronger ties with their subjects? Why were many Hinda political units small? What were the advantages and disadvantages to farmers of being ruled by pastoral aristocrats?

3. Kingdoms Rise and Fall in Zimbabwe

Much of the territory between the Zambezi and Limpopo rivers in the Republic of Rhodesia (which Africans call *Zimbabwe*) is a highland plateau. For centuries before Europeans or Asians had set foot there, it had been one of the routes used by the Bantu in their southward migrations. Before 1000 A.D. the forerunners of the Sotho and Ngoni people passed through. Groups of Sotho people settled and mined here; in fact, nearly every gold mine in Rhodesia today was first opened by the Sotho miners. The section of Rhodesia called Mashonaland was occupied by ancestors of the present-day Shona (*shoh'*nuh) from about 1100 A.D. on. These people mastered metalworking and dry stone-building techniques which evidence amazing skill. Their buildings survive as ruins, bearing mute witness to the once-powerful kingdoms which flourished in this part of the African continent before the colonial era.

"Stamped Ware" peoples settle north and south of the Zambezi. The first wave of Bantu migrants were simple farmers who had acquired an Iron Age culture, and who mixed with the Stone Age people (Bushmen and Hottentots) already there. Some had arrived at the Zambezi River by 500 A.D., and the more spirited groups crossed the river into Rhodesia about this time. They chose sites in the open country, where they could graze their cattle and more easily protect them from marauders. The people cultivated various kinds of millet and fashioned dish-shaped hand mills made of stone with which to grind the millet into meal. Their simple pottery was at first made with grooved decoration. Later on, the pottery had stamped and incised (cut) motifs — hence the reason for assigning the name "Stamped Ware people" to this culture.

Village life was simple. During the first millennium A.D., these rural peoples lived out their lives at a bare subsistence level. In southern Zambia, not far from Victoria Falls, archaeologists have excavated one of their settlements, Isamu Pati (is-*sah*'moo *pah*'tee), and have reconstructed the probable appearance of the village. Huts, made of poles and mud were built around a central enclosure. Grain bins were located close by, and the whole village was enclosed by a thorn fence for protection from wild animals and raiders. The isolation of these settlements from the outside world is suggested by the fact that in the excavated area, 28 glass beads were the only articles found which originated outside the village.

In 1960, another early settlement was discovered, that of Ingombe Ilede (in-*gahm*'bee ill-*lee*'dee). The discovery was made by accident during the construction of a water-pumping station in south-central Zambia, on the north bank of the Zambezi, some thirty miles below the Kariba Gorge. This village has been dated by radiocarbon techniques to between the seventh and tenth centuries A.D.

Trade was carried on with neighboring peoples. In the earlier levels of Ingombe that have been excavated, imported objects, such as glass beads, are rare. But in the later stages of Ingombe Ilede's development, imported goods are more common. The inhabitants made fine bowls and beakers quite unlike the early crude pots. The graves of Ingombe's leading citizens, located in the center of the site, have yielded additional evidence of contacts with the outside world. Strings of gold, glass, and shell beads were found around the necks and waists of dead persons. Their limbs were encased in copper bangles. The metal has preserved fragments of cotton and bark-cloth, some of which was imported. Near the heads and feet of several skeletons lay copper ingots, trade wire, and iron implements for making bangle wire, as well as imported ceremonial hoes and gongs. Other bodies were buried with large quantities of pottery or sea-shells. These goods are evidence of emerging trade activity. The iron gongs — used among certain Congo peoples to announce the presence of the chief — as well as the copper crosses (similar to old Katanga money), prove that trade relations had begun with the Congo. The strategic location of the village in an elephant-infested area (hence the source of ivory, which was much sought after by traders on the Zambezi) and near gold, copper, and salt mines, also suggests that the people of Ingombe Ilede were middlemen between Zambezi traders and the miners of the Mashonaland plateau.

Perhaps Ingombe would have become a much more important commercial center had it not been for the emergence of the states on the highland plateau to the south (in modern Rhodesia). The decline of Ingombe, so far as is now known, started when these stone-building states began to expand their gold trade. As was noted earlier (page 127), gold mining was in full swing in the middle of the tenth century A.D., when the metal was exported from Sofala. Although the gold trade began to decline in the sixteenth century, mining was continued by the Bantu inhabitants until the present century.

Elaborate stone ruins in Zimbabwe suggest early commercial contacts with the East. Archaeologists have not yet solved the riddle of the more than 300 stone ruin sites which are scattered throughout south-central Africa, and especially in Rhodesia. Several of these ruins have foundations which date from the eleventh to the fifteenth centuries and exhibit techniques of masonry which surpass in excellence all other structures known to have existed in Central or Southeast Africa during this period. A number of scholars, including Dr. Gertrude Caton-Thompson, have suggested that the primary stimulus for the development of the Zimbabwe culture was trade.

But why should a technically more advanced culture develop in the hinterland of south-central Africa? Why not farther north — in Tanzania or Kenya, for example — where there was easier access to trade with Arabia and India? The question cannot be answered with certainty. Perhaps it was because copper and gold were plentiful in Rhodesia and almost nonexistent in the north. Early traders prized African gold and copper, and they were frequently willing to travel far inland to get it. Thus the traders might have exercised an important influence for growth and change in this region. We still do not understand precisely how trade, mining, and the stone-built settlements were related to each other. Some scholars even question that there is any direct connection. But Basil Davidson's judgment has gained widespread acceptance. "[The] Iron Age civilization of south-central Africa," he writes, "was above all . . . a mining civilization; and its course and development were linked with the fortunes of the coastal trade. . . . [The] importance of these old mine workings . . . remains central for the whole growth and flowering of the Zimbabwe culture. The hammer of its iron-shop picks and the glow of its charcoal-fired ovens are as much the essential background to medieval Rhodesia as were the railways to the growth of nineteenth-century Europe."[9]

The Lost Cities of Africa (Boston: Little, Brown, 1959), pp. 258–259.

What was "Great Zimbabwe"? In this book the term "Zimbabwe" is used to identify the early stone-building culture of Rhodesia. "*Great* Zimbabwe" refers to the most important of the numerous ruins. Situated near the modern town of Fort Victoria, it consists of three groups of buildings:

1. *The "Acropolis."* Located on the top of a small rocky hill, this building may have been a fort, but could also have been, as Basil Davidson suggests, "a place of sanctity guarded merely from the profane."[10] There are a number of walls and terraces built on this hill. A stepped pathway forms the main ascent.

2. *The Elliptical Ruin* (or "*Temple Ruin*"). Built on a gentle slope in the wooded valley below the "Acropolis," this ruin comprises a massive, free-standing outer wall. It had a maximum height of 32 feet and was 17 feet thick in places. It was built dry (without cement) and had no foundations, although the ground had been leveled before building. This wall enclosed a second smaller wall and a cone-shaped tower about 31 feet high. Strewn about are fallen stoneworks which suggest the outlines of other structures. The ground plan of this area is shaped like an ellipse (see photographs, page 144), which accounts for the designation given it by archaeologists.

3. *The "Valley Ruins."* These consist of a mass of walling and smaller stone enclosures situated between the "Acropolis" and the Elliptical Ruin.

"Zimbabwe" is the anglicized form of the Shona word *dzimbahwe*, which literally means "stone houses." Sixteenth-century Portuguese explorers noted that the name was applied to the headquarters of Shona chiefs. The archaeologist J. Desmond Clark, however, interprets the word to mean "the place where the chiefs [kings or rulers] are buried." According to the son of a chief who lived there in 1890, only one section of the ruins, an area secluded by a wall and by natural high rocks, was entitled to be called Zimbabwe. It was there that a group of famous soapstone figures of birds (now kept in several different museums) stood. It is thought that these birds were memorials to departed kings. Since every Shona chieftainship has its dzimbahwe, or revered place where representatives of the people gather to pray for intercession with the spirits of their ancestors, quite possibly Great

[10] *Africa in History* (New York: The Macmillan Company, 1969), p. 133. The term "Acropolis" is a designation which modern scholars have assigned to this portion of the Great Zimbabwe ruins. It is not an African term. In the absence of written records, it is not known what the original builders intended it to be called.

ELLIPTICAL ENIGMA: From the air the Great Zimbabwe enclosure appears as a great ellipse. Its inner walls, platforms, and monoliths suggest that this "Elliptical Ruin" may have been a temple. The mysterious cone-shaped tower, partly obscured by foliage in the aerial photo, is shown in a close-up at right. Many archaeologists hold that the ruin was a royal residence, wherein the king performed certain priestly functions.

Zimbabwe's bird figures may represent the fish eagle, sacred to the Karanga people. Its cries were thought to be the oracular utterances of departed kings' spirits, which priests could interpret.

Zimbabwe was simply the most important of many dzimbahwe which existed before the nineteenth century Zulu invasions destroyed the Shona confederation. (See page 152.)

The ruins afford a picture of what life in Great Zimbabwe was like during its years of greatness. There is now general agreement among scholars that the people who built and inhabited Great Zimbabwe were Africans of Negroid (and Bantu-speaking) stock. Professor J. Desmond Clark's researches led him to draw the following picture of life in fifteenth-century Zimbabwe:

The "Temple" [Ruin] was probably the "palace of the chief," and in this connection it is interesting to compare the ground plan with that of the present-day village of the Paramount Chief of Barotseland [in Zambia]. Within the maze of walls and passages, made of stone at Zimbabwe but of reeds or pole and thatch in other chiefs' villages, lived the sacred "God-Chief," surrounded by barbaric splendor and protected from prying eyes. His actual houses were circular, built of pole, *daga* (daub), and thatch, . . . and on a special platform where several monoliths [stone slabs] have been found he may have held his court and given his audiences. His relic hut, which housed the sacred tribal relics, would also be in the "Temple" as would the huts of his wives and immediate entourage. The common people lived in similar, though probably smaller, huts among the walls and passages of the "Valley Ruins." Each group of huts would belong to a self-contained family unit, a man living with his wives, family, and possibly his slaves. The cattle kraals [corrals]

145

were also probably in the "Valley Ruins"; and on the slopes outside they must have cultivated their millet garden and pastured their stock. In times of danger the whole population probably retired to the fortified strong point of the "Acropolis" from which to withstand enemy attack.

From the many imported objects found in the excavation of [Great] Zimbabwe it seems certain that it was at one time an important center of trade and barter with visiting merchants from the coast and from other inland areas.[11]

The Shona peoples gradually displace the Sotho. The first main building phase of Great Zimbabwe came to an end in the early fifteenth century. This first important stone-building culture has been tentatively connected with the Sotho people. They had occupied Mashonaland for at least 200 years, having themselves driven out the aboriginal Bushmen, perhaps because the Bushmen's arrows were a threat to the settlers' cattle herds. The Bushmen took refuge in the Matopo (muh-*toh'*poh) Hills of western Rhodesia, or moved even farther west to the swampy fringes of Lake Ngami (ung-*gah'*mee) in Botswana, to hunt the wild game which abounds in that otherwise inhospitable land.

Now it was the Sotho people's turn for "eviction." Many of them decided not to compete with the vigorous and more ambitious Shona clans who were advancing in ever larger numbers into the territory between the Zambezi and Limpopo rivers. Some of the Sotho moved to other parts of Rhodesia and continued to mine for gold, although their new rulers received the profits. But many retreated across the Limpopo and made their homes in what is now the Transvaal (trans-*vahl'*) in South Africa where some of their descendants still live. They established themselves behind rough-hewn fortifications — the most impregnable of which were the rocks of Mapungubwe (mah-pun-*goob'*-wee). Excavations carried out on this site have yielded gold objects and pottery comparable to the best of such articles found at Great Zimbabwe. The archaeological evidence suggests that the Sotho held out in this border area through the fifteenth century. They were eventually displaced by the Venda people from across the Limpopo. The Venda people remained until they, too, were ruined by the Zulu invasions of the nineteenth century. Meanwhile, other Sotho groups went south to the Drakensberg range near South Africa's eastern coast, and still others to Botswana, where they mingled with

[11] J. Desmond Clark, *The Prehistory of Southern Africa* (Baltimore: Penguin Books, 1959), pp. 291–292.

Moshoeshoe I (1790–1870) forged a nation from Sotho groups fleeing Zulu regiments. Lesotho, independent since 1966, issued a stamp showing the nation's founder and its present ruler, his descendant. The Sotho preserve such traditions as the drum dance.

the Bushman and Hottentot communities. In the 1820's, the Sotho people of the Drakensberg range were united under an able ruler named Moshoeshoe (moh-*shway'*shway). Later, Moshoeshoe's mountain kingdom became the British protectorate of Basutoland and in 1966 it was proclaimed the independent nation of Lesotho, with Moshoeshoe's great-grandson as constitutional monarch.

Some Shona clans evolve ideas of kingship. About the same time as the decline of the early stone-building culture (early fifteenth century) there was another important development which was to lead to the building of much larger stone structures, as well as to grander conceptions of political power. The early Shona invaders of Rhodesia had been divided into separate clans. One group of Shona clans which settled in the south was known collectively as the Karanga (kuh-*rahn'*guh). They were, in the main, small-scale farmers and cattle raisers who lived in stockaded villages of thatched mud huts and granaries. They were united in their common religious beliefs, which included ancestor worship — probably introduced by their forebears from the "great lakes" region in the eleventh and twelfth centuries.

The Karanga clans took their lead from a dominant clan called the Rozwi (*rahz'wee*), which had developed a belief in a strong, divinely-inspired king. The Karanga rallied around the Rozwi "kings and barons" (to use Davidson's phrase), and embarked on a series of conquests. The result was the emergence of a new empire in southeastern Africa — the empire of Monomotapa (mah-noh-muh-*tah'*puh).

Two strong kings found the empire of Monomotapa. Careful comparison of local traditions, Portuguese records, and archaeological remains has enabled scholars to reconstruct the political history of this second, or Shona, period of precolonial Rhodesia. The decisive phase in the formation of the Karanga Empire occurred about 1440. It was then that Mutota (moo-*toh'*tuh), the Rozwi king of the Karanga, began a war of conquest to extend his rule over the entire plateau between the Zambezi and the Limpopo. Within ten years he had achieved his ambition and had gained control of most of the gold mines of the plateau and of the trade routes to the East African coast. Like the king of Ghana, he imposed duties on all goods coming into the empire — textiles, beads, porcelain, brassware, and other imports from overseas — as well as on exports.

Mutota died around 1450 before he could consolidate his conquests or secure control of the coastal ports and market towns. But his brilliant son and successor, Matope (mah-*toh'*pee), carried on his work. Over a period of 30 years, Matope extended his rule far into Mozambique to the harbors of the east coast trade — Sofala being the most important such harbor. Matope was acknowledged widely as the most powerful sovereign in the southern part of the African continent. One of the conquered people gave him the title Mwene Mtapa (muh-*way'*nee muh-*tah'*puh), which means "lord of the conquered lands." The Portuguese corrupted this title to "Monomotapa" in the sixteenth century — the name by which the empire, as well as the dynasty of kings which ruled it, is now generally known.

Internal rivalries weaken Monomotapa. In organizing his empire, Matope entrusted the two southern provinces to two Rozwi vassals,

BANTU ON THE MOVE. Green arrows show the directions followed by the Bantu as they gradually spread out from Cameroon to found kingdoms in central and southern Africa. Rock paintings were left by the Bushmen whom they replaced as inhabitants. Arabs continued to trade with the Bantu who occupied the Zanj coast. The small map shows the routes of Nilotic invaders who later passed through Uganda, mingling with the Bantu to establish new kingdoms.

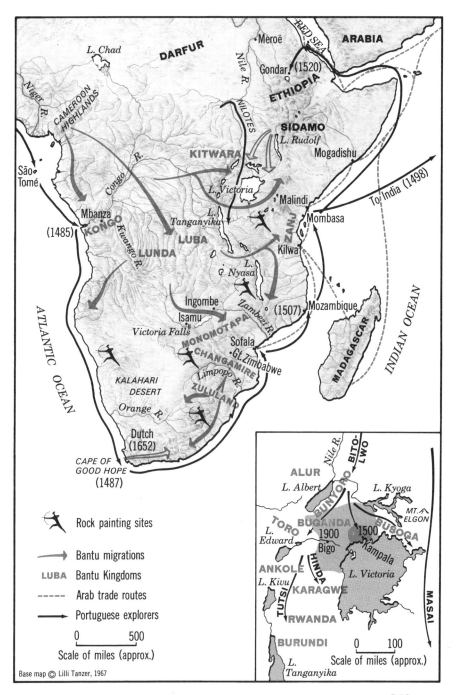

L. Chad

DARFUR

Meroë

RED SEA

ARABIA

Niger R.

CAMEROON HIGHLANDS

Nile R.

Gondar (1520)

ETHIOPIA

NILOTES

SIDAMO

L. Rudolf

KITWARA

L. Victoria

Mogadishu

São Tomé

Congo R.

Mbanza

KONGO

(1485)

Kwango R.

LUNDA

Tanganyika

L. Tanganyika

LUBA

Malindi

ZANJ

Mombasa

To India (1498)

Kilwa

L. Nyasa

Ingombe

Isamu

Victoria Falls

ATLANTIC OCEAN

KALAHARI DESERT

Orange R.

Dutch (1652)

CAPE OF GOOD HOPE (1487)

Zambezi R.

(1507)

Mozambique

MONOMOTAPA

Sofala

CHANGAMIRE

Gt. Zimbabwe

Limpopo R.

ZULULAND

MADAGASCAR

INDIAN OCEAN

Rock painting sites

Bantu migrations

LUBA   Bantu Kingdoms

Arab trade routes

Portuguese explorers

0   500

Scale of miles (approx.)

Base map © Lilli Tanzer, 1967

ALUR

Nile R.

L. Albert

BITO-LWO

BUNYORO

L. Kyoga

MT. ELGON

TORO

BUGANDA

1900

Bigo

1500

BUSOGA

Kampala

L. Edward

ANKOLE

HINDA

L. Kivu

TUTSI

KARAGWE

L. Victoria

MASAI

RWANDA

BURUNDI

L. Tanganyika

0   100

Scale of miles (approx.)

149

Torwa (*tohr'*wuh) and Changa (*chan'*guh). He placed other newly-won provinces in the hands of sons and trusted relatives, while he and his brothers retained the northern provinces, adjacent to the Zambezi Valley, under their direct control. The seat of government was thus centered in the northern part of the empire rather than in the area surrounding Great Zimbabwe. Once the Monomotapa's administration was regularized, greater attention could be given to increasing the economic well-being of citizens. Besides farming and cattle-raising, gold, copper, iron, and ivory were sources of income.

When King Matope died about 1480, there followed a long period of rivalry and political intrigue among the ruling "barons." Even before Matope's death, Changa had taken advantage of his relatively isolated position in the southern provinces to make himself an independent ruler. He now openly flouted the authority of Matope's son and successor, King Nyahuma (nyah-*hoo'*muh). Arab advisers had flattered Changa by conferring on him the title of *emir* (see page 76). Joining this title to his name, he became Changamire (*chan'*guh-meer), and thus emphasized his independence from the Monomotapa's authority. In 1490, Changamire's policy led to a direct confrontation with the ruling Monomotapa, resulting in the latter's death in battle. For four years, Changamire usurped the seat of the empire, only to be killed in turn. But Changamire's son and successor was able to retain control of the southern provinces, and, by adroit diplomatic maneuvering, he managed to detach the other provinces from loyalty to Monomotapa. By the 1570's, the northern area of Rhodesia was divided into several parts, and only one small portion was controlled by the Monomotapa.

The Portuguese take advantage of Monomotapa's troubles. After the Portuguese had established themselves in Sofala in 1505, they sought to control the profitable inland trade. But the Swahili coastal cities had long held a monopoly of this trade, Kilwa being the dominant city of that period. Kilwa's sister city, Sofala, was the principal export harbor for the gold of the interior. Cautiously, the Portuguese traders began to sail the Zambezi in the hope of finding gold and silver. In a short time they had established trading posts and markets near Mount Darwin. Their initial success emboldened them to impose their military and political authority over the African population of the area. Here, as elsewhere, the Portuguese were partially successful — thanks to their policy of playing off one side against the other in the dynastic struggles of the Monomotapa Empire. Indeed, without Portuguese intervention, the Monomotapa might well have achieved a political stability such as that enjoyed by the Rozwi kings of the south. As it was, the Monomotapas began to lean on the Portuguese for help. In 1607, for example, the Monomotapa, when faced with a revolt of powerful vassals, sought Portuguese aid. He received it, but only after he had made the following promise, preserved in a document dated August 1, 1607:

> I, the emperor Monomotapa, think fit and am pleased to give to his Majesty all the mines of gold, copper, iron, lead, and pewter which may be in my empire, so long as the king of Portugal, to whom I give the said mines, shall maintain me in my position. . . .[12]

Subsequent relations between Africans and Europeans were characterized by many such "deals" which were to prove costly to many generations of Africans.

The Portuguese destroy Monomotapa's independence. The steady encroachment of the Portuguese on Monomotapa's power met with resistance. The Monomotapa warriors rose up against the Portuguese in 1628, attacking their trading centers at Sena and Tete. The Portuguese, in turn, won two decisive battles — the first in December, 1628, and the second in May, 1629. The defeat of the Karanga forces enabled the Portuguese to displace the ruling Monomotapa with Mavura (mah-*voor'*uh), a puppet ruler of their own choosing. On May 24, 1629, Mavura signed a new "treaty" with the Portuguese, by which he agreed to accept the overlordship of the king of Portugal and to allow Christians full freedom to carry on missionary work and build churches. In effect, the Monomotapa Empire had ceased to exist as an independent political entity.

The Changamire Kingdom becomes the dominant African power in Rhodesia. While Monomotapa power was waning, that of its southern offshoot, the Changamire Kingdom, was growing. At its greatest extent — between 1695 and 1830 — Changamire became an empire about the size of the older Karanga holdings of Monomotapa. The Portuguese left Changamire territory relatively unmolested; there-

---

[12] From G. M. Theal, *Records of South-eastern Africa* (Pretoria [South Africa]: Government Printer, 1900), vol. 3, p. 376. Quoted in Basil Davidson, *The African Past: Chronicles from Antiquity to Modern Times* (New York: Grosset and Dunlap [Universal Library Edition], 1967), p. 164.

While most of the Ngoni Bantu were forced to flee the armies of the Zulu king, Chaka, the Swazi people resisted him successfully. Their territory was not incorporated into the Union of South Africa, but remained directly under the British. In 1968 Swaziland became independent. Here warriors of Swaziland go to pay the traditional tribute to their king. They will serve in his personal guard or work in the royal fields.

fore the seventeenth and eighteenth centuries were for Changamire a time of peace and progress. During this period the Rozwi rulers had moved back into Great Zimbabwe and continued to erect stone structures there. Few purely defensive works were erected, however, except those at Inyanga (in-*yahn*′guh) and its neighboring sites in the eastern hills. Stone ruins in the west — at Khami (*kah*′-mee), for example — seem to have been dwelling-places of powerful chieftains or governors rather than fortifications.

Changamire succumbs to invasions from outside. Perhaps the natural barriers protecting Changamire lulled its Rozwi rulers into a false sense of security. At any rate, they were ill prepared to cope with the rampaging Ngoni Bantu who invaded Rhodesia (then Southern Rhodesia) during the 1830's. These Ngoni had been forced to flee from the wrath of Chaka (*chah*′kuh), the great Zulu king. Before settling down near Lake Nyasa, the Ngoni had cut a wide path of destruction through the Changamire Empire, which eliminated it as a political state of any importance. Here again, however, the blame for this development rests ultimately with Europeans. For Dutch settlers from Cape Town had advanced along the fertile coastal plain of South Africa, preventing the Zulus and other peoples from expanding southward. Since their population continued to grow, the Zulus resorted to warlike expansion.

Meanwhile, other Bantu states were evolving in Central Africa.

• CHECK-UP

1. What evidence is there that Ingombe traded with peoples of the Congo and with the miners of the plateau?

2. Describe "Great Zimbabwe." What conclusions can be drawn from these ruins? Describe the relations of the Shona to the Sotho.

3. How did the Karanga clans found the empire of Monomotapa? Describe its government and economy. Why did the empire fall apart?

4. Why did the Changamire Kingdom prosper during the 1700's? What misfortunes overtook it in the 1830's? Why?

4. New Bantu States Evolve in the Congo Basin

In the late 1400's Portuguese traders came in contact with a coastal kingdom at the mouth of the Congo River. They described it as "great and powerful, full of people, having many vassals." The noted African scholar Jan Vansina has said of this civilization: "[There] is no tale more exciting to the contemporary scholar than the history of the Kingdom of Kongo during the fifteenth and sixteenth centuries."[13] This was so because by the fifteenth century Kongo had become a fully sovereign state, and because, acting on its own initiative, it attempted to incorporate Christianity and other elements of European culture into its own social fabric. Not until recent decades would an African nation again make such a large-scale attempt at the selective borrowing for its own use of elements from a foreign culture. To determine why this was so requires a closer look at developments in this part of tropical Africa. Only the most powerful states of the Congo Basin, however, will be considered: the kingdoms of Kongo, Luba, and Lunda.

A powerful kingdom emerges from small beginnings. The founders of the kingdom of Kongo came from the northern bank of the Congo estuary late in the fourteenth century. At that time, according to tradition, a young prince, the son of the ruler of the small state of Bungu (*bun'goo*), emigrated with some of his companions to the plateau of Kongo — today a part of Angola. The prince, whose name was Wene (*way'nay*), managed to conquer the plateau, and he and his companions married the daughters of the leading families

[13] Jan Vansina, *Kingdoms of the Savanna* (University of Wisconsin Press, 1968), p. 37. Note that the spelling "Kongo" designates the early kingdom. The modern form, Congo, refers to (1) the Congo (or Zaire) River; (2) the area of the Congo Basin; (3) the state of Congo (capital city: Brazzaville); and (4) until recently, the state of Congo (capital city: Kinshasa), which now calls itself Zaire.

of the region. Wene then took the title of *manikongo* (mah-nee-*kahn'*goh),[14] or king, and subdued the surrounding countryside. He also incorporated the two kingdoms of Mpangu (um-*pahn'*goo) and Mbata (um-*bah'*tuh) into his own empire. At his capital the mani-kongo maintained an elaborate court, with numerous slaves, pages, and personal attendants. He was an absolute monarch, believed to possess superhuman powers not dependent on earthly sources. Perhaps for this reason, no one was permitted to observe him eating or drinking, on pain of death.

Mbata had voluntarily recognized the manikongo's overlordship, and as a reward, Wene granted the leading Mbata clan the privilege of hereditary governorship of this province. The governors of the other provinces were appointed by the king. During the course of the fifteenth century, other smaller kingdoms and chiefdoms became vassals of the Kongo king. By the sixteenth century, the empire consisted of (1) a nucleus, bounded by the Atlantic Ocean and the Congo and Kwango (*kwahng'*goh) rivers and (2) a surrounding cluster of smaller states which acknowledged the supremacy of the manikongo.[15]

Diplomatic relations are established with Portugal. Late in 1482, Portuguese navigators exploring the West African coast made their first appearance at the mouth of the Congo River. From a distance, their strange craft appeared to onlookers as a new species of marine life. And so it was reported to Nzinga (uhn-*zing'*guh), the reigning manikongo, that whales of a special sort had been sighted off the coast. It soon became apparent that the "whales" were in actual fact Portuguese sailing vessels, and their occupants the men of Captain Diogo Cam (*dyoh'*goo *koun'*), one of the greatest of Portuguese navigators. In 1483, Diogo Cam himself put to shore with some of his men and established friendly relations with the local community. Cam left four Portuguese companions to be conducted to the court of the mani-kongo at Mbanza (um-*bahn'*zuh) — now the Angolan town of São Salvador (*sah'*oon sal-vuh-*thohr'*) — bearing gifts and messages, while he pursued his coastal voyages. On his return, Cam discovered that the four Portuguese had been retained at the court against their

[14] The prefix *mani-* designated an important officeholder in the kingdom. Thus the *manilumbu* was the governor of the king's quarters, the *manikabunga* was chief elector, etc.

[15] The title of the most important ruler in the Ndongo (un-*dahng'*goh) region at the time of the first Portuguese contacts was Ngola (un-*goh'*luh), which became the name of the later Portuguese colony (Angola).

wishes, whereupon he seized four Africans. Though the four Kongolese were taken as hostages for the safety of his own men, Cam attempted to make it clear to the local prince — a relative of the manikongo — that his subjects would be returned alive in fifteen months. When Cam sailed back to Portugal with the four Kongolese, the Portuguese king, John II, decided to seek an alliance with the manikongo as a means of penetrating the interior of Africa. John II, like earlier Portuguese rulers, was keenly interested in finding the legendary Christian kingdom of Prester John (see page 174). Accordingly, a concerted effort was made to impress the four hostages with the wealth and spiritual values of Portugal. Thus the victims of kidnapping, four black visitors from Africa, would be transformed into messengers of goodwill.

Diogo Cam's return trip to Kongo in 1487 was intended, therefore, as a diplomatic mission rather than as a voyage of exploration and conquest. He carried rich presents for King Nzinga and messages of hope that the manikongo would adopt the Christian religion. The manikongo proved to be a reasonable man and decided that an ambassador should be sent to Portugal with a small staff of Kongolese to learn European ways. John II was asked to send missionaries and builders to instruct the people of Kongo in new techniques. Payment for this service would be made in ivory and raffia cloth. John obliged by sending a fleet of three ships in 1491, carrying priests, skilled workers, tools, and religious objects. The mission was instructed to evangelize and to seek alliance rather than conquest. Catholic missionary priests did manage to baptize Nzinga Kuwu as King John I, and the royal family and most of the nobility became Christian. The Portuguese commander then joined the king in a successful war against a troublesome neighboring people. He returned to Portugal in 1492, leaving in Kongo enough Portuguese Catholic missionaries to run a newly-built school and to care for the many converts to Christianity.

Religious differences and political rivalry lead to civil war. Despite the efforts of the Portuguese missionaries, the conversion of the Kongo people to the Christian religion was by no means complete by the end of the fifteenth century. The manikongo himself reverted to traditional African forms of worship, as did his son Mpanzu (muh-*pahn'*-zoo). The queen mother, however, and another son named Mbemba (muh-*bem'*buh) — called Affonso (uh-*fohn'*soo) by the Portuguese — remained Catholic. Each side of the family had its following, and religious differences became linked with a political struggle over the

FORBIDDING REDOUBTS. Fort São Miguel (*right*) and Fort São Sebastian (*below*) date from Portugal's early adventures in Angola and Mozambique, respectively. They serve as grim reminders to Africans of Portugal's continued domination of those countries, where the Portuguese made little show of peaceful alliance with the inhabitants —as they had done in Kongo—but from the beginning used force to assert their authority. Slave traders carried on a lucrative business in Angola, while in Mozambique the main objects of Portuguese interest were gold and control of trade with the Far East.

royal succession. As the cleavage widened, Affonso left the capital but maintained contact with Portugal. In 1506, the Manikongo Nzinga died. Kongo traditions state that before his death he had instructed the electoral college — the nine to twelve leading officials who chose a successor to the throne — to choose his Christian son, Affonso, as the new king. But Mpanzu occupied the capital first and was supported in his bid for the throne by the manikabunga, who was both the leading elector and the chief priest of the old religion, and stood to lose his position if the Catholics were successful. A military confrontation between the two contenders for the royal power was to settle the religious and political differences which plagued the kingdom. In a battle fought in the main square of the capital, Affonso was victorious. He believed that he had been aided in his victory by the invisible forces of St. James and his heavenly knights.

Affonso I tries to Europeanize the Kongo nation. To strengthen his claim to the throne, Affonso ordered the execution of his brother. Shocking as this may seem to us, it was a not uncommon practice among ruling families in Europe and Asia. In fact, the bloodshed often was much greater in comparable European crises. Affonso did order that the life of the manikabunga be spared following the latter's conversion to the Catholic faith. Rather than being the "earth priest," as the manikabunga had been earlier, he was now appointed "keeper of the holy water."

As a Catholic with broad European tastes and attitudes, Affonso I determined to convert the whole nation to European ways. Between 1506 and 1512 a brisk exchange of letters, ideas, and goods developed between Kongo and Portugal. Affonso asked for more Portuguese priests, teachers, masons, and technicians, and he in turn sent more young Kongolese to Lisbon for education. In Portugal, King Manuel I began to take an interest in the remote African kingdom, now on the verge of becoming Christian. Manuel thought that Kongo was adjacent to the legendary Christian kingdom of Prester John. If this were true, he reasoned, the Muslim world would soon be surrounded by Christian forces. It was clearly advantageous to cultivate friendly relations with Kongo.

The slave trade brings about a deterioration in relations between Portugal and Kongo. But Affonso's plans for the Europeanization of his people failed. They were undermined by one of the side-effects of the Portuguese civilization Affonso had embraced — slavery and the slave trade. This trade was centered on São Tomé (*sah'*oon toh-*may'*), an island under the control of Portuguese adventurers who also had a monopoly on trade with Kongo. Fearing that closer relations between Kongo and Portugal might undercut this monopoly, the rulers of São Tomé conspired to cripple communication between Portugal and Kongo. Letters and gifts were intercepted. The messages which did get through to Lisbon were often ignored. In his letters to the Portuguese king, Affonso complained bitterly of the immorality and the illegal activities of the São Tomé freebooters. In 1526, for example, he wrote: "There are many [slave] traders in all corners of the country.

They bring ruin to the country. Every day people are enslaved and kidnaped, even nobles, even members of the king's own family." In addition to this, the Portuguese traders in the bush country were urging local chiefs to rebel against the manikongo's authority. Affonso tried to remedy the situation by ordering the expulsion of all whites from Kongo territory except teachers and missionaries. But by this time (July, 1526), the situation had become impossible to control, and Affonso revoked the expulsion measure after a few months. Kidnaping was now being carried on by some of the Kongolese themselves! Presumably, these were rival territorial leaders. It is true, however, that "slavery" as practiced and understood by Africans was something quite different from the European conception of slavery (see Chapter 5, page 183).

The king of Portugal issues the *regimento*. The one attempt which the Portuguese king, Manuel I, made to salvage the Kongo situation was his issuance in 1512 of the *regimento* (rezh-ee-*men*'too). This was a set of detailed instructions designed to reorganize the Kongo Kingdom, and in effect to help Affonso establish a Portuguese court at Mbanza. The document was delivered to Affonso by a special ambassador who also had with him the text of the Portuguese law code, which, it was thought, Affonso might wish to adopt. The ambassador had orders to act as the Kongolese king's adviser, and to expel any Portuguese subject from Kongo who was not leading an exemplary life. It was suggested that payment for services rendered by the Portuguese be made in slaves, copper, or ivory.

But Affonso refused to accept most of the proffered "reforms." He knew that his people were not prepared to go along with so many sweeping changes. He would accept technical assistance and missionaries to help spread the Christian gospel, but he did not wish to implement the *regimento* in other respects. Furthermore, Affonso was doubtless suspicious of Portuguese intentions. The skilled workers sent from Portugal were refusing to work and were living like nobles. Many of them were buying or selling slaves. In addition, the Portuguese seemed convinced that there were mines of silver, gold, and copper in the Kongo provinces, and were continually trying to learn their whereabouts from the local inhabitants. Affonso knew that there were indeed copper mines, but he also knew that the discovery of these mines would cause the Europeans to invade his country; hence he remained silent when questions were put to him about the mines.

How effective was Affonso's policy? In the oral traditions of the

Kongolese people, Affonso's reign stands out prominently. And yet his policy of Christianization and Europeanization was largely a failure. He wanted passionately to see his kingdom converted to Catholicism and to see his people literate and educated, and for this he was prepared to accept all the problems and injustices stemming from relations with the Portuguese. A small number of Kongolese did learn to read and write the Portuguese language, one of them Affonso's own son, Dom Henrique (dohm hen-*ree'*kay). Dom Henrique became the kingdom's first and only black bishop, but his role in the conversion of his people was insignificant. His father would not permit him to leave the capital, where Dom Henrique was forced to witness the laxity and selfishness of the white clergy and to suffer their scorn. He died in the 1530's.

The representatives of King Manuel at the Kongolese court now joined with Affonso in appealing to Lisbon for help. They swore that the pride and greed of the Portuguese were largely responsible for the troubles with the African population, and they advised their king to replace every civil and religious officer in Kongo, and to place the slave trade directly under Affonso's control. But these appeals went unanswered, and Affonso's reign ended with his death in the early 1540's. By that time Kongo chiefs were openly rebelling against their king, and disorder and corruption were widespread.

Later efforts at Europeanization fail. Affonso's reign set a pattern in Kongo history for more than a century. The slave trade, the quest for mines, the opposing factions of resident Portuguese, and efforts toward educating and converting the Kongolese continued into the 1640's. It is noteworthy, however, that the Portuguese did not at any time during this period attempt armed intervention — usually not even when it was requested by the manikongo to restore order. Officially, Portuguese intervention was limited to commerce and religion. There were, on the whole, cordial relations between the Kongo rulers and the Portuguese kings. The slave trade, though often deplored by the manikongo, continued to thrive. It was this trade, more than anything else, which blocked later attempts to Europeanize the Kongo. Efforts of Dutch and Italian traders and missionaries during the seventeenth and eighteenth centuries met with similar failure, though by this time Christian ideas were making an impression on many more Kongolese. Some people, for example, were beginning to fuse elements of traditional African religion with what they found most appealing in Christianity. The majority, however, felt that the

Christian missionary offered little of value to the African, and many more found the Christian religion, with its prohibitions and disciplines, distinctly distasteful.

Kongolo founds the first Luba kingdom. At about the same time the Kongo Kingdom had reached its peak, another major kingdom was being organized among the peoples living west of Lake Tanganyika. These peoples were, until the nineteenth century, remote from European contacts and could develop their own societies as they saw fit. The initial impetus for the Luba (*loo′*buh) Kingdom is ascribed to a hero named Kongolo (kahn-*goh′*loh), who came down from the north about 1500 and subdued the scattered villages and tiny chiefdoms. During this initial period, a son was born to Kongolo's half-sister. This child, whose name was Kalala (kuh-*lah′*luh), was given every opportunity to become a great warrior. Indeed, Kalala was so successful in the art of war that he incurred the jealousy of his uncle, Kongolo, who tried to kill him. But Kalala fled and returned before long with an army. Now it was his uncle's turn to flee. Kongolo tried to hide in caves but was betrayed by his own sisters, captured, and killed. Kalala

This Luba tribesman has come to Lubumbashi (formerly Elisabethville) in Katanga province to attend a political rally. He has donned ceremonial attire in anticipation of a visit from a Luba political leader. The history of the Luba Kingdom goes back to the sixteenth century, when strong leadership emerged in the Bantu-speaking settlements of the eastern Congo grasslands.

now became king. The story of Kongolo and Kalala has become the national Luba epic.

Luba society and government become highly organized. During his long reign Kalala implemented two goals: (1) the expansion of the royal domains and (2) the organization of a system of government which, with certain modifications, was to last until modern times and influence the social and political organization of many other peoples of Central Africa.

Luba's society was *patrilineal* — meaning that people traced their descent through the male line. A village was made up of one or more extended family groups. The village was administered by a headman chosen from the main lineage in the settlement. The headman was assisted by a council of all the heads of the lineages in the village. Several villages combined to form a chiefdom, headed by a *kilolo* (kih-*loh'*loh), a territorial chief. Several chiefdoms formed a province with a provincial chief, and all the provinces together made up the kingdom. There were some exceptions to this hierarchy. Several chiefdoms were directly responsible to the king, as were some villages. A number of chiefdoms were hereditary, while others were appointed by their immediate superiors and confirmed in their office by the king. Some chiefdoms were assigned for life, others for only a period of four years. The king had the authority to depose any chief, however. The king ruled his capital directly, and every king was expected to found his own new capital.

Luba kings rule by "divine right." Like many of their counterparts in Europe and Asia, Luba kings were believed to rule by divine sanction. The Luba word for this idea was *bulopwe* (boo-*lohp'*wee). It referred to a sacred quality stemming from the blood lines of Kongolo or Kalala — the founders of the Luba kingdom. It was a power vested in the blood, but a power, too, which could only be transmitted through males. No one could rule without this ancestral blood tie, and anyone who had it was expected to rule, even if only in a subordinate capacity — such as provincial chief.

The Lunda people evolve a matrilineal society. West of the Luba Kingdom another equally important state was established by the Lunda (*lun'*duh) peoples. It differed from the Luba Kingdom in that its families traced their descent through the female line, a *matrilineal* society. The Lunda government received its basic organizational structure under the reign of King Luseeng (*loo'*seeng) between 1630 and 1660. His son, Mwaant Yaav Naweej I, who ruled from about 1660 to 1690, continued his work, and his personal name, Yaav, became a general term signifying the Lunda kingship — somewhat as the name Caesar in the history of Rome. The Europeanized form of this name is Mwato Yamvo (*mwah'*tuh *yahm'*voh). *Mwato* is a title signifying "hereditary kingship."

By the end of Naweej's reign, the Lunda Kingdom had expanded to include a large area in what is now southwestern Katanga province in Zaire. During the eighteenth century it further expanded in all directions, coming to include an area of some 40,000 square miles. Local chiefdoms were allowed a considerable degree of autonomy, so long as they regularly paid their taxes to the king. The king maintained a large staff of traveling chiefs, each with a small force of men, to collect the taxes and to bring the king's orders to distant parts of the kingdom. Apart from these traveling agents, there was no standing army, a fact which makes the Lunda expansion over such a large part of Africa all the more amazing.

The village is the center of the Lunda political structure. The basis of the Lunda political system, like that of its Luba forerunner, was the village and its surrounding lands. The villagers were ruled by a council of elders and by a hereditary headman who also performed certain religious functions which gave him a special importance. He could not be removed from his office except by the king, who was believed to possess even greater religious powers. Different villages were united in groups according to the ties of kinship which existed between their headmen. The headmen, in turn, were subject to the elders of their group (elder headman, or *mbay* [um-*bay'*]), and the elders were grouped into political districts governed by a chief whose main duty was to collect the taxes and forward them to his superior in the capital.

The Lunda king had many advisers. At the capital, the Lunda king was assisted by three types of officials: (1) a council of fifteen, made up of the headmen of the fifteen oldest villages in the kingdom; (2) a group of resident officials who were linked to the king by ties of "perpetual kinship"; and (3) tributary chiefs from the countryside who were represented at the capital by permanent delegates. Within each category, there were title-bearing officials with specific assigned duties. Some of these duties stand in marked contrast to those which we might associate with a highly developed society, but they served important and useful roles in the Lunda social structure: for example, there was a magistrate in charge of the tombs of deceased kings, and

LUNDA: In 1960, old names and rivalries emerged from history to divide the new Congolese republic. Moïse Tshombe (*right*) drew his support from the Lunda people in the province of Katanga. He tried to secede from The Congo and establish Katanga as an independent state.

LUBA: Albert Kalonji (*left*) was a leader of the Luba people in Kasai province. After fighting broke out between the Luba and a rival tribe backed by the Congolese government, he tried to proclaim himself king of an independent Luba state.

KONGO: Joseph Kasavubu (*right*), first president of the Congo Republic, addresses an independence day celebration. Other Congolese were suspicious of Kasavubu because he was a leader of the Kongo people, descendants of the Bantu who had established the ancient kingdom of Kongo.

a guardian of the borders between the Lunda and Luba lands. The historic importance of the queen mother and other women is suggested by such titles as "Perpetual Mother of the Lunda" and "Perpetual Aunt."

Offices were of two general types — positional and those based on ties of "perpetual kinship" with the king. Both types of offices could be inherited, but offices which were based on a real blood relationship with the king were permanent. To understand how this system worked, we need to think of a European parallel. The European nobility was based either on blood ties with the crown (e.g., prince, duke) or on titles invested by the crown which could then be passed on to one's children, as in the case of barons and counts. This dual aspect of the Lunda political system enabled it to be adapted over a far wider area than would have been possible otherwise, because "foreigners" could be assimilated into the system of political offices. The Lunda system was in this respect an improvement over that of the Luba, in which *bulopwe*, or royal blood, was a "must" for officeholders. It helps to explain why the Lunda system expanded over a vast part of Central Africa — westward to Angola and southeast into Zambia. The Luba, on the other hand, did not expand far beyond their original homeland.

- CHECK-UP

1. What were the origins of the kingdom of Kongo? How did the Portuguese establish relations with it? What was their goal?

2. How did religious conflict lead to civil war in the Kongo? What were the goals of Affonso I? What was the *regimento*? Why did efforts to Europeanize and Christianize the Kongolese fail?

3. What were the origins of the Luba Kingdom? Compare Luba and Lunda government at the local, provincial, and national levels.

Summing Up

The migrations of Bantu-speaking groups in Central Africa began some 2000 years ago and continued to modern times. Bantu languages are only remotely related, however, and the term "Bantu" (the word means "people") fails to suggest the great differences in language, physical type, and culture among those peoples of Central Africa.

The Bantu migrations were gradual and may have resulted from an increase in the population of the original Bantu homeland, the

Cameroon highlands. Occupying first the Congo Basin (where the Pygmies eventually were displaced), the Bantu fanned out eastward and southward, moving into Uganda, Kenya, Tanzania, Zambia, Rhodesia, and lands farther to the south and southwest. Encounters with coastal peoples (the "Zanj empire"), and with Cushite and Nilotic cultures, stimulated the development of new skills and promoted trade. In Uganda, long interaction between the Bantu-speaking farm population and cattle-herding Cushite and Nilotic pastoralists produced the strong Bito monarchies — Bunyoro, Buganda, Ankole and others — which have persisted to this day. In other areas, including parts of Kenya and Tanzania, no such development occurred. Farther south — in Rwanda and Burundi — the differences between the aristocratic pastoralists and the farmers frequently resulted in bloodshed.

Some Bantu migrants reached the Zambezi River as early as 500 A.D. Excavations at Ingombe Ilede, in south-central Zambia, suggest that in addition to agriculture, trade in gold and ivory was carried on with peoples of the Congo Basin after 1000 A.D. These early trading settlements were superseded as commercial centers by the larger "stone-building" states of the Rhodesian plateau. The latter carried on extensive gold mining and trade from the eleventh to the sixteenth centuries. The stone ruins of Great Zimbabwe seem to have been structures built by two distinct Bantu-speaking groups — the Sotho and the Shona — who successively occupied this area. One branch of the latter, the Karanga, moved northward to found a kingdom headed by members of the Rozwi clan. The early decades of the fifteenth century saw this kingdom extend its sway over much of Rhodesia and Mozambique. It became the most powerful kingdom in the southern part of the continent. But Monomotapa, as this empire was called by the Portuguese, was weakened by internal rivalries. One member of the royal family led the succession of the southern provinces, and established an independent kingdom named after himself — Changamire. By 1570 Changamire had overshadowed Monomotapa. It became the dominant African power in Rhodesia following the Portuguese attacks on Monomotapa in 1628 and 1629, and survived until the 1830's. Then it was invaded from the south by Ngoni peoples fleeing from attack by King Chaka's Zulu warriors.

Late in the fourteenth century, a strong monarchy emerged just south of the Congo River estuary. There a Bantu prince managed to make himself manikongo, or ruler, of the local inhabitants. During the next century, Kongo made vassals of several small neighboring states, and by the sixteenth century it ruled much of what is now western Zaire. The Portuguese who arrived in 1482 came at first as friendly explorers seeking Prester John's legendary kingdom. Impressed by the Portuguese, the Kongolese king (Affonso I) embraced Christianity, sought a European education, and tried to introduce certain European practices into his kingdom. But Portuguese greed and duplicity, mainly in connection with the slave trade, brought to an end the Kongolese policy of voluntary Europeanization. It also doomed such efforts later.

West of Lake Tanganyika, the Luba people began to unite villages under a strong warrior-king about 1500 A.D. The kingdom was organized into several provinces, each made up of a number of chiefdoms consisting of one or more villages. The Luba monarchy was patrilineal — hereditary through the male line. The Lunda political structure proved more flexible than that of the Luba, in that blood ties with the king were not a prerequisite for holding office. The Lunda system thus was able to expand over a wider area and was able to absorb foreigners.

The number and variety of societies which developed in Central Africa during the precolonial era prove that the Bantu groups which settled there had the vigor and imagination necessary for establishing rich civilizations — even in an environment that posed many problems for human survival.

CHAPTER REVIEW

Can You Identify?

radiocarbon analysis	Affonso I	Matope
empire of Zanj	*bulopwe*	Bantu
Great Zimbabwe	Zambezi	Hima
Changamire Kingdom	Bushmen	Shona
manikabunga	kilolo	Sotho
Mwato Yamvo	Cushites	Luba
Monomotapa	kabaka	Lunda
manikongo	Ingombe	

What Do You Think?

1. In what ways were African governments similar to contemporary regimes in feudal Europe? Why?

2. How did the Arab and Portuguese presence on the coast affect the Bantu peoples of East Africa?

3. Would the Kongolese have benefited from more thoroughgoing Christianization and Europeanization? Explain.

4. What are the chief sources of our information about the history of Central African peoples?

5. Why have the migrations of pastoral peoples been more "explosive" than those of tillers of the soil?

6. Why was trade likely to strengthen the power of the king and to encourage territorial expansion?

Extending and Applying Your Knowledge

1. The Zanj cities in the 1400's had grown wealthy by expediting the exchange of Oriental products for trade goods from the African interior. Portugal put an end to Afro-Arab trade. Draw up a description of Zanj, consulting pages 101–104 of *Africa: Selected Readings.*

2. "Great Zimbabwe" poses many problems for the historian. What questions are unanswered? See relevant passages in T. Desmond Clark's *Prehistory of Southern Africa,* and in *Africa: Selected Readings,* pages 105–109.

3. How the Portuguese opened up the Old Kingdom of the Congo, or Kongo, and what they found are told on pages 115–119 in *Africa: Selected Readings.*

4. Compare feudal relationships in Europe and Africa. To do so you may first need to read about the mutual obligations of lord and overlord in medieval Europe. Consult a textbook in world history or such a book as *Knights, Castles, and Feudal Life* by Walter Buehr.

THE ERA OF
AFRICAN SLAVE
TRADE

Except for the discussion of Roman and Islamic influences in North Africa and of Portugal's relations with Kongo, little has been said about Africa's relations with the rest of the world. In this and succeeding chapters this side of African history will be examined.

During many centuries, except for the slender tie linking ancient Ethiopia to Europe, there was hardly any contact between the peoples of Africa south of the Sahara and the rest of the world. European development of the science of maritime navigation plus major improvements in shipbuilding helped shift the center of European trade and exploration from countries bordering the Mediterranean to lands facing the Atlantic.

This chapter considers the forces which led countries in Europe and Asia to explore the coasts of Africa. During this period of discovery there was an extraordinary expansion of Arab influence and of the Muslim religion in Africa. An understanding of the European impact on Africa requires an analysis of how the exploits of Portuguese and, later, other European seafarers affected peoples in Africa. They came to Africa largely for purposes of profit — to acquire gold, ivory, and slaves to be sold on the world market. An understanding of modern Africa requires that attention be paid to the effects of these encounters between Africans and non-Africans. In this connection one must inquire what were the consequences of the brutal slave trade — instituted by the newcomers and carried on for centuries — upon African developments.

At first the Europeans limited exploration to the coastal lands of Africa and to an occasional expedition inland. But by the mid-nineteenth century, interest had shifted to exploration of the interior and to imperial conquest. The last section in this chapter considers some of the factors underlying this sudden "scramble for Africa."

1. Europeans and Asians Become Interested in Trade With Africa

Muslim power comes to an end in western Europe. The year 1492, associated with Columbus's discovery of America, was also the year that Spain put an end to Moorish rule in Granada. (The Moors were Muslims from North Africa, who had conquered and ruled part of the Iberian Peninsula for more than seven centuries.)

The Muslims had developed a high civilization in lands extending from the Middle East across North Africa and into Spain. (See Chapter 2, pages 69–75.) They controlled the trade with Europe in Asian luxury goods and brought these to ports in the eastern Mediterranean. During the Crusades, the forces of western Europe failed to drive the Muslims out of the Holy Land. And in 1453, Muslim armies completed the conquest of the Byzantine Empire. As the sea power of Christian states bordering the Atlantic grew, they became increasingly eager to share in the rich trade with the East. That is why Portugal began to look for an all-water route to Asia around Africa, and Spain backed Columbus's search for a westward route to the Indies. In 1492, when Columbus reached the New World, he thought that he had reached the Indies. Six years later, Vasco da Gama landed in Calicut (*kal'*ih-kut) on India's west coast, thus giving Portugal an all-water route to the East. By sailing around Africa, this Western sea captain "discovered" a new world.

New inventions facilitate European expansion. European technology contributed to the conquest of Africa and the Americas. The magnetic compass and celestial navigation — contributions of Asian and North African cultures — enabled the Portuguese seafarers to venture farther out to sea. But more than improved navigation was needed if western Europe was to triumph over the indigenous peoples of Africa and the Americas. Superior weaponry was achieved during the fifteenth century by combining gunpowder invented by the Chinese with the harquebus, a forerunner of the musket. The printing press, which was perfected at about the same time, greatly facilitated the dissemination of useful knowledge. Thus the book and the gun — rather strange partners — enabled Europeans ultimately to penetrate Africa and to conquer new territory.

The development of international trade increases contacts with Africa. The expansion of trade led to the growth of cities and to the rise of more powerful monarchies in Europe. Countries such as Portugal, Spain, England, and France developed the resources to support expensive voyages of exploration and to undertake commercial ventures. From the Muslims, the Spaniards and the Portuguese had heard of the existence of mighty empires in the interior of Africa. Both Spain and Portugal were eager to tap the fabulous wealth of the Orient described by Marco Polo and others. Africa could be explored along the way, and African ports would be useful as stopping places for the vessels of Portugal (and soon other nations) en route to the East.

Although the early European explorers and traders found the stories of African gold and great inland kingdoms intriguing, they discovered no broad and gently-flowing rivers to facilitate exploration of Africa's interior. It is not surprising that early maps of Africa pictured a well-defined coastline but showed only a vast unknown interior.

Merchants from India and the East had long traded with East Africa. Merchants and seafareres from India and Southeast Asia plied the ocean lanes between the Orient and East Africa long before the Portuguese began to explore the West African coast. Indeed, traders from the Far East probably had some knowledge of East Africa many centuries earlier. The Chinese scholar Tuan Ch'eng-shih, writing in the ninth century, referred to a region in Africa as "Po Pa Li," a land where "the people do not eat any cereals but they eat meat; more frequently, even, they prick a vein of one of their oxen, mix the blood with milk and eat it raw. . . . From of old this country has not been subject to any foreign power."[1] It seems unlikely, however, that during these early centuries Chinese sailors had ventured as far west as Africa. More likely, the Chinese knew of Africa through intermediaries — the Arab, Indian, Malayan, and Indonesian traders with whom they dealt. Direct commercial contacts between China and East Africa probably were begun in the early 1400's.

---

[1] Quoted in G.S.P. Freeman-Grenville, *The East African Coast* (Oxford: Clarendon Press, 1962), p. 8.

A dhow, the traditional sailing vessel used by Arab traders along the Zanj coast, enters the port of Dar es Salaam in Tanzania. Amid the palm trees can be seen cranes used to unload modern freighters.

Mogadishu (moh-guh-*dih′*shoo), the capital of modern-day Somalia, became a major port of call for early Chinese merchants. A number of references are made to this African port in the histories of the Ming dynasty. In 1427 Mogadishu sent an ambassador to China, and three years later it is reported that a large fleet of Chinese junks dropped anchor in the harbor. Early Chinese coins and crockery have been found along the East African coast.

The monsoon winds facilitate navigation between Africa and the Far East. Seaborne trade between Africa and the peoples of Asia began long before the Portuguese explorations. The distance from Mombasa to Bombay across the Indian Ocean is 2500 miles — a great distance in ancient and medieval times. But more important than the distance are the monsoon winds. From December until February these trade winds blow steadily from the north-northeast; from April until September, the direction is reversed. Sailors from Africa could count on the monsoon winds to take them to India and the Persian Gulf and to bring them home again. Their ships did not need to be as large or as heavily provisioned as those of west European nations which ventured into the more dangerous Atlantic Ocean.

The regularity of the monsoons helps to explain the extraordinary diffusion of peoples and ideas in the basin of the Indian Ocean. The people of the Republic of Malagasy (formerly Madagascar), for example, are a mixture of African mainland and Malayan stock. There is evidence that Arabs, Indians, and Malayans were visiting and colonizing the East African coast and islands as early as the sixth century B.C. At the dawn of the Christian era, slaves from Africa were common in India and, somewhat later, in Arabia, Persia, Indonesia, and China.

Arab influence becomes strong in East Africa. It was the Arabs who became the most firmly established traders in East Africa. Arab merchants as well as refugees from inter-Muslim wars, settled along the East African coast in the eighth and ninth centuries. From the middle of the thirteenth century to the end of the fifteenth, the East African coast experienced great prosperity. Mombasa, Kilwa, Mogadishu, Lamu, and Malindi were important ports where iron ore, ivory, and slaves from the interior were exchanged for cotton cloth from India, stoneware from Siam, and porcelain from China. This expansion of Arab influence and the continuing contact with Muslim civilization had an extraordinary impact on many parts of Africa. In the Indian Ocean, European explorers who came in the 1500's and after followed a trail already blazed by Arab sailors, merchants, and missionaries.

Arab traders spread the Muslim religion in East Africa. As already mentioned (page 127), Arab and other Asian traders had visited the East African coast long before the advent of Islam. At first the permanent settlements established along the coast by such traders had little effect on the interior. But the presence of Arab trading communities led to the spread of Islam among the coastal Bantu-speaking peoples, and the intermarriage of Arab traders and Bantu-speaking Africans gave rise to dynamic Swahili-speaking peoples. As elsewhere, Muslim civilization enriched the culture with which it came into contact. The Arabic script provided the coastal peoples with a means of recording their history and of developing their own literature. Swahili, which is today one of Africa's most important languages, is a mixture of the Arabic and Bantu tongues.

Arab contacts with the East African interior remain limited. Because trade was the reason for the Arab presence in East Africa, no

IVORY. One of Africa's most ancient exports is ivory, used for ornaments and, in the 1800's, for piano keys and billiard balls. Africans used ivory themselves: In Guinea elephant tusks were elaborately carved and hollowed out to serve as cups for water, oil, and palm wine (above). The picture below shows combs, serving ladles, and ceremonial knives carved out of ivory by the Mangbetu people of northern Zaire.

concentrated efforts were made to expand into the interior or even to convert the Bantu peoples to Islam. The Arabs were not interested in most of Africa's raw materials. Their chief reason for establishing contacts with the interior was to acquire ivory, slaves, and gold, and they preferred to obtain these through African intermediaries. In other words, the Arabs of the east coast were traders, not conquerors. But they did not hesitate to use force if peaceful methods failed in their dealings with Africans.

Arab dominance over missionary and commercial activities in East Africa came to an end when the Portuguese penetrated into the Indian Ocean. They were determined to wrest supremacy in the East African trade from the Arabs. For nearly three centuries there was sporadic warfare between the Portuguese and the Arabs in this area.

● CHECK-UP

1. What were Columbus and Da Gama seeking? Why? Why had these great voyages not been made centuries earlier?

2. How was it possible for merchants from India and China to trade with East Africa before the coming of Da Gama?

3. Why had Arabs traded with East Africa and founded towns along the coast?

2. Portugal Establishes an Empire in Africa

The legend of Prester John excites the imagination of Portuguese navigators. Fifteenth-century Portugal was greatly interested in reaching the fabled Christian kingdom of Prester John somewhere in the interior of Africa. Prince Henry the Navigator prayed that his sailors would discover this kingdom. Africans captured along the west coast were taken to Portugal, given an education, and then brought back to Africa to look for Prester John. Emissaries were also sent overland to East Africa. While Columbus was sailing westward across the Atlantic, Pedro de Covilhão (*pay'*throo day koo-veel-*yown'*) was on a mission to Jerusalem to make inquiries about this mysterious and powerful kingdom. Eventually, having first gone to India, he found his way to the court of Ethiopia's Emperor Alexander. He married an Ethiopian lady and remained in Ethiopia until his death in 1525. Although unsuccessful in locating the legendary kingdom of Prester John, Covilhão had accomplished a significant feat in systematically exploring a part of the east coast of Africa.

Meanwhile, Portuguese explorers sailing along Africa's west coast in 1445 had reached the Cape Verde Islands and the land at the mouth of the Senegal River. By 1471 they had reached the Gold Coast and begun to build forts along the coast. After contacts had been made with the powerful empires in the interior, the African trade became increasingly profitable. The successful rounding of the Cape of Good Hope by Bartholomew Días (1487) and the reports received from Pedro de Covilhão on the East African coast meanwhile paved the way for the epoch-making voyage of Vasco da Gama.

Portugal discovers an all-water route to India. On the eighth of July, 1497, a Portuguese fleet of four ships commanded by Vasco da Gama put to sea. After many adventures the flotilla rounded the Cape of Good Hope and sailed northward along Africa's east coast. Da Gama, too, hoped that he might find the Christian kingdom of Prester John, to whom he had a letter of introduction from the king of Portugal. But when Da Gama anchored at what is today the port city of Mozambique, he discovered that the inhabitants of that town were non-Christian Africans and Arabs. The Portuguese ships cruised northward, and despite trouble from Arab traders managed to pick up a pilot who knew the route to India. The expedition then sailed across the Indian Ocean to Calicut. Before returning to Portugal, Vasco da Gama again paid East Africa a brief visit. This two-year voyage was a great success. True, only 55 members of the original crew of 148 men survived to tell the story. But Portugal's prospects seemed bright, for the value of the cargo brought to Lisbon was worth 60 times the total cost of the voyage. The era of Portugal's commermercial empire in Africa had begun.

The Portuguese gain control of trade with the East African coast, India, and the Spice Islands. As a result of Da Gama's success, the Portuguese fitted out new fleets and made plans to wrest the spice trade from Arab control. In 1510 a Portuguese expedition took over Arab, Indian, and Malaysian trading centers in India. Portuguese ships, soldiers, and merchants soon established a commercial monopoly in the vast area bounded by Mozambique in East Africa, Goa (*goh′*uh) in India, and Malacca (muh-*lak′*uh) on the Malay Straits. Portuguese ships carried slaves and ivory from Africa to India where they were exchanged for spices, cloth, and glassware. Then the ships sailed back to East Africa for water, food, and repairs and to trade for the gold which found its way to the coast from Zimbabwe in the interior. This done, the fleet sailed back to Lisbon with a king's ransom in gold and spices.

Superior arms strengthen Portugal's bid for commercial monopoly.
No one was left in doubt about Portugal's intention to control trade in the Indian Ocean. On his second voyage in 1502, Vasco da Gama threatened to burn the town of Kilwa (in present-day Tanzania) unless the ruling sultan acknowledged the supremacy of the king of Portugal and paid an annual tribute in gold. Lacking the power to resist, the sultan capitulated.

Three years later, a fleet of more than 20 ships and 1500 soldiers left Lisbon to establish Portuguese supremacy in the Indian Ocean. The port of Sofala in Mozambique, long famous for its export of gold, was the first to fall. This gave Portugal control of the gold shipped from the interior. When the port of Kilwa tried to resist, it was laid waste. The same fate befell other coastal towns. Mombasa, in present-day Kenya, was one of the largest and oldest of these towns. Reinforced by some 1500 African archers recruited in the interior, Mombasa bravely fought the Portuguese. But firearms triumphed over bows and arrows. The victorious Portuguese, after looting the ancient and wealthy city, put it to the torch and sailed away. The survivors of Mombasa were left with the smoldering ruins of their homes and the bodies of hundreds of their fellow citizens. The king of Mombasa, in his grief, wrote to the neighboring king of Malindi (mah-*leen'*dee), Sayyid Ali (*sah'*yeed *ah'*lee), describing what had befallen his kingdom and warning him against the invaders:

> May God protect you, Sayyid Ali. I have to inform you that we have been visited by a mighty ruler who has brought fire and destruction amongst us. . . . [No] one, neither man nor woman, neither the old nor the young, nor even the children, however small, was spared to live. His wrath was to be escaped only by flight. The stench from the corpses is so overpowering that I dare not enter the town, and I cannot begin to give you an idea of the immense amount of booty which they took from the town. Pray hearken to the news of these sad events, that you may yourself be preserved.[2]

[2] Justus Strandes, *The Portuguese Period in East Africa* (Nairobi: Kenya Historical Society, East African Literature Bureau, 1961), p. 73.

CHRISTIAN ETHIOPIA. The church of St. George, in the form of a cross, was carved in one piece out of solid rock below ground level. A dozen churches were built in this style at Lalibela in the 1200's, after Muslims had captured Jerusalem. Lalibela was intended to replace Jerusalem as a holy city. Below, a high-ranking priest is escorted by Ethiopian clergy.

In a few short years the Portuguese conquered the major ports and made Mozambique Island the center of Portuguese authority in East Africa. In 1542, a small Portuguese expeditionary force prevented the ancient Christian kingdom of Ethiopia from being overrun by a neighboring Muslim state. Portuguese missionaries tried unsuccessfully to bring the Ethiopian Coptic Christian Church into the orbit of Roman Catholicism. But except for a few missionaries living at the court of the emperor of Ethiopia, and an occasional expedition to obtain gold from the people along the Zambezi River, the Portuguese limited their contacts with East Africa to the mainland ports and the coastal islands.

Portuguese sea power cuts Africa's traditional ties with Asia. Unlike the Arabs, the Indians, and the Malayans, who for centuries had sailed the Indian Ocean and competed for trade, the Portuguese were determined to rule the sea and monopolize maritime commerce. Portuguese control of the East African ports effectively cut that coast's traditional ties with China, India, and the Middle East. It was not until the seventeenth century, when Portuguese control grew weaker, that these old relationships began to revive. The Arab colonies in East Africa, deprived of their lucrative trade, declined in importance. What had promised in the fourteenth century to emerge as a major east coast civilization gradually disintegrated. To escape Portuguese control, many Indian and Arab merchants moved to Madagascar or to African Red Sea towns.

Arab cultural influences diminish. The coastal ports of southern East Africa soon lost most of their Arab cultural flavor. Today Mombasa, Malindi, and Mogadishu, where Arab cultural influences survive, are as different from Portuguese coastal towns in Mozambique as they are from Lisbon itself.

No one knows how Africa might have developed if European conquerors had not cut short the expansion of Islam in East Africa and the hinterland. By their actions, Europeans destroyed the older system of Indian Ocean trade which had brought wealth and cultural enrichment to many parts of Asia and Africa. Portuguese merchants soon replaced the Arabs as the chief traders of the Indian Ocean. They took over the importing of calico and beads from India, which they exchanged for gold, ivory, and slaves in Africa. But if anything, Portuguese contacts with peoples in the interior of Africa were even more infrequent than had been those of the Arabs. The Bantu-speaking coastal peoples were regarded by the Portuguese as lower caste and were relegated to menial jobs. But because Portuguese men did not bring their families to East Africa, there was considerable intermarriage with local Arab and African women. Jesuit missionaries from Portugal made few converts among Arabs or Africans.

Portuguese control in East Africa begins to decline in the early 1700's. The early success of Portugal was made possible by lack of unity among the many Muslim kingdoms and principalities along the

Persian Gulf and the Indian Ocean. But by the early seventeenth century Portuguese interests began to be threatened by England and Holland. These countries established trading posts in India and the East Indies and their ships sailed the waters of the Indian Ocean in increasing numbers. And from 1580 to 1640 Portugal was ruled by Spanish kings who were more interested in protecting Spain's sea routes to the New World than in defending the Portuguese commercial empire in the East.

Another reason for the decline of Portuguese influence in the Indian Ocean was the emergence of Oman (oh-*man'*) — a principality in the southeastern part of the Arabian peninsula — as a major sea power. Originally an inland Arabian people, the Omani captured the Portuguese-held port of Muscat (*mus'*kat) in 1650. By uniting the seafaring peoples along the Persian Gulf coast under one flag, Oman acquired the strength to challenge Portugal on the seas. Using ships captured from the Portuguese or purchased from the English and the Dutch, who were glad to help the Omani fight their European rival, these Arab seafarers proceeded to drive Portuguese shipping from the Persian Gulf. Soon Omani ships were attacking Portuguese holdings along the East African coast and in the offshore islands, and even had the audacity to raid Mozambique. By 1660, therefore, Portuguese strength on the East African coast centered on Mombasa, where a powerful fort protected this island city.

It was not until 1696 that the Arabs considered their resources adequate for an attack on Mombasa. This time, it was the Portuguese who sought allies among the African peoples. Although some Africans responded to this appeal, Mombasa, after a three-year siege, fell to the Omani Arabs.

East Africans strike a fatal blow against the Portuguese. Portuguese forces managed to recapture Mombasa in 1728. But they were soon expelled, not by the Arabs from across the sea, but by Swahili-speaking Africans living along the coast. On November 26, 1729, the garrison of Fort Jesus in Mombasa, taunted with laughter and insults, sailed for Mozambique, taking only those possessions they could carry. Some years later an attempt to re-establish Portuguese influence along the northern coast met with little success. Portugal's "golden age" of domination in East Africa was at an end.

Portugal's influence on Africa was largely negative. Portugal's interest in Africa was narrowly commercial. The Portuguese had sought not to establish permanent colonies but to maintain only a few

The slave market at Zanzibar flourished under Arab rule. Black captives from the mainland were sold either to the owners of clove plantations on the island or to traders who reshipped them to Arabia.

strategic coastal bastions. Their rule was harsh and did not foster appreciation of European civilization among Africans. The Jesuit priests, little inclined to penetrate the forbidding interior, were hardly more successful than the soldiers. Portugal's greatest impact was on the Arab colonies in coastal East Africa and on the ties that Africa had established with Asia. The once prosperous Arab ports were destroyed, or decayed from lack of trade; the important contacts which these ports had maintained with India, Malaya, and China were severed.

Arabs promote a growing slave trade in East Africa. In the eighteenth century, the city-states of East Africa emerged once more. This time they were essentially Swahili-speaking African communities under Arab dynastic rulers who owed allegiance to Oman. When a representative of the sultan of Oman established his capital in Zanzibar in 1840, political contacts with the Arabian peninsula virtually came to an end. By that time the cities were inhabited by Africans who, although they shared an Arabian heritage, were more interested in expanding their commercial ties with the interior of Africa than across the sea with India or China. During the eighteenth century, Arab-

Swahili caravans had begun in increasing number to penetrate the interior. At first they went in search of ivory, but with the growing demand for slaves, they turned increasingly to the interior as a source of human merchandise.

• **CHECK-UP**

1. Why was Da Gama's voyage important to Portugal? How was Portuguese supremacy established in the Indian Ocean? What were the results in Asia and Africa?
2. Why did Portuguese control of the Indian Ocean trade decline in the 1600's? Evaluate Portuguese influence in East Africa.
3. Why did the East African coastal cities increase trade with the interior during the 1700's?

3. The Slave Trade Cripples Africa's Progress

Africa's development was impeded by the coming of the most dreadful era in that continent's history: the long centuries of forcible transport which took millions of Africans from the land of their birth to another continent and life in bondage. In the Americas black people were to provide the sweat and muscle to build a new civilization while their own civilization in Africa declined.

Descendants of 50 million and more African slaves who were forcibly taken from their continent are visibly present in the populations of Brazil, the United States, Cuba, and most other American republics. The peoples of the Western Hemisphere, in the main, are descended from the indigenous Indians, slaves brought from Africa, and European settlers. All of them on occasion hark back to their land of origin. The black American, who cannot know precisely *where* in Africa his ancestors came from, may nevertheless feel a sympathetic tie with that continent. The poet Claude McKay (1891–1948), who was born in Jamaica and came to the United States in 1912, has expressed this feeling with rare eloquence:

> For the dim regions whence my fathers came
> My spirit, bondaged by the body, longs.
> Words felt, but never heard, my lips would frame;
> My soul would sing forgotten jungle songs.
> I would go back to darkness and to peace,
> But the great western world holds me in fee,
> And I may never hope for full release

While to its alien gods I bend my knee.
Something in me is lost, forever lost,
Some vital thing has gone out of my heart,
And I must walk the way of life a ghost
Among the sons of earth, a thing apart.

For I was born, far from my native clime,
Under the white man's menace, out of time.[3]

The demand for African slaves becomes widespread. Long before
Africans were carried in chains to the New World, they were being
sold in the slave markets of the East. Large numbers of African
slaves were living in medieval India, Indonesia, Egypt, Turkey, and
Persia. A fifteenth-century Muslim ruler in Bengal (ben-*gawl'*) was
reported to have held as many as 8000 African slaves. This ruler,
whose name was King Barbak (*bahr'*bak) of Gaur (*gah'*oor), appointed some of his African slaves to important positions in the kingdom. In 1486, the slaves rebelled and placed one of their leaders on
the throne. These former slaves ruled Gaur for a number of years
before they were overthrown.

There is also evidence that African slaves held positions of leadership in Muslim principalities in what is present-day Iraq. In 869, a
Persian prince, aided by thousands of African slaves, is said to have
gained control of the entire Tigris-Euphrates delta.

Arab traders commercialize the African slave trade. Slavery in
one form or another seems to have existed from the dawn of history.
Slaves were found in Rome, Greece, China, and elsewhere before the
Christian era. But it was not until the twelfth century, after the
Arabs had conquered the kingdoms of the sudan, that fairly large
numbers of Africans were captured and sold as slaves in North Africa
and the Middle East. These slaves apparently were not regarded by
the Arabs as inferior. Indeed, some were held in high esteem because
of their superior intelligence or skills. Slaves in Muslim households
frequently were granted their freedom and raised to positions of responsibility. A European observer, commenting on what he had seen
in the Middle East and Africa, reported that "the Negro is treated
. . . like one of the family rather than as a slave. . . . [Muslims] have
no scruples about acknowledging as their superior in any respect a
man with black skin and wooly hair." Such treatment was consistent

[3] Claude McKay, "Outcast," from *The Selected Poems of Claude McKay.*
Used by permission of Twayne Publishers, Inc., New York.

with the tenets of Islam. For the Koran exhorts Muslims: "Clothe thy slaves with thine own vestments, and feed them thine own food."

Africans had a concept of slavery different from that of Europeans. Within Africa, wars sometimes led to the enslavement of the captured. But most of these slaves in time were absorbed into the victor's society rather than relegated to perpetual bondage. Unlike the Arabs and Europeans, the Africans did not regard slavery as total ownership of another human being. In fact, such a condition was inconceivable to them.

An increased demand for slaves develops in the coastal cities of East Africa. Until the end of Portuguese domination in East Africa, the number of African slaves exported to the Middle East and North Africa was never great. The new system of trade which emerged afterwards was focused on the exploitation of the resources of Africa itself. The growing willingness of both Arabs and Swahili-speaking Africans to exploit the hinterland led to a rapid increase in "slave-raiding" — attacking or raiding African villages, seizing captives, and selling them

The ruthlessness of a slave raid was dramatized in a drawing by the American artist Frederic Remington. Raiders shot down any blacks who resisted and burned the village to force survivors into the open.

to slave traders. Often slave-raiding was carried on to provide the porters needed to carry heavy tusks of ivory and other wares from the interior to the coast. It was also the means for meeting the growing demand of the Arab overlords of Zanzibar, Pemba, and other islands off the East African coast for slaves to harvest cloves and other newly introduced crops. In 1811 it was estimated that mainland slaves made up one fourth of Zanzibar's population of 200,000. Nor was slavery limited to the offshore islands. In 1835 African slaves constituted an estimated one-third of Oman's entire population.

Slave-raiding causes indescribable suffering. Today it is difficult to imagine the suffering brought on by the slave raids. One eyewitness account tells of families hiding in underground burrows until they were smoked out like animals. If no one emerged from such a burrow, the slave raider would assume that:

> [the] mother has suffocated her children, the father has killed her, and then killed himself. . . .

The same eyewitness went on to recall:

> Some [of the captured], grasping their feet with their hands, refused to rise. Others, bracing themselves against trees, [would] resist with all the force of their muscles; or [entwined] themselves with their wives and children [in] knots which nothing short of a sword [could] untie. . . . Those . . . hardest to deal with [were] yoked by the legs to horses and thus dragged away from their village.[4]

The number of Africans victimized by slave-raiders increased tremendously when the New World demands for slaves were added to those of the Arabs in the East.

The European market for slaves declines. The demand for African slaves in western Europe was small compared to that which later developed in the Americas. The first West African slaves were taken to the king of Portugal as a gift. But the number of African slaves purchased for labor in Europe remained small, partly because there was a plentiful supply of cheap labor in Europe. Furthermore, the traffic in human flesh was only marginally profitable when a copper or brass basin, for example, could be exchanged for approximately 150 dollars' worth of gold on the Guinea coast.

---

[4] Colonel L. DuCouret, *Recollections of Travel in Asia and Africa* (New York: Mason Brothers, 1860), p. 104.

The first slaves sent to America by the Spaniards to work on plantations and in the mines were whites who probably had been captured and enslaved by Arabs. It was only when large numbers of slaves were needed that the Spaniards and Portuguese turned to Africa for their supply. It soon became clear that fortunes could be made by using African slaves in exploiting the riches of the New World. By the mid-1500's, the slave trade had grown enormously. Slaves were to provide the plantation labor to meet the growing European demand for sugar and tobacco.

Some Europeans reap great wealth from the slave trade. The wealth that slavery brought first to Portugal and Spain, and later and increasingly to Holland, England, and France, helped to finance technical and industrial advances in Europe. Cheap manufactured goods were shipped from Europe to the Guinea coast where they were traded for slaves captured by African slave raiders. The slaves were brought to the New World where they were exchanged for tobacco and sugar to be sold in Europe. The profits were enormous. Not only the industrialization of western Europe but the rapid settlement and agricultural development of the Americas were facilitated by the profits from the slave trade and the labor of millions of African slaves.

By the early seventeenth century the Portuguese and Spanish monopoly of the slave trade had been broken by the British, Dutch, and French. The establishment of American colonies by these northern European countries further increased the market for slaves. Because mortality among the slaves was very high, the market was never saturated. Basil Davidson quotes a contemporary estimate that in the British West Indies "the whole race of 50,000 healthy slaves . . . [is] totally extinct once every twenty years."

For three centuries the slave trade was the major factor in European relations with Africa. Although slavery had been important in the commerce of the Indian Ocean, it had not dominated the relationship between Africans and Asians. But in West Africa from the sixteenth to the nineteenth century, Europe's primary interest in Africa was procuring slaves — "black ivory." Except for the few coastal centers to which slaves were brought from the interior, no real colonies were established by Europeans in West Africa until the end of the slave trade. Relations between European governments and the rulers of African kingdoms were limited to agreements for the procurement of slaves. There was no significant exchange of culture and knowledge. One of the reasons why few missionaries or explorers visited Africa during this period was that the slave trade was so in-human that those involved in it wanted no observers who might report its horrors.

The slave trade leads to the disintegration of African societies. Before Portugal acquired its American colony, the country had established relations with the African kingdom of Kongo, and Portuguese missionaries sought to convert the king to Christianity (see Chapter 4, pages 154–155). As in Ethiopia, the Portuguese at first dealt with the Kongolese king and his government as equals and co-operated with them in seeking to further trade. The Portuguese even assisted in the building of a new capital city. Later, when it had become clear that thousands of slaves were needed to work on plantations in Brazil, Portuguese relations with the Kongolese people underwent a drastic change. The sword and the musket replaced the Bible and the cross. African kingdoms were armed and pitted against one another so that prisoners of war might be enslaved. Africans living in coastal villages received firearms from Portuguese slavers, and were encouraged to make slave raids in the interior. Consequently, the center of African power and wealth tended to shift from the interior to the west coast.

Benin succumbs to the lure of the slave trade. Gradually the states of West Africa became involved in the slave trade. Benin, located in present-day Nigeria, was one of tropical Africa's great cultures. But Portuguese slavers came and provided Benin with firearms that would enable the country to conquer its neighbors. Then, after the surrounding lands had been laid waste and denuded of potential slaves, the Portuguese withdrew their support. During the seventeenth century, Benin declined. Its art, prosperity, and efficient government were all but lost in the bloodletting, capricious militaristic rule, and economic chaos which followed.

New African states rise to wealth and power. European luxuries, increasingly regarded by the coastal peoples as necessities, could be purchased only in exchange for slaves. As a consequence, some African peoples undertook to enslave their neighbors. One writer describes the situation in these words:

Competition among African groups for slave profit encouraged a marked increase in warfare, particularly in senseless and desperate warfare. No longer was war primarily for grievances or for honor; no longer was it limited by mutual agreement or by religious codes. Warfare in Africa was transformed from a local, often ceremonial

Slaves on the way to the West African coast were bound or yoked together to prevent them from escaping. If sickness or exhaustion caused a slave to lag on the march, he might be taken out of line and killed.

operation into a desperate struggle for senseless conquest, tribal wealth, and ultimate decimation [destruction] of the enemy.[5]

Some states — such as Ashanti and Dahomey — were located strategically between the coast and the interior with its vast supply of potential slaves. Because of their position, they became powerful and wealthy. Ironically, they were among the few African peoples able to offer effective resistance once imperialist expansion became the major goal of European powers in Africa.

Africa's population is greatly depleted by the slave trade. Until recently, most textbooks in American history included an account of the waves of immigration from Europe to the United States, but paid scant attention to the enforced migration of millions of Africans to the Americas. The exact number of enslaved Africans transported to the Western Hemisphere cannot be known. It is not impossible that some 50 million were sold into bondage over a period of three centuries. The sparse population of many parts of Africa even today is a constant reminder of the terrible drain on that continent's human resources caused by the slave trade. The estimate that one sixth of the slaves died during the voyage across the Atlantic makes clear that the traffic was carried on in a callous and brutal manner. How many

[5] Donald L. Wiedner, *A History of Africa, South of the Sahara* (New York: Random House, 1962), p. 58.

millions of Africans were killed or died of starvation because of the slave raids probably cannot be accurately determined.

Africa is deprived of many able inhabitants. Many of the slaves sent to America had been persons prominent in their home societies — political leaders, artists, and craftsmen. They were men and women who possessed talents highly esteemed by their countrymen. Numbers of Africa's finest and healthiest citizens were taken captive on the assumption that they would make the most valuable slaves. The cruelties and humiliations inflicted on them were designed to strip Africans of their pride and self-respect. Slaveowners tried to instill in young Africans a feeling of inferiority. The sufferings endured by Africans brought about a deep-seated bitterness which lingers among their Afro-American descendants down to the present. An eyewitness tells how the slaves were treated before boarding ship for the terrible voyage across the Atlantic. They were stripped of all clothing and examined by ship doctors for infirmities or diseases which would reduce their value on the slave market.

> These [unfit] being so set aside, each of the others which passed as good [was] marked on the breast with a red-hot iron, imprinting the mark of the French, English, or Dutch companies, so that each nation [could] distinguish [its] own.[6]

On the journey to the New World, slaves who became seriously ill were thrown overboard; the others were given barely enough food, water, and exercise to survive. During the five weeks or more of the voyage, their sufferings were beyond comprehension.

Western countries abolish the slave trade. The slave trade officially came to an end in West Africa early in the nineteenth century. In 1796 Denmark decreed an end to slave-trading by 1802. Parliament passed a law in 1807 abolishing the slave trade in the British colonies. Other European countries followed this example. In the United States the importation of slaves became illegal after 1808. But an illicit slave trade continued after that date.

Ironically, the end of the slave trade caused almost as much dislocation in Africa as its inception had created. Much of Africa's economy had become dependent on the slave trade — for human beings were by far the most valuable of the continent's exports. African kingdoms lost a sure source of revenue. The result was economic and political chaos in many areas. These conditions, in turn, provided a

---

[6] Quoted in Basil Davidson, *Black Mother: The Years of the African Slave Trade* (London: Victor Gollancz, 1961; Boston: Little, Brown, 1961), p. 97.

The coming of the white man as a slave trader was reflected in the art of West Africa. This wooden headdress, carved by an Ibo sculptor on the Nigerian Slave Coast, shows a European, identified by his sun helmet, driving a bound African captive in front of him.

pretext for European powers to intervene, as they said, to restore order in Africa.

The slave trade had a profound effect on race relations. Racial prejudice was an outgrowth of African slavery and not its cause. Arguments purporting to establish the inherent inferiority of Negroes began to appear when guilt-ridden Europeans and Americans who had profited from or acquiesced in the slave trade felt compelled to find reasons to justify their inhuman actions. Captains and owners of slave ships, middle-class investors in the slave traffic, and perhaps even kings and queens slept better after persuading themselves that slavery was justified on the grounds that Africans were "not quite human."

The American historian who concerns himself with the problem of race relations may well conclude that the persistence of the myth of racial superiority is the greatest evil stemming from this country's experience with slavery and the slave trade. Basil Davidson argues that slavery "produced among Europeans the mentality of race superiority that helped to hasten colonial conquest, and still lingers like a poison in our midst."[7] If anyone wishes to understand why Africa is only now emerging into the modern world, and why the problem of race relations is so complex, he must trace the impact on Africa and America of centuries of slavery.

[7] Davidson, *op. cit.*, p. 246.

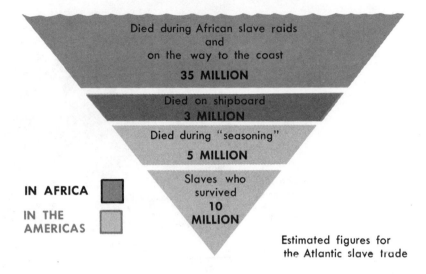

Manpower Lost in the Slave Trade

Died during African slave raids
and
on the way to the coast
35 MILLION

Died on shipboard
3 MILLION

Died during "seasoning"
5 MILLION

Slaves who
survived
10 MILLION

IN AFRICA

IN THE
AMERICAS

Estimated figures for
the Atlantic slave trade

Loss of life was high at all stages of the slave trade, even "seasoning,"
when new slaves were "broken in" on West Indian plantations.

● CHECK-UP

1. What are the origins of slavery? Of the African slave trade? Why
   did the east coast slave trade increase during the 1700's? How did the
   African concept of slavery differ from that of Arabs and Europeans?

2. Why was there a great demand for slaves in the New World? Why
   was the slave trade highly profitable? What nations profited most
   from it? How? How did the slave trade affect Africa? European
   relations with Africa?

3. What was the effect of slavery on the slaves? On the owners of slaves?
   On race relations? When was the Western slave trade abolished?
   What were the results?

4. Several Factors Lead to Direct European Involvement in Africa

Until the nineteenth century, European relations with Africa were
largely limited to commercial contacts along the coast. European
ships entered the mouths of rivers or anchored close to the shore only
long enough to obtain supplies and to buy and load slaves. This
situation changed greatly in the nineteenth century, and a new period
in African history began.

Rivalry for control of the water route to India leads to a Dutch colony on the southern tip of Africa. The Portuguese, the first Europeans to round the Cape of Good Hope and tap the riches of the Orient, were able to maintain their monopoly of this trade for little more than a century. Then they found themselves competing with the Dutch, the English, and the French. Unlike the Portuguese, who could anchor at East African ports for rest and supplies, the Dutch, who had no other overseas bases en route, came to stop at the Cape of Good Hope before sailing across the Indian Ocean northeastward to India or the East Indies. Other European countries tended to follow this latter route. England, France, and Holland — unlike Portugal — did not combine African trade with commercial ventures to India, Malaya, or China.

In 1652 the Dutch established a colony at the Cape of Good Hope to supply meat, fresh food, and water to their ships. The number of Dutch settlers at the Cape increased as Holland moved to protect the colony against attacks from Africans by land and rival European countries by sea. The fertile land gradually induced the descendants of these early settlers to move inland to improve their lot in life. About a hundred years after the first settlement, the Boers (bohrz), as

In 1720 a Dutch artist painted this view of the harbor at Cape Town in South Africa, with Table Mountain looming in the background. At right, a British ship fires a salute before dropping anchor.

these Dutch began to be called, came into conflict with African peoples moving southward. A series of hard-fought wars resulted which did much to crystallize the existing relations between Africans and Boers. When the British took over the Cape Colony in the 1800's, the descendants of the Dutch settlers moved farther into the interior to establish independent frontier republics.

Britain tries to end the African slave trade. Having lost much of its American empire following the Revolutionary War, Great Britain concentrated on its growing Asian trade. British interest in Africa was limited to establishing way stations where India-bound ships might stop, or bases from which the Royal Navy could operate to suppress the slave trade.

After the Napoleonic Wars, Great Britain was the undisputed mistress of the seas. During that conflict the British had sought the co-operation of the sultan of Oman to block a possible attempt by Napoleon to invade India by advancing across the Middle East. But Britain and Oman failed to see eye to eye on the question of the slave trade. Britain had outlawed slave-trading in 1807, but Sultan Seyyid Said (*say'* yid sah-*yeed'*) was reluctant to give up the money derived from selling African slaves in the Middle East. As Great Britain extended its control over India, Said's market for slaves declined. The British finally compelled the sultan to sign a series of treaties limiting his slave-raiding and slave-trading activities. But it was not until 1873, and then only under the threat of naval bombardment, that the sultan of Oman finally signed a treaty outlawing the slave trade.

The antislavery movement leads to British involvement in Africa. The British antislavery movement took on the fervor of a crusade. Not only did middle-class British citizens oppose the slave trade and demand the abolition of slavery in British colonies, they also sought to end slavery everywhere. British pressure was responsible, for example, for treaties under which Portugal and Spain in the early 1800's officially ended their participation in the slave trade. But the demand for slaves in the Middle East and in the Americas did not abate simply because Great Britain opposed the slave trade. It soon became apparent that if Great Britain wanted to end this sordid traffic, it must take steps to end the exportation of African slaves. For more than fifty years the British navy hunted down slave ships in the Atlantic Ocean. Final victory was achieved only when the demand for slaves ceased. This came about after the defeat of the South in

ANTISLAVERY PATROL. A picture from a British magazine of 1860 (*above*) shows a paddle-wheel steamer of the Royal Navy halting a sailing ship off the West African coast. A total of 874 slaves were found on board. Below, British sailors are fired upon by Arab crewmen when they try to board a dhow suspected of carrying slaves below deck.

the American Civil War (1865), and when slavery was abolished in Cuba and Brazil in the 1880's.

The antislavery movement contributed to a new kind of involvement in Africa, not only for Britain but for other countries. In Britain, there had developed a curiosity about the land and peoples of Africa. Both in England and in France the Church moved naturally from a crusade to save Africans from slavery to one that would save their souls from "paganism." Explorers began to move into the interior of Africa. Missionaries soon followed, as did businessmen interested in selling mass-produced wares in an African market. These and still other reasons caused European governments to become increasingly interested in Africa.

An upsurge of nationalism and missionary zeal leads to increased European interest in Africa. The Industrial Revolution not only led to increased interest in sources of raw materials and in markets for manufacturers. It was also accompanied by a religious revival. Protestant churches vied with one another and with the Catholics to "save the souls" of Africans and Asians. Influential religious leaders joined with middle-class industrialists and businessmen in urging the government to undertake overseas ventures. The resulting rivalry among the European powers gave added impetus to this drive for overseas empires. The fact that the French and Germans also became interested in establishing colonies and developing new foreign markets for their goods made the British determined to secure their "share" of Asia and Africa.

Although Africa ranked below Asia in its economic importance to Britain, the continent did supply important raw materials and provided a growing market for exports as well as unusual opportunities for investment. Thus colonies were established to meet the demands of missionaries and businessmen and at times simply to keep another country from getting a foothold in an area.

Englishmen, Frenchmen, and Germans vied with one another everywhere. Africa needed exploring; Africa needed Christianity; Africa needed European goods; the roaring European factories needed raw materials from African mines and forests. The "scramble for Africa" was about to begin.

● CHECK-UP

1. Why did the Dutch establish a settlement in South Africa? How did they come in conflict with Africans?

2. What was Britain's interest in Africa originally? How did the British antislavery movement come to involve that country in Africa?
3. Why did Europe's interest in Africa increase greatly during the 1800's?

Summing Up

Beginning in the late 1400's, Africa was visited by increasing numbers of Europeans and Asians. Encouraged by improvements in shipbuilding and navigation, and eager for adventure and wealth, Portuguese seafarers made their way along the West African coast. Even earlier, seamen from India and the Persian Gulf had plied the sea lanes between their countries and ports in East Africa and Madagascar. For a time, the Arabs maintained a near monopoly of missionary and commercial activities in East Africa. But after Vasco da Gama's famed voyage rounding the Cape of Good Hope, a growing number of Portuguese vessels put in at East African ports. Eventually Portugal gained control of the East African trade.

The Portuguese were interested primarily in Africa's gold and ivory, although they vied with the Arab traders in the lucrative and expanding slave traffic. The Portuguese made few cultural contacts with Black Africans, regarding them as lower caste. In the seventeenth century, Portuguese monopoly of Indian Ocean trade and her commercial interests in East Africa began to be challenged by the English, Dutch, and Omani. The final expulsion of the Portuguese from their stronghold at Mombasa was accomplished by Swahili-speaking Africans.

The traffic in slaves — carried on by both Arab and European traders — drained Africa of much of its best manpower, and caused Africans unspeakable suffering. The mortality rate among the enslaved — especially during the ocean crossings — was very high. The damaging effect of the slave trade in arresting the cultural and political development of African kingdoms was incalculable. The collaboration of some Africans with white slave traders only made matters worse. In time, much of Africa became economically dependent on the slave trade.

The antislavery movement of the eighteenth and nineteenth centuries finally succeeded in outlawing the slave trade. This action caused economic and political distress in parts of Africa. These conditions, in turn, provided a pretext for European intervention. Arguments put forward in justification of slavery had been based on the alleged inferiority of Africans. Thus a tradition of racism got its start. It has persisted in various forms to the present day.

The nineteenth century saw a further deterioration in European-African relations as rivalry for commercial supremacy in Africa led to European colonization along the African coast. Antislavery and missionary sentiment in Britain, which reached a peak of intensity in the early 1800's, stimulated British efforts to suppress the Arab slave trade. But these also led to increasing British involvement in East Africa and to conflict with some Arab rulers.

. . . .

CHAPTER REVIEW

Can You Identify?

Cape of Good Hope	Mogadishu	Calicut
slave-raiding	Mombasa	Da Gama
missionary zeal	Swahili	Días
nationalism	Covilhão	Oman
Mozambique	monsoon	Boers

What Do You Think?

1. How was slavery among the ancient Greeks and Romans, and later in Muslim lands, different from the institution that developed in the New World?

2. Why did the concept of racial inferiority gain acceptance with the expansion of slavery and the slave trade?

3. Why were the Portuguese at first little interested in the slave trade but later deeply involved in it?

4. How did Europe and the Americas profit from slavery and the slave trade?

5. Why was the slave trade a curse to Africans?

6. Why did European interest in Africa increase following the abolition of the slave trade?

Extending and Applying Your Knowledge

1. The inhumanity of slave-raiding and the selling of slaves is brought out graphically in *Africa: Selected Readings*, pages 120–125.

2. *Africa: Selected Readings*, pages 126–131, may be consulted for information about the "business aspects" of the slave trade.

3. Africans sold into slavery endured unspeakable suffering in the Atlantic crossing to the New World. Compile an account of the crossing by reading pertinent passages from *Black Cargoes* by Daniel Mannix and Malcolm Cowley (Viking Press). A selection from this book may be found in Richard C. Wade ed., *Negroes in American Life* (Houghton Mifflin). The latter volume also contains several selections dealing with life under slavery.

6

CONQUEST AND COLONIAL RULE

This chapter considers the events and forces which in a comparatively short time led first to the exploration of Africa and later to its partition among the great European powers. This was the period during which the secrets of Africa's interior were unlocked to Europeans. The paths blazed by the explorers were soon trod by missionaries. And then European soldiers and governors followed in the footsteps of the explorers and missionaries until all of Africa was partitioned.

1. European Explorers and Adventurers Turn to Africa

During the early nineteenth century, Africa was, for most non-Africans, a virtually unknown world awaiting exploration. In this section will be mentioned the European explorers who most directly affected the subsequent course of events in Africa.

James Bruce reaches the source of the Blue Nile. James Bruce may be regarded as the first major European explorer of Africa. He was a sturdy, red-haired Scotsman, more than six feet tall. His 1768 expedition up the Nile to find the river's source was halted by an African war. Undaunted, he returned after spending some months in Arabia. Before beginning the long and difficult expedition into the Ethiopian highlands, he visited the ruins of ancient Axum. Ninety-five days later he arrived in Gondar (*gahn'*der), the capital of what was then the principal Ethiopian kingdom. The king received him in a reception hall which was 120 feet long. Bruce reports that when he first saw the king and his prime minister they were busily engaged in plucking

LANDMARKS FOR BRUCE. An Ethiopian guide (*above*) surveys the falls over which the Blue Nile tumbles soon after it exits from Lake Tana. In 1770 a Scotsman, James Bruce, scouted round the lake and followed one of its feeder rivers to a marsh. This he proclaimed to be the source of the Nile. He did not realize that another branch of the river, the White Nile, had its source a thousand miles farther south. Bruce made his headquarters at Gondar, capital of the Ethiopian ruler. At Gondar a young Ethiopian girl (*right*) leads tourists to the tower of the castle of King Fasildas. The castle and palace at Gondar were built for the King during the 1600's. Ethiopian workmen adapted styles of building which had been introduced earlier by Portuguese missionaries.

199

out the eyes of prisoners captured in recent battles. Bruce's description suggests that the Ethiopia he visited was but a pale reflection of the Ethiopian Kingdom of earlier centuries. Bruce found a number of petty principalities fighting one another in a bloody struggle for supremacy.

In Gondar, Bruce was at the same time both a prisoner and an honored guest. He finally received permission to head an expedition to nearby Lake Tana, whence he proceeded up the Little Abai (ah-*bye'*) River to its marshy source. Standing up to his ankles in the cold marsh, James Bruce in 1770 was certain that he had found the source of the Nile.

> . . . Standing in that spot which had baffled the genius, industry, and inquiry of both ancients and moderns for the course of near three thousand years, . . . [I], a mere private Briton, . . . in my own mind [had triumphed] over kings and their armies.[1]

But Bruce was mistaken. The ultimate source of the White Nile is Lake Victoria in present-day Uganda, a thousand miles south of the place where Bruce was standing.

Bruce returned to Gondar where he lived as a prisoner-guest for two more years. Then he began the return to Europe by moving down the Nile to Cairo. After being at death's door on numerous occasions from disease, thirst, and attacks by hostile tribesmen, Bruce reached Europe in 1773. The story of his exploits fell on incredulous ears. Ridiculed as a fraud, Bruce returned a bitter man to his estates in Scotland. But Bruce was not a failure, for he had stirred the curiosity of a younger generation.

Mungo Park reaches the Niger River. Next to the Nile, the Niger River and its fabled city of Timbuktu generated the most interest in Britain. Mungo Park, another Scotsman, dedicated his life to unraveling the mystery of its precise location.

In 1796 Mungo Park moved inland from the West African territory of Gambia until he reached Segu (say-*goo'*) on the Niger. Although he returned to England for a short stay, Mungo Park, like so many others before and after him, could not resist the lure of Africa. He returned to seek the source of the Niger and to visit the mysterious city of Timbuktu. In 1805, this Scotsman again reached the Niger, and with his remaining companion began his explorations. In a scuffle

[1] Quoted in Alan Moorehead, *The Blue Nile* (London: Hamish Hamilton Ltd., 1962), p. 26.

From Here to Timbuktu

For many Americans, Timbuktu is another word for remoteness. Actually, it is a West African town with a fabulous past. In recent years, the town has begun to awaken from its long sleep of obscurity.

Timbuktu was settled by Tuareg Berbers in 1087, but during the twelfth century it fell under the rule of the Mandingo kings of Mali. Tuareg invaders conquered it in 1434, but in 1469 Timbuktu was captured by the Songhai ruler, Sunni Ali. During the reign of his successor, Askia (1493–1528), the city reached its highest state of development and splendor. Located at the southern edge of the Sahara near the bend of the Niger River, Timbuktu was a crossroads of caravan trade routes, and thus became known as "the port of the sudan in the Sahara." Its growing wealth enabled the city fathers to summon architects from Moorish Spain to build mosques and schools; these, in turn, helped Timbuktu to become a great center of Islamic culture and scholarship. But in 1591, the Sultan of Morocco captured the city during a war with the Songhai Empire. An oppressive rule was begun which gradually stifled the city's business and cultural activity. The population shrank. By 1800, conditions in Timbuktu had become chaotic. At this point Tuareg of the desert swooped down upon and captured the once-proud city. Thereafter it was conquered by several neighboring states in succession, and in 1893 it became French; but by this time Timbuktu had become little more than a trading post.

Today, Timbuktu is enjoying popularity as a tourist center, and the government of Mali is doing what it can to revive the town's economy. A Mali airmail stamp (*above*) shows a view of Timbuktu and its famous Sankore mosque which is intended to catch the eye of foreign travelers.

with Africans, Mungo Park either leaped or fell from his raft and drowned. The river he loved had claimed him forever, even before he could discover its source or reach Timbuktu.

René Caillié rediscovers Timbuktu. The first European explorer to enter Timbuktu and return alive was René Caillié (ren-*ay'* cah-*yay'*), a Frenchman. Caillié tells us that as a young man, "All my spare time was taken up with books of travel. The map of Africa which . . . showed only desert or unexplored regions, fired my imagination above all others."[2]

When Caillié entered Timbuktu in 1828, this city was only a shadow of its earlier self. The Frenchman did not stay long in Timbuktu, but joined an Arab camel caravan preparing to cross the western Sahara to Morocco. No European had ever accomplished this feat, and Caillié prayed that he would be "the first European who succeeded in crossing this sandy ocean from the south to the north."[3]

When he finally arrived in Morocco, Caillié was more dead than alive, and so disheveled that the French consul at first refused to confer with him. On his return to Paris, Caillié initially was received as a hero. Later, questions were raised about the report of his journey, and he was publicly accused of lying in claiming to have reached Timbuktu. A sick and broken man, René Caillié died at the age of 39. But as in the case of Mungo Park and James Bruce, the account of his expeditions stimulated interest in the exploration of Africa.

The "Mountains of the Moon" attract explorers. Even before the Christian era, rumors of a mighty mountain of snow near an enormous lake circulated throughout the Mediterranean world. A Greek merchant told a Syrian geographer how after journeying inland from the East African coast for 25 days he "arrived in the vicinity of the two great lakes and the snowy range of mountains whence the Nile draws its twin sources." In 150 A.D., Ptolemy (*tahl'*uh-mee), a geographer and mapmaker, included this description in his map of Africa. He called the sources of the Nile the "Mountains of the Moon." For more than a thousand years, Ptolemy's crude map was the chief source of information about the interior of Africa. It was not until 1848 that a European, Johann Rebmann, actually saw Mount Kilimanjaro and

---

[2] Quoted in Heinrich Schiffer, *The Quest for Africa* (New York: G. P. Putnam's Sons, 1957), p. 289.

[3] J. P. Moffett (ed.), *Handbook of Tanganyika* (Dar es Salaam: Government Printer, 1958), p. 40.

confirmed the story of great snow-covered mountains on the equator.

Rebmann reaches Mount Kilimanjaro. Johann Rebmann, a mild-mannered German missionary, lacked the gusto of men like Mungo Park and James Bruce. The purpose of Rebmann's explorations was merely to find a place where he might serve God. Carrying a Bible and an old gun which rarely worked, his most effective weapon was a huge umbrella. On one occasion he used this umbrella to frighten a lion and on another to put to flight some would-be attackers. Rebmann was the first European to keep a careful record of a journey into the interior of East Africa. Together with his partner, Johann Krapf, he paved the way for later explorers. The life of the missionary explorer was even more difficult than that of the adventurer. For his lot was not to return home to a hero's welcome but to continue work in a distant land. A very sick man, Johann Krapf finally left Africa in 1853. Twenty years later an Englishman traveling to the coast from Zanzibar found Rebmann, blind and solitary, at Rabai (in modern Kenya) surrounded by about half a dozen converts. One consequence of the work of these two German missionaries was that the focus of

The snow-capped crest of Kilimanjaro is seen through the flower stalks of sisal plants on a Tanzanian plantation. Africa's highest peak, Kilimanjaro is an extinct volcano which rises more than 19,000 feet.

European exploration shifted for a time from western to eastern Africa. Doubtless many believed that since the secrets of the Niger had already been revealed, and fabled Timbuktu had been visited, the time had come to seek once more the sources of the Nile. They wished to see for themselves Ptolemy's "Mountains of the Moon" and the great lakes of Central Africa.

Livingstone's missionary efforts lead him into Central Africa. The vast unexplored area between the Congo and the settled area of South Africa fired the imagination of Dr. David Livingstone (1813–1873). As a boy of ten, Livingstone worked twelve hours a day in a textile factory in England. While working, he also began the study of medicine and theology. In 1840 he began his career as a medical missionary on the South African frontier. At first he worked in a mission established among the Sotho just west of the Orange Free State, and in 1844 he married the daughter of the head of the mission station. Because Livingstone had repeated disagreements with the Boers, he decided to leave the mission and to explore the interior. He and his wife established several mission stations on the southern fringes of the Kalahari Desert. In the course of this work, Livingstone mastered several African languages and demonstrated a genuine concern for the Africans, making an earnest effort to help them meet their bodily and spiritual needs. More than most Europeans of his day, Livingstone was able to identify with Africa and its people. In 1849, two wealthy game-hunters, William Oswell and Mungo Murray, invited Livingstone to act as interpreter on an expedition northward across the desert. In two months, they reached Lake Ngami in what is now Botswana, probably the first Europeans to see this region.

Livingstone carefully surveyed the surrounding area and put his observations into writing. The account of this expedition excited great interest in England. Livingstone was eager to continue northward, but was forced by news of illness in his family to return to South Africa for a year (1850). Once the family was well and supplies had been gathered, the Livingstones resumed their explorations. Dr. Livingstone had heard tales of the mighty Zambezi River and he was determined to see its rushing waters. Finding the river, he naturally wanted to ascertain the river's source and its outlet. The urge to find answers to such questions never left him.

Livingstone seeks the sources of the Zambezi. To insure the safety of his family, Livingstone sent them to England. Then he returned to his mission station only to find it destroyed by Boers who resented the influence the missionaries exerted over the Africans. Livingstone wasted little time in gathering supplies and moving once more into the unknown interior. There he lived off the country and made friends wherever he went, eating the food and learning the languages of the Africans he visited. Searching for the sources of the Zambezi, Livingstone traveled across Africa to the west coast. There Portuguese merchants, observing his gaunt condition, advised him to sail for England. But Livingstone refused, stating that his task was only half completed and that he intended to go back to the east coast. Having already covered more than two thousand miles, and despite the fact that he was tired and ill, Livingstone again plunged into the interior. In November, 1855, the missionary-explorer saw for the first time the world's greatest waterfall, which he named Victoria Falls, in honor of Britain's queen. In 1856 he finally reached the east coast. From there Livingstone sailed home to England.

Livingstone returns to Central Africa. When he returned to England in 1856, Livingstone received a hero's welcome. But two years later, he returned to his beloved Africa for another six years of exploration — this time with backing from the British government. At the beginning of 1862, Livingstone's wife on her return to Africa died of a tropical fever. With her death, the missionary-explorer resolved to remain in Africa. In 1865, he accepted the invitation of the Royal Geographical Society to return to Africa to settle "a question of intense geographical interest, . . . namely the watershed or watersheds of South [Central] Africa." The following year Livingstone was given the title of "Consul of the Independent Negro Tribes of the African Interior." Sick and frequently delirious, Livingstone sought to make his way to Ujiji (oo-*jee′*jee) in present-day Tanzania. Deserted by all except three of his servants, he lay seriously ill for six months in an African's hut. Livingstone had been in the interior for eight years, and the outside world only occasionally had heard of his whereabouts and health. Newspaper readers were eager to learn more about him.

Stanley goes to Africa to find Livingstone. In 1869 Henry M. Stanley, a 28-year-old foreign correspondent for the *New York Herald*, was summoned to Paris to confer with his editor, James Gordon Bennett, Jr.[4] Mr. Bennett quickly came to the point: "I am going

---

[4] Stanley's real name was John Rowlands. In 1857, at the age of sixteen, he had stowed away to New Orleans from his native Wales. He was befriended by a rich New Orleans merchant who became his protector, and whose name — Henry M. Stanley — the young man adopted as his own.

The Zambezi River, at this point more than a mile wide, drops 350 feet into a narrow chasm, thus creating Victoria Falls. David Livingstone, the explorer, named the falls in 1855. Rising clouds of spray, which can be seen at a distance, already had given the waterfall its African name of *Mosiloatunya*, or "the smoke that thunders."

to send you out to look for him [Livingstone]." Thus began Stanley's lifelong preoccupation with Africa.

After a 236-day trek from the East African coast, Stanley's elaborately-equipped caravan finally reached Ujiji, where Livingstone was resting. The meeting of the two men has gone down as one of the most dramatic moments in the history of exploration. Stanley later described it as follows in his book, *How I Found Livingstone:*

As I slowly approached I noticed that he looked pale and tired. He was wearing a bluish cap with faded gold band, a shirt with red sleeves and grey breeches. I could have fallen on his neck, but I didn't know how he, as a Briton, would take it. So I did what cowardice and false pride indicated as the best thing, walked slowly towards him, took off my hat, and said: "Dr. Livingstone, I presume?" "Yes," he replied with a kindly smile, and raised his cap. We shook hands warmly and I said aloud: "I thank God, Doctor, that I have been allowed to meet you." "And I am thankful to be able to welcome you here."[5]

[5] Quoted in Schiffer, *op. cit.*, p. 174.

Although at least a generation separated the two men in age, they became fast friends. Livingstone insisted to Stanley that his work in Africa was not finished, and refused to accompany him to the coast. But there was to be only a short time left for Livingstone to finish his work. In 1872 he packed his worn and patched gear and wearily began his last expedition to explore the lakes and rivers of Central Africa. In April of the following year, on the southern shore of Lake Bangweulu (bang-wee-*oo'*loo) in Zambia, he asked his assistants to build him a hut, so that he could die in it. On May 1, he was found dead kneeling in prayer beside his bed.

Livingstone is remembered as both a humanitarian and a scholar. The love and loyalty Livingstone inspired in others was remarkable. His most devoted friends, and those whom Livingstone loved most, were Africans. His closest African associates, after preparing the body, carried their dead leader to the East African coast — a journey which took nearly nine months. Livingstone's body was then returned to England for burial in Westminster Abbey. There he lies in the company of Britain's most honored dead.

Livingstone's maps and carefully documented research — brought to England by Stanley — enabled geographers to fill many gaps in their knowledge. Large regions in southern and central Africa were no longer a mystery to non-Africans because of the work done by David Livingstone — missionary, scientist, and explorer.

- **CHECK-UP**

   1. What did each of these explorers add to Europe's knowledge of Africa: Bruce, Mungo Park, Caillié, Rebmann, Livingstone?
   2. Which of these men made the greatest contribution to Africans? To interest in and knowledge about Africa? Why?

2. Renewed Search for the Sources of the Nile Leads Europeans to the Great Lakes

Burton and Speke determine to solve the riddle of the Nile's source. Two Englishmen, sometimes in co-operation and at other times competing, finally located the source of the White Nile and satisfied the mounting curiosity of Europeans on this question. Richard Francis Burton already had the reputation of being a bold adventurer when he came to East Africa in 1854. Disguised as an Arab, Burton made the pilgrimage to the Muslim holy city of Mecca, an adventure in which discovery would have brought death. With him on the Somali coast was another young Englishman, John Hanning Speke, whom Burton had met in India. Together they planned to explore the interior of Somaliland (now Somali Republic).

Speke had long dreamed of exploring Africa and secretly hoped to discover the elusive fountainhead of the Nile. When the two men set off into the interior, they were attacked by Somali warriors. Their wounds compelled the two men to return to England. After recovering, Burton and Speke began preparations for another expedition. This time the Royal Geographical Society subsidized their expedition and instructed them to clear up the mystery of the great lakes. The two explorers advanced from Bagamoyo (bah-gah-*moh*′yoh) on the coast of Tanzania, inland along the Arab slave route to Tabora (tuh-*bohr*′uh), then continued westward to seek a large lake about which they had heard so much. Disease, malnutrition, and the hostility of the inhabitants plagued the expedition. It took Speke and Burton five months to reach the land of the Nyamwezi, a relatively peaceful and united people in central Tanzania. Finally, in February, 1858,

Murchison Falls in Uganda is formed where the Nile River bursts with a roar through a steep cleft in the rocks only 18 feet wide. The first Europeans to see the falls were Sir Samuel Baker and his wife, who completed the task of tracing the White Nile to its source.

they reached Lake Tanganyika, the deepest lake in the world, never before visited by Europeans. Because he was suffering from eye trouble, Speke ironically could not gaze upon the beautiful lake before him. As he wrote in his journal: "From the summit of the eastern horn, the lovely Tanganyika Lake could be seen in all its glory by everyone but myself."

Speke names Lake Victoria. Both explorers became increasingly ill. Speke suffered from an ear infection, while Burton was a constant victim of malaria and other fevers. When they returned to Tabora to recuperate, the two adventurers were no longer friends. In July, 1858, Speke, leaving the still sick Burton behind, set out alone to find the other large lake, reported to lie several hundred miles to the north. At length he reached a lake which the Africans called Ukerewe (oo-keh-*ray'*way). Speke wrote: "I no longer felt any doubt that the lake at my feet gave birth to that interesting river, the source of which had been the subject of so much speculation. . . . [This] magnificent sheet of water I have ventured to name *Victoria* after our gracious Sovereign." But Burton, anxiously awaiting Speke's return, was not convinced that his erstwhile friend had actually located the source of the Nile.

Speke's claims are accepted in England. When Speke returned to England in May of 1859, his report that Lake Victoria was indeed the source of the Nile was accepted by the president of the Royal Geographical Society. He, therefore, was commissioned by the Society to learn more about the Nile's source. Burton's contributions, on the other hand, were barely recognized. When he challenged his former friend's claim to have found the source of the Nile, Burton was ridiculed and accused of jealousy. Thus Speke, the junior partner, received most of the glory. In 1860 Speke and his new companion, James Grant, set out for Africa. On this expedition Speke visited the powerful African kingdoms located along the shores of Lake Victoria, and his reports describing them did much to stimulate missionary interest. Once again Speke used Tabora in Tanzania as a base. From there he moved northward along the Uganda side of Lake Victoria until he arrived in Buganda, the most powerful of the lake kingdoms. After tarrying in this pleasant land, he followed the shore of Lake Victoria, seeking the outlet which was the actual source of the Nile. On July 28 Speke achieved his goal. "I saw that old father Nile without any doubt rises in the Victoria N'yanza, and as I had foretold, that lake is the great source of the holy river which cradled the first expounder [Moses] of our religious belief."

Speke returned to England again a hero. Burton bitterly challenged Speke's claims, and a public meeting was arranged to permit the two former friends to present their respective positions. This confrontation never took place, however, for Speke, who had gone hunting earlier that day, fell in climbing over a wall and accidentally shot himself.

The Bakers reach Lake Albert. After sighting Lake Victoria, Speke had hoped to push on to the northwest, where still another large lake stretched along the Congo's northeastern border. Passing through Uganda, Speke met Sir Samuel Baker and his wife, whose expedition had reached Uganda by way of the Nile route. The Bakers obtained maps and other useful information from Speke. After many hardships and a particularly difficult period at the court of King Kamrasi (kahm-*rah′*see) of Bunyoro, the Bakers finally reached their goal in March, 1864. Exclaimed Baker: "England has won the sources of the Nile!" He decided that the stream flowing northward from the northern end of the large lake was the White Nile. Baker named the lake after Queen Victoria's late husband, Albert. (The river which emerges from Lake Victoria is known as the Victoria Nile. It flows into Lake Albert, and when it emerges is known as the White Nile.)

For future European mapmakers, Africa was rapidly being filled in with lakes, rivers, mountains, and the location of important kingdoms. The European explorers assigned European, rather than African, names to many of the locations on their maps. Taking credit for "discovering" Africa's interior lakes, rivers, and mountains, they seemed to overlook the fact that these landmarks had been known for centuries to Africans and had received distinctive African names long before the coming of the white man.

Stanley crosses Africa from east to west and explores the Congo. When Stanley received the news of Livingstone's death in April, 1874, he had just completed an assignment to cover the British campaign against the Ashanti in West Africa (in present-day Ghana). He hastened to London to act as one of the pallbearers. At this point the thought struck him that, if he returned to Central Africa on his own, he might complete Livingstone's work of exploration. At the same time, he would reap glory for himself and, he hoped, put an end to the view held by some — that his earlier mission to find Livingstone had been prompted by selfish motives.

In November, 1874, the former newspaper reporter left Bagamoyo, Tanzania. It took him nearly three and a half months to reach Lake

Victoria, where he visited Mutesa, king of the powerful Baganda, and took time to explore the region around Lakes Victoria and Tanganyika. He then reached the decision to go to the Lualaba River and to follow it to the source of the Congo — a mighty stream which had interested Livingstone to the day of his death. Stanley's porters had brought in boats which were assembled, and canoes were purchased from the local inhabitants. The expedition made slow progress down the Lualaba. Each time the expedition was halted by rapids, supplies and boats had to be carried until the latter could again be launched. The expedition suffered many casualties from poison arrows fired by startled Africans. But the rifle each time proved superior to the bow. After nearly a month on the river, Stanley reached the immense rapids today known as Stanley Falls. The river still seemed to run almost due north, but finally it swung westward toward the Atlantic.

A misunderstanding leads to bloodshed. Downstream from Stanley Falls, more than fifty huge canoes, each carrying eighty oarsmen and a detachment of black warriors, bore down on the expedition. When Stanley's men began to panic, he ordered them to fire. Taken by surprise, the Africans fled to the shore. Stanley, angered, pursued them. "My blood boiled and a savage hatred overwhelmed me. . . . I reduced their ivory temple to ruins and in breathless haste set fire to their huts; then I sank their canoes in midstream."[6]

Some years later a French priest, in talking to the king who had led this supposed attack on Stanley's expedition, discovered that the people in fact were rushing out to *welcome* the strange white man! One can only imagine their surprise and bitterness when they were fired upon and their buildings destroyed. The following is King Mojimba's version of the massacre:

> But as we drew near his canoes there were loud reports, bang! bang! and firestaves spat bits of iron at us. We were paralyzed with fright; . . . [these] were the work of evil spirits! . . . Several of my men plunged into the water, . . . some screamed dreadfully, others were silent — they were dead, and blood flowed from little holes in their bodies. "War — that is war!" I yelled. "Go back!" . . . That [Stanley] was no brother. That was the worst enemy our country had ever seen. . . . When we returned that evening our eyes beheld fearful things: our brothers, dead, dying, bleeding, our village plundered and burned, and the water full of dead bodies.[7]

[6] Stanley, as quoted in Schiffer, *op. cit.*, pp. 188–189.
[7] Schiffer, *op. cit.*, p. 197.

In Stanley's time, Africa was explored by big, well-armed expeditions, and the European acquired a new image in African eyes. A Yoruba sculptor carved this typical figure of a European on horseback, his rifle at the ready. Note his long nose, mustache, and sun helmet, the front brim of which has broken off this old carving.

More dangers awaited Stanley's expedition when it reached the rapids below Stanley Pool, a widening of the lower Congo. It took his men 131 days to make this difficult portage. Food became increasingly scarce, for this region had been devastated by the slave raids. In August, 1877, a thousand days out of Zanzibar, Stanley dispatched a message toward the coast, addressed to "Any Gentleman who speaks English" at Boma (a town near the river's mouth):

> I have arrived at this place from Zanzibar with 115 souls; men, women, and children. We are now in a state of imminent starvation. We can buy nothing from the natives, for they laugh at our . . . cloth, beads, and wires. . . .[8]

His request for supplies fortunately arrived just in time to save the group from starvation. Stanley survived to recount his adventures and win the acclaim he sought as the first European to trace the Congo's course.

Exploration paves the way for conquest and colonialism. Except for some small and inaccessible pockets, the interior of Africa was known to Europeans by about 1880. It remained for missionaries to follow the trails blazed by the explorers. And soon would come armed forces to divide the continent among the European powers.

[8] Stanley, as quoted in Lamar Middleton, *The Rape of Africa* (New York: Harrison Smith & Robert Haas, 1936), p. 14.

Stanley, the last of the great explorers, links the age of exploration with that of partition. He hoped that the widely-read account of his explorations — especially that of his Congo expedition — would arouse British interest in the Congo. But in this he was disappointed. Failing to get British backing, he then turned to King Leopold of Belgium, who was eager to establish an overseas empire. The Belgian king recruited Stanley to help him lay claim to the Congo. Stanley, therefore, returned to Africa in the service of King Leopold. He was largely responsible for bringing the Belgian Congo, a territory 75 times the size of Belgium and rich in mineral resources, under Leopold's control.

● CHECK-UP

1. What did each of these explorers add to Europe's knowledge of the great lakes region: Burton, Speke, Baker, Stanley?

2. In what sense did European explorers make discoveries in Africa?

3. What dangers, real and imaginary, were encountered by Stanley?

4. How did the age of exploration lead to the age of partition?

3. Missionaries Become Involved in the Scramble for Africa

The evils of the slave trade stimulate missionary interest in Africa. The English Protestant churches, along with Christian churches in other European countries, wished to follow up the abolition of slavery with a massive missionary endeavor. Their purpose was not only to spread the Christian gospel, but to help stamp out Arab slave-raiding carried on from the island of Zanzibar. Since Zanzibar had long been a leading slave market, the early Christian mission stations just inland from the East African coast became havens for runaway slaves. The missionaries, often at great risk to themselves, harbored these fugitives and refused to surrender them to their Arab owners. Friction between English missionaries and Arab slave-dealers, subjects of the sultan of Zanzibar, was one factor that eventually led the British government to establish control over Zanzibar.

Missionaries endure hardships and suffering. The first wave of missionaries who came to Africa had been impelled by an intensity of religious faith which is hard for us today to comprehend. This faith led whole families to leave their European homes to move into the interior of Africa. Since the death rate among Africans was staggering, it is not surprising that missionaries, unaccustomed to life in the tropics, perished in large numbers. Of the Baptist missionaries in the

Belgian Congo during the decade 1878 to 1888, for example, approximately half died.

Missionaries interpreted the world to Africa and Africa to the world. Although they described the rivers, mountains, and lakes of Africa, most explorers did not really come to know the peoples of Africa. But the missionary who came to stay had to learn the languages of the people among whom he and his family would work and live. The missionaries were thus in a position to picture African culture and society to Europeans. They became the interpreters of Africa to the world. A steady stream of missionary reports, journals, memoirs, and descriptive literature was published and received widespread circulation. In general, the Western world accepted this missionary interpretation of Africa as true. Actually, it was shot through with bias, factual errors, and value judgments that disapproved of African ways. Without doubt, many widely held stereotypes about Africans and African life originated in this literature. Views of a primitive and even "savage" African population fed the vanity of Europeans who already cherished deep-seated convictions of their own "superiority." Europeans were eager to read materials which they interpreted as proving their own excellence.

Many Africans learned to read and write at missionary schools. To tell their parishioners the story of Jesus and the church which he founded, and to convert them to its tenets, the missionaries had to provide instruction in reading and writing. Thus, from the very outset, general education as well as religious training became a primary goal of missionary activity. A few of the early mission schools became in time substantial institutions of higher learning. The Fourah Bay College, established in 1827 by the Christian Missionary Society in Sierra Leone, is an example. Similar institutions in Ghana, Nigeria, and Uganda provided Africa with a whole generation of national leaders educated in the Western tradition.

Most African languages that have been reduced to writing owe their written form to the dedicated work of missionaries. Once there was a written language, Christian religious stories and hymns could be translated into the African vernacular. In the course of their work, missionaries also learned a great deal from the Africans. Once they were able to speak to the people and understand their history and culture, they discovered how inaccurate had been many earlier descriptions of Africans. Stanley and most other explorers had simply called them "savages." But individual missionaries wrote detailed descrip-

An old photo shows a French mission school. Here the teacher is an African convert and the pupil at the blackboard is learning to read his own language. Note the teacher's alarm clock and the bell on the floor.

tions of what they saw and heard, and carefully recorded the customs and histories of Africa's many peoples.

Rivalry between Protestants, Catholics, and Muslims becomes a source of conflict in East Africa. After Stanley had visited the court of King Mutesa of Buganda, he sent back to England the following widely read newspaper dispatch:

> Until I arrived at Mutesa's court the King delighted in the idea that he was a follower of Islam; but by one conversation I flatter myself that I have trampled the newly-raised religious fabric to the ground, and if it were only followed by the arrival of a Christian mission here, the conversion of Mutesa and his court to Christianity would, I think, be complete.[9]

This plea for missionaries fell on eager ears. But Stanley's description of the type of missionary needed was not heeded. Almost in the words spoken by Livingstone many years before, Stanley warned:

[9] *The Daily Telegraph* (London: November 15, 1875)

A Protestant church in Uganda is built in Western style, but its members are called to worship by the sound of drums from the tree-house at right. Drum towers are one example of a new use of African music in services.

> . . . [What] is wanted . . . is the practical Christian who can teach people how to become Christians, cure their diseases, construct dwellings, understand . . . agriculture, and turn his hand to anything. . . . He must be tied to no church or sect. . . .[10]

Mutesa welcomed the first Christian missionaries, but he was surprised that they were not prepared to enter into profitable trade, as were Muslims. Because of this unusual behavior, the king suspected the missionaries of being spies. No sooner had the English Protestant missionaries settled in his kingdom than the Catholic French made their appearance. Although both groups professed to be Christian, Mutesa observed that there were sharp differences between them. At the same time, the Muslims were troubled by this intrusion of Christians. It seemed to the Muslims that this was a plot to stamp out Arab and Islamic influence in East Africa. If allowed to continue,

[10] *Ibid.*

European interference would eventually deny Arabs their profitable income from the slave trade.

A new king turns against the missionaries. When the old king died in 1884, Mwanga (muh-*wahn'* guh), his eighteen-year-old son, proved less patient with the missionaries than his father had been. Soon after his accession to the throne, Mwanga executed two young African men who had been converted to Christianity. In 1885, when the Anglican Bishop Hannington was traveling to Uganda to visit his missionaries, he approached Uganda over the route traditionally taken by invaders. The suspicious Mwanga ordered the bishop killed, and later burned many young converts at the stake.

A period of violence followed, during which the king was deposed and the Christians driven from the kingdom. When the Christians returned, Protestants competed with Catholics, and both fought the Muslims. By 1890, Christians were in control. The kingdom's major provinces were divided equally between Protestant and Catholic chiefs. The same year, and partly as a consequence of the religious wars, Great Britain and Germany signed a treaty under which Uganda came within the British sphere of influence and Tanganyika (present-day Tanzania) under that of the Germans.

Missionaries provide European powers with a pretext for intervention. The establishment of a missionary outpost in the African interior might cause a European government to dispatch troops to insure the safety of the missionaries. At times, the presence of mission stations provided an excuse for direct political or military intervention in the affairs of an African kingdom. Commercial companies received charters from their home governments that permitted them not only to carry on trade but directly or indirectly to govern Africans in large areas. Individual missionaries often opposed the harsh policies of the companies, but their interests could coincide. For example, the missionaries, eager to raise the standard of living, encouraged Africans to cultivate such crops as coffee which could be sold for cash. Cash-crop farming, in turn, provided money which the Africans could spend to buy the manufactured goods sold by the charter companies, and to pay the taxes levied by the colonial governments.

Missionaries become the pioneers of empire. In a remarkably short time, church missions in Africa had grown from Livingstone's solitary witness to what was becoming an international religious crusade. In 1910, when the first worldwide missionary conference was held in Edinburgh, African missions were well represented. Of the "sixty-five

Pope Paul VI and Cardinal Rugambwa of Tanzania (*right*) meet the actors after a restaging of the martyrdom of young Christian converts in Uganda 85 years ago. The "villains" in the drama carry spears with rubber blades. The Pope came to Uganda to honor the martyrs, who have been named saints by the Roman Catholic church.

societies and boards at work on the [African] continent, . . . twenty-two were [domiciled] in Great Britain, twenty-one in the United States and Canada, nineteen on the continent of Europe, . . . and three . . . in South Africa."[11] At the turn of the nineteenth century, more than 4000 Protestant missionaries were working in Africa. The Catholic church reported a total of 6000 workers, including 1500 priests.

● CHECK-UP

1. What motives stimulated missionary activity in Africa? What problems did missionaries have to overcome? What services did they render? What disservice?

2. Why did missionary activity at times lead to religious rivalry? To conflict? To intervention by a European power? To exploration?

[11] C. P. Groves, *The Planting of Christianity in Africa: Vol. 3, 1878–1914* (London: Butterworth Press, 1955), pp. 282–285.

4. Rivalry Develops Over Control of Africa's Resources

During the 1870's and 1880's, France, Belgium, and Britain were feverishly expanding their holdings in Africa. It was inevitable that their interests would clash, although none of the European powers involved wished to risk a general war over Africa. Operating from bases in Senegal, the French were extending their claims into the region of the upper Niger. At the same time, Britain was extending West African coastal stations far into the interior. There was a real danger that these probings into the interior, when added to competition for trade, might lead to war. Rules for the division of the booty were needed lest rival powers fall to fighting among themselves.

International conferences attempt to regularize European interests in Africa. King Leopold of Belgium, whose great ambition was to acquire an African empire, took the initiative in calling the first major European conference on Africa. It was to be held at Brussels in September, 1876. Quite clearly the purpose of the conference was to gain recognition for Leopold's claim to the Congo, and in this he was largely successful. But by 1885 rivalry in Africa again threatened the peace of Europe. In that year Germany took the initiative and invited the major powers to a conference in Berlin. (The United States was represented at this conference by Stanley and another American, both of them in the employ of the Belgian king.)

✶ This assembly of European statesmen showed little concern for the peoples of Africa; indeed, it acted almost as if that continent were uninhabited. Called to deliberate about the Congo Basin and the conflicting interests of European countries in that part of the continent, the Berlin Conference merely regularized the scramble. Most of Leopold's claims were recognized, but it was agreed that all nations would have the privilege of trading in the watershed of the Congo. Similar agreements were reached with respect to the Nile and the Zambezi. The traffic in gunpowder and alcohol was deemed too profitable to be the monopoly of any one nation. Agreements were also reached with respect to procedures for making land claims on the coast and in the interior. As an afterthought, the conferees added to the 60,000-word text of the conference proceedings about 200 words expressing concern for the welfare of African peoples.

France acquires the largest African empire. The French reaction to Stanley's reports was that France must acquire part of the Congo. De Brazza, a French explorer, had led an expedition which reached

MALAGASY QUEEN. Ranavalona III, the last queen of independent Madagascar, was a Christian. She posed for her portrait with her royal scepter lying on a huge Bible. After the French conquered her island in 1896, Ranavalona was sent into exile.

The queen's palace crowned a ridge in Tananarive, capital of Madagascar. Missionaries built a memorial church (*center*) on the cliff where a pagan ancestor of the queen had hurled Christian converts to their death.

Stanley Pool before Stanley made his appearance. De Brazza also urged France to move into the region of the Niger.

Earlier, France had staked a claim to vast areas across the Mediterranean Sea in North Africa. After a long war, Algeria was conquered in 1847. In 1881 Tunisia became a French protectorate, much to the annoyance of Italy which also desired this North African territory. Not until the first decade of the twentieth century did Morocco come under French rule — with a small zone in the north later "sublet" to Spain. In 1889, the Ivory Coast was declared a French protectorate. And in 1894, after a series of brutal wars, the African kingdom of Dahomey was annexed. At this time, the French had greater influence in the interior of West Africa than did Great Britain. On more than one occasion, France and Britain were near war. In Nigeria the British managed to move into the interior, but only after a dangerous military confrontation with France in the Niger region.

France and Britain become rivals for control of Africa. France sought an empire which would stretch across Africa at its widest point from Dakar in Senegal to the Red Sea. The British also had a dream of an empire running the length of Africa from Cape Town to Cairo. It was in the heart of Africa that the conflicting aspirations of Great Britain and France nearly led to war. In 1898 Colonel Marchand, after an amazing march across the desert, reached the Nile, where he soon found himself face to face with Britain's General Kitchener. Kitchener ordered Marchand to withdraw, and after a period of brinkmanship, France backed down. The "Cape-to-Cairo" dream was to become a reality. France had to be content with a huge West African empire including nearly a quarter of the entire continent. This vast region, however, had a population of perhaps 25 million, a smaller population than British-controlled Nigeria. Approximately one-third of the French West African empire was desert.

Britain's empire was scattered throughout the continent. It has been said that Britain acquired her African empire in a fit of absent-mindedness. A look at the map seems to support this point of view. In West Africa, British holdings, except for Nigeria, were but islands in a French sea. Except for way stations along the West African coast, established in the days when sailing ships had to go around the Cape to India, Britain's first colonial venture was in the extreme south. During the Napoleonic Wars, the British conquered Cape Town (1806), and eight years later formally gained possession of the Cape Colony in the Treaty of Paris. From these beginnings, Britain's

African empire grew to become first in population and second in size.

The Boers leave Cape Colony. The Boers, descendants of the Dutch settlers of South Africa, did not find the new British rule to their liking. There was an influx of English settlers, English was made the official language, and slavery was abolished — developments which the Boers resisted. To escape British rule, the Boers moved out in the Great Trek (1835–39), and established the Republic of Natal (nah-*tahl'*) in the interior. Later they also settled along the Orange River and in the Transvaal. But in 1843, Britain declared Natal a British colony and five years later annexed the Boer Orange River settlements. However, the independence of the Boers in Transvaal was recognized (1852), and two years later the British also withdrew from the territory north of the Orange River. This was then proclaimed the Orange Free State by the Boers. In 1856 the Boers of Transvaal organized the South African Republic, and the two Boer states (Orange Free State and South African Republic) recognized each other's independence.

The discovery of diamonds and gold creates problems for the Boers. The independence freely granted the Boers came to an abrupt end in 1877 when the British annexed the South African Republic. Ten years earlier diamonds had been discovered in lands controlled by the Orange Free State. News of the strike brought in thousands of adventurers, most of them British. The governor of Cape Colony simply annexed the diamond region, although it had been under the authority of the Orange Free State since 1854. The Orange Free State vigorously protested the British action. Despite Boer protests, the remaining Boer lands were annexed six years later (1877). In 1880 the Transvaal Boers, under the leadership of Paul Kruger, rose in revolt and declared their independence. When the Boers defeated British forces sent against them, the British government was ready to negotiate. Under the Treaty of Pretoria (1881), the South African Republic was granted independence, but Britain was to control the Republic's relations with foreign countries.

In 1886, incredibly rich gold fields were discovered in the southern Transvaal. Cecil Rhodes, who later became governor of the Cape Colony, and his associates soon gained financial control of the gold mining industry. A few years later, the British government granted a charter to the British South Africa Company headed by Rhodes. It was given almost unlimited rights and powers in the region north of the Transvaal.

PLANTATIONS. Colonial rule introduced the growing of cash crops for export. *Above, left:* Nigerians gather coffee beans on an African-owned plantation. In East Africa, Africans usually worked on plantations owned by European settlers. *Above, right:* A Tanzanian sets out sisal plants, while (*below*) women pick tea in Malawi.

Increasing tensions lead to the South African War. The fact that "outlanders" (non-Boers) enjoyed no political rights in the South African Republic aroused much resentment. Authorities in the Cape Colony, determined to bring the Boer states under British control, encouraged a conspiracy of outlanders to be reinforced by a small body of South Africa Company "volunteers" led by Dr. Leander Starr Jameson — Cecil Rhodes's right-hand man (1895). When Jameson's force was defeated and captured, Kaiser Wilhelm of Germany sent a telegram of congratulations to Boer President Kruger. This action aroused a storm of indignation in Great Britain, and caused the British to press the Boer government to grant the vote to foreigners who had lived in the Transvaal for five years. Kruger, in turn, demanded that Britain surrender its control over the Republic's foreign relations.

Because neither side was willing to yield, war broke out in 1899 and continued for three years. Before the 75,000 Boers were defeated, Britain had to send in more than a quarter of a million troops. When the Boers finally surrendered, the independent Boer states became the British crown colonies of Orange River and Transvaal. In 1910, they became members of the Union of South Africa, a white self-governing dominion under the British crown.

Britain extends its control over Central and East Africa. Cecil Rhodes, then director of the British South Africa Company, believed that the area north of the Transvaal might also be rich in gold and diamonds. With the aid of a private army, Rhodes defeated the local African chieftains and gained control over the vast region which bears his name. When no valuable minerals had been discovered in Southern Rhodesia (now the Republic of Rhodesia), a land with fertile soil and a good climate, Rhodes encouraged the immigration of European farmers. As a consequence of this policy, Southern Rhodesia became a major area of white settlement. Today it is one of the few areas where a white minority continues to rule the African majority. In 1891, the British extended their control over what is now Zambia, calling it Northern Rhodesia.

In 1890, meanwhile, Great Britain had reached an agreement that removed a source of friction arising from Germany's intrusion into East Africa. In that year, a treaty was signed whereby Great Britain recognized Germany's pre-eminence in Tanganyika (Tanzania), as well as France's rights in Madagascar. In return, Germany agreed to

Britain's protectorate over Zanzibar and gave up German claims to Uganda and Kenya. Now Great Britain was free to move inland in East Africa without fear of conflict with Germany. In 1890, Sir Frederick (later Lord) Lugard helped to lead a British force into Uganda. After some hesitation, the British government decided in 1894 to extend its rule up to the great lakes. Actually the operations in this part of Africa had been carried on by the British East African Company. But since it had lost money over the years, the Company was happy to turn over its problems and responsibilities in the region to Her Majesty's Government. Kenya was proclaimed a British protectorate in 1895. Seven years later, the Uganda Railway, running from Mombasa on the east coast to Lake Victoria, was completed. This railroad passed through some of the best farming country in the world. How better to help pay for this expensive railroad than to encourage the English settlers to seek their fortune in the "White Highlands"? Enormous tracts of land were reserved for Europeans, and within ten years Kenya was well on its way to becoming a major area of white settlement and, in consequence, a region of tension and conflict between the races.

The British become more deeply involved in Egypt and Sudan. The Suez Canal, which was opened to international commerce in 1869, had been built on Egyptian territory with a combination of African, French, and British labor and capital. In 1875, however, Great Britain became the principal shareholder in the Canal. Because of Egypt's increasing financial instability, Britain and France, acting on behalf of European creditors, jointly intervened in the affairs of the Egyptian government and established a "condominium," or joint rule, over it. Doubtless the controls imposed on the Egyptian government and the presence of so many foreigners in Cairo contributed to the growing nationalist movement of the 1880's and the uprising of Egyptian officers. Britain's response to violence was to bombard Alexandria and to occupy Cairo (1882). From a legalistic viewpoint, Egypt was Turkish territory. It was governed by the khedive (keh-*deev'*), who owed allegiance to the Turkish sultan. But real power was in the hands of the British representative. When war broke out between Britain and Turkey (1915), Egypt became a British "protectorate."

Because of its association with the khedive of Egypt, Great Britain also became involved in the Egyptian territories in Sudan. British officers commanded the Egyptian army which was trying to hold this

In the Sudan, Beja nomads fought for the mahdi against the British. Their camel cavalry also fought dismounted, each man seizing his sword and round leather shield for a bold rush into the British lines.

immense region for Egypt. In 1883 these British-led forces were attacked by Mahdi (*mah'*dee)[12] Mohammed Ahmed (*ah'*med) of Dongola (*dahn'* goh-lah), leader of a radical and militant Muslim sect. In a bloody battle only 300 of Britain's 8000 men managed to escape. Reluctantly, Great Britain told the Egyptian government to evacuate Sudan. General Charles ("Chinese") Gordon was sent to Sudan to oversee the withdrawal of the Egyptian garrisons and to try to reach an agreement with the mahdi. But the mahdi rejected Gordon's proposals and laid siege to Khartoum. Early in 1885 the city was captured; Gordon and the garrison were massacred. For more than a decade, Sudan was left to the rule of the mahdi's followers. But a growing realization of the region's importance to assure Egypt's water supply — as well as the interest of France and others in Sudan — moved the British to action. In 1896, British General Herbert Kitchener, leading an Anglo-Egyptian army, began the reconquest of Sudan. He proceeded slowly, building a railroad along the Nile as he advanced. When he reached Fashoda (fuh-*shoh'*duh) — now Kodok (*koh'*dahk) — Kitchener found the town occupied by a

[12] **mahdi:** In the religion of Islam, the *mahdi* (or "rightly-guided one") was the expected ruler who was destined to bring about the final victory of Islam by divine intervention, after which the reign of righteousness would be established throughout the world. Mohammed Ahmed was one of several men who had claimed this title in the course of Islamic history.

French force. When the French commander refused to evacuate the town unless ordered to do so by his government, an international crisis ensued. Not prepared to fight Britain alone, France had no choice but to withdraw.

Britain extends its holdings on the west coast. British interests in West Africa date back to the early nineteenth century. The British — together with the Portuguese, Spanish, French, Dutch, Danes, and Swedes — had earlier maintained forts or posts along the coast where they engaged in the slave trade and the trade in gold, ivory, and palm oil. When the slave trade was abolished, many of these stations fell into disuse.

1. *Gambia and Sierra Leone.* Britain's oldest colony in Africa, Gambia, was a tiny enclave surrounded by French-held territories. In 1807, it was put under the government of Sierra Leone, but was separated and made a crown colony in 1843.

Sierra Leone, for a time, had been used by the Portuguese as a base for the slave trade but was taken over by Great Britain and made a crown colony in 1808. In the 1780's Sierra Leone became a haven for slaves from the United States who had fought for Britain during the American Revolutionary War and had been promised freedom. Freetown, the capital of Sierra Leone, was established by the British in 1788 on land purchased from a Temne (*tem'*nay) chief. It has an excellent harbor, and was a base used by British warships seeking to stamp out the slave trade. When a slave ship was captured, its slaves were brought to Freetown and set free. Gradually Britain's control in this area was extended inland.

2. *The Gold Coast.* The Gold Coast (Ghana) had a colonial history much like that of Sierra Leone. From the fifteenth century on, its coast had been visited by Portuguese, Dutch, British, and Danish seamen engaged in the slave trade. A number of Ashanti rulers, located a considerable distance inland, had co-operated in this trade in order to make money. Early in the nineteenth century the powerful Ashanti Federation moved southward and attacked the coastal region. After a number of unsuccessful attempts to defeat the Ashanti, the British would have pulled out but for the merchants and traders who urged the British government to continue the war and remain in the Gold Coast. The British government yielded to their pressures, but it was not until 1896 that British troops finally defeated the Ashanti and occupied their capital of Kumasi (koo-*mah'*sih). British governors then rubbed salt on Ashanti wounds by seizing the famous Golden Stool,

Kumasi, capital of the Ashanti kingdom, was burned in 1874 by British troops. They had marched inland, not to occupy the country, but to halt Ashanti raids on British trading posts along the Gold Coast.

or throne, symbol of the Ashanti nation. War broke out anew and the British had to rush in reinforcements to avert yet another defeat by the Ashanti army.

3. *Nigeria.* Britain's most populous and important colony in Africa was Nigeria, now one of independent Africa's largest countries. As late as 1870, Britain held only the port city of Lagos (*lah'*gus) on the Nigerian coast. Companies interested in developing palm nut agriculture were largely responsible for the penetration of the interior. The Royal Niger Company, like similar German and French companies, had secured a charter from the British government authorizing it to sign treaties with local African rulers. Such agreements were usually accompanied by a gift of money, gin, cloth, or rifles. France at first competed with Britain for control of this immense area, but in 1890 the two powers signed a treaty giving Britain the lion's share of the lower Niger region. In 1899, the British government took over Nigeria from the Royal Niger Company and on January 1, 1900, declared it a British protectorate. Between 1900 and 1906, the High

FIGHTING LADIES. European travelers who visited King Gezo of Dahomey (*right*) were surprised to find him guarded by several thousand women armed with muskets. An illustration in an English book published in 1851 showed one of his woman soldiers wearing a neat uniform and holding the head of a defeated enemy (*below, left*). By the 1860's when Richard Burton visited Dahomey, the women's army corps had suffered several defeats in the incessant warfare with other kingdoms along the Slave Coast. An illustration in Burton's book (*below, right*) showed one of the surviving veterans.

Commissioner, Sir Frederick Lugard, subdued the Fulani rulers and their Hausa subjects. After that, British control in Nigeria was complete.

Germany's African empire is short-lived. Even before Germany had carved out a slice of East Africa (see page 224), a German mer- chant had started to sign treaties with African chiefs along the West African coast. Once German Chancellor Otto von Bismarck gave official approval to this tiny settlement, it grew rapidly into what came to be known as German South-West Africa. The familiar pat- tern was followed: treaties were signed with chiefs in the interior in exchange for guns, whiskey, and cloth, and gradually the boundaries of the German colony were extended. German South-West Africa, though large in area, was sparsely settled, and so dry that only cattle ranches promised to be successful. The militant Hereros (huh-*ray'*- rohs) people rebelled against German rule between 1904 and 1908, and only after several bloody campaigns, involving some 20,000 Ger- man troops, was the insurrection put down. General von Trotha (fun *troh'*tuh) issued his notorious Extermination Order, calling for the killing of every Herero man, woman, and child. By the end of the war, the Herero population had been reduced from over 80,000 pros- perous cattle-herders to 15,000 starving fugitives. But the Germans reaped some financial satisfaction from their conquest when rich dia- mond deposits were found in 1908. The colony then became more nearly self-sufficient and attracted a sizable number of German settlers.

Elsewhere in Africa the Germans were also busy. They were aided and abetted by a German government that was eager to divert the attention of England and France from Europe to Africa. In the 1880's, Germany acquired control over extensive lands in what came to be known as Togo and Cameroon. Because the British and French had claimed most of the coast, these German colonies had little frontage on the ocean. But this narrow foothold became a gradually widening wedge inland. The Germans were heavy-handed in ruling their African wards. There were frequent rebellions in nearly all German-held colonies, and memories of German oppression lingered on for years afterwards in these areas. In 1905, for example, the Maji Maji rebellion broke out among African laborers drafted to work on a German cotton plantation near the southeastern coast of Tanganyika (modern Tanzania). The movement quickly spread, and many missionary stations were attacked and burned. In suppressing the rebellion, "villages and crops were ruthlessly destroyed, cattle were carried off, and the German Askaris [African mercenary soldiers] were granted absolute license to rob, kill, or enslave the inhabitants. Famine [broke out] . . . and the numbers who died as a result of it and in actual warfare are said to have reached the figure of 120,000."[13]

Italy also seeks to acquire colonies in Africa. In Italy, as elsewhere in Europe, national pride dictated many decisions. Patriotic Italians, clamoring for a colonial empire in Africa, had hopes of getting Tunisia. These were dashed by French occupation of that country. Italy's opportunity came when Great Britain advised Egypt to withdraw from Sudan. Assab (*ass'*sub), a Red Sea port acquired by an Italian shipping company, was taken over by the Italian government in 1882. It became a base for Italian colonization and the nucleus of the Italian colony of Eritrea. In 1889 Italy seized a large part of Somaliland, then under the sultan of Zanzibar. From these footholds on the coast, Italy had high hopes that through negotiation and a show of force more territory could be acquired. But unfortunately for Italy, inland from Eritrea was Ethiopia, a country able to defend itself. Blocked to the north and south by the British and French, the Italians decided to move farther into Somaliland.. But here, too, expansion into the interior was blocked by Ethiopia. It was evident that if Italy was to create an empire in Africa, Ethiopia, Africa's oldest kingdom, would have to give way.

France, ever eager to check Italy, secretly began to help Emperor Menelek to prepare his country for an invasion. It was reported that the French supplied Ethiopia with some 30,000 rifles. Over the centuries Ethiopia had acquired experience in defensive warfare, fighting off Arab attacks from Somalia and Eritrea. When Italy invaded Ethiopia in 1895, her troops met determined resistance and suffered a crushing defeat at Adowa (*ah'*doo-ah) early the following year. Emperor Menelek's army of 90,000 men, armed with rifles and spears, routed the Italian forces, killing some 6000 and taking 2000 prisoners. The Italian prime minister resigned, and his successor agreed to a peace treaty, signed in Addis Ababa, the Ethiopian capital, which acknowledged the complete independence of the ancient kingdom. The fact that Africans had won a great victory over a European army stunned Europe.

Italy's defeat in Ethiopia did not end its designs for expansion in Africa, however. In 1911 an Italian army occupied the Libyan coast. Turkey, the nominal overlord of Libya, was not able to stop the Italian

[13] Moffett, *op. cit.,* p. 76.

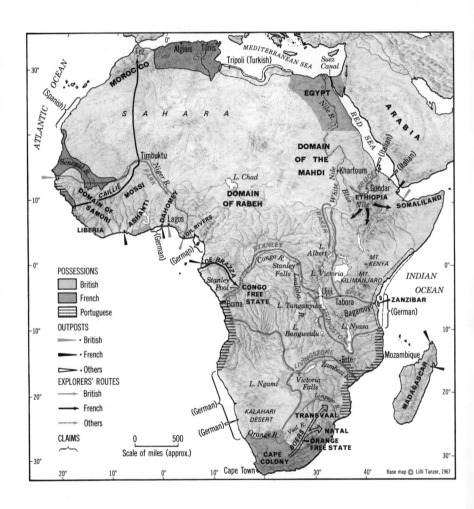

POSSESSIONS
- British
- French
- Portuguese

OUTPOSTS
- British
- French
- Others

EXPLORERS' ROUTES
- British
- French
- Others

CLAIMS

0   500
Scale of miles (approx.)

Base map © Lilli Tanzer, 1967

COLONIAL FOOTHOLDS — 1885. Europeans had been in contact with Africa for 400 years, but they had occupied only the edges of the continent. Most of their holdings in tropical Africa were isolated outposts, left over from slave-trading days. When the explorers of the 1800's left the coast, they plunged into an interior that still was African and unknown. By 1885, however, Britain, France, and Portugal were using their coastal outposts as bases for empire-building, while Italy and Germany were laying claim to vast stretches of unoccupied coastline.

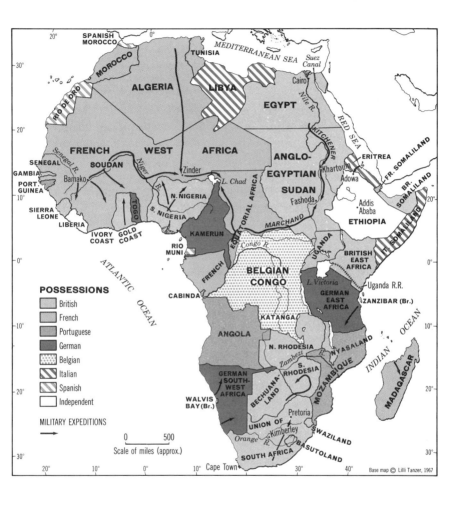

COLONIAL EMPIRES — 1914. On the eve of World War I, Africa had become a patchwork of European colonies. Only two African countries, Ethiopia and Liberia, remained independent. Rival European powers had rushed to consolidate their claims, often based on a trading post or the route of a single explorer (see routes shown on facing page 232). The Europeans who pushed inland met strong African resistance. The arrows on this may show the direction of major campaigns, but guerrilla warfare continued in many areas for years, and local revolts were frequent.

aggression, but the Arabs of the Libyan interior fiercely resisted Italy for decades. By the 1920's Italy had gained control of Eritrea, Italian Somaliland, and Libya, and in 1935 was ready to make another stab at Ethiopia.

Belgium ruthlessly exploits the Congolese. Under the guise of ending the slave trade and bringing civilization to the Congo, King Leopold of Belgium established himself as the leader of an "international association" to further exploration and settlement in the region. Stanley was employed to continue his explorations and was provided with a number of blank treaty forms. In the name of Leopold, Stanley concluded more than 500 treaties with unsuspecting African chieftains and established trading posts and settlements.

In the Berlin Act of 1885, King Leopold and his "international association" had gained recognition from the European powers as administrators of the "Congo Free State." Leopold ruthlessly exploited this vast land. The wild rubber trees in the forest had to be tapped to provide latex (liquid rubber), human labor was needed to do this work and to transport the latex, as well as ivory and other valuable products, to the coast. This was accomplished by means of a "labor tax" on all Congolese. In practice, this meant that each Congolese chief had to turn over to Belgian supervisors as many workers as the latter demanded. Leopold simply chartered companies, giving each control over the peoples in a given area. Rumors of the excesses committed by Leopold's private army and by the chartered companies soon found their way to a shocked world. Ostensibly Leopold had been authorized to bring the benefits of civilization to the people of the Congo. In reality he had amassed an enormous private fortune at an estimated cost to the Congo of nearly 100,000 lives a year.

● CHECK-UP

1. Why were international conferences held to reconcile conflicting claims to African territory? What agreements were reached? What areas were claimed by France? Britain? Why did the goals of the two countries conflict?

2. Why did the Boers leave Cape Colony? Why did the British seek to re-establish control over them? Why did war break out? What solution was worked out to satisfy the Boers?

3. How were conflicting imperial goals in East Africa resolved? In West Africa? In Egypt and Sudan?

4. What problems were encountered by Germany in South-West Africa? By Italy in its quest for colonies? How was the Congo exploited by King Leopold?

5. African Nationalism Emerges During the Post-World War I Period

By 1910 the partition of Africa, which had begun in earnest about 1880, was over. For the next 45 years, decisions affecting Africa and its peoples were made not in Africa, but in London, Paris, Lisbon, Brussels, or Berlin. Africans had never acquiesced in this policy of European imperialism and had steadfastly fought against it. But not until after World War I did Africans begin to unite on a large scale. It was during this interwar period that modern African nationalism was born.

Imperialism is a potent force in international relations. The partitioning of Africa provided the great powers with pawns for their game of international chess. When a crisis developed, it often was possible to reach a compromise by trading a piece of Africa for a concession elsewhere. Thus imperialist expansion in Africa not only strengthened the industries of France, Belgium, Germany, and Britain, but insured a degree of flexibility in their competitive relations. World War I did not break out until all of Africa had been divided among the great European powers. There remained no unclaimed or loosely held territories which could be used to appease an aggressor nation.

The Allies strip Germany of her African colonies. The Treaty of Versailles, which ended World War I, stripped Germany of all her colonies. However, the imperialist policies of the victorious powers had changed hardly at all. To President Wilson's dismay, Britain, France, and Italy — allies in World War I — scrambled to gain control of defeated Germany's colonies. Italy, resentful because France earlier had frustrated her imperial ambitions in Africa, felt outraged when she received none of Germany's former colonies. In 1935, the Italian dictator, Mussolini, tried to redress this grievance by a brutal assault on the African nation (Ethiopia) which had inflicted humiliating defeat on the invading Italian army some forty years earlier. The League of Nations listened in sympathy to Emperor Haile Selassie's appeal for help against Italy's open act of aggression, but did nothing to stop it. Italian machine guns, poison gas, tanks, and planes finally prevailed over Ethiopia's unmechanized army, and Italy formally annexed the country in 1936. Ethiopia then was combined with Eritrea and Italian Somaliland to form Italian East Africa.

Had it not been for President Wilson's insistence that the League of Nations exercise some degree of control over Germany's former colonies, it is likely that Germany's African territories simply would have been added to the French and British colonial empires. Under the mandate system, control over colonies formerly held by Germany or her allies was entrusted, or "mandated," to one of the victorious powers. Accordingly, German South-West Africa was mandated to the Union of South Africa, which was then a dominion within the British Empire. The Cameroons and Togoland were divided into French and British mandates. German East Africa, renamed Tanganyika, was mandated to Great Britain, except for the heavily populated area bordering the Congo, which was mandated to Belgium under the name of Ruanda-Urundi. The colonial powers were supposed to report periodically to the League of Nations on the economic and political progress being made by their respective mandates. But the attitude of the nations charged with this responsibility showed that in Africa there was actually very little difference between a colony and a mandate.

The partition of Africa introduces artificial boundaries. If one looks at a map of Africa, one will note that many of the boundaries are straight lines which bear little relationship to mountain ranges or rivers — lines which take into account none of the many differences in African cultures and languages. Present-day African countries retain the shape given them by the imperial powers at conferences in Berlin, Brussels, Paris, and London. Knowing very little about the interior of Africa and nothing about the people who lived there, these imperialist statesmen in a few short hours made far-reaching decisions affecting the lives of tens of millions of Africans.

A major problem facing the newly independent countries of Africa is the fact that national boundaries, rather than enclosing similar peoples and cultures, in fact often divide them. It is not surprising, therefore, that conflicts have plagued the new nations of Africa. People seeking reunification with their kinsmen sometimes are forced to agitate against the government under which they live. New governments, striving to preserve their frontiers, are likely to deal harshly with those who take part in such agitation. Many of these problems are Africa's legacy from the colonial period.

Africans begin to develop a feeling of unity. The political units which the European powers created in Africa for purposes of administering their overseas empires often became, willy-nilly, units reflecting the new African nationalism. In their common opposition to foreign rule, many Africans began to look beyond purely local ties and

After years in exile, Emperor Haile Selassie of Ethiopia was restored to his throne during World War II. A combined drive by Ethiopian freedom fighters and British troops ended Italian rule over his country.

to develop a sense of comradeship. Local languages or dialects, loyalties to clans, and differences in customs came to be subordinated to the overriding principle of nationalism. Although disputes arose among Africans over precise boundaries — especially those which separated peoples sharing the same culture — the new African nationalism has served as a counterforce against a return to the earlier African particularism, or exclusive attachment to very small local units. The leaders of the new nationalism have usually argued that the borders of the newly independent countries should be accepted as permanent.

Africans deliberately retain some features of European culture. Wherever France established schools in her African colonies, the French system of education was adapted to the African environment. Great Britain, Belgium, and Portugal followed a similar policy. Because of the multiplicity of African languages, French, English, and Portuguese became the official languages in the respective French, English, and Portuguese territories. Children educated beyond the first three or four years of school were required to learn the language of the European governing power. And today, when the representatives of member states of such African bodies as the Organization of African Unity assemble, those who shared British rule converse in English while those who come from former French-held territories talk to one another in French. Interpreters are required to translate not hundreds of African languages, but only Arabic, English, and French.

The impact of European rule covered the entire range of social, political, and economic relationships. The Ghanaian or Nigerian who has been educated in Britain drinks tea, likes roast beef, and can easily find his way around London. The educated elite of Senegal or the Ivory Coast probably enjoy French cooking in addition to African specialties. Traditional customs and cultures frequently acquired a European veneer. At the same time many Africans have consciously sought to revive their own cultural traditions. African nationalists usually have not rejected every vestige of European culture, but have retained whatever has been useful to them and can complement local African practice.

● CHECK-UP

1. What was the mandate system? Why was it introduced?
2. Why have the artificial boundaries drawn when Africa was partitioned created problems for present-day states?
3. What are the causes and characteristics of the new African nationalism? What evidence of the impact of European rule remains?

Summing Up

The end of the eighteenth century marked the beginning of a long period of European exploration and exploitation of Africa. Curiosity about the still-uncharted African interior was growing, and European businessmen hoped that the exploration of Africa would pave the way for establishing lucrative markets for European manufactured goods.

Much of this curiosity about Africa was centered in the Nile and Niger rivers. Conflicting theories about the source and course of each river needed to be resolved. James Bruce reached the source of the Blue Nile and explored the sites of ancient Ethiopian cities. But it remained for Richard Burton, John Speke, and Samuel Baker and his wife to show that the Nile was fed by great lakes in the heart of Africa.

Mungo Park's journeys in West Africa during the 1790's had given England proof of a great interior river — the Niger. His subsequent explorations, and those of René Caillié, stimulated further interest in lands south of the Sahara. Johann Rebmann and Johann Krapf tracked down the legends of high East African mountains by reaching Mount Kilimanjaro. Their real goal, however, was the conversion of Africans to Christianity. This goal was devoutly shared by David Livingstone, the great English explorer-missionary, whose long journeys through Central Africa spanned some 30 years. In a three-year trek beginning in 1853, Livingstone traveled from Barotseland (Zambia) to the mouth of the Zambezi, and saw and named the spectacular Victoria Falls. Doubting the claims of Speke and Baker, Livingstone determined in 1866 to find the Nile's watershed, a task he did not live to finish. His last journey brought him in 1871 to the Lualaba River. It was Henry M. Stanley, who, having set out to establish Livingstone's whereabouts for an anxious newspaper-reading public, confirmed Speke's contentions concerning the Nile's source. Stanley's vivid accounts of his African journeys stimulated further European exploration of the interior. But whereas Livingstone was loved by Africans for his humanitarian efforts on their behalf, Stanley's tactics aroused African suspicion and hostility. It was Stanley, too, who was chiefly responsible for making the vast area of the Congo the domain of Belgium's King Leopold.

European missionary endeavors evoked a mixed response from Africans. On the positive side of the ledger were the efforts of missionaries to translate the Bible into African tongues, which caused these languages and dialects to be reduced to writing. Medical missionaries brought special knowledge and techniques for combating dreaded tropical diseases. On the negative side, missionaries often made enemies by what appeared to be a condescending and patronizing attitude toward the "natives." Sometimes, too, missionaries provided a pretext for foreign military intervention. Furthermore, rivalry among missionaries of different faiths — Catholic, Protestant, Muslim — weakened the impact each might have had on the African people.

The nineteenth century was a period of intense international rivalry for control of Africa. England, France, Germany, Belgium, and to a lesser extent, Italy and Spain took part in the scramble for colonies. Portugal already had established an empire on both sides of the continent. France eventually acquired the largest African territory, much of it desert. In terms of wealth and population, Great Britain came out best among the European empire-builders in Africa. This was especially true after the discovery of diamonds and gold in Boer-held territory — territory which became British as a result of the costly Boer War. Cecil Rhodes, the leading spokesman for British imperialism, encouraged European immigration into the fertile highlands of East Africa, thereby dispossessing Africans of their best ancestral lands and entrenching British authority in that entire region. Meanwhile, British investments in the Suez Canal had led to involvement in Egypt's internal affairs and, ultimately, to the establishment of a British "protectorate" over that country. After a long struggle with the mahdi and a confrontation with the French at Fashoda, British control was extended to include the Sudan. In West Africa, British holdings came to include Gambia, Sierra Leone, Gold Coast, and Nigeria. Germany, too, carved out an African empire that included South-West Africa, Togo, Cameroon, and Tanganyika. These lands, taken from Germany after its defeat in World War I, were turned over as League mandates to Britain, France, and the Union of South Africa. Italy's ambitions for empire were focused on the one African country which had retained its independence — Ethiopia. In the 1890's an Italian army was ignominiously defeated. But Italy then annexed Eritrea and most of Somalia. In 1911, Italy seized Libya from Turkey. Continuing to nurse resentment against Ethiopia, Italy on the eve of World War II used its air power and armor to conquer that country.

The European takeover of Africa makes clear the role of imperialism and colonialism in giving direction to international affairs. Obviously the reaction of Africans to these forces was very different from that of Europeans. To Africans it became imperative to break the imperialist yoke and to restore "uhuru" (freedom). To accomplish this goal, Africans drew together as never before. In the course of their struggle for independence, powerful new nationalist movements were born.

CHAPTER REVIEW

Can You Identify?

Ashanti	mahdi	Transvaal
Ethiopia	Fashoda	Rhodesia
Adowa	Tunisia	South-West Africa
mandate	khedive	Orange Free State
Lugard	Paul Kruger	Congo Free State
Nigeria	Cecil Rhodes	labor tax
Livingstone	protectorate	colonialism
Mutesa	Kitchener	imperialism

What Do You Think?

1. Why did French and British colonial goals in Africa conflict? Why were they reconciled in time?

2. Why might a colonial governor and Africans disagree on the advantages and disadvantages of colonial rule?

3. Why did the Africans prefer independence to British rule? Why were the British unwilling to concede independence?

4. What conclusions can be drawn from the fact that Africans — Ashanti, Ethiopians, Sudanese, Zulus — at times defeated European troops?

5. What were the assumptions underlying missionary activities in Africa? Were these activities acceptable to Africans?

Extending and Applying Your Knowledge

1. "Two Views of Colonial Rule" will help the reader to understand why Africans and Europeans did not agree on this subject. See *Africa: Selected Readings*, pages 166–172.

2. Africans who adopted European ways often found themselves "Between Two Worlds." See article with this title, pages 172–179, in *Africa: Selected Readings*.

3. Illustrate the evils of economic imperialism. (See pages 182–187 of *Africa: Selected Readings*.)

4. Chinua Achebe is one African writer who can help others to see the missionaries through African eyes. See *Africa: Selected Readings*, pages 155–166.

7

TOWARD LIBERATION

In 1960 the Nobel Peace Prize for the first time was awarded to an African, Chief Albert Luthuli, a leader in the struggle against white domination in South Africa. In his speech of acceptance, Luthuli provides a theme for this chapter:

> Our continent has been carved up by the great powers; alien governments have been forced upon the African people by military conquest. . . . Strivings for nationhood and national dignity have been beaten down by force; traditional economies and ancient customs have been disrupted. . . . But now, the revolutionary stirrings of our continent are setting the past aside. Our people everywhere from north to south . . . are reclaiming their land, their right to participate in government, their dignity as men, their nationhood. . . .

In 1941, during World War II, President Franklin Delano Roosevelt and Prime Minister Winston Churchill met secretly at sea and affixed their signatures to the Atlantic Charter. The Charter stated that all people would henceforth have a right to choose "the form of government under which they would live." Once the dust of World War II had settled, Europe's colonies — first in Asia and then in Africa — began to demand the freedom promised them.

1. The Spirit of Independence Catches Fire Throughout Africa

By 1950 there were still only four independent countries in Africa: Egypt, Ethiopia, Liberia, and white-dominated South Africa. At first the pace of freedom was slow. The North African countries were the first to attain freedom. The former Italian colony of Libya became a sovereign nation in 1951. And in 1956, Sudan, Morocco, and Tunisia were granted their independence. But for tropical Africa the promise did not come true until 1957, when the Gold Coast became independent Ghana. Over the next twelve years, 34 independent nations were born. Portugal, however, still held Angola, Mozambique, and Guinea-Bissau (Portuguese Guinea); and the Republic of South Africa controlled Namibia (South-West Africa). Spain held on to Spanish Sahara. Rhodesia proclaimed its independence, but under a government dominated by whites. The tiny Territory of the Afars and Issas was the only African country whose people voted to continue under foreign (French) control (see map on page 255).

World War II brought Africa into the mainstream of world affairs. More than a half million Africans were trained to help Britain and France in the war against Germany, Italy, and Japan. Thousands of Africans, assigned to duty in the far corners of the earth, returned home with new knowledge of the world beyond Africa. After World War II, Africa was not the same. African soldiers had learned that the white soldier was neither braver nor abler than the African. Those

Albert Luthuli wore the traditional fur cap of a Zulu chief when he accepted the Nobel Peace Prize at Oslo, Norway. He was honored for his stand on behalf of racial justice and understanding in South Africa.

who had not already attended school soon learned to read and write, fire rifles, drive trucks, and more important, to work together until a job was done. In short, the postwar period witnessed the return to Africa of thousands of young men who now were aware of their own humiliating status and who possessed an idea worth fighting for. Henceforth the African's watchword was *uhuru* (freedom), by which he meant liberation from foreign rule.

African manpower, raw materials, and supply routes helped the Allies win the war. The demands of the war had compelled Great Britain and France to reduce the size of their administrative and technical staffs in the colonies. It was necessary, therefore, to train Africans to assume important positions in the administration of the colonies. Furthermore, the Allied powers desperately needed raw materials from Africa to carry on the war. More than half of the world's annual production of gold — vital for maintaining the monetary systems of the world — came from Africa. Half of the world's production of chrome and radium — essential to the armaments industry — was African. Much of the uranium needed to develop the atomic bomb was mined in the southern Congo. Copper and industrial diamonds, palm oil and cobalt flowed from Africa to Europe and the United States, and were important contributions to Allied victory.

To get around German and Italian forces in the Mediterranean area, the Allies built a series of air and sea bases in tropical Africa stretching from the west to the east coast. American planes landed tons of supplies in West African ports for transshipment to the North African front. During the height of the war some 300 planes a day flew in and out of Accra, the capital of the Gold Coast. This huge undertaking was a success in large measure because of the assistance of Africans.

The war causes the colonial powers to examine themselves. Wars are revolutionary in that they make extraordinary demands upon people and bring about fundamental changes both in the victorious and the vanquished nations. It is not surprising that the Allies found it difficult to reconcile moral pronouncements made during the war with the continued existence of colonial empires. Having opposed the Nazi idea of Aryan racial superiority, it became difficult to justify the view that whites had an inalienable right to rule blacks. In theory, the Allies were defending the freedom of European nations. Could they then deny freedom to Africans? The very principles for which the war had been fought seemed to demand that the victorious powers set free their colonies.

During World War II, French colonial troops fought their way across the Sahara and helped to liberate France from Nazi rule. Under the command of European officers, African regiments had long been used by France and other powers to defend their colonies in Africa. In wartime more thousands of Africans were recruited and learned to handle the most modern weapons and equipment.

As a result of the war, most of the imperial powers—but not Portugal — reluctantly concluded that self-government in some degree for their colonies was inevitable. But they disagreed with their colonial wards, and with the United States and the Soviet Union, as to how quickly self-government should be granted and what form it should take. Thus, even though the *idea* of freedom for Asia and Africa was accepted, the powers were not prepared to grant independence to their colonies immediately or unconditionally. Struggle and sacrifice would be required before the inevitable would become a reality. Meanwhile, in order to demonstrate good faith, France and Great Britain launched a series of economic and political reforms in their African colonies. Roads, hospitals, and schools were built, and Africans were invited to take a larger part in the administration of the colonies.

Africans demand an early end to colonialism. In spite of these reforms, Africans saw that social and racial equality would come only with political equality. African leaders listened to the words of Kwame Nkrumah (*kwah'*mee en-*kroo'*mah), American-educated leader of the independence movement in the Gold Coast: "Seek ye first the political kingdom and all other things shall be added unto it." The African people believed that when they were free, they could create the kind of society they wanted. African nationalists — the leaders of the independence movement — saw their struggle as a necessary step in achieving racial liberation and ending alien domination.

The UN Charter held a promise of freedom for colonies. The men who gathered in San Francisco in 1945 to draft a charter for a new world organization recalled that the ill-fated League of Nations began to disintegrate when it failed to heed Ethiopian Emperor Haile Selassie's plea to stop Mussolini's aggression. This time the interests of the African and Asian people could not be ignored; the United Nations would have to assume a major responsibility for decolonization. Therefore, Article 73 was included in the Charter of the United Nations. This article states that nations which ruled over dependent territories had an obligation — a "sacred trust" — to

> promote to the utmost . . . the well-being of the inhabitants of these territories, and to this end . . . to develop self-government; to take due account of the political aspirations of the peoples, and to assist them in the progressive development of their free political institutions. . . .

Africans and Asians saw this provision of the Charter as a promise of freedom. The Charter also provided for an "International Trusteeship" system to govern the former colonies of the defeated Axis powers. For example, the United Nations was to decide the future of Italian possessions in Africa — Libya, Somaliland, and Eritrea. Furthermore, the one-time German colonies which had been held by Britain, France, Belgium, and South Africa under the mandate system of the League of Nations now became United Nations Trusteeships. The UN temporarily assigned responsibility for most of these territories to the colonial powers. But Africans could appeal directly to the UN Trusteeship Council if they believed that their "trustees" were not advancing them toward self-government, and they were quick to take advantage of this right.

African nationalists appeal to the UN. Some of the African leaders came to the United Nations as penniless petitioners. They frequently lived in New York City tenements until they had an opportunity to present their case. Despite these inconveniences, the information and petitions which they brought to the Trusteeship Council and to the General Assembly's Committee on Information from Non-Self-Governing Territories helped to call attention to conditions in Africa. This kind of pressure induced the colonial powers to move more quickly than they otherwise might have done.

In 1960 Ghana's delegation to the United Nations Assembly in New York was headed by President Kwame Nkrumah (*left*). He wore robes made of colorful *kente* cloth woven in Ghana. Nkrumah and other African leaders urged the UN to hasten independence for all African nations.

African and Asian states form an important power bloc within the UN. So long as the United Nations was made up largely of countries in North and South America and Europe, African problems received little consideration. The first annual report of the UN Secretary General contained in its 66 pages only two sentences about Africa. But after 1955, newly independent African nations began to take their places as member states of the UN. By 1964, the African states had the largest continental representation in the General Assembly. Today in the General Assembly, where each member state has one vote, the former Asian and African colonies dominate the proceedings. Nearly one-half of the 1962 annual report was devoted to African affairs. As more and more Asian and African countries entered the United Nations, its many committees and agencies began to publicize the growing demand for independence.

African leaders are encouraged by the success of Asian independence movements. Most of Europe's Asian colonies had been agitating for independence even before World War II. Great Britain had offered India its future independence in exchange for the latter's aid in defeating the Axis powers. The struggle of Gandhi and Nehru to win freedom for India was well known in Africa, and many African nationalists patterned their independence movements on the Indian example. True to her promise, Britain granted India independence in 1947. A year before, on July 4, the Philippines became an independent nation, in fulfillment of a promise made by the United States before World War II. The French and Dutch, returning to their Asian dependencies after the Japanese were defeated, had to use force in their effort to re-establish control. The Dutch, however, were forced out of Indonesia in 1949. The struggle for independence in Indochina and Indonesia contributed to the rising tide of nationalism in Africa. Ahmed Ben Bella, who guided Algeria along the road to independence, received his military training in Indochina while serving with the French army. Several African leaders had spent considerable time in India; some were even involved in India's struggle for freedom. Kwame Nkrumah, who became the first prime minister of the Gold Coast (renamed Ghana), once said: "I have been influenced in much that I have been able to carry out by the ideas of that great man Mahatma Gandhi."

The Cold War speeds independence for Africa. Africans had the advantage of outside help from the United States and Russia in the fight for independence. But because of this fact they became involved in the Cold War before they had a chance to settle their internal problems. Both camps in the Cold War sought the support of the uncommitted nations. The Soviet Union used its position on the Trusteeship Council of the UN to pose as the champion of non-Western peoples and to demand that colonial powers liberate their colonies immediately. Out of deference to its European allies, however, the United States felt that it could not take such a strong stand for African independence. In 1960, the UN adopted a Soviet-supported resolution demanding that steps be taken to end colonialism. Because the United States abstained from voting on this resolution, the Soviet Union won an important propaganda victory.

Most African nations refuse to take sides in the East-West struggle. Both the Western and Communist camps have tried to increase their influence in Africa and to align African peoples on a pro- or anti-Communist basis. Communist China, too, has made an effort to establish a special sphere of influence in Africa. The new nations of Africa recognize their need for outside assistance and their strategic importance in the international power struggle. But they have been careful to make no definite commitments to any one power bloc, preferring to play one side against the other and thus reap maximum advantage. The new states, in short, are prepared to accept friendship — in the form of cultural exchange, economic aid, and technical assistance — from any country that offers it. But for the most part, they have stopped short of joining military alliances in order not to upset other potentially friendly nations. Similarly, the new African nations have avoided taking sides in the Sino-Soviet dispute.

Both China and the Soviet Union take an interest in Africa. Both the Soviet and Chinese governments have aided the new nations of Africa. Both, moreover, also have helped the groups fighting in the white-dominated countries of southern Africa (page 278). Usually the Chinese have aided the more radical groups.

The Soviet government contends that its interest in Africa is based on anti-imperialism. Therefore, the USSR has helped countries which do not even have a socialist government. Mainly because of the Soviet Union's stance in the Arab-Israeli dispute, Arab countries in North Africa have accepted much economic and military aid from the Russians. The fact that African nations continue to value their pride more than any amount of aid is illustrated by Soviet-Egyptian relations. In 1970, Russia installed missiles in Egypt to defend against Israeli air attacks, and the Russians practically took over Egypt's air defenses. At one time there were 20,000 Russian military and technical personnel in Egypt. Then in 1972 President Sadat of Egypt suddenly announced that, although the two countries would remain friendly, all Soviet personnel would leave Egypt. Evidently the Russians would not give all the military equipment Egypt requested, and the Egyptians felt insulted by this refusal.

Meanwhile, China has greatly extended its influence in Africa. In the early days of independence, the Chinese concentrated on supporting radical groups within African countries, but in recent years the Chinese have stressed aid for economic development and have taken less interest in internal political struggles. A major Chinese project in Africa has been the financing and building of the Tanzam Railroad in Tanzania. When this 1100-mile-long railway is completed, Zambia will be able to ship its copper to a port on the Indian Ocean without sending it through white-controlled Rhodesia or Mozambique.

The way in which the Chinese conduct themselves in Africa wins them much respect from Africans. They dress, eat, and live simply, in direct contrast to American and European officials, most of whom drive cars, have servants, and live in relatively luxurious homes. The Chinese can say to the Africans that they, too, are colored and come from a poor country.

INFORMATION. Above, leaders of local radio-clubs in Dahomey receive new radios from the government. They will return to their home villages and organize their neighbors into clubs so that they can listen together to broadcasts about new farming methods. The United Nations is helping Dahomey to set up this agricultural extension service by radio. Left, a newsdealer offers a choice of papers to Nigerians on their way to work in the morning rush-hour. Nigeria has a lively press which led the struggle for self-government in colonial days.

Modern means of communication have multiplied the effect of outside influences on Africans. Each week Communist countries beam hundreds of hours of radio programs in many different African languages into Africa. On a lesser scale, so do other countries. Africans who own radios may listen to Radio Moscow, the British Broadcasting Corporation, the Voice of America, or programs originating in their own countries. Radio brings to peoples everywhere ideas about the rights of man and of self-determination, as well as Communist teachings. News bulletins dealing with race relations in the United States and the struggles of black Americans for equal rights may be heard in most of Africa. Today, African radio programs are being broadcast in more than 100 African languages. Leaders of anticolonial movements, broadcasting from neighboring countries, continuously exhort fellow Africans to strike for freedom and independence from foreign domination. Such methods were effectively used by the Tanzania Broadcasting Company to speed independence for neighboring Kenya and Zambia.

Not only can ideas and slogans be communicated instantaneously, but people themselves can now be transported from one place to another anywhere in the world in less time than formerly was needed to travel from one part of a country to another. Before freedom came to most of Africa, the leaders of independence movements had visited the major world capitals and appeared before agencies of the United Nations. They had pleaded their case, bargained with both Communist and non-Communist leaders, and sought and obtained the support of the major powers.

Newspapers play an increasingly important role in shaping opinion. With the spread of literacy to rural areas, it is expected that the press will exert increasing influence in the political life of the newly independent nations. The United Nations reported in 1971 that there were 218 daily newspapers in all of Africa, with a combined circulation of 2.7 million copies.

Aside from poverty and illiteracy, the main obstacle to the growth of newspapers is the great number of languages. A further factor hindering the growth of the press is that originally the newspaper was a white and Western import that had no roots in African life. A few countries still lack their own press, but Nigeria, for example, boasts more than 20 newspapers. To Americans, the reported total circulation of African newspapers may seem small. But their importance must not be underestimated. These papers reach the best-educated segment of the population, the group that is most influential in any developing country.

● CHECK-UP

1. How did their World War II experience strengthen the desire of Africans for freedom? What role did Africa play in the war?
2. Why were most imperial powers after the war ready to grant colonies a measure of self-government? What promises to that effect were made in the UN Charter? Why were Africans most concerned about getting political equality?
3. How did the Cold War speed African independence? What was the effect of Asian independence movements? What role did mass media play in shaping African views?

2. British Colonies in West Africa Win Independence

In preparing their colonies for independence, the European powers introduced governments that reflected their own political systems. The colonial rulers also tried to maintain close relations with their former colonies after independence. Former British-held territories automatically became members of the British Commonwealth, while French colonies were included within the French Community. But once the African states became independent, they tended to alter their governments to suit their needs.

The manner in which independence was obtained varied from country to country. And in developing their political and economic systems, some countries followed institutions inherited from the colonial past more closely than others.

Ghana sets the pattern for British Africa. Ghana, in British-held West Africa, was first to win its freedom. The Gold Coast, as it was called before independence in 1957, had become one of Britain's wealthiest colonies. Gold and cocoa had brought wealth to many, but they also created a bitter division between the people and their traditional rulers. The rise to important positions of young educated Ghanaians was a challenge to the power of the traditional chiefs supported by the British colonial government.

After World War II, Great Britain turned over responsible administrative positions to Africans as a necessary step in preparing the Gold Coast for independence. But the British timetable for independence was much more gradual than that envisioned by the African nationalists. In 1945, the Gold Coast parliament had a majority of African members. These, however, were not elected by the people but appointed by the British governor. In 1947 the first nationalist movement, the United Gold Coast Convention (UGCC), was established. Its aims were: (1) immediate independence and (2) elimination of the influence traditionally exercised by the chiefs. These two goals were closely related, for the British had long ruled the country through these local chieftains.

The Ghanaian nationalists gain strength rapidly. An unexpected event played an important part in speeding change in Ghana. During the postwar era, thousands of farmers in the south were hard hit by the dreaded "swollen shoot" disease of cocoa. The British launched a campaign to cut down the infected trees as a means of halting the spread of the disease, but the farmers bitterly opposed this action. Ill will generated by this campaign was an important factor in the rise of anti-British feeling and activity. Because British policy was administered by and through the local African chiefs, these chiefs became the prime target for nationalist criticism and hostility.

Nkrumah mobilizes nationalist sentiment. In 1947 Kwame Nkrumah (page 245) returned to Ghana, having completed ten years of university study in the United States. During these years he had worked as a dishwasher, waiter, and day laborer in order to support himself. In the United States, and later in England, he had become involved in Pan Africanism, a world movement of blacks aimed at promoting unity among Africans and Afro-Americans and at putting an end to colonialism. In Ghana, Nkrumah quickly became the leader of the nationalist elements. He had prepared himself well for the historic task ahead; for, as he said in his autobiography, Nkrumah "devoted much energy to the study of revolution." In the tradition of Gandhi, he launched a campaign of nonviolent civil disobedience against British authority. Founding a new party, he organized branches throughout the country in preparation for the first national election to be held in 1951. Nkrumah was jailed for a time, but was released when his party won a decisive victory at the polls.

The nationalists overcome obstacles and win independence. British policy called for the granting of independence in four stages. In the first stage, Africans were to become involved in the legislative branch of the government and were to participate in the development of democratic local government. At the second stage, Africans would be permitted a majority in the legislature — although the real power would still remain in the hands of the British-controlled colonial administration. In the third stage — the stage of "internal self-government" — the governor would turn over most of his powers to an African prime minister, but would keep the right of veto and would be responsible for foreign relations. The final stage would be the granting of complete independence. Ghana's independence thus was to be delayed by British gradualism. The independence movement was also handicapped by competing groups, reflecting, in part, ancient ethnic divisions.

Actually Ghana won complete independence on March 6, 1957, and in 1960 it became a republic, with Nkrumah as president. By 1964, Ghana had been transformed into a one-party state with strong government controls over the economy. The coercive tactics used by Nkrumah to bring this about earned him the reputation of a dictator and drew the criticism of the United States and its allies, the more so since Nkrumah actively cultivated the friendship of Communist China and Soviet Russia. Opposition to Nkrumah's methods also increased within Ghana. In 1966, while he was on a visit to China and the Soviet Union, a group of generals took over the government. Nkrumah was forced to seek asylum in Guinea, where he died in 1972.

After Nkrumah's overthrow, Ghana was governed by a council headed by army officers until 1969, when free elections were held. Nkrumah's spending policies had left Ghana with a debt of 800 million dollars, and the civilian government devalued the currency, thereby setting off a sharp rise in the cost of living. In 1972 a bloodless military coup overthrew the civilian government. A new, army-dominated government vowed to end the "economic mismanagement" of the previous government.

Regional differences pose serious obstacles to Nigerian unity. Nigeria was Britain's largest colonial holding in West Africa. Actually, the country called "Nigeria" was a European creation, for within its artificial boundaries were included at least 150 ethnic (or "tribal") groups. Despite this complexity, however, the country may be divided into three major geographical regions.

Northern Nigeria — which contains more than half of the country's 60 million inhabitants — is larger in area and population than the other two regions combined. This region is the home of the Hausa and the Fulani, and is predominantly Muslim. Here Sir Frederick Lugard, the first governor general of Nigeria, implemented

AFRICA TODAY. Independence came swiftly to most of Africa during the late 1950's and the 1960's. The struggle continues in territory under Portuguese rule. Elsewhere in Africa: (1) Namibia (formerly known as South-West Africa), entrusted years ago to South Africa as a mandate, was annexed by that country instead of being prepared for self-government. The United Nations voted to end South Africa's rule but could not enforce this decision. (2) Rhodesia declared its independence in 1965, but Britain refused to recognize this act until Rhodesia's black citizens accept the terms of independence. (3) Although South Africa is an independent country, there is little freedom for the 80 per cent of its people who are black. (4) The Sinai Peninsula has been occupied by Israel since Israeli troops captured it from Egypt in 1967.

the principle of "indirect rule" with which his name and British colonial policy were associated. Indirect rule simply meant that the colonial power recognized existing African governments and exercised control by ruling the people through traditional institutions. In northern Nigeria, the traditional rulers are Fulani nobles, called *emirs*. The emirs, although they were part of the British administrative system, were little affected by British rule. The north's scanty natural resources, together with its adherence to the ancient Islamic social system, help to explain why the region remained poor compared to the south.

Although the British built roads and a railroad to connect coastal Nigeria to the north, the Hausa peasants eked out only a meager existence. But in the south, the Yoruba cocoa planters and Ibo palm oil traders began to prosper, since these products commanded good prices in the export trade. Over the years the British developed a practice of sending to the northern region as clerks and administrators southerners largely educated in Christian mission schools. These newcomers were resented by the Hausa and Fulani because their education fitted them to take the best jobs in government and business.

Southern Nigeria, where perhaps half the population is Christian, is divided into two regions. In the eastern portion the six million Ibo people are the major group. The British controlled the small, autonomous Ibo villages through the local chiefs. But more direct control was imposed on the urbanized Yoruba people who dominate the west. Centuries earlier, the slave trade had brought the Yoruba into contact with Europeans. Thus, there were marked economic and religious differences between the northern region and the two southern parts of Nigeria, a fact which led the British to govern north and south differently. But this seemingly enlightened policy led to problems when Nigeria became independent.

Agitation for Nigerian independence begins in the south. As early as 1922, the British had allowed Africans to serve on the Nigerian colonial legislative council. The emirs in the north, however, opposed southern agitation for independence, fearing that an independent Nigeria would be dominated by the better educated and wealthier people of the south. Because of differences between the regions and their mutual suspicion and fear, the British felt that Nigeria should become a federal union in which the different regions retained much self-rule. In 1960 a Nigerian federation of the three

CIVIL WAR. Proclaiming their region to be the independent republic of Biafra, the Ibo people sought to secede from Nigeria in 1967. Ibo soldiers (left) tried to hold back the advance of government troops. In the bitter civil war, perhaps two million people died. Crowds in Lagos (below) celebrated the cease-fire that ended the fighting in 1970 and reunited Nigeria as a twelve-state federation.

governments was granted independence. Three political parties, each drawing its major support from one of the three regions, competed in the 1959 national elections. Nigerian politics ever since have reflected the necessity for balancing power between these competing peoples, regions, and parties.

As in the United States, the powers of government were divided between the central government with its capital at Lagos and the regional governments. The central governments had a Senate providing equal representation for the regions, and a House of Representatives based on population. But, unlike the United States, the executive power in Nigeria was in the hands of a prime minister and cabinet selected from the majority party in the House of Representatives. Each of the regional governments had two houses, one representing the traditional chiefs and the other elected on the basis of population.

Regional differences sharpen into open hostility. Nigeria's new government found it impossible to overcome deep-seated antagonisms and rivalries. Civil unrest led to an army rebellion in 1966. An Ibo general proclaimed military rule and planned a stronger central government. But the Hausa, fearing Ibo domination, staged a countercoup. The new leader, Colonel Gowon, then tried to limit Ibo power in the central government at Lagos. As a consequence, the eastern region seceded and proclaimed itself an independent republic called Biafra (bee-*ahf*'ruh). The resulting civil war lasted three years and caused untold suffering among the people. In January, 1970, Biafran resistance finally collapsed, and the secession came to an end.

Today Nigerians are optimistic about the future of their country. The reconciliation of Biafra and Nigeria was surprisingly smooth, without much of the retaliation and bitterness which so often follow civil wars. Nigeria's military leaders have set up a twelve-state federation to help prevent domination of small ethnic groups by larger ones. Meanwhile, Nigeria has become one of the world's top ten oil producers. Full of self-confidence, government leaders are determined to put Nigeria into the category of "developed nations."

Sierra Leone becomes independent. Sierra Leone, a small country on the west coast, won independence from Britain in 1961. Although it has fewer than three million people, Sierra Leone has not been spared the usual problems arising from strong local ties and traditions. The most powerful people in the new nation are the descendants of slaves who were freed and resettled in Freetown, the capital city, between 1787 and 1870. Politics in Sierra Leone reflect the rivalry between these descendants of slaves and the rest of the population.

Political parties reflecting local interests emerged after World War II and demanded independence. Great Britain gradually increased the involvement of the people in the government, and in 1961 complete independence was granted. Since then, the government has proceeded on a shaky basis, with several coups forcing changes in power. As a result, Sierra Leone's economic development has suffered.

Gambia gains independence. Britain's only other West African colony, Gambia, received independence in 1965. A tiny country, little more than a narrow wedge jutting from the coast into the center of Senegal, Gambia has fewer than half a million people. Though the Gambians are related to the people of Senegal, they have emerged as an independent country since they were ruled by Britain, whereas Senegal was a French colony.

The road to independence and nationhood has been difficult for tiny Gambia. Ethnic group differences present obstacles to national unity, and poverty slows economic development. Gambia is still not self-sufficient in production of rice, its basic foodstuff. Despite these handicaps, the country has shown determination to succeed. Peanuts are its chief export, and tourism is also important to the economy. Gambia and Senegal have held conferences to discuss the difficult problems in their relationship.

● CHECK-UP

1. How had Britain sought to prepare Ghana for independence? What was the reaction of the nationalists in Ghana? Why were the nationalists successful?

2. What obstacles to national unity were present in Nigeria? Why was a federal union established? How successful was it?

3. How did Sierra Leone and Gambia become independent? What problems has each had to cope with?

3. France's Colonial Empire in Africa Opts for Independence

France's African empire was divided into two groups of colonies — French West Africa and French Equatorial Africa. The West African colonies included Senegal, Mauritania, Soudan (now Mali), Guinea, Ivory Coast, Niger, Upper Volta, and Dahomey. The four Equatorial colonies were Gabon, French Congo, Ubangi-Shari (now the Central African Republic), and Chad. Although each colony had its own governor and colonial administration, the eight West African territories were collectively responsible to headquarters in Dakar. The four colonies of Equatorial Africa were linked in a similar fashion. This association of neighboring colonies was important. Because of this experience, the independent former French territories today are more closely associated than are the former British possessions.

The French strive to change Africa through their "civilizing mission." The French approach to colonial government was quite different from Britain's philosophy of indirect rule. France preferred to govern the colonies directly. Unlike the English, the French believed that they had a "civilizing mission" to perform, one that would require them to remake their African wards into black Frenchmen. Accordingly, carefully selected Africans were sent to France, where they received an education that thoroughly grounded them in French culture. These Africans then became involved not only in the government of the colonies but often in the government of France.

Most French colonies follow the example of Guinea. France viewed her empire as an integral part of Greater France. After World War II, arrangements were made for qualified people in the colonies to elect more representatives, not only to their own colonial government, but to the French National Assembly as well. The French conception of freedom for the African territories did not mean independence but rather increased participation and enhanced status within the French Community. In 1958, General Charles de Gaulle attempted to satisfy the demand of the colonies for self-government and, at the same time, to keep the new nations within the French Community. He asked the people in each of the colonies to decide by ballot whether they wanted complete independence and separation from France, or self-government in their own territory, with the mother country remaining responsible for foreign affairs, defense, and finance.

When Guinea, led by Prime Minister Sékou Touré (*seh'koo too-ray'*), voted for complete separation, France immediately withdrew its administrators, doctors, and teachers. This was supposed to bring home to the eleven other new nations the disadvantages of forsaking France. But it was a lesson lost on all of them. Guinea did not capitulate, and when Sékou Touré sought aid elsewhere, the Soviet Union was quick to provide it. Guinea's experience encouraged the

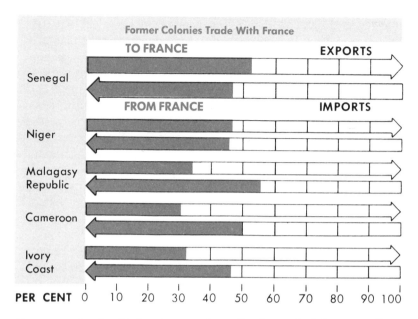

France remains the chief customer and supplier for most of the new nations born out of former French Africa, as shown by these percentage figures from typical countries. French aid helps to finance two-way trade.

countries which earlier had voted to remain with the French Community to change their minds. In 1960, the other eleven states requested and were granted complete independence, while maintaining close economic relations with France.

France's African colonies have much in common. Because the French colonies were neighbors and because under French colonial policy political and economic development had meshed, the independence movement in French Africa originally was more regional than national. From 1946 until the move toward independence came to French Africa after 1958, a single political party was dominant. This party was the RDA (*Rassemblement Démocratique Africaine* — or African Democratic Union), whose president Felix Houphouet-Boigny (oo-foo-*ay' bwah'*nyee) was even then demanding "the liberation of Africa from an odious tutelage — imperialism." (Houphouet-Boigny later became president of the Ivory Coast.)

A common cultural experience fails to insure political unity. Many of the former French colonies wished to make the most of the common bonds which had been forged during generations of living under French imperialist rule. They also shared a valuable unifying link in the French language. But this common denominator of French culture could not be translated into a new political unity. Attempts to form federations of two or more independent states enjoyed only short-term success — such as the merging in 1959 of Senegal and Soudan into the Mali Federation. Although this federation was dissolved in 1960, less ambitious attempts at co-operation have been successful. Some of the former French territories joined together in a customs union, and co-operated in financing an airline. They have formed military alliances and in other ways tried to assist each other. Representatives of their governments regularly meet to discuss mutual problems. To facilitate these meetings, they founded an association which is now called the Common Organization of Africa, Malagasy, and Mauritius, or OCAM for short.[1] The OCAM states are Cameroon, Central African Republic, Chad, Dahomey, Gabon, Ivory Coast, Malagasy Republic, Mauritius, Niger, Rwanda,

---

[1] The initials stand for the French name, *Organisation Commune Africaine et Malagache*.

Meeting in Paris in 1966, these African leaders had no difficulty talking to French Premier Pompidou *(left)* and President De Gaulle. All spoke French, since the Africans had grown up under French colonial rule. President Hamani Diori of Niger stands between Pompidou and De Gaulle; third from the right is President Houphouet-Boigny of Ivory Coast.

Senegal, Togo, and Upper Volta. (Congo and Zaire, former members, withdrew in 1972.)

The "Casablanca Bloc" disagrees with the OCAM group. The willingness of the OCAM nations to maintain close military and economic ties with France brought criticism from other African states. Guinea and Mali, for example, did not support their sister states. Instead they became more closely linked with Ghana, Egypt, Morocco, Libya, and Algeria, in what was often referred to as the "Casablanca Bloc."

In Western eyes, the countries comprising the Casablanca Bloc were the "radicals" of Africa, though none were Communist. From the Casablanca Bloc's point of view, there were good reasons for their anti-Western sentiment: (1) The invasion of Egypt by Israel, Britain, and France in 1956 seemed to them an act of imperialist intervention. (2) They resented French efforts to cripple the economy and government of Guinea when it withdrew from the French Community. (3) Sympathy for Algeria ran high when the French army sought to crush that country's independence movement. Moreover, the Casablanca nations wanted to come out squarely in support of Patrice Lumumba's leadership in the former Belgian Congo (page 273). On other issues, too, the Casablanca Bloc was more vocal than the OCAM states: Israel was denounced as "an instrument in the service of imperialism," and France was condemned for testing nuclear weapons in the Sahara. The Casablanca Bloc was dissolved officially in 1963 with the creation of the Organization of African Unity (OAU).

The French Trust Territories win their freedom. Togo and Cameroon, two former German colonies in West Africa, had become League of Nations mandates after World War I and were divided between the French and the British for administrative purposes. French Togo and Cameroon set the pattern of constitutional advance toward independence which soon was followed by the older French colonies. Both of these Trust Territories obtained internal self-government in 1957, ahead of the other French colonies. Independence came to both in 1960, though territorial boundaries remained to be settled. After British Togoland in 1956 had voted for unification with Ghana, President Nkrumah exerted pressure to persuade the former French-administered section to join Togo's western portion in accepting Ghanaian rule. But the newly independent Togo — one of the smallest and poorest countries in Africa — resisted Ghana's blandishments. Instead, it signed agreements with France covering defense, finance, and diplomacy. In recent years Togo's economic growth has been great enough to increase government services without having to increase taxes.

Madagascar becomes the Malagasy Republic. Madagascar, the world's fourth largest island, is situated far off the southeast coast of Africa. It was settled some two thousand years ago by people from Indonesia. Later, with the arrival of Arabs and Africans, Malagasy achieved its unique blended population.

France had claimed Madagascar as early as the seventeenth century and conquered the entire island in 1896. 'After World War II, the people of Madagascar revolted against French rule (1947), and the French government sent a large army to restore order. An estimated 80,000 people died in this rebellion. After the revolt, Madagascar's nationalist movement found a moderate leader in Philbert Tsiranana (fil-*behr'* tseer-ah-*nah'*nah), who believed that the island had more to gain by co-operating with France. He organized an effective political party which favored having Madagascar remain a member of the French Community. Not until 1960 was complete independence negotiated.

President Tsiranana's government was in power until 1972 when violent demonstrations by student and worker groups disrupted the country for several weeks. The students wanted the educational system to stress national culture over French culture, and the workers had economic grievances. Tsiranana handed over the reins of power to a military government.

Although a potentially rich country, Madagascar is underdeveloped. Its population of over seven million people are occupied primarily in herding and growing food for local use. Coffee, the country's major export, is sold almost exclusively to France.

● CHECK-UP

1. What did France see as its mission in Africa? How was this view reflected in French relations with colonies and colonials?
2. What did the French African colonies have in common? Why did the concept of a French Community fail?
3. How have some of the former French colonies co-operated with each other? Why did the Casablanca Bloc reflect anti-French views?
4. What was the background to independence of Togo and Cameroon? Of the Malagasy Republic?

4. Independence Comes Slowly in Areas with Large Numbers of European Settlers

The highlands of Africa, running from Kenya in the north to the Veld in South Africa, attracted large numbers of European settlers. In the colonies formed in these regions, the mother country was often under heavy pressure from white settlers not to turn the government over to the African majority. In this section we shall see how, nevertheless, six black nations won independence — five from Britain and one from Belgium.

The struggle for independence in British Central Africa creates problems. Northern and Southern Rhodesia were added to Britain's empire by Cecil Rhodes who, as director of the British South Africa Company, encouraged thousands of white settlers to seek their fortune in the region. Southern Rhodesia became a self-governing colony in 1923, and the following year Northern Rhodesia, which had fewer white settlers, was declared a British Protectorate.

Nyasaland (now Malawi) never attracted many Europeans, primarily because it was densely populated and lacked mineral wealth. In the 1930's, some of the white settlers in the Rhodesias and Nyasaland sought to persuade Great Britain to unite the three territories in a single white-dominated federation. The African population of Northern Rhodesia and Nyasaland bitterly opposed federation, fearing domination by white-controlled Southern Rhodesia. Nevertheless, in 1953 Great Britain united the two Rhodesias and Nyasaland in a Central African Federation. Despite massive African opposition, the British government held that federation was in the economic interest of all concerned. Southern Rhodesia was wealthy and white planters owned large and fertile farms. Northern Rhodesia, although poor, had enormous copper deposits. Nyasaland was poor and overpopulated. A federation, it was argued, could use the talent and wealth of Southern Rhodesia in developing the rich mineral resources of Northern Rhodesia. Nyasaland would provide the labor needed in Rhodesia. The Africans continued to protest. They believed that under federation, workers from Nyasaland would be exploited to enrich white Europeans living in Southern Rhodesia. Although Africans made up more than 95 per cent of the total population, they were denied any effective participation in the new federal government.

Continued opposition to the Central African Federation leads to its dissolution. In Northern Rhodesia, the Zambia African National Congress, led by Kenneth Kaunda (kow-*oon*'duh), boycotted white stores and did what it could to sabotage the new federation. In 1958, the Nyasaland Africans were cheered by the return from England of Dr. Hastings Banda, their long-absent leader. The following year, when rioting broke out, Banda and his supporters were jailed. African opponents of the federation in Southern and Northern Rhodesia were also arrested. The situation became so explosive that the British agreed to re-examine the whole idea. As a result, Great Britain in 1963 permitted Nyasaland to withdraw from the federation, and on the last day of that year, the Central African Federation was dissolved. In 1964 Nyasaland became a fully independent state with the new name of Malawi. Later in the same year Northern Rhodesia shed its colonial name and, under the leadership of Kenneth Kaunda, won its independence as Zambia.

Southern Rhodesia, meanwhile, is still dominated by its white minority. Now called simply Rhodesia, this state remains unwilling to extend political rights to Africans. The white government declared independence from Great Britain in 1965. But Britain refuses to recognize this action because the Rhodesian government has not given the African population fair representation in the government (pages 281–282).

Africans oppose a white-dominated federation in the eastern highlands. The beautiful and fertile Kenya Highlands attracted thousands of English and Afrikaaner settlers. Many Indians also settled in Kenya. Although few in number compared to the Africans, the Europeans and Indians controlled both the government and the economy until 1963. Seeking to strengthen their hold on the land, Kenya's European settlers also wanted a federation. They urged Great Britain to form an East African Federation, linking Kenya with Uganda (where there were no white settlers) and with Tanganyika (which had a number of English and German farmers).

As in the Central African Federation the Africans resisted, fearing that Kenya's white-dominated society would bring about a denial of African rights in Tanganyika and Uganda. Above all, the Africans in these two colonies feared that white settlers would take over their land, as had happened in Kenya. In Uganda, the kabaka (king) of Buganda led the opposition to an East African union. Because Tanganyika, a pre-World War I German colony, had become a

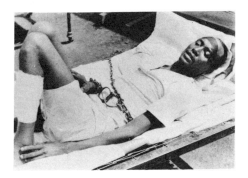

MAU MAU. In the 1950's a rural police headquarters in Kenya was defended against Mau Mau raiders by barbed wire and sharpened stakes set close together in the ground. The Mau Mau resistance to British rule in Kenya was determined and desperate. Left, a wounded rebel captured by British troops was chained to his hospital bed to prevent him from trying to escape.

United Nations Trust Territory after World War II, Britain felt that it did not have a completely free hand to change its status.

Thousands of lives are lost during the Mau Mau rebellion. The Kikuyu (keh-*koo*'yoo) people of Kenya had long protested that their country had been taken illegally. Europeans had grabbed nearly 17,000 square miles of the best land, which in earlier years had been open to Kikuyu settlement. While the Europeans, using African labor, actually farmed only a small part of this immense area, the Kikuyu grew desperate because they were denied land needed to support their rapidly growing population. As a result of this feeling, a secret movement called *Mau Mau* was formed and gained a large following among angry Kikuyu tenant farmers. It carried on terrorist acts against white settlers and stressed that African religion and traditions were to be preferred to European. In 1952 the lid blew off this explosive situation and there was a full-scale Mau Mau rebellion. Jomo Kenyatta, a nationalist leader who had been educated in England, was tried and convicted on the charge of organizing the Mau Mau uprising and kept in prison until 1961. Kenyatta steadfastly denied involvement in the Mau Mau rebellion.

Whether or not Kenyatta was implicated in the rebellion, the majority of the Kikuyu supported it — actively or passively — from a general sense of grievance and frustration. Much was made in the Western press of Mau Mau atrocities against Europeans. These occurred, but not to the extent claimed. In all, 43 white civilians were killed and about 100 white troops. In an effort to mobilize all the Kikuyu in support of the rebellion, the Mau Mau had killed many more African "loyalists" than Europeans. Thousands of Africans were hanged by the British government for carrying firearms or *pangas* (large knives). In April, 1954, the British launched the notorious "Operation Anvil" in the Nairobi area. Some 26,000 Kikuyu men from that city and an additional 100,000 people from the highlands

"BURNING SPEAR." Jomo Kenyatta was known by this name to his early followers in Kenya. He posed for the photograph at right in the 1930's when he was studying anthropology in London. There he wrote an important book about his Kikuyu people, entitled *Facing Mount Kenya*. Below, after becoming the first president of independent Kenya in the 1960's, Kenyatta posed with the heads of neighboring nations who had met to form an East African economic union. From left to right: Milton Obote of Uganda, Julius Nyerere of Tanzania, Kenyatta, and Kenneth Kaunda of Zambia.

were rounded up and packed off to already overcrowded detention camps, where they suffered great hardships. Perhaps the ugliest phase of the Mau Mau war took place in 1953, when Kikuyu villages turned against each other in bloody reprisals for suspected "loyalist" sympathies. A combination of British military reinforcements and divisions within Mau Mau ranks finally brought the war to a close by late 1955. But emergency restrictions imposed on the African population remained in force until 1960.

Kenya and Tanganyika finally attain independence. The Mau Mau rebellion made it clear to the British that reforms were needed. First, the "white highlands" were opened to settlement by people of all races, much against the wishes of the white farmers. Africans were increasingly brought into the government, and a new constitution was framed, granting wide suffrage. By the time elections were called in 1960, two major political parties had been formed. The Kikuyu and Luo peoples were allied in the Kenya African National Union (KANU), organized by Tom Mboya along moderate democratic lines. It attracted strong support in the urban areas. Tom Mboya, a Luo, had insisted on the release of Jomo Kenyatta, perhaps to win Kikuyu support. The rival party, the Kenya African Democratic Union (KADU), included a number of less numerous agrarian peoples. The European minority also formed a party which firmly opposed African control of the government. KANU won the election, but Mboya refused to form a government until Kenyatta was released. Fearful that the split between the two African parties would lead to civil war, Great Britain proposed independence for Kenya under a constitution which provided a considerable degree of independence for the country's eleven regions. In 1963, KANU, under the leadership of the now-free Jomo Kenyatta, won the national elections, and Kenya finally became independent. Kenyatta, whom the British had kept under guard for nine years, became his country's first prime minister and a year later its president.

Two years earlier, Julius Nyerere (nye-er-*rehr*'ree), leader of the Tanganyika African National Union (TANU), had led his country to independence. Nyerere formed a working alliance with leaders of Tanganyika's white and Indian minorities. Since Tanganyika was not divided by serious internal differences or rival parties and had no large white population, its road to independence was relatively smooth. In 1964, Tanganyika and Zanzibar joined to become Tanzania. Nyerere continued to lead TANU and the new nation.

Uganda wins independence but is plagued by internal rivalries. In Uganda the establishment of independence was complicated by rivalry between the kingdom of Buganda and the rest of the country. But in 1962 an independent government was formed, and Milton Obote (oh-*boh*′tee) became the first prime minister. The friction between Buganda and the rest of the country, and the special rights granted to the ancient kingdoms, made it desirable to establish a federation in Uganda. As the most powerful member, Buganda enjoyed a special status. In 1963 the kabaka of Buganda was made president of the new nation, while Milton Obote continued as its prime minister. Despite this compromise, a crisis developed in 1966. Charging that there was a plot to overthrow him, Obote suspended the constitution and proclaimed himself president. When the kabaka refused to accept this change, the Ugandan army attacked his palace. The kabaka escaped into exile, leaving Obote in control.

A dictator takes over in Uganda. In 1971, while President Obote was out of the country, a general named Idi Amin seized control of the Ugandan government. At first, the people of Buganda were delighted. General Amin agreed to have the body of the kabaka, who had died in Britain, brought back to Uganda for a state funeral. He released all political prisoners, about a hundred, most of them followers of the kabaka. But later he disappointed the people of Buganda by announcing that Uganda would be a republic; there would be no Kingdom of Buganda.

Under General Amin, Uganda has become a harsh dictatorship. Amin suspended the constitution, dissolved parliament, and proclaimed himself head of state. Military rule will continue, he has said, until Uganda's affairs have been "put in order."

Meanwhile, President Nyerere of Tanzania had welcomed Milton Obote in that country. When fighting broke out near the Tanzania-Uganda border, General Amin accused Tanzanian troops of making the attack, along with Ugandan troops loyal to Obote. As the confusing skirmishes went on, President Kenyatta of Kenya tried to bring about peace between the two countries but failed. In 1972 Ugandan airplanes even bombed several towns in Tanzania. The two countries signed a peace accord later that year.

An extreme nationalist, General Amin announced his determination to rid Uganda of all outside influence. After seizing a number of British-owned companies, he declared that Britons in Uganda would have to sell their businesses to Africans by January, 1973. He

General Idi Amin came to power in Uganda after overthrowing Milton Obote's government in a military coup. Amin promised useful reforms for Uganda but instead began a reign of terror.

closed the borders to all tourists. Declaring that he was going to Africanize the churches, he began expelling missionaries. And he ordered every Asian who was not a Ugandan citizen to leave the country within 90 days.

Uganda's relations with other countries have deteriorated. When General Amin ordered the expulsion of the 50,000 Asians with British citizenship, Great Britain canceled a $24.5 million loan to Uganda. The United States announced that it would send no more aid to Uganda after General Amin publicly praised Hitler's. treatment of Jews during World War II.

Within Uganda, the effects of Amin's reign are severe. Some of the country's best-educated and ablest citizens, including the chief justice and the vice-chancellor of the university, are missing and presumed dead. Top army officers have "disappeared." The economy is suffering badly from the end of the tourist trade and the lack of business know-how, formerly supplied by the Asians who were expelled.

An East African Community is organized. When independence in the early 1960's removed the threat of white domination, the three East African countries again began to examine the possibility of federation. Under British rule, transportation, communications, and postal service in the three areas had been jointly managed. In 1963, the three prime ministers, Kenya's Kenyatta, Uganda's Obote, and Tanzania's Nyerere, signed a declaration of intent to federate. In 1967 the three nations established the East African Economic Community and Common Market. This provided for a customs union, economic co-operation, and a common assembly to legislate on Community matters. Ethiopia, Zambia, Somalia, and the Sudan have expressed an interest in becoming members. But political difficulties within the East African Community threatened its stability, especially after the border fighting between Uganda and Tanzania in the early 1970's.

The independence movement in the Belgian Congo comes as a surprise to Belgium. One of the largest colonies in European-dominated Africa was the Belgian Congo. After World War II, Belgium placed major emphasis on the economic development of the Congo. The Belgians did little to prepare the colony for self-government, believing that such a development was a half-century or more in the future. Unlike the Ghanaians, Guineans, or Kenyans, the Congolese had not formed modern political parties and apparently were not pressing for freedom.

Almost no Africans in the Belgian Congo were educated beyond primary school, for the Belgians expected to fill all leadership positions in the Congo for many years to come. But no matter how hard they tried, the Belgians could not keep their subjects from hearing the cries for freedom shouted in other parts of Africa. Freedom is contagious, and soon the Congolese, too, were demanding an independence for which there had been little preparation. Whereas the French and the British had introduced local representative government in their colonies before World War I, it was not until 1957 that the Congolese were permitted to vote for local councils. In 1959 dangerous riots broke out in the capital city of Leopoldville (now Kinshasa), and the Belgians realized for the first time that the Congolese were determined to gain their freedom.

Congolese independence is accompanied by factionalism and bloodshed. After the 1959 Leopoldville riots, Belgium had invited prominent African leaders to discuss the issue of independence. Then, after a brief meeting in early 1960, Belgium agreed to give the Congo its independence in June of that year. This hasty decision was in sharp contrast to the British plan for decolonization — a gradual granting of increasing responsibility leading to full independence. The first Congolese national elections were held a few weeks before the scheduled independence celebrations. The only organization which stressed maintaining the Congo as a unified country was the National Congolese Movement led by Patrice Lumumba. Other parties tended to represent only one section of the country or only one of its many different peoples.

Because a great number of parties had put up candidates, and because the Congolese lacked experience with democratic processes, the election was indecisive and chaotic. The two leading figures that emerged were Kasavubu (kah-suh-*voo*′boo), who drew his strength primarily from the Bakongo people near Leopoldville, and Patrice Lumumba, who attracted support here and there throughout the entire country. At the last moment, a coalition was formed that made Lumumba, whose party had won the most seats (though not a majority) in the new legislative body, the prime minister, and Kasavubu president. Within three days of independence, the Congolese Army rebelled against its Belgian officers, demanding greater freedom and higher pay. Independence became a farce when within two weeks Belgian paratroopers occupied the capital city on the pretext of protecting their countrymen. Next, Moïse Tshombe (moh-*ees′ chahm*′bay), prime minister of the Katanga Regional Government, declared that his immensely rich mineral region had seceded from the newly independent Congo. Since Belgian (and to some extent, British) business interests controlled the economy of Katanga, Belgians contributed white mercenary soldiers, money, and arms to Tshombe's secessionist move.

The Congolese appeal for outside help. Amid rising disorder, Prime Minister Lumumba sought outside aid. First, he sent a plea to President Eisenhower, asking the United States to prevent Belgium from reoccupying his country. Then, Lumumba appealed to the United Nations. After considerable debate, the UN Security Council resolved that Belgium should remove its troops from the Congo and that the United Nations should send an international force to help keep order. Disappointed by the American response to his request, and doubtful that the United Nations could meet its commitment, Lumumba addressed a third plea — this time to the Soviet Union.

Whereas the United States and independent African countries channeled their help to the Congo through the United Nations, the Soviet Union delivered materials directly to Lumumba. Guns and ammunition, trucks and supplies, technicians and advisers were flown to the Congo from Moscow. Lumumba's close relations with the Russians alarmed some of his fellow politicians. With encouragement

After the murder of Patrice Lumumba, first premier of The Congo, he became a hero to many Africans in other countries. In their eyes, Lumumba was a symbol of resistance to foreign intervention and of the drive for national unity in new African countries. A postage stamp showing the fallen leader and a map of his troubled country was issued by Morocco, at that time a member of the "radical" Casablanca Bloc.

from Belgium and other Western nations, President Kasavubu dismissed Lumumba from his post as prime minister. An army officer named Joseph Mobutu (moh-*boo'*too) then stepped in and ordered the Russians to leave the country.

The Lumumbists form a new national government. Lumumba and his followers planned to establish their own government in Stanleyville, the capital of Oriental, or Eastern, Province. But, while trying to escape to Stanleyville, Lumumba was captured by Mobutu's troops and imprisoned. His supporters, however, did reach Stanleyville. So strong was Lumumba's support that this rebel government soon gained control of Oriental and large sections of other provinces. Consequently, by the beginning of 1961, the Kasavubu/Mobutu government found itself increasingly insecure. Not only was half the country outside its control, but there was a feeling in the United States (under the new Kennedy administration) and among United Nations officials that the Lumumbists were too strong to be excluded from power. The continuance of two rival regimes, however, obviously provided an opportunity for Communist intervention.

Fearing that the growing support for Lumumba might topple their regime, the Leopoldville authorities ordered the transfer of their very important prisoner to Katanga. Thus Lumumba came into the hands of his archenemy, Tshombe. Soon after Lumumba's arrival in Katanga, he was murdered. His death touched off a wave of anger throughout the continent, where Lumumba had become a symbol of independent Africa's struggle to win freedom from foreign domination. At this juncture, the United Nations passed a strongly worded resolution that the Congo be returned to parliamentary rule and that the UN be granted necessary powers to deal with outside intervention. This resolution led to a temporary alliance between the Kasavubu regime and Katanga. But it was clear that Tshombe had no real intention of ending his separatist rule over Katanga, and the Kasavubu regime opened negotiations with the Lumumbists. As a result of these negotiations, parliament reconvened under UN protection and a new national government was formed.

Civil war is renewed. Meanwhile, Tshombe, with the help of Belgian officers and mercenaries from many Western countries, had created a powerful army in Katanga. Negotiations to remove these foreign troops were going on in 1962 when fighting broke out between the Katanga army and UN troops. This fighting caused controversy all over the world — with the role of UN forces being called into question. The UN effort was further shaken when UN Secretary-General Dag Hammarskjöld (*hah'*mar-shuld) was killed in an airplane crash while flying to negotiate with Tshombe. Under his suc-

Soldiers from African nations served in the international force created by the United Nations to keep order in The Congo. Here an Ethiopian general reviews UN troops stationed in the rebellious province of Katanga.

cessor, U Thant (*oo' tahnt'*), however, the UN passed an even stronger resolution against Katanga. The fighting which again broke out in Elisabethville (the capital of Katanga) was ended temporarily when Tshombe agreed in principle that Katanga's secession should be ended and the whole Congo reunited. Discussions to achieve these ends dragged on and once again fighting broke out. Not until January, 1963, did the secessionist movement in Katanga come to an end. Tshombe was sent into exile.

Differences over Katanga lead to another split in the government. Guerrilla bands trained by a Lumumbist, however, continued to resist the national army. When it became clear that the army could not control this spreading rebellion, President Kasavubu, in desperation, agreed to appoint Tshombe prime minister until an election could be held. The president's reasoning was that Tshombe commanded sufficient support, especially in Katanga, that the government with his help could restore order. Tshombe, however, was unable to make good his promise to negotiate with the rebels. As rebel strength continued to grow, Tshombe called on the United States for military aid.

This move was a tragedy for all concerned. True, American aid plus large numbers of white mercenaries enabled Tshombe to push back the rebel forces into the eastern Congo. But as the rebels grew more desperate, their reprisals against white hostages became more brutal. Rebel resistance to government forces began to crumble in 1965, and by the middle of the year this second Congolese rebellion was all but ended. The causes leading to it had not been dealt with, but an uneasy peace had come to the troubled Congo.

Tshombe is convicted of treason. Disagreement between President Kasavubu and Prime Minister Tshombe resulted in the latter's dismissal from office. But Tshombe's influence in the Congolese parliament was so great that he was able to block the confirmation of a new prime minister. At this point a bloodless coup, led by General Mobutu, deposed Kasavubu. Tshombe's travels abroad and his dealings with Belgian businessmen had aroused widespread suspicion that he was in league with the Belgians. And it was rumored that once again Tshombe was recruiting a mercenary army to take over power. A mutiny of pro-Tshombe soldiers in Kisangani[2] seemed to confirm this suspicion.

---

[2] In 1966, the Congolese government changed the names of Leopoldville, Stanleyville, and Elisabethville to Kinshasa, Kisangani, and Lubumbashi.

Presidents Mobutu of Zaire and Senghor of Senegal (right and left) conferred with President Sadat of Egypt in 1971. In their conflict with Israel, Arab leaders welcome support from black Africans.

After the Congolese Parliament ousted Tshombe from membership in that body, he went into exile in Spain. A three-man military court in Kinshasa tried Tshombe *in absentia*, found him guilty of treason, and sentenced him to death. During the summer of 1967, a white-led mercenary force launched a rebellion against Mobutu's government in eastern Oriental and Kivu provinces. This insurrection was linked to the kidnaping of Tshombe in June, when a plane in which he was flying was hijacked and diverted to Algeria. Mobutu, however, charged that Tshombe had planned the new uprising before his seizure. He asked Algeria to turn Tshombe over to the Congolese government. Meanwhile, the United States announced its support of the Mobutu government. The UN Security Council adopted still another resolution condemning foreign intervention, and by the beginning of 1968, Mobutu's government had restored order. The troubled nation seemed at last to be at peace.

The Congo finds stability and economic recovery. When General Mobutu had taken over the Congo government, the economy was chaotic. Trained foreign personnel had fled the country during the years following independence, and inflation and a heavy foreign debt further hurt the economy. But since Mobutu has been in power, the economy has been making rapid strides. His formula for success has been to stress rapid industrialization and monetary stability. He has energetically encouraged private foreign investment, but at the same time has kept a close watch on the activities of foreign companies already in the country. Foreigners, especially Belgians, were allowed to take over the management of public enterprises whose managers had not been able to do a good job — for example, in the Katanga copper mines.

A growing confidence in the country was reflected in the decision in 1971 to change the name of the country (and the Congo River) to *Zaire;* this had been the name of the river before the white man arrived in Africa.[3] There have been some minor disturbances, such as student demonstrations and accusations of an attempted coup. But, compared to the early 1960's, recent years have been marked by peace and stability. Mobutu has made Zaire a one-party state, and in 1970 he was elected to a seven-year term as president.

● CHECK-UP

1. Why was the Central African Federation established? Why was it dissolved?
2. How did Kenya achieve independence? Tanganyika? Uganda? What is the East African Community?
3. Why was the Belgian Congo poorly prepared for independence? Why did factional strife break out? What was the reaction of the UN and the great powers? What part did Katanga play?
4. How has the Congo, now Zaire, fared under Mobutu?

5. African Liberation Is Not Complete

By 1968, 42 nations of Africa were independent. Two of these, Rhodesia and South Africa, had white governments, which allowed little freedom to the Africans living there. In these two countries, as well as in Angola, Guinea-Bissau, Mozambique, and Namibia, the struggle for freedom has continued, but resistance to African independence is much stronger in these lands than it was in other African countries. The freedom movements are bound to bring violence and bloodshed; and some experts doubt if South Africa, the major stronghold of white rule, will be liberated in this century.

Portugal still has an empire in Africa. The Portuguese, who have been in Africa longer than any other European power, still rule three

[3] Also, the president changed his own name from Joseph Mobutu to Mobutu Sese Seko, a more authentic African name.

African countries: Guinea-Bissau (Portuguese Guinea), Angola, and Mozambique. Portugal's future in Africa is in doubt, however, since the liberation movements in these three countries are strong enough to force Portugal to spend almost half its yearly budget in fighting them.

The most successful liberation movement is in Guinea-Bissau, a small, poor country wedged between Guinea and Senegal. Beginning in 1962, a liberation group launched a well-organized guerrilla movement to liberate the countryside. The PAIGC, as this group is known, has won control of nearly two-thirds of the territory. This military success is impressive, but even more impressive have been the social and political successes of the PAIGC. By the end of 1967 its spokesmen claimed that the number of children in school in the liberated areas was eight times greater than in 1962. In 1972 the PAIGC held elections for the National Assembly in the liberated areas, with 90 per cent of the registered voters participating. A blow to the movement was the assassination of a talented leader, Amilcar Cabral, in 1973.

Angola is a large country rich in diamonds and iron ore. Its liberation movement began in 1961 with a sudden uprising in which

In 1961 the first two Congolese doctors graduated from Lovanium University in ceremonies attended by the Belgian faculty. Lovanium, the first university in The Congo, had been founded only seven years before, so few professional men were trained under colonial rule.

poorly armed and undisciplined nationalist soldiers terrorized the white population. The Portuguese army set about restoring order and claimed to have reconquered the country by mid-1963. Some 350,000 Angolan refugees fled into the Congo, from which they have operated two competing guerrilla movements. The friction between these two has weakened efforts to liberate Angola. By the early 1970's the Portuguese seemed to have the upper hand, though guerrillas continue to inflict damage from time to time.

The third Portuguese colony is Mozambique, an agricultural nation whose population is only 1 per cent white. An African group that has operated in this colony is the Mozambique Liberation Front, or FRELIMO for short. Under the leadership of Dr. Eduardo C. Mondlane, who was later assassinated, FRELIMO claimed in the 1960's to control several areas of Mozambique. Operating out of Tanzania, FRELIMO has centered its efforts on sabotaging the construction of the Cabora Bassa Dam, a huge project in northern Mozambique. The Portuguese, who are hoping the hydroelectric dam will transform the economy of Mozambique, plan to bring one million whites from Portugal to settle there. Deciding to go on the

Black Angolan guerrillas continue their efforts to overthrow the Portuguese government in their country. This photo shows guerrilla forces of the ARGE (Angola Revolutionary Government in Exile) attacking a Portuguese military convoy.

offensive, in 1970 Portugal used 35,000 troops to break up the rebel strongholds in the Cabora Bassa area. The Portuguese claim that the drive was so successful that FRELIMO has now all but stopped military activity in the north. FRELIMO, plagued with leadership troubles since Mondlane's death, has now splintered. A new group, MOLIMO, takes its inspiration from Mao Tse-tung and Fidel Castro.

The success or failure of the liberation movements in Portuguese Africa depends in part on how long Portugal can continue to bear the financial burden of fighting African guerrillas. Though a relatively poor country, Portugal gets large sums of money from the United States and France for the use of military bases in the Azores. Also, Portugal's partners in the North Atlantic Treaty Organization (including the United States) give Portugal military aid. Officially, no NATO aid is to be used in Africa, but the Portuguese get around this by declaring that the African provinces are actually part of Portugal.

Rhodesia and Great Britain fail to agree on independence. To the west of Mozambique lies Rhodesia (formerly Southern Rhodesia), another area where white rule continues. In 1965 the Rhodesian white minority government declared independence from Great Britain, but the British refused to recognize independence since the 4.8 million blacks had no effective voice in the government. (Only about a quarter million people in Rhodesia are white.) Britain imposed economic sanctions against Rhodesia in an effort to force negotiations and called on other nations of the world to stop trade with Rhodesia as well. The United States co-operated with Britain in an embargo on oil, which forced one of Rhodesia's refineries to close. But for the most part the economic sanctions have not worked because of lack of support from the majority of countries, including the United States.

After several attempts at negotiations had failed, in 1971 Rhodesia and Great Britain reached an agreement on a constitution for Rhodesia. It provided for voting qualifications of salary, property, or education that the vast majority of black Rhodesians could not fulfill. Britain agreed to honor the constitution if a survey of Rhodesia showed that the majority of all Rhodesians accepted it. A commission traveled to Rhodesia and held public meetings and private discussions to determine public opinion. Its conclusion, reported to the British government, was that while the proposals were acceptable to the great majority of whites, the majority of Africans

Apartheid, or racial segregation, is strictly enforced at a bus terminal in South Africa. As the sign says, this ticket window is for whites only. *Blankes* means "whites" in Afrikaans, the language of the South African Boers, which is based on Dutch. The two languages on the sign are required by law. This reflects another kind of division in the country — that which exists between South Africans of Boer descent and those of English ancestry.

rejected them. When the British government accepted this report and announced it would continue sanctions, Rhodesia and Britain were back in the same old stalemate that had existed since 1965.

Rhodesian liberationists have not been effective. The liberation movement in Rhodesia has not been strong. The Zimbabwe African Peoples Union (ZAPU) and the Zimbabwe African Nationalist Union (ZANU)[4] have been banned in Rhodesia, and now have their headquarters in Zambia. Conflicts between ZAPU and ZANU have further weakened their effectiveness. Since 1968, however, guerrilla activity has been troublesome enough for the Rhodesian government to ask South Africa for help in policing the border with Zambia.

White rule in South Africa is based on total segregation. Except for Rhodesia, South Africa is the only independent African country ruled by a white minority. Of its more than 22 million inhabitants, less than 4 million are white. About 60 per cent of the whites speak Afrikaans (ahf-rik-*ahnz'*), a language which has evolved from the Dutch spoken by the original white settlers. In 1948 the Afrikaaner Nationalist Party won control of the government and began to implement its policy of total racial segregation, called *apartheid* (uh-*pahr'*tayt), meaning "apartness." The Afrikaaner answer to the rising tide of black nationalism and the emergence of free nations

[4] Black nationalists in Rhodesia want to change the country's name to Zimbabwe.

to the north has been to deny Africans any right to participate in the government which controls their lives.

The South African government has established some 300 reserves — somewhat similar to Indian reservations in the United States — for the Black African "Bantu" population. In theory, the reserves are eventually supposed to become "Bantustans," semi-independent countries in which all Africans in South Africa would live. At present, about seven million Africans live in the homelands. These areas comprise only 12.9 per cent of the land — and it is the poorest land. Jobs and opportunities for a good life on the reserves are few.

Eight million Africans now live in "black" areas near the cities; they provide the labor which is necessary for the South African economy. Any African who enters a white area must carry his "registration book"; moreover, if it is not correct in every detail, he may be arrested. Those Africans who do have jobs in the white areas may work only on one-year contracts and can never bring their families to live with them. The families must stay behind in the homelands. Since South Africa's highly developed economy depends on

Opposition to rigid government control occasionally erupts in South Africa. Here a white student hurls a tear-gas canister back at police during an anti-apartheid demonstration in Cape Town.

the labor of millions of Africans, it seems unlikely that complete separation will ever come about.

The African liberation movement hardly exists within South Africa. Refugees from that country have formed the African National Congress in other nations, but within South Africa an efficient police force with many paid informers manages to stifle any expression of dissent.

South Africa refuses to give up control of Namibia. The United Nations has repeatedly demanded that South Africa give up control of Namibia, a diamond-rich country which borders South Africa. This is the country that, under the name South-West Africa, was mandated to South Africa during World War I (page 236). The South Africans have refused to leave Namibia, even ignoring a ruling by the International Court of Justice that their rule of the area is illegal. In fact, the South Africans have already introduced apartheid and Bantustans in Namibia. A liberation group operating out of Zambia, SWAPO (South-West African People's Organization), seems to have had little impact. But it has continued guerrilla activity, especially in northern Namibia.

The liberation groups depend on outside aid. Remembering the humiliation of being ruled by colonial powers, most African nations make some contribution to the liberation movements in the white-ruled countries. Tanzania, Guinea, Zambia, and Zaire have played a crucial role in any successes the liberation groups have had by allowing them to train on their soil and granting them access to the borders of the white-ruled countries. The major source of financial aid has been the Communist nations. The Scandinavians have made direct government grants to the liberation movements, but other aid from western countries has come primarily from private sources, such as church groups or humanitarian organizations.

Will the liberation movements be successful in the white-ruled countries? The whites are determined not to share their political power with the black majority, and the liberation groups seem weak, divided by infighting, and hampered by lack of funds. However, some of them have been operating for ten years or more. In Mozambique and Angola they cost Portugal a tremendous amount of money, and they seem to be getting support from a number of Africans from within most of the white-ruled countries. No one can say what the future of white rule is in these countries, but it appears that the liberation movements will never give up the struggle.

• CHECK-UP

1. What successes have liberation movements had in the Portuguese-ruled countries of Africa? What problems do they face?
2. Why did Great Britain not recognize Rhodesia's declaration of independence?
3. What has been South Africa's policy toward non-whites? Why is it so difficult for a liberation movement to get under way there?
4. What is the political status of Namibia?
5. From what sources do the various liberation groups in Africa get aid? Why is it difficult to predict their future?

Summing Up

The principles of freedom enunciated in the Atlantic Charter were put to severe test by the postwar African liberation movements. Libya became a sovereign nation in 1951, and five years later Sudan, Morocco, and Tunisia were granted independence. South of the Sahara, however, a few more years were to pass before the yoke of foreign domination was thrown off.

The African experience in World War II had added leaven to the widespread yearning for independence. The Allied war effort was greatly aided by African manpower and natural resources. The very fact of these contributions to Allied victory called attention to the contradiction between the victors' earlier pronouncements about freedom and their continuation of colonial rule in Africa. Such spokesmen for African liberation movements as Kwame Nkrumah and Jomo Kenyatta pressed this moral advantage to the full in demanding complete and immediate independence. The United Nations, furthermore, provided a forum for African complaints against colonial "trustees" who were dragging their feet in carrying out the UN charge to prepare Africans for self-government. African nationalists were encouraged, too, by the spectacular successes of Asian independence movements.

In general, African countries remained aloof from the Cold War. Most African leaders avoided taking sides in the East-West power struggle, preferring to accept economic aid from any country that offered it. Radio and the press have played an increasingly important role in shaping African public opinion. Certain African countries have managed to achieve independence relatively peacefully; others have won it at the cost of much bloodshed; several are still struggling to escape from white domination.

Of the former British colonies, Ghana was first to win its freedom (1957). By granting Africans a measure of political responsibility prior to independence, the British hoped to prepare them for self-rule, and to insure an orderly transition to freedom. But this gradual process was too slow for the new nationalist leaders, including Ghana's Kwame Nkrumah. Largely in response to pressure exerted by him and his followers, elections were held in 1957 to decide the makeup of the new government. Nkrumah obtained the presidency, which he held until he was overthrown in 1966. Nigeria posed a different set of problems. In that country, artificially created boundaries enclosed three distinctly different regions. For a time the British solution — a federation of three independent states — seemed to work, but by the 1960's, regional antagonisms had erupted into civil war. The eastern province seceded in 1966, calling itself the Republic of Biafra. The war lasted until 1970, when Biafra surrendered. Since then, Nigeria has made steady progress toward political stability and a healthy economy.

In East Africa white settlers tried to thwart national liberation movements. One tactic, which failed, was the formation of an East African Federation, linking Kenya, Uganda, and Tanganyika. The federation was to have been under the thumb of the white minority. The Mau Mau rebellion (1952–1955) made clear the necessity for an early transfer of political power to Africans. In elections held in the 1960's, Kenya and other nearby states did attain freedom from British rule. This could not be said of Rhodesia, however. There the white minority defied British directives to form a coalition government of whites and blacks.

France at first sought by various means to retain some degree of control over its African colonies. An offer of internal self-rule, with membership in the French Community, was rejected first by Guinea, and then by a succession of other French colonies. While ridding themselves of French political control, these countries have retained some economic ties with France and certain useful cultural traditions inherited from their colonial background. Furthermore, this common legacy has tended to bring former French colonies together into regional groupings (such as OCAM) for mutual economic advantage.

The struggle of the Belgian Congo (present-day Zaire) for independence was complicated by (1) Belgium's reluctance to keep hands off the Congolese economic and political situation after formal independence had been granted, and (2) a long, drawn-out struggle for power among Congolese factions, complicated by foreign intervention and ideological differences. By the late 1960's, however, peace had come to the troubled country under President Mobutu's government, and Zaire began to build a stable, healthy economy.

In the white-ruled countries of southern Africa and in Guinea-Bissau, Africans have yet to gain their freedom. African liberation movements have used guerrilla tactics to harass Portugal and the governments in Rhodesia and Namibia, but these movements remain basically weak. South Africa's white-minority government remains in complete control of that country.

In the African countries which did achieve independence, the leaders and their people had to undertake the enormous tasks of nation-building. In this endeavor they needed a sense of unity and purpose as well as economic aid from the developed nations.

. . . .

CHAPTER REVIEW

Can You Identify?

liberation movement	Touré	Lumumba
indirect rule	Mboya	Mobutu
"civilizing mission"	Kenyatta	Biafra
French Community	Nyerere	Namibia
Casablanca Bloc	apartheid	OCAM
East African Community	Bantustans	FRELIMO
Luthuli	Mau Mau	Idi Amin
Nkrumah	Kaunda	

What Do You Think?

1. Why were African states courted by both sides in the Cold War? How did they react?

2. Which conception of its role as a colonial power was probably better for Africans — that of Britain or France? Explain.

3. Why did South Africa adopt its policy of apartheid?

4. Why was Nkrumah, the man who led Ghana to independence, later ousted from the presidency?

5. After independence, why did internal conflicts plague Nigeria? The former Belgian Congo?

Extending and Applying Your Knowledge

1. The poem "Dawn in the Heart of Africa," by Patrice Lumumba, a leader in the Congo's independence movement, reflects the bitterness Africans felt toward colonialism. Read and report on this poem. See *Africa: Selected Readings*, pages 206–207.

2. The emotional appeal of Nkrumah's campaigning is brought out in "Freedom Now," in *Africa: Selected Readings*, pages 201–206.

3. Excerpts from the writings of Julius Nyerere present this leader's hopes and plans for African self-reliance in economic development. See *Africa: Selected Readings*, pages 213–219.

PROBLEMS OF NATION-BUILDING IN AFRICA

For most African countries, independence marked the beginning of the difficult process of creating a modern unified nation out of a colony that included many different ethnic groups. Diverse African populations were often lumped together within artificial boundaries drawn by agreements among imperialist powers. In Chapter 7 attention was focused principally on the political and economic problems confronting a given colony as it struggled toward independence. In this chapter the major emphasis is on the demands confronting substantially all newly independent states engaged in nation-building.

1. Emerging Countries Must Overcome Many Economic and Social Barriers to Achieve a Viable Nationhood

Far-reaching economic changes are needed. Since World War II, the two-thirds of the human race living in Africa, Asia, and Latin America have become increasingly aware of their poverty and are demanding that something be done to alleviate their condition. The more this two-thirds of the world's population recognize the possibility of improvement, the greater will be their demands on governments — their own and those of wealthier lands — to transform the dreams into reality. The steadily growing demand for a better life for the world's poor has been called "the revolution of rising expectations."

Nation-building means modernization, and this in turn means creating the wealth necessary to end the humiliating condition of poverty, ignorance, and disease. Although it is the second largest continent, Africa has only a small proportion of the world's improved roads and railways, telegraph and telephone lines, automobiles and trucks, power plants and factories. For example, of the world's total of more than two billion ton-miles of railway traffic, Africa in a recent year accounted for less than 2 per cent. Only 2 per cent of the world's motor vehicles are in Africa, and the continent accounts for less than 6 per cent of the world's total imports and exports. The problem of transportation takes on meaning when one notes that a large country such as Madagascar has less than 600 miles of railway, Nigeria about 10,000 miles of paved roads, and Mauritania fewer than 5000 motor vehicles. Some African countries have no railroads at all. Electricity, a good indicator of the degree of modernization, tends to be limited to Africa's capital cities. In a recent year, all of Africa consumed less than 2 per cent of the world's production of electrical energy. The total for tropical Africa — excluding the Republic of South Africa — was less than one-half of 1 percent!

Technical skills are in short supply. The shortage of human resources, in the sense of skilled and educated people, is even more

Africa needs more modern technicians, such as this TV cameraman who works at Station VOK (Voice of Kenya) in Nairobi. Not all African nations have television, and broadcasts often are limited to the capital city.

serious. For even if minerals, hydroelectric power, and investment capital to pay for plant and machines were available, skilled workers would have to be found to insure efficient production. Many years are needed to train a skilled technician. Thousands of schools are required to provide Africans with elementary and high school education. Then there must be colleges and universities to prepare Africans for the professions and government service. This requires buildings, equipment, and research facilities. Even more important, a trained professional staff of teachers must be found for each new school or university that is built.

Africans want to Africanize jobs held by foreigners. After more than a decade of independence, African nations are dismayed that so many important positions in their economies are held not by Africans but by Europeans, Asians, Syrians, and Lebanese. Most countries quickly Africanized their civil services (government jobs), but many foreigners remained in private business. Africans as businessmen have several handicaps. Generally, they lack the capital or property needed to set up a business. They also lack technical training and practical business experience. Many countries have passed laws to restrict certain businesses to citizens, but these laws do not always work. In Liberia, whites have set up Africans as the front men for businesses, while the whites remain in control.

Asians have been forced to leave some countries. In Central and East Africa, Africans have especially resented Asian businessmen. The Asians first came to East Africa from India in 1902 to build a railroad from Kampala, Uganda, to Mombasa, Kenya. In the 1920's and 1930's more Indians came; these were artisans and shopkeepers. The Asians worked hard and prospered and soon completely controlled trade in the area. In cities one could see shop after shop owned by Asians and few, if any, owned by Africans. The feeling grew that the middle-class Asians were exploiting Africans, and it was also resented that the Asians, who held onto their foreign customs, showed no desire to become part of the African community. Relations between Africans and Asians worsened when most Asians backed the British during the independence movements.

As the British colonies became independent, the British offered the Asians living in these countries the chance to become British citizens. More than half chose British citizenship in preference to citizenship of the country in which they were living. They did not go to Britain to live, however, because their livelihood was in Africa.

Because of racial tension in Great Britain, the British ruled in 1968 that a British passport would not guarantee the right to enter Britain for permanent residence. They limited the number who could enter Britain each year to 5000 families. At the same time, Kenya passed laws to speed up the Africanization of trade. Faced with the loss of livelihood, 15,000 Kenyan Asians left for Britain, fearing that British restrictions would soon increase. The fact that very few Asians chose Kenyan citizenship at the time shows how little faith Asians had in African governments.

Asians fared even worse in Uganda. The Ugandan dictator, General Amin (page 270), voiced all the complaints that Africans have had about Asians. He charged that although Asians had been in Uganda for 70 years, only six Asian women had married African men; that Asians regarded Ugandan citizenship only as an act of convenience; and that many Asians were guilty of bribery, corruption, income-tax evasion, hoarding, profiteering, and sabotaging the government's efforts to get Africans into business. In 1972 General Amin rocked the Asian community of his country when he announced that all Asians who were not Ugandan citizens would have 90 days to leave. At that time there were about 80,000 Asians in Uganda, 30,000 of them Ugandan citizens.

Over the next three months, Asians formed mile-long lines at travel and immigration offices in Uganda. The lines at immigration offices moved slowly since Africans who were not familiar with the procedures replaced Asian immigration officers who were standing in line to get their own papers approved. Most of the departing Asians went to Britain, though other countries also offered to receive them.

Amin ordered any Asians who remained in Uganda to leave the cities and settle in the countryside. Uganda's economy was bound to suffer from the Asians' departure. General Amin announced a government crash program to train retailers, wholesalers, distributors, and importers, but he admitted that Uganda lacked qualified teachers to carry out this program.

Agricultural development is getting more attention. In the first decade of independence, most new African nations stressed industrial development as the way to raise living standards. But by the early 1970's many leaders were realizing that they had not placed enough emphasis on rural development. In most nations industrial development had not been a success. There was a scarcity of capital within the countries, and some leaders wanted to avoid overdependency on outside aid. Even if there had been new factories producing, for example, bicycles, cloth, and radios, most Africans were so poor that they could not have bought them, and consequently the factories would have failed.

Since at least 80 per cent of all Africans are subsistence farmers, rural development seemed to be a wiser investment than industrial development. It costs much less to distribute fertilizer or improved seeds to hundreds of farmers than it does to build a factory which might employ only a hundred people. In the 1970's, therefore, most African countries began to budget more money for rural development than they had in the first ten years of independence.

Life for most Africans is not easy. The leaders of new African nations invariably pointed out that their homelands were underdeveloped primarily because colonial rulers had exploited their resources and deprived them of an opportunity to become modern states. With independence achieved, these leaders had to prove to their people that they could "deliver the goods." Somehow they must break through the maze of poverty, ill health, and ignorance.

One of the first problems the new governments had to tackle was hunger. Food is often limited in African countries, and hunger is a constant companion of the majority. Meat is seldom eaten. Even if an animal is slaughtered, its flesh must be consumed immediately or it will spoil, especially in the tropical countries. The diet of many Africans is not a healthful one; it tends to be high in starches and low in protein.

Because modern medications are now available for many diseases, population has grown rapidly. But when more babies live past infancy, there are more mouths to feed from the same acreage. Although the production of food in Africa has increased since World War II, the increase has not been greater than that in population. As a result, the amount of food *per person* has not increased.

Moreover, disease is still a serious problem. An inadequate diet, a difficult climate, and lack of knowledge of sanitation and preventive medicine are chiefly responsible for the diseases that plague Africa. Malaria, for example, is common everywhere except at high altitudes. Although it rarely kills its victims, malaria saps the strength and energy of millions. On the hopeful side, certain dreaded diseases which once were widespread — such as leprosy and sleeping sickness — are now being controlled. Unfortunately, others, such as bilharzia, seem to be on the increase. This malady is contracted from snails found in African rivers and lakes. The snails thrive in the slow-moving waters resulting from modern dams and irrigation ditches. People afflicted with bilharzia usually become very anemic and weak. It is estimated that three-quarters of all the people who live near the great lakes of Africa suffer from this debilitating illness. Other diseases, such as tuberculosis, worm infestation, and syphilis, are also widespread.

Furthermore, ignorance hampers efforts to improve health. Debilitating diseases sap the energy of the people and contribute to their continued poverty. Poverty makes it all but impossible to extend education to those who need it badly. It is a vicious circle which can be broken only by dedicated effort on the part of the African peoples and aid from abroad. But Africans are increasingly aware of these health problems and are striving to improve their medical and public health facilities.

A shared feeling of national identity is required. More is involved in nation-building than improvement in the standard of living. Man requires pride in himself if he is to survive as a man. For a long time many Africans seemed to accept comparative poverty and lack of education. But during World War II, large numbers of Africans were made painfully aware — through books and radio, personal experience, and word of mouth — that they were economically and politically deprived. They bitterly realized that they were treated as people incapable of ruling themselves. They first requested, then demanded, independence. But, after obtaining it they no longer felt any compelling need for unity against a colonial power. Thus, ironically, national independence sometimes was followed by an upsurge of old local and tribal loyalties.

Nation-building in Africa, therefore, requires not only new roads, factories, schools, and hospitals, but an attachment to the nation itself, a feeling of "we-ness" on the part of all who live within the national boundaries. Of course these two aspects of nation-building are closely related. Roads are necessary to link the capital city to the outlying provinces in order that buses and trucks can operate to bring the people more closely together. Radio stations are needed to broadcast programs which will promote the appreciation of cultural values — especially those which can be shared by all citizens. Above all else, schools are needed to teach citizens to read, for the printed

NATIONAL LITERACY CAMPAIGN .....LIBERIA

LEARNING. Many African adults are starting their education by learning to read, like these women in Ghana (*above, left*). Handmade posters (*above*) are part of a campaign to end illiteracy in Liberia. The United Nations aided Cameroon in founding a school to train high school teachers where (*left*) a future biology instructor learns to prepare microscope slides. From modern universities such as Ibadan in Nigeria (*below*), graduates are emerging to meet Africa's urgent need for teachers and technicians, but some new nations are too poor to provide jobs for them.

word can foster the knowledge and the emotional awareness of a common heritage and national identity.

Africans are eager for knowledge. Immediately after independence most African governments spent more money on education than on any other item in the budget. Leaders had promised free universal education to the people, and, moreover, they believed that education was one of the best ways to build a nation. More children (though not all) were able to attend school than ever before. Africans were enthusiastic about learning. Even adults would travel great distances to attend classes in reading, agricultural techniques, or child care.

Emphases in education have changed. After several years, African leaders began to have doubts about their earlier emphasis on mass education. After elementary school, an African student must pass a very difficult test to be able to attend secondary school. Only a small percentage of the students are accepted for secondary school, and the rest — called school-leavers — cannot further their education. The school-leavers, who have learned to read and write and know something of the outside world, are not content to stay and farm in their villages. They head for the big cities, where they think they can find excitement and a respectable job. But, in countries where there are so few factories, jobs are just not available. In the United States the great migration to the cities occurred at a time of rapid industrial development. A young person with very little skill who left the farm 50 or 100 years ago could easily find a job in Chicago or New York. In 1970 in Ghana 20 to 35 per cent of the labor force was unemployed, and 70,000 to 80,000 school-leavers were entering the job market each year!

Faced with these realities, Africans began to reassess their educational programs. In Tanzania, President Nyerere decided to emphasize agriculture in the curriculum, instead of the usual academic subjects, since farming would undoubtedly be the main livelihood of the great majority of Tanzanians for years to come.

Other African governments have chosen not to spend as much on education as before. Now the budgets stress such items as roads, ports, and electricity, and more money is going into the rural areas. Another item that has been greatly increased is military expenditures.

Boys get more schooling than girls. In most African countries, education is not yet either universal or free. Parents often have to choose which of their children to send to school. In many parts of

WOMEN. The women of modern Africa carry on old roles, such as farming, but also learn new ones. Left, this Kenyan farm woman, dumping a basket of tea leaves, works along with her husband on a small tea co-operative. A demonstration in Tanzania (below) shows that many women want an expanded role in building the "new Africa."

Africa, the betrothal of a young woman calls for the father of the prospective groom to present a dowry in the form of cattle or money to the parents of the bride-to-be. If a girl is in school beyond the age of about fourteen, she may, in effect, be depriving her family of the wealth she would bring if she married. This fact, plus the cost of education, helps to explain why most African students are boys.

African cities are growing fast. The millions of young Africans who stream into the cities help make Africa's cities the fastest growing in the world. In general, the population is increasing faster in the big cities than in the small ones. Like the rest of the world, Africa is now having to deal with the problems usually found in rapidly growing cities, such as unemployment, crime, and inadequate water supplies and sanitation systems. In cities all over Africa one can see youths waiting outside employment offices or standing near shops and restaurants with odd bits of merchandise to sell — watchbands or small pieces of hardware. Often they sell nothing all day long. Heavy unemployment, of course, leads to crime.

Governments are trying different methods to solve these problems. In Nairobi, the Kenyan government ordered employers to hire 10 per cent more workers, whether they needed them or not. Educational television in the Ivory Coast portrays farming as an occupation worthy of respect. The aim is to change the notion that it is beneath the dignity of an educated person to farm for a living. Nigeria has begun publicly executing thieves to try to discourage theft.

Economic development requires the investment of wealth which somebody has earned but not consumed. How can the poor African countries find wealth to build the schools, clinics, and roads that the people need to raise their standard of living? If a new government were able to increase food production by 10 per cent, it would find it difficult to persuade farmers living at a bare subsistence level not to live better by eating more. But if the additional food *is* consumed at home, the country will be short of exports needed to earn foreign exchange. And without foreign exchange, the country cannot import other necessary commodities, or buy equipment needed to modernize and expand its economy. When a new nation starts with very little, economic development is frustratingly slow and difficult. The average annual income in tropical Africa is rarely higher than 300 dollars per person and in some countries is as low as 60 dollars. Under such conditions, little can be saved or skimmed off through taxation to use for economic development.

Two photos reflect the Western-style growth found in many African cities. Above are modern streets and buildings in downtown Dar es Salaam, Tanzania's capital. Below, young Africans watch planes land at the airport in Douala, Cameroon. The Cameroonian government has improved its urban airports, hoping to attract more tourists.

The African economies are affected by price fluctuations on the world market. Another problem of the African economies is that, like those of other countries, they have to depend on the world market for their exports. If the world price for copper, for example, falls sharply, the economy of Zambia, which depends heavily on the export of copper, will suffer. The drop in the price paid for the mineral might lead to the closing down of mines. If the mines close, much of the labor force will be thrown out of work. Another country that is heavily dependent on a single export is Sierra Leone. It gets as much as 75 per cent of its export income from the sale of diamonds. Elsewhere on the continent, Tanzania depends heavily on coffee, cotton, and sisal; Uganda on coffee and cotton; Upper Volta on cattle; Guinea on aluminum ore; Congo on timber; and Ghana on cocoa.

Most crops are sold by the farmers through co-operatives to the government, which in turn sells them on the world market. When

Many nations depend on one mineral or export crop to earn most of their foreign exchange. If the price of this product drops a few cents, a nation may be unable to pay for the manufactured goods it must import.

	"Single Export" Economies									
	◄────── TOTAL VALUE OF EXPORTS ──────►									
Zambia	Copper									
Chad	Cotton									
Liberia	Iron Ore									
Ghana	Cocoa									
Guinea	Aluminum Ore									
Sierra Leone	Diamonds									
Uganda	Coffee									
Somalia	Livestock									
Senegal	Peanut Products									
Dahomey	Palm Oil and Nuts									
PER CENT	0 10 20 30 40 50 60 70 80 90 100									

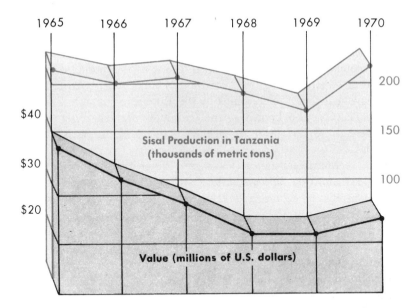

As synthetic fibers replace sisal in making twine, the price of sisal goes down. In 1965 and 1970 Tanzania produced about the same quantity of sisal, but 1970 income was almost half that of 1965.

prices fall drastically, as they have in recent years in the case of cocoa and coffee, the government pays farmers less than in former years. It is difficult to explain to uneducated farmers that the government has no choice in the matter, especially when agitators may be telling them that the government is deliberately cheating them. Economic problems of this nature can easily lead to political instability and revolt.

Nation-building depends in part on aid from abroad. In 1962 the United Nations resolved that the developed nations should dedicate themselves to "a decade of development" to help underdeveloped countries. Great Britain and France recognized that their former colonies had to continue to depend on them for economic and technical assistance. French aid to Africa is larger than that of Great Britain or the United States. Some 10,000 French specialists help the former French African colonies south of the Sahara. Aid also can be "good business" for the former colonial powers, since British and French firms still have large investments in Africa. They are a major source of imports and services, such as transportation, needed by the new countries. In some cases, Britain and France continue to buy African export crops at subsidized high prices, dating from the period when colonial products were developed for use by the mother country.

Another hopeful sign is the fact that 24 independent African nations have associate memberships in the European Economic Community (EEC), also known as the Common Market. A large development fund has been set aside by the EEC to assist these countries.

With technical assistance, loans, and other types of help from developed countries, African nations are expanding production and selling surplus food, minerals, and other products on the world market. In this way they acquire the funds to finance part of their own development. Nevertheless, the need for assistance continues to be far greater than the capacity or the willingness of the developing countries to provide it.

Africa receives aid from the United States. In 1972, United States aid to the African continent amounted to 163 million dollars. This is a substantial sum, even if it is small compared to the assistance given to Asian countries. The developed countries are selective in deciding which African countries to assist. Naturally France and Great Britain channel aid to their former colonies. The United States, on the other hand, seeks to support friendly countries, particularly those in which economic assistance seems most likely to result in successful development. In recent years, the bulk of American aid to Africa has gone to Morocco, Nigeria, Tunisia, Zaire, and the Ivory Coast.

Some African nations have made a choice between reliance on outside aid and on their own resources. African leaders are caught in a dilemma. If a nation welcomes large-scale aid from a foreign country, France, for example, the economy will probably prosper, but Frenchmen will stream into the country and the nation will not feel entirely free in making decisions. On the other hand, if a nation does not encourage aid from outside, it has greater freedom in making policy decisions but the people's standard of living will not improve very much.

Though most African countries try to strike a balance between these two extremes, others have made a definite choice. Ivory Coast, for example, has chosen economic progress over freedom from foreign influence. The French control almost all businesses, and the economy has been growing at a rapid rate. In 1970 there were 40,000 Frenchmen living in the Ivory Coast, four times as many as before independence. Even sales clerks and bank tellers are French. President Mobutu of Zaire appears to be making a similar choice in encouraging foreign investment in that country. In Tanzania, President Nyerere has chosen self-reliance. Tanzania should not depend on money to solve its problems, he says. Instead, it should rely on what it has — land and agriculture and people — to build a better life for Tanzanians. Nyerere's philosophy is shared by President Touré of Guinea, who once told General de Gaulle of France, "We prefer liberty in poverty to opulence in slavery."

● CHECK-UP

1. What is a "revolution of rising expectations"? What are major obstacles to modernization in Africa?
2. Why have so few Africans been businessmen in their own countries? Why is rural development getting an increased amount of attention?
3. What health problems are still severe in Africa?
4. Why is attachment to the nation essential in nation-building? What are some obstacles to this goal?
5. Why does price fluctuation on the world market pose a serious problem for African countries? Why is capital accumulation difficult? What are developed nations doing to help?

2. The Fabric of Traditional Life Is Threatened by Many Changes

Africa is undergoing a social revolution as a consequence of independence and economic development. People are taking new jobs, children are going to school, parents are attending literacy classes, new crops are being planted and sold, and money is being used as a medium of exchange everywhere. But when great changes take place rapidly, serious problems of dislocation and adjustment often result.

Social change is occurring at a fast pace. In Africa the rate of social change has been very rapid. Within a single generation men have moved from an isolated and often simple existence to jet airplanes and involvement in international affairs. People who 20 years ago had never seen a car or an airplane, or ventured more than a few miles from their small villages, today drive powerful trucks long distances and live in modern houses. But the rate of change has

NEW WAYS. Above, a Kikuyu elder holds a fly-whisk, traditional symbol of his authority. But it does not extend to Nairobi, Kenya's busy capital, where a Kikuyu "meter-maid" (*right*) hands out parking tickets.

been uneven. For example, in Tanzania the coffee-growing Chagga people had achieved a relatively high standard of living long before independence. They own better houses than many found in parts of southern and eastern Europe. Only 50 miles away, the nomadic Masai graze their cattle and live, for the most part, just as they did 200 years ago.

When a society undergoes rapid change, the rules regulating behavior often no longer apply. A major problem in rapidly changing Africa is the difficulty of transferring loyalty, respect, and obedience from local (or "tribal") units to larger associations. Today, African farmers belong to co-operative societies. Workers on the large plantations, in the mines, or in urban centers belong to labor unions made up of people from many regions and ethnic groups. Who is to settle a dispute when the traditional law of one group clashes with that of another? A modern nation requires each person to consider himself first and foremost a citizen of that nation. But the process of transferring one's basic loyalties from village or clan to a larger, overarching community requires education and psychological readjustment. It cannot be done overnight. The African people, accustomed to family and local allegiances, cannot be expected to make the transition to national allegiance at a single stroke.

Political instability poses a threat to many new nations. Americans should avoid snap judgments about whether the new African countries are democratic or really ready for independence. Like the Ghanaians and the Nigerians of today, our forefathers struggled to rule themselves — to be free of domination from across the sea. The Articles of Confederation — America's first attempt at national self-government — were unsuccessful and lasted only seven years. The years immediately after independence brought a depression and not prosperity. The Constitution was adopted only after considerable controversy. The Whiskey Rebellion of 1794 indicated that western American farmers saw little reason for paying to the national government a tax which had not been levied by the state governments. Our Alien and Sedition Acts of 1798 severely limited democratic rights.

The new African nations have experienced similar problems. Zaire, Nigeria, and Sudan, for example, had bitter civil wars. In Burundi continued tension between the Hutu majority and Tutsi minority erupted in violence in 1972. An estimated 5000 Tutsi and 100,000 Hutu were killed. In addition to civil disturbances, Africa has been troubled by attempted assassinations of political leaders. Among those assassinated have been presidents of Togo and Somalia and prime ministers of Zaire, Burundi, and Nigeria.

The legacy of France and Britain to their former colonies included the rudiments of democratic government. Democracy is a difficult system of government to institute and maintain in a newly independent, developing country. Should the leader of such a new country tolerate an opposition party which preys on the ignorance of the masses in order to win power? When an African leader is desperately trying to unify a new nation and raise its standard of living, what should he do if the leader of an opposition party accuses him of being dishonest or of depriving the people of the fruits of independence? In the United States, if a candidate for office were to say that the President could make everybody rich by simply printing more money, people would laugh at him. But in a country where the level of education is very low, the majority of people might believe such a statement. Some African leaders reluctantly, and others perhaps willingly, have set aside democratic constitutions and severely limited the rights of an opposition party to combat this kind of irresponsibility. Under these conditions it may prove very difficult for an honest leader to maintain democratic institutions at all times.

Throughout Africa there is a tendency to permit only one political party. Those who led the struggle for independence regard themselves as founders of a nation and tend to regard opposition to their programs as treason. Because many Africans still are unable to distinguish between loyal opposition and political opportunism, the heads of state sometimes must use the powers of government to limit the rights of the opposition. It often is difficult to tell whether a given leader is silencing irresponsible opportunists, or taking steps to keep himself permanently in office. Single-party systems of government are the rule in most African states today; opposition parties function freely in a few countries.

But even though a country may have only one political party, it is possible for democratic procedures to operate within that party. Leaders like Touré and Nyerere argue that their parties are run democratically, but once a decision is made, there can be no opposition. In Tanzanian elections, for example, the party supports an official slate of candidates, but other candidates are allowed to run against them, provided that they, too, are party members. Thus the voters have at least a limited choice, and in a number of contests have voted party leaders out of office in favor of "new faces." Political leaders contend that a weak developing state cannot afford to have an opposition party. All must work together.

Many African nations are now ruled by military governments. In many countries the promises of a golden age made by nationalist leaders during the independence movement have not come true. Instead, many Africans have found their countries beset by inflation, civil disturbances, and corruption in the government, and they see little improvement in the lives of the masses of the people. As has happened in developing nations on other continents, army officers have often stepped in to take over the troubled governments. Since 1960, there have been more than twenty military coups in Africa, and by 1973, one-third of Africa's population was under military rule.

Though each of the military coups was unique, there were similar aspects to all of them. At independence, most African armies still

Military leaders like General Ramanantsoa of the Malagasy Republic have won control of a number of African governments in recent years. Here Ramanantsoa waves to a crowd after taking power in 1972.

had quite a number of European officers, but they were gradually replaced by African officers. In some countries, as the armies became Africanized, the African officers became more and more concerned about worsening problems. Realizing that no other country would interfere, they took over the civilian government by force, often when the president or prime minister was on a trip abroad. The army officers were probably encouraged by the contagious effect of seeing other African armies easily topple civilian governments. Typically, the army leader who took over the country pledged to end inefficiency and corruption in the government.

With few exceptions, military governments do not seem to be more honest or effective than the civilian governments they replaced. But who is going to get rid of them to try to form a better government? Who can force them out without guns? Only rarely do military governments return control to civilians. Once military leaders have tasted the power and excitement of running a country, they do not want to give it up. In Sierra Leone and Dahomey civilian rule was restored when younger army officers, disappointed with the military rule of older officers, led coups and handed over the power to civilians.

Sometimes military governments change their character by becoming more civilian. The military leader wears a business suit instead of a uniform, builds a political party, and holds elections. President Mobutu in Zaire is a prime example of a military leader who became a president and adopted a civilian tone for his government.

Many African countries are seeking larger spheres of unity. Despite Africa's many ethnic groups and difficult problems of nation-building, there exists a powerful movement to link countries into larger units and even to build a United States of Africa. There are many reasons why such unity is desirable. Present boundaries are artificial and there is no long history of defending these frontiers against an enemy. Moreover, most African states do not have a sufficiently large population to support a modern economy. For example, can Gambia, with a population of less than half a million, support its own university, airline, and army? Excluding South Africa, there are only ten African countries — Egypt, Algeria, Morocco, Nigeria, Zaire, Sudan, Ethiopia, Tanzania, Kenya, and Uganda — which have a population over ten million. Small populations and low national incomes help to explain why many African leaders are seeking to forge bigger units of economic and political co-operation through the twelve regional organizations that exist within Africa today.

● CHECK-UP

1. What problems have resulted from rapid social change in Africa? What problems contribute to political instability?
2. Why has a single-party political system developed in many countries? What opportunities for democracy does this system provide? Why have military leaders often taken over governments?
3. Why do African leaders wish to organize larger units of economic and political co-operation?

3. Africans Strive to Preserve Their Cultural and Political Integrity

The newly emergent states of Africa recognize the need to develop greater cohesion and political unity within their borders and to experiment with new forms of political and economic co-operation.

But they also want to rid Africa of unwanted foreign controls. This threefold struggle will doubtless continue for some time. Non-African countries must try to see these problems of nation-building from an African viewpoint.

What form should the movement for African unity take? Should the African countries form regional associations like the East African Community and OCAM (pages 262 and 272), hoping that these large groupings eventually will merge to form a single Pan-Africa? President Nyerere of Tanzania favored such a step and said of the East African Community: "It must be a step towards total African unity."

Ousted President Nkrumah of Ghana thought otherwise. He believed that regional federations would retard the emergence of a continental federation. He proposed, instead, the formation of a United States of Africa. In 1963, a move in this direction was made when the heads of Africa's independent states met at Addis Ababa and signed the charter of a new continent-wide association — the Organization of African Unity (OAU). The charter provides for a permanent secretariat and for regular meetings of the prime ministers of member countries.

Over the years the OAU has become an organization based on voluntary co-operation, with an emphasis on unanimous decisions.

Delegates meet in the new headquarters of the Organization of African Unity at Addis Ababa in Ethiopia. The OAU provides a forum from which African nations can speak with one voice on international issues, and also where they can try to solve their own disputes.

Modern artists in Africa are often inspired by traditional art from the past, such as the wooden mask (*far left*) which was carved in Ivory Coast. A sculptor in Gabon fashioned the eyes of a stone head (*left*) in a way which resembles the slit eye-holes of an old-time mask. Note that the hairdo is carved in slanting lines like those around the edges of the mask which suggest a beard.

NEW LIFE
IN OLD ARTS

African dancing is an art practiced by the whole community, but it includes spectacular leaps and balancing acts by individual performers, such as the Dahomeyan pole-dancer shown at right. New African governments sponsor official troupes of dancers. Their performances, based on traditional folk dances, have been seen in Europe and America.

Left, in Nigeria, dormitories built in African style house students at a new school for training museum personnel. The United Nations helped to establish this center where Africans can study ways of preserving their cultural heritage. It is located near the site where sculptures of the Nok culture were first unearthed.

In Ivory Coast, dancers of the Tropical Ballet re-enact an old legend in pantomime. Note that the king is shaded by a beach umbrella.

Above, artists at the University of Ife in Nigeria paint murals on the walls of a courtyard where dances and plays are presented. Theirs is a modern version of the old African art of decorating clay-plastered walls with colorful designs. The mural at left was photographed in a hut in the Central African Republic and shows a man drinking from a gourd or pot with a long neck and handle.

One of its finest accomplishments has been to serve as a common ground where member countries can solve their disputes. The OAU's membership now consists of every independent African country except South Africa and Rhodesia. It has been particularly outspoken in condemning the white-ruled countries of Africa and supporting the liberation movements in those nations.

Free African countries are determined to rid Africa of the vestiges of colonial rule. The compulsion to eliminate white rule where it still survives is one of the most powerful forces moving Africa towards continental unity. Member nations of OAU see as their goal independence for a race long denied human rights; total victory calls for all of Africa to be free. As Sékou Touré of Guinea put it:

> . . . [So] long as all Africa is not free, Guinea will feel threatened. Consider the man who has injured a finger. The finger alone does not feel pain; if there is pain, it is the whole body of the man that feels it.[1]

In their crusade to rid the continent of the last vestige of white domination, the independent nations of Africa are seeking the assistance of the United Nations and the major world powers. South Africa, Rhodesia, and Portugal are equally determined not to give in and are strengthening their armed forces. Independent African nations, as well as nations outside Africa, support "governments in exile" set up by the liberation movements to care for refugees and train soldiers in the independent nations bordering on white-controlled countries.

The African revolution is a racial as well as a political struggle. The intensity of African feeling about the continued presence of colonialism on the continent reflects the pent-up emotions of peoples who have been exploited by whites. In the early 1960's, although the new African nations shared with the United States and the UN the conviction that the former Belgian Congo should be pacified and unified, they were bitterly opposed to the use of white mercenaries to help achieve this goal. Anti-American feeling in free Africa increased enormously because Africans were led to believe that the United States supported Tshombe's efforts to pacify the Congo rebels. When he was prime minister, Tshombe made use of South

---

[1] Quoted in Paul E. Sigmund, Jr. (ed.), *Ideologies of Developing Nations* (New York: Praeger, 1963), p. 157.

Upstaging the African Dance

In Africa the dance has long been a central feature of community life. From the time a child learns to walk, he also learns the steps of traditional dances, progressing from simple to highly intricate rhythms. The correct execution of a ritual movement can be a physically demanding feat, requiring exceptional vigor and mind-body co-ordination.

The movements in ritual dance are symbolic representations of great themes, and comprise a language clearly understood by the participants. Masks, signifying the presence of a deity or spirit, are often worn to heighten the dramatic impact of the ceremony. Dances also have been used to mark important stages in the life cycle: birth, initiation, marriage, death. And then there are purely social dances, when people dance just for the fun of it.

But education and the shock of contact with foreign cultures have undermined the sacred character of many such dances. In certain areas, dancers are discovering the field of commercial entertainment. An increasing number of the more gifted perform at government-sponsored art festivals or before foreign audiences. As a consequence, traditional dances are undergoing profound changes. They now tend to emphasize the most dramatic movements and to play down the subtler gestures once so meaningful to the participants. As African dances become more self-conscious and spectator-oriented, they sometimes lose in spontaneity. On the other hand, they may gain in skill and technique, and acquire an appeal that is more truly universal.

African mercenaries who were equipped with American arms and ammunition. There was also widespread African resentment against the white people of Europe and the United States who rallied to the support of Biafra, the section of eastern Nigeria which tried to secede in 1967. Although the aid was given to Biafra on humanitarian grounds, American motives were suspected and resented almost everywhere in Africa outside the secessionist state itself.

Charges of "neo-colonialism" have been made. Not only do the new African nations hate the continued white domination of southern Africa; they also fear the reintroduction of outside rule in the liberated nations. The term *neo-colonialism* is used to describe any measure that tends to make an African nation economically or politically dependent on a foreign country.

Suspicious of the motives of the great powers, and feeling compelled to demonstrate their power and independence to their own people, leaders of the new African countries from time to time have made serious accusations against the United States and other countries. In 1964, Tanzania charged that the United States was plotting its overthrow and in 1965 expelled two American diplomats from that country. When two tiny Uganda villages were bombed in 1965 by Congolese using American-built and Cuban-piloted aircraft, the Ugandan government accused the United States of "genocide" and recalled its ambassador from Washington. The food and medical aid which American relief organizations sought to provide Biafra were seen as efforts to re-establish foreign influence in Africa. The unspoken assumption that white people must still do for blacks what they are unable or unwilling to do for themselves is deeply resented.

Americans find it difficult to understand the reasons for anti-Americanism in Africa. Americans recall that the United States has provided millions in aid, sent many Peace Corps volunteers, and invited thousands of Africans to study in this country. Should not Africans be grateful? The fact that Americans expect gratitude is, of course, one reason why anti-Americanism exists. Nobody, and particularly the poor and very sensitive Africans, wants to be indebted to someone. Africans realize that they cannot get along without aid from developed nations, but that does not mean that they like to accept it.

Many Africans have always regarded the United States as an anti-colonial power, and as a country which has demonstrated what rapid modernization can do for the common man. Long before colonialism took over Africa in the 1800's, Africans knew about America's struggle for freedom. In 1784, a British citizen reported that Africans revolting against their colonial overlords in the Mozambique area justified their action with the words: "America is free! Cannot we be?" Today the United States finds it necessary to support positions in world affairs which often are opposed by the majority of new African countries. For example, the fact that Portugal is a member of NATO and therefore an ally of the United States doubtless has tarnished the American image in Africa. Africans also resent our trade with South Africa and importation of chrome from Rhodesia (which continues despite the United Nations' sanctions against trade with Rhodesia).

An American photographer and two Liberian girls visit the Roberts monument, which overlooks Monrovia, Liberia's capital. A sculptured panel shows black settlers from America who landed in Liberia in the 1820's. The monument honors Joseph Roberts, born in Virginia, who became first president of the black republic when it declared its independence in 1847.

A new phase of liberation awaits Africa. The new states of Africa are seeking the complete liberation of their continent. They are striving to build themselves into modern nations. In the process, old practices and beliefs are constantly being challenged by the new. Yet their very insecurity often leads people to cling desperately to old and tried ways. What lies in the future for the dynamic people of this vast continent? How will the emergence of Africa affect the world?

Chapter 7 opened with a quotation from Albert Luthuli's speech in accepting the Nobel Prize. Another quotation from that eloquent address will form the conclusion to this book. For in Luthuli's words are reflected both the strength of Africa's past and the promise of its future:

> . . . [Let] me invite Africa to cast her eyes beyond the past and and to some extent the present with their woes and tribulations, trials and failures, and some successes, and see herself an emerging continent, bursting to freedom through the shell of centuries of serfdom. This is Africa's age — the dawn of her fulfillment, yes, the moment when she must grapple with destiny to reach the

summit of sublimity, saying: Ours was a fight for noble values and worthy ends, and not for lands and the enslavement of man.

● CHECK-UP

1. What are the various directions that the search for African unity might take? What has OAU accomplished?
2. Why are Africans determined to eliminate white rule where it still exists? Why does this issue seem of crucial importance to Africans? What is neocolonialism? Why is it feared by Africans?
3. Why has anti-Americanism increased in Africa?

Summing Up

Shortage of technical skills, limited resources, and lack of a common feeling of national identity handicap nation-building in the African states which have acquired independence since World War II. Popular pressure for quick solutions to Africa's economic and social ills sometimes brings to power political leaders who are unable to fulfill campaign promises. Frustration over lack of progress has led Africans to restrict activities of foreigners, especially Asians in East Africa. The education and training needed to combat such problems as disease and poverty cannot be obtained overnight.

Developed nations have provided economic aid in the form of loans and capital investments to African countries. In general, Africans are wary of aid that might conceivably result in a new form of colonialism for the recipient. Perhaps the most acceptable form of aid is a guaranteed price for the products sold on the world market.

Modernization is coming first to the large centers of population, bringing with it radical changes in the traditional African social fabric. Especially difficult for Africans has been the transference of individual loyalty from kinship groups to the state. Western-style democracy, which presupposes the existence of opposing political parties, has not found ready acceptance in the new African states. Instead there has been a trend toward one-party systems and an increase in the number of military governments, with little chance for a return to civilian government.

Some political leaders view mounting pressures to form regional or continental associations of states, such as OCAM and OAU, as detrimental to the development of strong nationhood. And foreign interference in African affairs, regardless of the motivation behind it, is regarded with suspicion.

CHAPTER REVIEW

Can You Identify?

revolution of rising
    expectations
governments in exile
political opportunism

developed countries
investment capital
national identity
neo-colonialism

world market
bilharzia
genocide
OAU

What Do You Think?

1. Africa is rich in natural resources. Why is per capita income low?

2. Why have many African nations adopted a one-party political system and state socialism?

3. Why have the Soviet Union and China made friends in Africa?

4. Some Africans do not like to accept foreign aid even when they know their country needs it. Why? Would it be better for both sides if aid were channeled through the UN? Why or why not?

5. To speed development in the emerging countries, it has been suggested that developed nations each year contribute 1 per cent of their gross national product. Would you approve? Why or why not?

Extending and Applying Your Knowledge

1. *Africa: Selected Readings* includes selections on six major themes developed in this book. Summarize each. The themes are:
  a. African reactions to colonialism and continued white rule: pages 155–166, 169–179, 181–187, 201–209, 219–231.
  b. Problems confronting African nations: pages 6–10, 20–23, 210–219, 232–244.
  c. African culture: pages 24–44, 53–56, 76–82, 148–149, 246–257, 265–266.
  d. Economic imperialism: pages 180–187.
  e. Slavery and the slave trade: pages 114–131.
  f. Rise of the great African kingdoms: 45–76, 93–114, 136–138.
(The page references are to *Africa: Selected Readings*.)

2. For current information about Africa, refer to *Africa Reports*, a journal of African affairs which is published nine times a year, and includes a chronology of events. Write to Suite 500, Dupont Circle Building, Washington, D.C. 20036, for subscription information.

BIBLIOGRAPHY

Note: The books recommended in this list are for the general reader. More specialized works are cited in the text footnotes.

Historical and Economic Development

Burke, Fred G. (ed.), *Africa: Selected Readings.* Houghton Mifflin, 1974. A varied collection of primary and secondary source readings, with introductory headnotes, on African history and civilization. Very useful companion to the present volume.

——, *Sub-Saharan Africa: Problems of Nation-Building.* Harcourt, 1968. A readable discussion of the emergence of modern Africa with emphasis on problems of economic development and nation-building.

Cowan, L. Gray, *The Dilemmas of African Independence.* Walker, 1968. Africa's struggle for independence and its later search for economic development, viable political structures, and national unity.

Davidson, Basil, *Africa: History of a Continent.* Macmillan, 1966. A survey of African history with excellent photographs of ancient sites, present-day cities and villages, and art.

——, *The Lost Cities of Africa.* Little, Brown, 1959. The development of kingdoms and cities in Africa before the coming of Europeans to Africa's shores.

Hance, William A., *African Economic Development.* Praeger, 1967. A good introduction to the economic problems of modern Africa.

Moorehead, Alan, *The White Nile.* Harper, 1960. An interesting account of the nineteenth century European explorations of Central Africa and efforts to solve the mystery of the Nile's sources.

Mboya, Tom, *Freedom and After.* Little, Brown, 1963. A personal account of the Kenyan independence movement and the problems of nation-building.

Nkrumah, Kwame, *I Speak of Freedom: A Statement of African Ideology.* Praeger, 1961. The personal statement of an outstanding African political figure with an account of Ghana's early achievement of independence.

Nyerere, Julius K., *Ujamaa — Essays on Socialism.* Oxford, 1968. Essays on the philosophy and policies of African socialism in Tanzania.

Oliver, Roland, and Fage, J. D., *A Short History of Africa.* Penguin Books, 1962. A readable survey of African history from ancient times through independence.

Shinnie, Margaret, *Ancient African Kingdoms.* St. Martin's, 1965. An account of African states before the arrival of Europeans.

Culture and Society

Bohannan, Paul, *Africa and Africans*. Doubleday, 1964. Concise survey of African cultural development by an outstanding anthropologist.

Drachler, Jacob (ed.), *African Heritage: An Anthology of Black African Personality and Culture*. Collier Books, 1964. Stories, poems, songs, folk tales, and essays illustrate the dynamic quality of African traditions.

Gibbs, James L., Jr. (ed.), *Peoples of Africa*. Holt, 1965. An inclusive reference book on various African tribes.

Kenyatta, Jomo, *Facing Mt. Kenya: The Tribal Life of the Gikuyu*. Random House (Vintage Books), [1962]. A study of life and customs among the Kikuyu people of Kenya.

Raum, Otto F., *Chaga Childhood: A Description of Indigenous Education in an East African Tribe*. Oxford University Press, 1967. An interesting account of the ceremonies and beliefs of Chaga childhood.

Turnbull, Colin M., *The Lonely African*. Anchor Books (Doubleday), 1963. A sensitive discussion of the African's struggle to retain his identity in an era of rapid social change.

Van Den Berghe, Pierre L., *South Africa: A Study in Conflict*. University of California Press, 1967. An analysis of South African society with emphasis on the dominant theme of social conflict.

Literature

Achebe, Chinua, *Man of the People*. John Day, 1966. An excellent novel set in Nigeria, which provides a picture of the African political structure.

———, *No Longer at Ease*. Obolensky, 1961. A novel revealing the problems of urban dwellers in Nigeria.

———, *Things Fall Apart*. Astor-Honor, 1959. A novel based on the conflicts resulting from the introduction of western influences into a traditional Nigerian village.

Ekwensi, Cyprian, *People of the City*. Humanities Press, 1966. An adult story of a young man who tries to find a point of equilibrium amid the pleasures and distractions of the city.

Knebel, Fletcher, *The Zinzin Road*. Doubleday, 1966. An entertaining novel about a Peace Corps volunteer in West Africa.

Mphahlele, Ezekiel, *The African Image*. Praeger, 1962. Literary criticism by an outstanding South African writer.

Ngugi, James, *Weep Not, Child*. Heinemann, 1964. A novel about a young boy growing up in Kenya.

Nolen, Barbara (ed.), *Africa Is People*. Dutton, 1967. An excellent anthology of the writings of African literary and political figures.

Paton, Allan, *Cry the Beloved Country*. Scribner's, 1948. A literary classic about South Africa, which reveals the black man's attraction to and alienation within "the white man's cities."

ACKNOWLEDGMENTS

Thanks are extended to the following organizations and persons for making pictures available for reproduction: A. F. P. from Picture Parade, 280; Afro Audio-Visual Co., 315; American Museum of Natural History, 58, 87, 111 (top), 113 (top), 123 (top left & right), 125, 173 (top & bottom), 189, 212, 310 (top left); Arab Information Center, 55 (top), 64 (bottom); Authenticated News International, 257 (top); Belgian Tourist Bureau, 137 (bottom); British Museum, 113 (bottom); Casa de Portugal, 156 (top & bottom); Culver, 183, 191, 193 (top & bottom), 226; FAO, 64, 128 (middle); FAO photos by G. Grégoire, 32, C. Bavagnoli, 35, 94 (top), and A. Defever, 250 (top); French Embassy Press and Information Division, 3 (top & bottom), 17 (top), 39, 90 (middle), 94 (bottom), 103 (middle), 111 (middle & bottom), 187, 215, 245, 310 (top right), 311 (top & bottom); Dorothy Horne, 77 (bottom), 120, 208, 216, 304 (right); Lynne Hartwell Horne, 282; Inforcongo photo by C. Lamote, 9 (left); Information Service of Dahomey, 310 (middle); Institute of African Studies, University of Ife, 311 (middle left & right); Charlotte Kahler, 94 (middle); Kenya Tourist Office, 26 (bottom); Keystone Press Agency, 46, 243, 262, 267 (bottom), 275 309; Marburg-Art Reference Bureau 48; Ivan Massar of Black Star for World Bank and IDA, 297 (top); Metropolitan Museum of Art, 51 (top); Mobil Oil Co., Inc., 17 (bottom); Museum of Fine Arts, Boston, 51 (bottom), 55 (right); New York Times, 299 (bottom); Radio Times Hulton Picture Library, 180, 220 (top), 267 (top); photos from Rapho-Guillumette by Marc and Evelyne Bernheim 59, 199 (top & bottom), Allyn Baum, 62, Georg Gerster, 90 (top), 177 (top), and Lynn McLaren, 171, 203; Rhodesia National Tourist Board, 206; Schlegel from Eastfoto 299 (top); B. P. Singer Features, 124, 134, 135, 137, 139 (left & right), 147, 268 (bottom), 290; S. Rhodesia Dept. of Tourism, 144 (top & bottom), 145; Tass from Sovfoto, 297 (bottom); Twentieth Century Fund, 3 (middle), 26 (top & middle), 77 (top), 97 (left), 123 (bottom), 177 (bottom), 223 (top right), 295 (top left & bottom); UNESCO photos by Dominique Roger, 44, Garraud, 74, P. Almasy, 82, 310 (bottom), and J. C. Bois, 295 (middle); United Nations, 9 (right), 12, 97 (right), 103 (bottom), 128 (top & bottom), 131, 160, 163 (bottom), 223 (top left & bottom), 237, 247, 250 (bottom), 295 (top right); UPI, 163 (top), 218, 257 (bottom), 268 (top), 271, 277; WHO, 279; WHO photos by D. Henrioud, 90 (bottom), 103 (top), 152; Wide World, 163 (middle), 283, 307. Maps by Lilli Tanzer and Dick Sanderson. Drawings by John Gretzer. Title page illustration: Eliot Elisofon.

INDEX

This index includes references not only to the text of the book but also to charts, maps, and pictures. These may be identified as follows: *c* refers to a chart; *m* refers to a map; *p* refers to a picture. The letter *f* following a page reference refers to a footnote.

Abbasids, 72, 73
Abidjan, *p* 17
Abolition, 188: of slavery, 213, 222; of slave trade, 188; impact of, on Africa, 188–189
Abraham, 67
Abydos, 46
Accra, 244
"Acropolis," 143, 146
Addis Ababa, 231, *m* 233, 309
Adebo, Chief S. O., 29
Aden, *m* 84
Administration, systems of, 71, 104; colonial, African participation in, 244, 253, 256
Adowa, *m* 233; battle of, 231
Adulis, 57, *m* 70
Aegean Sea, 45
Afars and the Issas, Territory of, *m* 7, 22, 243, *m* 255
Affonso I, king of Kongo, 155–159, 166
African Democratic Union. *See* Rassemblement Democratique Africaine (RDA)
African Negroes. *See* Negroid peoples
African religion. *See* Religion
Africans, origin of, 20, 29, 119
Afrikaaner Nationalist Party, 282
Afrikaans language, 282
Afro-Americans, 188, 253. *See also* Negro Americans
Afro-Asiatic language group, 25, 27
Agadès, *m* 84, 104
Agaja, king of Dahomey, 115
Age groups, 18, 33 (box)
Aghlab, Ibrahim ibn, 72
Aghlabids, 72
Agricultural civilization, 66. *See also* Farmers, farming
Agriculture. *See* Farmers, farming
Agricultural revolution, 21–22, 44, 45
Ahmed, Mohammed, mahdi of Dongola, 226
Ahmose I, pharaoh of Egypt, 50
Aïr, 104, 109

Airlines, *p* 77, 262
Aïr Mountains, *m* 6, *m* 70
Akan, 107, 110
Akwamu, 107
Alafin of Oyo, 112, 114
Albert, Lake, *m* 6, 8, *m* 232; named, 210
Alcohol, traffic in, 219
Alexander, emperor of Ethiopia, 174
Alexander the Great, 53, 69
Alexandria, 65, *m* 70; British bombing of, 225
Algeria, 61, 63, 69, 75, 308; conquered by France, 221; independence, 248, *m* 255, 263; in Casablanca Bloc, 263; Tshombe in, 277
Algiers, *m* 84, *m* 232, *m* 255
Ali, caliph, 71
Ali, mai of Kanem-Bornu, 109
Ali, Sayyid, king of Malindi, 176
Ali, Sunni, 101–102, 104, 117, 201
Allat, 68 *f*
Almohads, 72, 75, 79; empire of the, 75–77
Almoravids, 72, 75, 79, 89–91, 116
Alooma, Idris, mai of Kanem-Bornu, 108–109, 117
Alps, 63
Aluminum ore, 300
Alur, 136, *m* 149
Amadoo, 89
American Indians, 29, 181
Amhara people, *m* 7
Amharic, language, 27 (box); civilization, 59, 119
Amin, 109
Amin, Idi, 270–271, *p* 271, 292
Amir. *See* Emir
Amir, Arab commander, 69
Amun-Re, Egyptian sun god, *p* 55
Ancestors, 34, 41; worship of, 36, 38, 115, 143, 147
Anglo-Egyptian Sudan, *m* 233
Angola, 14, 153, 164, 243, 279–280
Animals, domestication of, 45, *p* 135; as sacrifices, *p* 113
Ankole, *m* 149
Antelope, *p* 21
Anthropologist(s), 20, 21, 25, 43, 43 *f*, 121; disagreement among, about "tribe," 30
Antislavery movement, 192–194, 195, 196
Apartheid, 24, 282–283
Apedemak, lion-god, *p* 55, 56

323

Arab Empire, 76. *See also* Arabs; Muslim empire
Arabian Peninsula, *m* 6, 8, 25, 69
Arabic language, 27, 28, 67, 72, *p* 77, 88, 172, 238
Arabic religions, 67, 68
Arabs, *m* 7, 19, 61, 67, 69, 79, 83, 85, 121; and Zanj, 127; in Monomotapa Empire, 150; settlements and cultural influences of, in East Africa, 19, 168, 172, 174, 178, 195; in Madagascar, 264; and Portuguese in East Africa, 175, 180, 195; and the slave trade, 183–184, 213, 216–217; attacks of, on Ethiopia, 231; resistance of, in Libya, 234
Archaeologists, 56, 82, 100, 122, 126, 141, 142, 143
Archaeology, 43, 120, 133 *f*, 148
Architecture, of mosques, *p* 74; sudanese, 99; of Zimbabwe, 142–146, *p* 144
Arians, 66
Arius, 65
Armies: Assyrian, 52, 78; of Ghana, 89; of Mali, 97; of Songhai, 102; Moroccan, 106; Baganda, 135; of Monomotapa, 150–151; Zulu, 152; Kongolese (civil war), 156–157; Muslim, 169; Portuguese, in Mozambique, 176–177; foreign, pretexts for intervention by, 217; British, in South Africa, 222, in Boer War, 224, in Gold Coast, 227; Anglo-Egyptian, 225–226; French and British, at Nile River, 221, and Fashoda, 226–227; Ashanti, 228; German, 230; Ethiopian, 231; Italian, defeated at Adowa, 231, occupies Libya, 233–234, and Ethiopia, 235; King Leopold II's, 234; Nigerian, 258; French, in Madagascar, 264
Arnekhamani, king of Meroë, 56
Art, 56, 82, 115, 117; prehistoric *p* 21; of Bushmen, 125; of Bantu, *p* 137; modern African, *p* 310, *p* 311
Aryans, defined, 24; and Nazi race theory, 244
Asantehene, 36
Ashanti, *m* 7, 35, 36, 37, 83 *f*, *m* 84, 107, 114, 115, 117, 187; British campaign against, 210, 227
Ashanti Federation. *See* Ashanti Union of Akan States

Ashanti Union of Akan States, 114, 227–228
Ashurbanipal, king of Assyria, 52
Asia, 19, 20, 28, 44, 49, 50, 52, 95, 194, 242; African contacts with, 2, 185; independence movements in, 247–248
Askaris, 231
Askia Mohammed, emperor of Songhai, 102, 104–105, 117, 201
Aspalta, king of Kush, *p* 55
Assab, 231
Associations, types of: occupational, 30, 291, religious, 30
Assyria, 52, 78
Aswan High Dam, *m* 6, *p* 44
Athanasius, 65
Atlantic Charter, 242
Atlantic Ocean, 5, *m* 6, 8, 62, 69, 154, 172, 211; crossing of, by slaves, 187, 188; British navy in, 192, *p* 193
Atlas Mountains, *m* 6, *m* 70
Audoghast, *m* 84, 88, 91
Augustine of Hippo, 65
Augustus, emperor of Rome, 65 *f*
Australia, 15
Axum, 57–59, *m* 70, 79, *m* 84; obelisks of, *p* 59; culture of, 57, 58; ruins of, visited, 198
Ayyubids, 73
Azania, *m* 70, 127

Bagamoyo, 208, 210, *m* 232
Baganda, 35, 36
Baghdad, 67, 72, 73, 79, *m* 84
Bahutu. *See* Hutu
Bairu, 131, 132
Baker, Sir Samuel, 210, 238, 239
Bakongo people, 273
Bakri, al-, 86, 88, 89
Balanced rocks, *p* 120
Baluba. *See* Luba
Bamako, *m* 233
Bambara, *m* 7
Bamileke, *m* 7
Bananas, 110, 122, 136
Banda, 110
Banda, Dr. Hastings, 266
Bangweulu, Lake, 207, *m* 232
Bantu language group, 25, 28, 121, 164
Bantu-speaking peoples, 121–129, 130–139, 140–152, 153–164; definition

of term, 121; migrations of, *m* 149; in Congo Basin, 124, 153–164; in savannah, 125; in Rhodesia, 126, 152; in East Africa, 126, 172, 178; kingdoms of, in "great lakes" region, 130–139, *m* 149; at Lake Nyasa, 152, intermarriage of, with Arab traders, 72; in South Africa, 283

"Bantustans," 283

Baptists, 213

Barbak, king of Bengal, 182

Barotseland, 145, 239. *See also* Zambia

Basutoland, 147, *m* 233. *See also* Lesotho

Baru, Sunni, ruler of Songhai, 102

Bashorun, 112

Bassi, ruler of Ghana, 91

Battuta, Ibn, 96

Batusi, 32 *f*, 138. *See also* Tutsi

Baule, *m* 7

Beads, 141, 148, 178

Bechuanaland, *m* 233. *See also* Botswana

Bedouins, 77, 78

Beja, *m* 7

Bekr, Abu, 75, 91, 92, 116

Belgian Congo, 213, *m* 233, 234, 263, 272. *See also* Congo Basin; Congo (Kinshasa); Zaire

Belgium, *c* 9, 213, 219, 234, 235, 237, 239, 272, 273

Belisarius, Roman general, 66

Bemba people, *m* 7

Ben Bella, Ahmed, 248

Bengal, 182

Benin, *m* 84, 107, 112, 114, 115; and slave trade, 186

Bennett, James Gordon, Jr., 205–206

Benue River, *m* 6, 82, 108

Berbers, *m* 7, 60–62, 63, 66, 72, 73, 74, 75, 76, 83, 85, 99, 101, 104, 110; origin of name, 60; horsemanship of, 61, *p* 62; in trade, 65; raid Roman towns, 66; plunder Mali towns, 99; capture Songhai capital, 101. *See also* Tuaregs; Nomads

Berlin, Conference of (1885), 219; Act of (1885), 234; conferences in, 236

Betsileo people, *m* 7

Biafra, *p* 257, 258, 314. *See also* Nigeria

Bigo, 133 *f*, *m* 149

Bilharzia, 294

Bilma, *m* 84, 107

Birds, figures of, 143, *p* 145

Birth rate, 16

Bismarck, Otto von, 230

Bito, 132–133, 134, 138, *m* 149, 165

Black Africans, 22, 81, 106, 110, 127, 155, 185, 195

Black Americans. *See* Negro Americans

Black nationalism, 282

Blue Nile, 5, *m* 6, *m* 70, 198, 238

Boats, construction of, 45, *p* 46; travel by, 47

Boers, 191–192, 222, 224, *m* 232, 240

Boer War, 222, 224, 240

Boma, 212, *m* 232

Bombay, 171

Bono, 110

Bornu, *m* 84, 104, 107, 109

Botswana, 14, 146, 204, *m* 255

Brazza, Pierre Savorgnande, 219, 221

Brazzaville, 3

Britain, 19, 62, 74, 83 *f*, 89, 170, 179, 185, 194, 217, 219, 222, 224, 227, 235, 236, 237, 239, 240, 265, 271, 281–282, 301–302

British East Africa, *m* 233

British East Africa Company, 225

British, 34, 110, 114, 192, 194, 195; in Uganda, 136, 225; antislavery activities of, 192–194; in West Africa, 227–230; colonial administration of, 244, 252, 253. *See also* British South Africa Company; British East Africa Company

British Empire. *See* Britain

British Somaliland, *m* 233

British South Africa Company, 222, 224, 265

British Togoland. *See* Togo

British West Indies, 185

Bronze casting, *p* 113, 115

Bruce, James, explorer, 198, 200, 203, 238

Brussels, 236; Conference of (1876), 219. *See also* Belgium

Buffaloes, 96, 126

Buganda, 134–136, 209; expansion of (1500–1900), *m* 149 (inset); Uganda's independence delayed by, 266; special status of, in Uganda federation, 270. *See also* Uganda

Bulopwe, 161, 164

Bungu, 153

Bunyoro, 133–134, *m* 149, 210

Burton, Richard Francis, 207–210, 238

Burundi, 32, 131, *m* 149, 165, *m* 255, 305; Bantu groups settle, 126; Hutu in 138; monarchy ended in, 139

Bush country, 13, 158

Bushmen, *m* 7, 19, 25, 120, *p* 125; language of, 27; occupations of, 31; contacts with Bantu, 125–126; rock paintings of, 125–126, *p* 125; in Mashonaland, 140, 146

Business, 28, 194, 291

Busoga, *m* 149

Byzantine Empire, 53, 66; Muslim conquest of, 169; rulers of, 69, 79

Cabinda, *m* 233

Cabora Bassa Dam, 280, 281

Cabral, Amilcar, 279

Cadiz, 77

Caesar, Julius, 65 *f*, 162

Caillié, René, explorer, 202, 239

Cairo, 11, 73, *m* 84, 98, 200, 221, *m* 233; museum at, 47; British occupation of, 225. *See also* Egypt

Calicut, 169, 175

Caliphs, 69, 71, 72, 73, 77, 78, 79, 104

Cam, Diogo, 154–155

Camel(s), 10, 64, 66, 85; introduction of, by Romans, 40. *See also* Caravans

Cameroon, 124; under German rule, 230, 240; mandated to France and Britain, 236, 240, 263; member of OCAM, 262; independence of, 263, *m* 255

Cameroon Highlands, 121, *m* 149, 165

Cape Colony, 191–192, 224; British takeover of, 192, 221, 222

Cape of Good Hope, *m* 6, 19, *m* 149; circumnavigation of, 175, 191, 195; Dutch settlers in, 191

Cape Palmas, *m* 6, 62

Cape Town, 2, 11, 152, 221, *m* 232

Cape Verde, *m* 6; Islands, 175

Caravans, 10, 17, 60, 85, *p* 90, 96, 181, 202. *See also* Trade routes

Carthage, 60, 62–63, 65, 66, *m* 70, 79; empire of, 62; destruction of, 63

Casablanca Bloc, 263

Cash-crop farming, 18, 217

Castes, 132, 178, 195

Catholics. *See* Roman Catholics

Cattle, 14, 34, 96, 130, 136; as dowry, 37, 298; domestication of, 45; exchange of, 32. *See also* Cattle herding

Cattle herding, 14, 18, *p* 32, 38, 41, 44, 110, 165; as way of life, 31; among Bantu of East Africa, 126–127, *p* 137; among Nilotes, 132–133, *p* 135, 165; among Shona, 147; among Hereros, 230

Caucasoid (or Caucasian) peoples, *m* 7, 22, 24, 25

Caucasus Mountains, 73

Central Africa, 13, 67, 119–166; Livingstone in, 204–205, 207, 239; Stanley in, 205–206, 210–213, 239

Central African Federation, 265

Central African Republic, *m* 255, 260, 262

Central Uganda, 130

Cereal grains, 45, 81, 96, 110, 126, *p* 128, 170

Chad, 16, *p* 97, 122, *m* 255, 260, 262; Basin, 4, 5, 40; Lake, *m* 6, 56, 107, 109

Chagga (or Chaga) people, 2, *m* 7, 304

Chaka, Zulu ruler, 152, 165

Changa, 150. *See also* Changamire

Changamire, 130, *m* 149, 150, 165; empire of, 151–152

Charles V, king of France, 98 *f*

Ch'eng-shih, Tuan, Chinese scholar, 170

Chewa people, *m* 7

Chiefdom, 138, 161, 162. *See also* Chiefs; Chieftainship

Chiefs, 34, 36, 112, 114, 131, 145; trappings of, *p* 111; as arbitrators, 136; services paid to, 137–138; stone houses of, 143; rebellion of, in Kongo, 159; among Luba, 161; Congolese, and Stanley, 234; supported by colonial government, 253, 256

Chieftainship, 105 (box), 143; in Buganda, 135; spread of, into Central Africa, 136. *See also* Chiefdom; Chiefs; Kingship

China (Communist), attempts of, to influence Africans, 248–249; Nkrumah's relations with, 254

Chinese, 57, 121, 170; use of African slaves by, 172, 182; in Indian Ocean, 178, 180

Chokwe, *m* 7
Christianity, 38, 40, 59, 65, 79, 194; impact of, in North Africa, 65–66; and Islam, 67; missionaries of, 114, 239; and Kongo, 153, 155–159, 166; and Buganda, 215–217. *See also* Christians; Religion; Missionaries
Christians, 38, 151, 213, 216; death of in Buganda, 217, 218. *See also* Christianity; Roman Catholics; Protestants; Missionaries; Religion
Chwezi, 131, 132, 133
Circassian slaves, 73
Cities, *c* 16, 17, 72, 100; growth of, in Europe, 170; of East Africa, 180; African, growth and problems of, 298. *See also names of particular cities*
Civil service, 75, 101
Civil war, 115; in Kongo, 155–157; in Nigeria, 258, 305; in Kenya, 266–269; Congolese, 272–278
Clan(s), 30, 35, 37, 41, 135, 147, 237; definition of, 37, 83; rivalries among, 138; Rozwi, 148
Clark, J. Desmond, 143, 145, 146 *f*
Classes, social, 45, 112, 139
Click language group, 26, 27, 125
Climate, 9, 10, 11–14, 14–19; changes in, 44; Mediterranean, 11; in Nile Valley, 45; subtropical, 12; temperate zone, 11; tropical, 45; and altitude, in Uganda, 130
Cloth, 96, 136, 172, 175, 230. *See also* Textiles; Cotton
Cloves, 184
Coastal plain, 4, 11
Coastline, 2, *p* 3
Cobalt, 244
Cocoa, 252
Coffee, 18, 264
Cold War, 248–249
Colonialism, 212–213, 240, 253. *See also* Colonial rule; Colonies; Imperialism
Colonial rule, 22, 23, 105, 115, 120, 313–314; effect of, on tribal lines, 30; Portuguese, 174–180; German, 230–231, 235–236; Italian, 231, 235; legacy from period of, 236, 237; early end of, demanded, 245
Colonies, European, in Africa, 191–192, 194, 196, 230–231; and mandates, compared, 236

Columbus, Christopher, 169, 174
Commerce, 28, 29, 96, 136, 165, 170, 175, 178, 185. *See also* Trade
Common Market. *See* European Economic Community
Commonwealth, British, 252
Communication, problems of, 27; media of, 251
Community, French, 252, 260, 261, 263, 264
Community organization, forms of, 18; Islamic ideal of, 74, 104
Compass, magnetic, 169
Condominium, French-British, 225
Congo Basin, 4, *c* 9, 13, 14, 40, 122, 127; forest of, 50; Bantu speaking people in, 124, 153–164, 165; and Stanley's explorations, 210–213; and subjugation of, 234, 239; Berlin Conference discusses, 219. *See also* Belgian Congo; Congo (Brazzaville); Congo (Kinshasa); Zaire
Congo (Brazzaville), 153 *f*, 260, 263
"Congo Free State," *m* 232, 234
Congo (Kinshasa), 153 *f*, 272–278, 312–313. *See also* Belgian Congo; Zaire
Congo peoples, 141, 153, 211. *See also* Kongo; Luba; Lunda
Constitutions, 105 (box), 306
Co-operatives, 304
Copper, 45, 59, 88, 96, 127, 141, 142, 151, 158, 184, 244, 300
Coptic church, 66, 177
Cotton, 18, 57, 136, 230, 300; dry goods, 107, 172
Council of Nicaea, 65, 66
Councils, of elders, 35, 36, 162; governing, 112; of Luba headmen, 161; of Lunda headmen, 162
Court systems, 97, 104
Covilhão, Pedro de, 174–175
Craftsmen, *p* 87, 88, 132, 188
Crops, 13, 15, 44, 45, 81, 96, 116, 122, 127, 300–301; yields, 13, 16; rotation of, *p* 35
Crusades, 73, 169
Cuba, 181, 194
Culture(s), African, 83; comparison of, with European and American, 22, 23; revival of, 238
Cushites, 126, 127, 131; influence on Bantu groups, 126, 130, *p* 137, 165; infiltrated by Nilotes, 132

Customs union, 272
Cyrenaica, 69, *m* 84

Daga, 145
Dagomba, 105 (box)
Dahomey, *m* 84, 107, 114–115, 187, *m* 232, 259, 308; French annexation of, 221; independent, *m* 255, 262
Dakar, *p* 3, 14, 25, 221, 260
Dam(s), *m* 6, *c* 9, *p* 12
Damascus, 67, 71, 72, 79, *m* 84
Dance, 115, *p* 139, *p* 147, 313 (box); *p* 311
Dar es Salaam, 127
Darfur, *m* 84, 108, 122
Davidson, Basil, 63, 86 *f*, 101, 108 *f*, 139, 142, 151 *f*, 185, 189
Death rate, 16
Deba, 86
Democracy, 305–306
Descent groups, 37
Desert Nile, 107
Deserts, 14, 40, 44, 221. *See also names of particular deserts*
Developing countries, 15; problems of, 289–315
Dia, 101
Diamonds, discovery of, 222, 230, 240; exported, 244, 300
Días, Bartholomew, 175
Dido, queen of Carthage, 60
Dinka people, *m* 7
Diseases, 293–294
District council, 36
Districts (nomes), 47
Diviner, 39, *p* 39, 41
Djenné, *m* 84, 99, 106
Domain of Rabeh, *m* 232
Domain of Samori, *m* 232
Domain of the Mahdi, *m* 232
Donatism, 65
Donatus, bishop of Numidia, 65 *f*
Dongola, 226
Dougga, 63, *m* 70
Dowry, 37, 298
Drakensberg Mountains, *m* 6, 146, 147
Drums, use of, 86, 133 *f*, p 147
Dutch, the, in South Africa, 19, *m* 149, 152, 195, 282; in Kongo, 159; and Cape Colony, 191–192, 222; role of, in west coast slave trade, 227; ousted from Indonesia, 248
Dzimbahwe, 143, 145

Earthworks, 133 *f*
East Africa, 11, 19, 59, *m* 70, 110, 122, 130, 148, 206, 207, 213, 214, *m* 233; languages of 28, 121–122; mountains of, 13, 16, 202, *p* 203; Bantu-speaking peoples enter, 126; contacts of, with Chinese, 171; with Arabs, Indians, and Malayans, 172, 178, 195; and Portuguese commerce, 174–179; British involvement in, 196, 205, 222, 224–225, 240; German interest in, 224, 230–231, 236, 239; Italy's adventures in, 231, 235; Asian settlers in, 291–292
East African Economic Community and Common Market, 272, 309
East Indies, 179
Ebony, 56, 57
Economic assistance programs, 301–302
Education, 99, 296–297
Edward, Lake, 8, *m* 149
Egypt, 22, 50, 52, 54, 56, 63, 66, *m* 70, 72, 73, 74, 76, 78, 79, 83, 95, 107, 108, 225–226, *m* 255; ancient civilization, 43–53; unification of, 47–48, Muslim Arabs invade, 69; Mansa Musa visits, 98; influence of, on Cushites, 26; slaves in, 182; and Suez Canal, 225, 240; as British "protectorate," 225, 240; and the Sudan, 231; Soviet interest in, 249; Israeli invasion of, 263; membership of, in Casablanca Bloc, 263
Eisenhower, Dwight D., 273
Elderly, role of the, 38
Elders, council of, 36, 162
Electoral college (Kongo), 156
Electric power, *c* 9, 290
Elephants, *p* 21, 53, 63, 96, 129, 141
El Kaar-el-Kabir, 106
Elliptical Ruin, 143, *p* 144, 145
Emir, 76 (box), 150, 256
Emirates, Fulani, 230, 256
Empires, African, 81, 86, 91, 107, 112, 148, 150–151; instability of, 100, 151; colonial, 170, 194, 219, 221, 236, 240, 244
England. *See* Britain; British
English language, 29
Equality, Muslim doctrine of, 71; racial, social, and political, related, 245–246; Black Americans' struggle for, 251
Eritrea, 231, *m* 233, 234, 235, 240

Esarhaddon, king of Assyria, 52
Ethiopia, 5, 8, 13, 14, 22, 27, *p* 57, 53–59, 79, *m* 84, 119, 126, 168, 178, 198, *m* 255, 272; cultural isolation, 59; Christianity introduced, 59, 66; defended by Portuguese, 177; James Bruce visits, 198, 200; Italy's wars with, 231, 234, 235; annexation of, by Italy, 235. *See also* Axum; Kush; Meroë
Ethnic groups, *p* 26, 29. *See also* Tribe
Euphrates River, 49, 50
Europe, 20, 74, 89, 121, 132; African relations with, 2, 99, 105 (box), 151, 168, 170, 185–186, 190–194; and slave trade, 184–188; and Arab and Eastern science, 168, 169–170; civilization of, 180
European Economic Community (EEC), 302
Europeans, in Africa, 24, 28, 99, 105 (box), 110 *f*, 114, 115, 152, 170, 184–188, 225, 240. *See also* Colonies; Colonialism; Imperialism
Evolution, 14, 15, 20
Ewe, *m* 7, 27
Excavations, 141, 146, 165. *See also* Archaeology
Exploitation, 183, 234, 238
Exploration, 168, 169, 170, 171, 174, 198–213, 238–239
Explorers, 110 *f*, 185–186, 198–213; Portuguese, *m* 84, *m* 149, 175. *See also names of individual explorers*
Exports, *c* 300; single commodity, 300
Export taxes, 88, 116, 148
Extended family, 18, 34, 35, 36, 37, 161. *See also* Kinship groups
Extermination Order, 230
Ezana, king of Axum, 58, 59

Fada-n-Gurma, 105 (box)
Fage, John D., 47 *f*, 98 *f*, 105, 114, 115
Family, 30, 37, 38, 41. *See also* Extended family; Kinship groups
Famine, 109
Fang, *m* 7
Farmers, farming, 12, 13, 34, 35, 41, 81, 116, 224, 292–293, 304; European, 28; in Egypt, 44; in Ethiopia, 56; in Ghana, 81–82, 91; in Mali, 93,

96; skills, 110; in Uganda, 130; in Zimbabwe, 140; in Zambia, 141
Fartua, Ahmed ibn, 108
Fashoda, 226, *m* 233, 240
Fatima, 71, 73
Fatimid Empire, 72, 73, 74, 79. *See also* Egypt
Federation, 114, 117, 262, 265
Feudalism, 132, 135
Fez, *m* 70, *m* 84, *p* 74, 75, 96, *m* 232
Fezzan, *m* 6, 107, 108
Figurines, 82, 115, 127
Firearms, 108, 114, 117, 170, 176, 186, 230. *See also* Weapons
First Dynasty, 47
Fishing, 19, *p* 131
Fon, *m* 7
Food, 10, 13, 15, 31, 44, 45, 96, 116, 117, 122, *p* 128, 212; surplus, production of, 47; shortage of, 293; for export, 298, *c* 300. *See also* Crops; Farmers, farming
Food-gathering, 19, 31, 41, 44, 81
Foreign exchange, 298
Forest products, 107
Forests, 110, 112, 122, 194. *See also* Rain forest
Fortifications, Cushite, 126; Chwezi, 133 *f*; Sotho, 146; Portuguese, *p* 156, 175, 179, 227; British and other European, on west coast, 227
Fort Jesus, 179
Fort São Miguel (Angola), *p* 156
Fort São Sebastian, *p* 156
Fort Victoria, 143
France, 19, 69, 74, 89, 170, 260; expansion of, in Africa, 219, 221, 235, 239, 240; and Suez Canal, 225; and the Sudan, 226, 231; and Nigeria, 228; and Ethiopia, 231; establishes schools, 237; colonial administration of, 244, 260; former colonies trade with, *c* 261; war of, with Algeria, 263; aids African nations, 301–302
Freetown, Sierra Leone, 227, 258
FRELIMO, 280–281
French, the, 105 (box), 185, 196, 202; as missionaries, 216; in Egypt, 225; in West Africa, 227. *See also* France
French Cameroon. See Cameroon
French Community. *See* Community
French Congo. *See* Congo (Brazzaville)

French Equatorial Africa, 259
French, language, 27, 262
French National Assembly, 260
French Somaliland, *m* 233. *See also* Afars and the Issas, Territory of
French Togo. *See* Togo
French West Africa, 259
Fulani, *m* 7, 27 (box), 31, 92, 104, 106, 110, 116, 230, 254

Gabon, *m* 255, 260, 262
Galla people, *m* 7
Gama, Vasco da, 127, 169, 175, 176, 195
Gambia, 200, *m* 255, 294; British acquisition of, 227, 240; achieves independence, 259
Ganda people, *m* 7. *See also* Baganda
Gandhi, Mahatma, 247, 248
Gao, *m* 84, 95, 99, 101, 102, 106
Garama, *m* 70
Garamantes, 61, *m* 70
Gaul (France), 62, 63
Gaulle, Charles de, 260, *p* 262
Ge'ez, 119
Geography, of Africa, 2, 14–19, 207
German East Africa, 224, 225, 230, *m* 233, 236
Germans, 24, 194
German South West Africa, 230, *m* 233, 236. *See also* South-West Africa
Germany, 19, 217, 219, 235, 239, 240; intrusion of, into East Africa, 224–225, 230–231; and southwestern Africa, 230, 236; African territories of, after World War I, 235–236, 240
Ghaba, al-, 86
Ghana, ancient: 30, *m* 70, 75, 79, 81–91, 92, 110, 116, 148; boundaries of, *m* 70, 83, *m* 84; government of, 35; modern: 83 *f*, 210, 300; Ashanti wars in, 227–228; independence achieved in, 252–254, *m* 255; in Casablanca Bloc, 263
Gizeh, *p* 51
Gold, 45, 50, 60 *f*, 65, *p* 86, 89, 95, 96, 106, 127, 170, 177, 195; trade, 85, 88, 91, 165, 168, 174, 176, 178, 184, 227, 244, 252; discovery of, in South Africa, 222, 224, 240
Gold Coast, 83, 109, 110, 175, 227,

m 233, 240, 243, 244. *See also* Ghana
Gold mines, *m* 70, 89, 140, 141, 148, 151, 165, 176; and Ingombe Ilede, 142. *See also* Gold; Mining
Golden Stool, 36, 114, 227
Gold-salt trade, 88, 91, 96, 116
Gondar, *m* 84, 198, 200
Gordon, Charles ("Chinese"), British general, 226
Goths, 69
Government, systems of, 69, 82, 86, 96–97, 112, 117, 136, 150; Luba and Lunda, 161–164; of colonial powers, 252; of modern countries, problems of, 306–308
Gowon, Colonel Yakubu, 258
Grain coast, 110 *f*
Grain growers, *p* 128, 132. *See also* Farmers, farming
Granada, 77, 99, 169
Grant, James, 209
Great Britain. *See* Britain
"Great lakes" region, 122, 127, 130, 135–136, 204, 207, 208, 225, 238
Great Pyramid, 43, 46–47, *p* 51
Great Trek, 222
Great Zimbabwe, 133 *f*, 143–146, *p* 144, *p* 145, *m* 149, 152, 165
Greece, *m* 70, 79; African slaves in, 182
Greeks, 53, 93; influence of, in Axum, 57; in North Africa, 69
Greenberg, Joseph, 25, 27, 120
Guinea, 5, 83, 93, 110, *m* 255, 259, 300; Nkrumah seeks asylum in, 254; opts for separation from France, 260; and Casablanca Bloc, 263
Guinea-Bissau, 243, *m* 255, 279
Guinea coast, 13, 16, 21, 81, 184, 185
Guinea states, *m* 84, 110–115, 117
Gunpowder, 170; traffic in, 219
Guns. *See* Firearms

Hadza, 27
Hafsid, 78
Hajj, 95, 97, 104, 116
Hammarskjöld, Dag, 275
Hannibal, Carthaginian general, 63
Hannington, Bishop James, 217
Hanno, Carthaginian navigator, 62; voyage of, *m* 70

Hatshepsut, queen of Egypt, 66
Hausa, *m* 7, 28, 120; language, 28; states, 81, *m* 84, 107, 108, 109–110, 117; subjects of Fulani, 230; in northern Nigeria, 254
Hegira, 68, 83
Henry the Navigator, 99, 174
Herero, *m* 7; massacre of, 230
Herodotus, 1, 43, 47, 53, 61
Herskovits, Melville, 121
Hieroglyphs, 56. *See also* Writing, systems of
Highlands, 13, 16
Hima, 131–133, 136
Hinda, 136, *m* 149
Hoe, *p* 35, 56, 83, 122, *p* 123, 141
Hoggar Mountains, *m* 6
Holland, 19, 179, 185, 191
Holy cities of Islam, 67, 68, 69, *p* 74. *See also* Mecca; Medina; Jerusalem
Holy Land, 169
"Holy War," 69
Homer, 93
Homo sapiens, 20, 22
Horses, 63, 88, 107
Horus, falcon-god, 48, 49
Hottentots, 25, 27, 140, 147
Houphouet-Boigny, Felix, 261, *p* 262
Hunger, 293
Hunters, 96, 135
Hunting economy, 19, 31, 44, 81
Huts, *p* 137
Hutu, *m* 7, 138, 139, 305
Hydroelectric power, *m* 9, *c* 9
Hyksos, 50

Ibn Fartua. *See* Fartua, Ahmed ibn
Ibn Yasin. *See* Yasin, Abdullah ibn
Ibo, *m* 7, 30, 256; and "Biafra," 258
Ice Ages, 10
Idris, 72
Idrisids, 79. *See also* Morocco
Ife, 110, 112, 117
Ihangiro, 136
Immigration, European, 222, 224, 240
Imperialism, 169, 219–234, 235, 240
Implements. *See* Tools
Import taxes, 88, 116, 148
Independence, 40, 115, 240, 242, 294; in North Africa, 243; in Asia, 247, 248; in British-held territories, 252–259, 265–272; France's colonial empire chooses, 259–264; Congolese

civil war accompanies, 272–277; role of UN in, 246–247
India, 19, 57, 74, 169, 221; African slaves in, 172, 182, 183, 192; East African contacts with, severed, 180; British control of, 192; independence of, 247–248
Indian Ocean, *m* 6, 19, 127, 179; Portuguese in, 174, 175, 176, 178, 195; slave trade in, 185
Indians, 127, 170, 178; settled in Africa, 28, 266; American, 29, 181
Indonesia, 110, 170; African slaves in, 172; Dutch rule of, ended (1949), 248; Madagascar settled by, 264
Industrial Revolution, 194
Ingombe Ilede, 141–142, *m* 149, 165
Inheritance, laws of, 102
Intellect, development of, 14–15
Intermediaries. *See* Middlemen
International relations, imperialism in, 235, 239–240
International trade, 170, *c* 261, *c* 300
Inyanga, 152
Iraq, African slaves in, 182
Iron, 56, 79, 81, 82, *p* 123, 130, 151, 172
Iron Age, *c* viii, 119, 123, 142; Pygmy culture of, 124; Bantu government during, 131; culture of, among Bantu of Zimbabwe, 140
Ironworking, 82, 88, 122, 132
Irrigation, 126
Isamu Pati, 141, *m* 149
Isis, temple of (Philae), *p* 44
Islam, 17, 40, 67, 69, 71, 72, 79, 91, 93, 101, 102, 104, 107, 109, 117, 124, 168, 172, 178, 215, 216, 226; and slavery, 182–183
Islamic civilization, 67–79, 169, 172; law in, 76, 96, 102; scholarship in, 104; science in, 168
Israel, 249, 263
Isthmus of Suez, 74
Italian East Africa, 235
Italians in Africa, 194; in Kongo, 159; in East Africa, 231, 234, 240
Italian Somaliland, *m* 233, 234, 235, 240
Italy, 63, 72, 239; covets Tunisia, 221, 231; and Ethiopia, 231, 233–234, 235, 240; resentment of, following World War I, 235, 240
Ituri Forest, 31, *p* 124

Ivory, 56, 57, 60 f, 65, 107, 129, 130, 136, 141, 158, 165, 168, 172, 174, 175, 178, 184, 195, 227, 234
Ivory Coast, *p* 12, 110, *m* 233, 238, *m* 255, 259, 261, 302–303; as French protectorate, 221; membership of, in OCAM, 262

Jameson, Dr. Leander Starr, 224
Jerusalem, 67
Jesuits, 178, 180
Jesus, 67, 214. *See also* Christianity
Jihad, 69, 91
John I (Kongo). *See* Nzinga Kuwu
John II, king of Portugal, 155
Judaism, 38, 66. *See also* Religion
Justinian, emperor of Rome, 66

Kabaka, 35, 134, 270
Kainja Dam, *m* 6
Kairouan, 69, *m* 84
Kalahari, Basin, 4, 5, 40; Desert, *m* 6, 11, 14, 19, 31, 41, *m* 149, 204
Kalala, 160–161
Kamba people, *m* 7
Kamerun, *m* 233. *See also* Cameroon
Kamrasi, king of Bunyoro, 210
Kampala, 134, *m* 149, *m* 255
Kanem, *m* 84, 107, 109
Kanem-Bornu, empire of, 61–62, 81, *m* 84, 104, 107–109, 117; decline of, 109
Kangaba, 92, 93, 100
Kano, *p* 17, *m* 84, 109, 110
Kanuri, *m* 7, 107
Karagwe, 136, *m* 149
Karanga, 147–148, 151, 165; empire of, 148–150
Kariba Dam, *m* 6
Kariba Gorge, 141
Karina, battle of, 93
Kasai, *p* 123
Kasai River, 4
Kasavubu, Joseph, 273, 274, 275, 276
Kashta, ruler of Kush, 52
Katanga, 9, 59, *m* 233, 273, 274, 275, 276, 278
Katerega, kabaka of Buganda, 134
Katsina, 109
Kaunda, Kenneth, 266
Kaya Maghan, 85
Kennedy, John F., 274

Kenya, 8, 13, 14, 19, 25, 28, 34, 120; nationalism in, 30, 266–269; Bantu groups settle, 127, 130, 165; Hima nomads in, 131; Portuguese conquests in, 176; British protectorate, 225; independence in (1963), 249, *m* 255, 268–269; Asians in, 292
Kenya African Democratic Union (KADU), 269
Kenya Highlands, 11, 13, 127, 130, 266
Kenyatta, Jomo, *p* 268; imprisonment of, 268; release of, 269; as prime minister of Kenya, 269; and Uganda, 270; and East African Community, 272
Khami, 152
Kharijites, 71, 72
Khartoum, 5, *m* 232, *m* 233; mahdi's capture of, 226
Khedive, 76, 225
Khoisan language. *See* Click language group
Khufu, pharaoh of Egypt, 46, *p* 51
Kikuyu people, *m* 7, 14, 34, 35, 36, 138, 267, 268, 269
Kilolo, 161
Kilwa, 127, *m* 149, 150; under Arab influence, 172; and Vasco da Gama, 176; Portuguese destruction of, 176
Kimberley, *m* 233
Kingship, *p* 111; in Egypt, 45, 47; in Ghana, 83, 86; in Songhai, 102; among the Mossi, 105 (box); in Benin and Oyo, 112; in Uganda, 131–136; among Shona clans, 147–148; in Kongo, 154
Kinissai, emperor of Ghana, 88
Kinshasa, 4, 5, 272, 273, 274
Kinship, groups, 41, 117, 162; patterns, 36–37, 161–162
Kintu, founder of Kitwara, 131–132
Kisangani, 5, 274, 276
Kitchener, Horatio H., 221, 226
Kitwara Kingdom, 131–133, *m* 149
Kivu, 277; Lake, 8, *m* 149
Kiziba, 136
Kodok, 226
Koki, 136
Kongo, *m* 7, 27 (box); kingdom of, *m* 149, 153–159, 165; spelling of, explained, 153 f; Portugal's relations with, 186
Kongolo, 160–161

Koran, 67, 68, 75, 77, 99, 102; teachings of, on slaves, 183
Koro Toro, 56
Krapf, Johann, 203, 239
Kru, *m* 7
Kruger, Paul, Boer leader, 222, 224
Kukya, 101
Kumasi, *m* 84, 114, 227
Kumbi, *m* 70, 85, 88, 89, 92
Kush, 50, 52, 54, 56, *m* 70, 78, 79; and Egyptian rule, *p* 55
Kwango River, *m* 149, 154
Kyamtwara, 136
Kyogo, Lake, *m* 149

Labor, organization of, 47
Labor tax, 234. *See also* Taxes
Labor unions, 304
Lagos, 228, *m* 232, 258
Lamu, *m* 84, 127, 172
Land, limitations of, 10; grants of, 136; disputes over, between Africans and white settlers, 283; ownership of, 34, 36, 136
Languages, African, 25; major language groups, 25–27, 121; number, 30, 41; as obstacle to progress, 27–28; and history, 120; written, 214; subordinated to nationalism, 236, 237, 238; and communications media, 251. *See also names of particular languages*
Law, 96, 102, 107, 304; Portuguese code of, 158
League of Nations, policy of, on Ethiopian question, 235, *p* 237, 246; and mandate system, 236, 240, 246
Leakey family (anthropologists), 20
Legends, 93, 95
Leopold II, king of Belgium, 213, 219, 234, 239
Leopoldville. *See* Kinshasa
Leprosy, 293
Leptis Magna, *p* 64, *m* 70
Lesotho, 147, *m* 255; achieves independence (1966), 147
Liberia, 22, 62, *m* 233, *m* 255, 291, *p* 315
Libya, *m* 255, 263
Libyans, 50, 52, *m* 70
Limpopo River, *m* 6, 40, 146, 148, *m* 149
Lion Temple, 56
Lisbon, 157, 159, 176, 178, 235
Little Abai River, 200

Livestock, 93, 96. *See also* Cattle
Livingstone, David, missionary explorer, 204–207, 210, 211, 239; reaches Lake Ngami, 204; and Victoria Falls, 205; meeting with Stanley, 206; death, 207
Loma Mountains, 5, *m* 6
London, conferences at, 235, 236
Lower Egypt, 47, *p* 48, 52
Lozi people, *m* 7
Lualaba River, *m* 6, 211, 239
Luba, *m* 7, *m* 149, 153, *p* 160, 166; kingdom of, founded, 160; society and government, 161; comparison with Lunda, 164
Lubumbashi, *p* 160, 276
Lugard, Sir Frederick, 225, 230, 254
Lumumba, Patrice, African political leader, 263, 273–275
Lunda, *m* 7, *m* 149, 153, 166; government of, 161–162; types of offices, 164
Luo (people of Kenya), *m* 7, 269
Luseng, Lunda king, 161
Luthuli, Chief Albert, 242, *p* 243, 315
Luxor, 49
Lwo, 132–133, 135, 136, *m* 149

Macro-Bantu, 121
Madagascar, *m* 6, 172, 195; Indian and Arab merchants in, 178; France's claims in, 224; achieves independence (1960), 264. *See also* Malagasy Republic
Maghreb, *m* 6, 72, 74, 75, *m* 84, 96
Magic, 38, 102. *See also* Diviner
Mahdi, 226 *f*, 240; defeat of British by, 225–226
Mai, 108, 109. *See also* Kingship.
Maji Maji, rebellion of, 230
Makonde people, *m* 7
Malagasy Republic, 120, 172, *m* 255, 262, 264. *See also* Madagascar
Malawi, 8, *m* 255, 266; inland water fishing in, *p* 131
Malayans, 172, 178
Malaysia, 122, 129 *f*, 175
Mali, ancient empire of, 81, 83, *m* 84, 92–100, 104, 105 (box), 107, 108, 110, 116, 201; definition of, 93 *f*; decline of, 99; modern republic of, *m* 255, 263
Mali Federation, 262

Malindi, *m* 84, 172, 176, 178
Malinke, *m* 7
Mamluks, 73, 74
Mandate system, 236, 246
Mande, 85
Mandingo, 27 (box), 92, 93, 99, 100, 104, 107, 116, 201
Mani-, significance of, 154 *f*
Manikabunga, 154 *f*, 156, 157
Manikongo, 154, 155, 156, 158, 159, 165
Manilumbu, 154 *f*
Mansur, al-, sultan of Morocco, 106
Manuel I, king of Potrugal, 157, 158, 159
Maps, 170, 207, 210, 236
Mapungubwe, 146
Marchand, Jean Baptiste, 221
Markets, *p* 94, 148, 150, 168, 194, 238
Marrakech, 75, *m* 84
Marriage, 36, 37
Martel, Charles, 69
Masai, *m* 7, *p* 26, 35; age groups among, 33 (box), 34; as cattle herders, 31, 32
Mashonaland, 140, 141, 146. *See also* Rhodesia; Zimbabwe; Shona
Masinissa, king of Numidia, 63
Mas'udi, al-, 129
Matadi, 5
Matope, king of the Karanga, 148, 150
Matrilineal society, 36, 161
Matrilineal succession, 86, 88
Mau Mau, 14, *p* 267, 267–269
Mauritania, *m* 70, 83, *m* 255, 259
Mauritius, 262
Mavura, ruler of Momomotapa, 151
Mbanza, *m* 149, 154, 158
Mbata, 154
Mbay, 162
Mbemba. *See* Affonso I
Mboya, Tom, 269
McKay, Claude, 181–182
Mecca, 67, 68, *p* 77, 95, 97, 98; Burton in, 208
Medina, 67, 68, 98
Mediterranean, *m* 6, *m* 70, 84; coast of, 16, 40, 56; cultures of, 60–66; "period," 66, 79
Memphis, 49, 52, *m* 70
Mende, *m* 7
Menelek, emperor of Ethiopia, 31
Menes, Egyptian ruler, 47

Merchants, European, 10; American, 10; of Songhai, 102; Indian, 170; Arab, 172, 174; Portuguese, 175
Merenra, pharaoh of Egypt, 50
Merina people, *m* 7
Meroë, 54–57, 58, 59, *m* 70, 79, 83, 122; as capital of Kush, *p* 55; culture of, 56–57; destruction of, 59, 122; iron industry of, 54–56, *p* 123; racial composition of, 56; trade, 56
Mesopotamia, 45, *m* 70, 72
Metalworking, 56, 83, 140
Middle East, 45, 67, 69, 73, 169, 178; African slaves in, 182, 183
Middle Kingdom, 50
Middlemen, 83, 115; Berbers as, *p* 62; in Ingombe Ilede, 141; in East Africa, 174
Migrations, of Bantu-speaking peoples, 121–127, 146, 164, 165; Cushites, 127; Hima, 131; Nilotes, 132–133; Shona and Sotho, 146
Ming dynasty (China), 171
Mining, 56, 127, 142, 165; by Sotho peoples, 140, 141; in Kongo kingdom, 158; effect of world prices on, 300
Missionaries, Portuguese, 151, 155, 158, 159–160, 177, 178; Arab, 172, 174, 195; slave traders opposed to, 185–186; in African interior, 194, 212–213; sufferings of, 213–214; schools of, 214; King Mutesa's treatment of, 215–216, and King Mwanga's, 217; rivalry among, 216, 217, 239; work of, evaluated, 239
Missions, 114, 215, 217, 230
Mobutu Sese Seko (Joseph), 274, 277, *p* 277, 303, 308
Mogadishu, *m* 84, 127, *m* 149, 171, 172, 178
Mohammed, 67–68, 67.*f*, 69, 73, 79, 83, 121
Mohammed, Askia, Songhai ruler. *See* Askia Mohammed I
Mojimba, Congolese king, 211
Mombasa, *m* 84, 127, 171, 172, 179, 195, 225; capture of, by Portuguese, 176; and Arabs, 178, 179
Monarchy, *p* 111, *p* 139; European, 170. *See also* Kingship
Mondlane, Eduardo, 280
Mongo peoples, 125
Mongols, 73, 95

Mongoloid race, *m* 7, 22, 24
Monomotapa, 130, 148–151, *m* 149, 165; Portuguese encroachment upon, 151, 165
Monsoon winds, 171–172
Moors, 77; in Spain, 169
Morocco, 61, 63, 72, 75, 79, 88, 106, 110, 202, 302; under France and Spain, 221; independence, 243, *m* 255; in Casablanca Bloc, 263
Moses, 67, 209
Moshoeshoe, Sotho ruler, 147, *p* 147
Mosques, at Fez, *p* 74; at Gao, 99; in Mali, *p* 103, in New Bussa, *p* 103
Mossi, *m* 7, 81, *m* 84, 101, 104, 105 (box), 107, 117, *m* 232
Motopo Hills, 146
"Mountains of the Moon," *m* 70, 202, 204
Mount Cameroon, *m* 6
Mount Darwin, 150
Mount Elgon, *m* 6, 131
Mount Kenya, *m* 6, *m* 232
Mount Kilimanjaro, 2, *m* 6, 202–203, *p* 203, *m* 232, 239
Mozambique, 148, *m* 149, 165; coastal plain of, 4 f, 8; language of, 28; state of, 127; towns of, 178; and Portuguese rule, 243, *m* 255, 301; independence movement in, 280–281
Mozambique Island, 175, 177
Mozambique Liberation Front, 280
Mpangu, 154
Mpanzu, Kongolese prince, 155–157
Mu'awiyah, 71
Mubende, 133
Murabitum, al-, 75
Murray, Mongo, 204
Musa, Mansa Gonga (or Kankan), 93, 95–99, 104, 116
Musawarat, *p* 55, 56
Muscat, *m* 84, 179
Music, *p* 111, 115
Musket, 170, 186
Muslim empire, *m* 70, 72, 79, *m* 84, 85, 157, 169
Muslim faith. *See* Islam
"Muslim period," 66
Muslims, 38, 68, 69, 71–79, 107, 177, 239; in Buganda, 215, 216, 217; in Sudan, 226. *See also* Islam; Religion
Mussolini, Benito, 235
Mutesa, king of Buganda, 211, 215, 216

Mutota, king of the Karanga, 148
Mwane Mtapa, meaning, 148. *See also* Monomotapa
Mwanga, king of Buganda, 217
Mwato Yamvo, 162

Nabib Desert, 41
Naga, 56
Nairobi, 268
Naivasha, Lake, 8
Namibia, 14, 243, *m* 255, 284
Nandi, *p* 135
Napata, 50, *m* 70
Napoleonic Wars, 192, 221
Narmer, Egyptian ruler, 46, 47, *p* 48
Natal (South Africa), 129, *m* 232; Boer Republic of, established, 222
National Congolese Movement (MNC), 273
Nationalism, 194; in Egypt, 225; emergence of, after World War I, 235–238, 240; African, spurred by Asian, 248; in Ghana, 252–254; in Madagascar, 264; in Congo, 272; in South Africa, 282
Nation-building, problems of, 289–315
Navigation, development of, 168, 169, 195; and monsoons, 171–172
Navigators, 168; Chinese, 170–171; Arab, 172; Portuguese, 154–155, 169, 171, 174–178, 195; Indian, 170, 195
Nazis, race theories of, 23, 244
Ndebele, *m* 7
Ndongo, 154 f
Negritude, 23
Negro Americans, 23, 24, 53, 181, 189; equal rights struggle of, 251
Negroid peoples, *m* 7, 22, 23, 24, 25, 121
Nehru, Jawaharlal, 247
Neocolonialism, 302, 313–314
Neolithic period, 21
New Kingdom (Egypt), 50, 51, 54, 78
Newspapers, 251
Ngami, Lake, 146, 204, *m* 232
Ngola, ruler of Ndongo, 154 f
Ngoni, 140, 152, *p* 152, 165
Niani, 93, 95, 99
Nicaea, council at, 65, 66
Niger-Congo language group, 25, 121
Nigeria, 5, 28, 82, 101, 119, 122, 186, *m* 233, 298, 302; tribes of, 30; for-

est of, 112; colonial powers dispute over, 221; British control of, 228–230, 240; major regions of, 254; independence, 254, *m* 255, 256, 258; civil war, *p* 257, 258, 305

Niger, Republic of, *m* 255, 259, 262

Niger River, 5, *m* 6, 40, 61, *m* 70, 82, 83, 92, 101, 102, 110, 204, 238; Basin, 4, 25; Delta, 4 *f*; Mungo Park reaches, 200, 239

Nile River, 5, *m* 6, 25, 40, 43, *m* 70, 107; cataracts, 5, 10, 50, 52, *m* 70; Basin, 4; branches of, 5; Delta, 47; overflowing of, 44, 47, 78; sources of, 207–213, 238, 239; international agreements about, 219; railroad constructed along, 226

Nile River Valley, 16, 43, 44, 45, *m* 70, 78, 130, 132

Nilotes, 31, *p* 135, *m* 149; influence of, on Bantu culture, 130–131, 165; pastoral economy of, 132; invade Uganda, 132–133, *m* 149 (inset); in southern Kenya, 132, 135

Nkrumah, Kwame, *p* 247; quoted, 245, 248; Gandhi's influence on, 248; Pan Africanism of, 253, 309; death, 254; as leader of nationalists, 253; as president of Ghana, 253–254, 263

Noba, 58

Nobel Peace Prize, 242, 315

Noblemen, 112

Nok, *m* 70; culture of, 82

Nomads, 61, 66, 83, 91, 101; Bushman, 125; Hima, 131; Nilotes, 132

Nomes, 49

North Africa, 8, 60, 61, 63–66, 78, 79, 83, 89, 107, 168; languages of, 28; Muslims in, 69, 169; slaves in, 182, 183; French in, 219, 221; and independence, 243

North Atlantic Treaty Organization (NATO), 281, 314

Northern Rhodesia, 224, *m* 233, 265, 266. *See also* Zambia

Ntemi, 138

Nuba people, *m* 7

Nubia, 45, 49, 50, 54, *m* 70, 78, 126; people of, *p* 51

Nuclear weapons, in Sahara, 263

Numidia, 61, *m* 70

Nyahuma, king of Monomotapa, 150

Nyamwezi, *m* 7, 208

Nyasa, Lake, *m* 6, 8, 152, *m* 232

Nyasaland, *m* 233, 265, 266. *See also* Malawi

Nyerere, Julius, *p* 268, 269, 270, 272, 296, 303, 309

Nyoro, 133. *See also* Bunyoro

Nzinga Kuwu, king of Kongo, 154, 155, 156

Oba, 112, *p* 113

Obote, Milton, 270, 272

OCAM. *See* Organisation Commune Africaine et Malagâche

Occupations, types of, 31, 41

Oduduwa (Yoruba god), 112

Old Arabic, 67

Old Kingdom (Egypt), 49

Oliver, Roland, 47 *f*, 98 *f*, 119, 120 *f*, 133

"Ol Morrani," 33 (box), 34

Oman, *m* 84, 179, 180, 195; slavery in, 184; British relations with, 192

Omari, al-, Arab scholar, 95

Oni, 112

Oral traditions, 93, 101, 120; of Kongo, 158–159. *See also* Legends

Orange Free State, 222

Orange River, *m* 6, 40, 222, 224, *m* 232

Organisation Commune Africaine et Malagâche (OCAM), 262, 309

Organization of African Unity (OAU), 238, 263, 309, 312

Orun, 112

Osiris, Egyptian deity, 48, 49

Oswell, William, 204

Othman, 71

Ottoman Empire, 74, 76, 108

"Outlanders," 224

Ovambo, *m* 7

Oyo, 107, 112, 114, 115, 117

Paintings, 45, *p* 311. *See also* Rock paintings; Art

Palm oil, 244, 256

Pan Africanism, 253

Pangas, 268

Paris, Treaty of, 221; conference of, 236

Park, Mungo, 200, 202, 203, 239

Partitioning of Africa, 198, 219–234, 235; artificial boundaries caused by, 236

Patrilineal society, 36; of Luba, 161, 166
Peace Corps, 314
Pemba, 127, 184
Peoples of Africa, *m* 7, 25–39. *See also names of particular peoples*
Pepi II, pharaoh of Egypt, 49
Persian Gulf, *m* 84, 179, 195
Persians, 25, 52, 79, 127; African slaves used by, 172, 182
Pharaohs, 46, 50, 52; power of, 48, 49
Phoenicia, 52, 60, 61, 63, *m* 70
Piankhi, king of Kush, 52
Pilgrimage, to Mecca. *See* Hajj; Holy cities of Islam
Plateau, 4, *m* 6, 8, 11, 40, 165; Ethiopian, 13; of Mashonaland, 141, 142, 165
Political parties, 305–306
Polo, Marco, 170
Polytheism, 67. *See also* Religion
Po Pa Li, 170.ˈ *See also* Chinese
Population, 12, 15, 16, 100; cities with largest, *c* 16; effect of agricultural revolution on, 44, 45, 81, 110; pressure of, as cause of migration, 124; increase of, in early Uganda, 130; diffusion of, in Indian Ocean basin, 172; depletion of, by slave trade, 187, *c* 190; of French West Africa, 221; nations with largest, 308
Ports, *p* 3, *p* 64, 28, 148, 170, *m* 232; of East Africa, 172, 176, 177, 180
Portugal, 100, 156, 169, 170, 174, 237, 245; king of, 151, 155, 176; Kongolese in, 155; African empire of, 174–180, 239, 243, 279; sea power of, 178; under Spanish rule, 179; influence of, evaluated, 179–180; ends slave trade, 192. *See also* Portuguese
Portuguese Guinea. *See* Guinea-Bissau
Portuguese, the, in Africa, 99, 148, 165; records of, 148; and Monomotapa, 150–152, 165; and Kongo, 153–159, 166; in Angola, 154 *f*; in Ethiopia, 174, 177; in West Africa, 175; and Mozambique, 175, 176, 178, 280; in Indian Ocean, 179; in Arabia, 179, 180; in East Africa, 178, 195; and slave trade, 185; commercial empire of, 178, 191, 195. *See also* Portugal
Pottery, 82, 126, 127, 132; "stamped ware," 140

Poverty, 289, 293, 294
Prester John, 155, 157, 166, 174, 175
Pretoria, *m* 233; Treaty of, 222
Primogeniture, 102, 112
Proconsul, 20
Property rights, 102
"Protectorate," British, in Uganda, 136; in Zanzibar, 225; in Kenya, 225; in Egypt, 225, 240; in Nigeria, 228
Protestants, 194, 213, 215, 216, 217, 218, 239. *See also* Roman Catholics; Christians; Religion; Missionaries
Provinces, 93, 114; in Mali, 97
Ptolemies, 53, 56, 57. *See also* Egypt
Ptolemy, Claudius, 202
Punt, 51, *m* 70
Pygmies, *m* 7, 19, 31, 50, *p* 124; territory of, occupied by Bantu, 124, 165
Pyramid(s), 43, *p* 46, 47

Queen mother, 155, 164

Rabai, 203
Rabat, 75, *m* 84
Race(s), *m* 7; meaning of, 22–25, *p* 26; theory of origins of, 15. *See also names of particular racial groups*
Race relations, 22, 23, 24, 312–313
Racial differences, 15, 22, 24; theories of, 23, 24, 189, 196, 244
Radio broadcasts, 251
Radiocarbon analysis, 119, 141
Radium, 244
Railroads, 28, 225, 226, 249, 290
Rainfall, 10, 11, 12, 13, 16; in Uganda, 130
Rain forest(s), 11, 13, 19, 31, 50
Rameses XI, pharaoh of Egypt, 52
Rassemblement Démocratique Africaine (RDA), 261
Raw materials, 174, 194; importance of, in World War II, 244
Re, Egyptian sun god, 48
Rebmann, Johann, 2, 202–203, 239
Red Sea, *m* 6, 8, 14, 51, 56, *m* 70, 221; African towns along, 178
Regimento, 158
Religion, traditional African, 38, 40, 41; in ancient Egypt, 48–49; in

Kush, 56; in Ghana, 91; in Mali, 93; in Songhai, 102; in Guinea states, 115; in Kongo, 155; Christian, 65–66, 114, 155–157, 159–160; Islamic, 67–69, 91, 109, 168, 172; conflicts over, 155–157; revival of, in Europe, 194; political rivalry and, 215–216

"Revolution of rising expectations," 289

Revolutionary War, 192, 227

Rhodes, Cecil, 222, 224, 240, 265

Rhodesia, Republic of (formerly Southern Rhodesia), 13, 14, 19, 119, 126, 130, 133 f, 140, 142, 150, m 255, 312; independence declared, 243, 266, 281; liberation movement in, 282. *See also* Zimbabwe

Ribat, 74

Rift Valley, m 6, 8, 40

Rio Muni, m 233

Rituals, 38, 39, 41, 138, 313 (box)

Rivalry, among colonial powers, 194, 196, 221, 239–240; among religions, 215–216, 217, 239

Rivers, 4, m 6, 40, 170; basins, 4; systems, 40. *See also names of particular rivers*

Rock paintings, p 21, m 70; Berber, 61; Bushman, p 125, 125–126

Roman Catholics, 155, 156, 177, 178, 194, 215, 216, 239; martyrs, 217, 218. *See also* Christians; Missionaries

Roman Empire, 53, 60, 62–66, 69, m 70, 71, 72, 162; ruins of, p 64; African slaves in, 182

Roosevelt, Franklin Delano, 242

Rowlands, John. *See* Stanley, Henry M.

Royal Geographic Society, 205, 208

Royal Niger Company, 228

Rozwi, 148, 151, 152, 165

Rubber trees, 234

Rudolf, Lake, m 6, 8

Rukidi, Isingoma Mpuga, 133, 134

Rumfa, Mohammed, Kano ruler, 110

Ruanda-Urundi, Belgian mandate, 236. *See also* Rwanda; Burundi

Rural culture, types of, 18

Rural development, 292–293

Ruwenzori Mountains, m 6, 130

Rwanda, 32, 131, 138, m 149, 165, m 255, 262; Bantu groups settle, 126; Hima in, 133; monarchy ended, 139

Saba, m 7

Sabaean script, 57

Sadat, Anwar, 249

Sahara Desert, 5, m 6, 10, p 21, 29, 60, 81, 83, m 84, 88, p 90, 106, 108; size of, 8, 11, 14

Saheli, es-, 99

Said, Seyyid, sultan of Oman, 192

Sailors. *See* Navigators

Sais, 52

Sakura, 95

Saladin, 73

Salisbury, p 120

Salt, 85, 88, p 90, 91, 96, 106, 107, 141; deposits, m 70

Samburu, p 134

Sané, 101

Sankore, 99

São Salvador, 154

São Tomé, m 149, 157

Sardinia, 72

Savannah, 11, 13, 19, 20, 41, 81, 110, 127

Schools. *See* Education

"Scramble for Africa," 169, 235, 239, 240

Sculpture, 57, p 298; of Nubia, p 51; of Meroë, 56; of Benin, p 113; of Guinea, 115

Seafarers. *See* Navigators

Sefuwa, dynasty, 107, 109, 117

Segu, 200

Selassie, Haile, 235, p 237

Semakokiro, Buganda ruler, 135–136

Semitic languages, 27

Sena, 151

Senegal, 28, 83, 88, 221, 238, m 255, 259, 263; River, m 6, m 70, 74, 83, 89, 175

Settlers, 14, 19, 130; English, 34, 265; of European origin, 22, 224, 225; German, 230; Afrikaaner, 282; in Kenya Highlands, 13, 168

Shana, 37

Shango, Oyo deity, 112

Sheba, m 70; queen of, p 57

Shi'ites, 71, 72, 73

Shire River, p 131

Shona, m 7, 140, 143, 145, 146–148, 165

Sidamo, 126, m 149

Sierra Leone, 5, m 233, m 255, 300, 308; British control of, 227, 240; independence achieved in, 258–259

Sinai Peninsula, 45
Sisse, 83
Skin color, development of, 15, 22
Slave Coast, 110 *f*
Slave market, 88, 168, 182, 184, 188, 192, 213
Slave-raiding, *p* 183, 183–184, 186, 188, 212
Slavery, 41, 108, 157, 158, 182, 183; African and European concepts of, compared, 183; British abolish in South Africa, 222
Slaves, 10, 72, 73, 114, 154, 158, 168, 169, 172, 181, *p* 187; in India and the East, 172, 182; Arab interest in, 174; transported by Portuguese, 175; rebellion of, in India, 182; in ancient Rome and Greece, 182; treatment of, 182–183, 188, 195; demand for, 182–183, 184; estimated numbers of, 187, *c* 190; in Freetown, 227; white, 185. *See also* Slavery; Slave trade
Slave trade, 114, 115, 117, 168, 185–186, 95, 208; in Kongo, 157, 159, 166; in India, 175, 192; in Portuguese-held East Africa, 178, 195; promotion of, by Arabs of East Africa, 180, 195, 196; crippling effect of, 181–190, *c* 190, 195; manpower lost in *c* 190; abolition of, 188, 192; impact of, on race relalations, 189; suppression of, 192, *p* 193, 196; in Uganda, 216–217; in West Africa, 227; African co-operation in, 186, 227
Social organization, 29, 37, 41, 130; in early Uganda, 132; of Kongo, 154–155; among Luba, 161; Lunda, 162–164; change in, 304–305
Sofala, 127, 129, 142, 148, *m* 149, 150; falls to Portuguese, 176
Soils, 13, 15, 6, 44, 45
Sokoto, *m* 84, 110
Solomon, king of Israel, *p* 57
Somalia (Somali Republic), 14, 51, 127, 171, 208, 231, 240, *m* 255, 272; national consciousness in, 30
Somaliland, 231
Somali people, *m* 7, 27
Somba people, *p* 35
Songhai, *m* 7, 62, 81, 99, 105 (box), 107, 108, 110; empire of, *m* 84, 100–106, 116–17

Soninke people, *m* 7, 83, 85, 91, 116
Sorcery, 27 (box), 39, 102
Sorghum, 45, 96, 122, 126, *p* 128
Sotho, *m* 7, 140, 146, 147, *p* 147, 165
Soudan, *m* 233, 259, 262. *See also* Mali
South Africa, Republic of, 11, 13 (climate), 14, 19; apartheid in, 24, 282; European population of, 28; Bantu-speaking groups in, 121; Bushmen in, 146; and South-West Africa, 243, 284; "bantustans" in, 283; intransigence of, 282–284
South African Republic, 222, 224
Southern Rodesia, 265. *See also* Rhodesia, Republic of
South-West Africa, under German rule, 239, 240; "mandated" to Union of South Africa, 236; Republic of South Africa holds, 243. *See also* Namibia
South-West African People's Organization, 284
Soviet Union, supports African liberation in UN, 248; technical assistance from, 249, 259, 301; and Congo crisis, 273
Spain, 60 *f*, 62, 63, 69, *m* 70, 72, 75, 76, 77, 88, 89, 99, 170, 221, 239; Moorish rule ended in, 169; and slave trade, 192, 227; African colonies of, 239, 243
Spaniards, 25, 170, 185
Spanish Morocco, *m* 233
Spanish Sahara, 243, *m* 255
Speke, John Hanning, 208–210, 238, 239; names Lake Victoria, 209
Spices, trade in, 175–176
"Spiritual double," 112
"Stamped Ware" peoples, 140
Stanley Falls, *m* 6, 211
Stanley, Henry M., 205–207, 210–213, 221, 234, 239
Stanley Pool, 221, *m* 232
Stanleyville. *See* Kisangani
Stone buildings, 127, 140, 141, 165; ruins of, 56, 142, *p* 144; culture of, 146–157; Rozwi erect, 152
Stoneware, 172
Strait of Gibraltar, *m* 70
Strandes, Justus, 176 *f*
Subsistence economy, 15, 18
Successor states, 89, 92
Sudan, 25, *m* 6, 7, 41, 65, 67, 81, 82, 83, 85, 104, 106, 107, 110, 124;

defined, 28; Nilotes of southeastern, 31

Sudan, Republic of, 5, 122, *m* 255, 272; language of, 25, 28; Anglo-Egyptian, 225–226, 231, 240; independence granted to (1956), 243; civil war in, 305

Sudanese (or Sudanic) kingdoms, *m* 84, 110, 124. *See also* Ghana; Mali; Songhai; Kanem-Bornu

Sudanic language group, 25

Sudd, *m* 6, *m* 84

Suez Canal, *m* 6, 74, 225, *m* 232, 240

Sultan, 73, 76, 96, 98, 106, 108; of Istanbul, 108; of Sokoto, 110; of Cameroon, *p* 111; of Kilwa, 176; of Oman, 180; of Zanzibar, 213, 231; of Turkey, 225

Sumanguru, Susu king, 92–93, 116

Sundiata, ruler of Mali, 92–95, 100, 104, 116

Sunni Ali. *See* Ali, Sunni

Sunnis, 71, 102

Susu (city), 92

Sussu, 93

Swahili, 28, 120, 121–122, 172, 179; East African communities of, 180, 183

Swazi, *m* 7, *p* 152

Swaziland, *p* 152, *m* 233, *m* 255; achieves independence (1968), 152

Syria, 66, 71, 72, 73

Tabora, 208, 209, *m* 232

Taghaza, *m* 84, 96, 104, 106

Tana, Lake, 5, *m* 6, 8, *m* 70, 200

Tanganyika, German colony, 230, 240; mandated to Britain and Belgium, 236; as British trust territory, 266; achieves independence (1961), 269. *See also* Tanzania

Tanganyika, Lake, *m* 6, 8, 160, 166, 209, 211, *m* 232

Tanganyika African National Union (TANU), 269

Tangier, 2

Tanzania, 2, 8, 19, 27, 28, 126, 127, 131, 165, 208, 210, 249, 284, 296, 300, 303; tribes in, 30; Masai pastoralists of, 31; political entities in, 138; under German authority, 217, 224–225; independence, *m* 255, 269; merger of Tanganyika and Zan-zibar, 269; relations with Uganda, 270; elections in, 306

Tanzania Broadcasting Company, 251

Tariffs, 88

Taro, 96

Taxes, 88, 92, 96, 108, 116, 162, 234, 302

Technical assistance, 158, 248, 249

Technical skills, 290, *p* 290

Teda, *m* 7

Tekrur, *m* 84, 88, 92, 93, 95, 104

Temne, *m* 7, 27, 227

Tenkaminen, emperor of Ghana, 88, 91, 116

Territory, categories of, in Mali, 97; expansion of, in Buganda, 136, *m* 149; Lunda, 162

Tete, 151, *m* 232

Textiles, 148. *See also* Cloth

Thant, U, UN Secretary General, 276

Thebes, 49, 52, *m* 70

Thutmose I, 50

Tibesti Mountains, *m* 6, *m* 70

Tigris-Euphrates Delta, 182

Timbuktu, 5, *m* 84, 99, 101, 102, 104, 106, 107, 200, *m* 232, 201 (box), 202, 204

Timgad, 63, *m* 70

Tipaza, 63, *m* 70

Tiv, *m* 7

Tlemcen, 75, *m* 84

Tobacco, 185

Togo (or Togoland), *m* 233; under German rule, 230, 240; mandated to France and Britain, 236, 240, 263, independent, *m* 255, 263

Tombs, 45, 60, 100, 162

Tools, 15, 20, 21, 44, 81, 88, *p* 123; of Cushites, 126

Toro, *m* 149

Torwa, 150

Touré, Sékou, prime minister of Guinea, 260; quoted, 312

Tours, France, 69

Towns, 45, 59, 72; conflict of, with rural areas, 100, 104, 116

Trade, in early sudan, 17; in early Egypt, 45; trans-Saharan, 64–65; in Ghana, 82, 83, 85, 88–89; in Mali, 96; Kanem, 107; in Central Africa, 130; of Buganda, 135; of East Coast, 148, 150, 183; Kongolese, 157, 159; with people of Asia, 171, 178; East African interior, 174; West African

coastal, 175; as cause of international rivalry, 178; missionaries encourage, 217. *See also* Commerce; International trade
Trade centers, *p* 17, 57, *m* 84, 85, 88, 148, 150, 151, 175
Trade routes, 60, 61, *m* 70, *m* 84, 91, 109, 117, 148; all-water, to East, 169, 175
Traders, 59, 102, 110 (*f*), 132, 142, 170; on Zambezi, 141, 150; Arab, in spread of Muslim religion, 72; in East Africa, 174
Trading posts, 60, 60 *f*, 127, 150, 165, 179, 234
Traditions, 95, 101, 148, 158, 238. *See also* Oral traditions
Transportation, problems of, 290
Transvaal, 146, 222, 224
Travel, 10, 47
Treaties, 151, 192, 222, 224, 228, 230, 234, 235
Tribe, *m* 7, 25, 29, 30, 34, 37, 41
Tribute, 88, *p* 152, 162, 176
Tripoli, 69, *m* 84, 107, 108, 109, *m* 232
Trojans, 93
Tropical laterite, 13
Tropical rain forest, 31. *See also* Rain forest(s)
Trotha, Adolf von, 230
Trusteeship Council (UN), 246, 248
Trust Territories, 263, 267
Tshombe, Moïse, 273, 274, 275, 276, 277, 312
Tsirinana, Philibert, 264
Tswana, *m* 7. *See also* Botswana
Tuaregs, *m* 7, 61, 74, 75, 89, *p* 90, 99, 101, 102, 104, 106, 109, 117, 201. *See also* Berbers
Tumart, Ibn, 75
Tumba, Lake, 4
Tunis, *m* 84, 109, *m* 232
Tunisia, 61, 63, 69, *m* 70, 72, 75, 78, 79, 302; Almohad rule of, 75; as French "protectorate," 221; independence, 243, *m* 255
Turé, Mohammad, 102. *See also* Askia Mohammed I
Turkey, 79, 108, 182, 225, 231, 240
Tutsi, *m* 7, 32, 138, 139, *p* 139, *m* 149, 305
Twa, *p* 124. *See also* Pygmies
Tyre, 60

Ubangi River, 4, *m* 6
Ubangi-Shari, 260
Uganda, 8, 35, 120, 130–136, 200, 209, 210, *m* 233, 300, 314; languages of, 28; Bantu-speaking groups settle, 126, 127, 130, 165; early Bantu government in, 131; Bito-ruled states in, 133; "protectorate" of, 136; missionaries in, 215–217; German claims to, 225; kabaka of, leads Africa's opposition to East African Federation, 266; independence, *m* 255, 270; under Amin, 270–271, 292
Uganda Railway, 225
Uhuru, 240
Ujiji, 205, 206, *m* 232
Ukerewe, Lake, 209. *See also* Victoria, Lake
Uli, Mansa, 95
Umayyad, 71, 72
Umma, 74
Unemployment, 298
Union of South Africa, 224, 236, 240. *See also* South Africa, Republic of
United Gold Coast Convention (UGCC), 253
United Nations, and decolonization, 246, 247; trusteeships of, 246; and Congo, 273, 274, 275, 276, 277, 312; promotion of development by, 301
United States, 11, 14, 29, 36, 53, 181; at Berlin Conference (1885), 219; African raw materials received by, 244; race relations in, 249; relations with Uganda, 271; Congo policy of, 273, 274, 276, 277; and Rhodesia, 281; aid to Africa, 302; Africans' feelings toward, 314
University of Sankore, 99
Upper Volta, 105 (box), 259, 263, 300
Uranium, 244

Vaal River, *m* 232
"Valley Ruins," 143, 145, 146
Vandals, 66, 69
Vansina, Jan, 153
Vassals, 133, 148, 166; revolt of, against Monomotapa, 151
Vegetation, *m* 6, 11–14
Veld, 13, 265
Venda, 146
Versailles, Treaty of, 235

Victoria, 209, 210; Falls, *m* 6, 141, *m* 149, *p* 199, 205, 239; Lake, *m* 6, 8, 130, 134, 136, 200, 209, 225, *m* 232
Village(s), 36, 45, 47; life of, in early Zimbabwe, 141, 147; Luba, 161; Lunda, 162; and slave-raiding, 183
Vizier, 73, 76 (box)
Volta Dam, *m* 6
Volta River, *m* 6, 40
Volta River Valley, 110
Voodoo, 38; defined, 27 (box)
Vumba, 127

Wagadu, 85
Wagadu-Bida, 89
Wagadugu, 105 (box)
Wak-Wak, 129
Waklimi, Zanj rulers, 129
Walata, *m* 70, 83, 93 *f*
Walvis Bay, *m* 233
Wangara, *m* 70, 85, 96
Warriors, 18, *p* 135, *p* 152, 211
Water, *p* 12, 16, *p* 131, 226; power, potential of, *c* 9; scarcity of, 11; storage, 57
Watusi, 32 *f*, 138. *See also* Tutsi
Wealth, differences in, 45
Weapons, 81, 88, 93, *p* 123, 130, 169, 235; nuclear, 263
Wene, Manikongo, 153–154
West Africa, *p* 3, 14, 28, 79, 81, 82, 89, 92, 93, 100, 106, 107, 109, 110, 210; pastoral societies of, 31; great kingdoms of, 65, 79, 81–117; exploration of, 170, 195; states of, and slave trade, 186–187, 227–230; British holdings in, 227–228, 230, 240; interior of, dominated by France, 221; chiefs of, and Germany's aims, 230
Western sudan, 81, 98, 99, 104, 108, 112
White Highlands, 13, 225. *See also* Kenya Highlands
White Nile, 5, *m* 6, 200, 207, 210, *m* 232
Wiedner, Donald L., quoted, 186–187
Wilhelm II, German kaiser, 224
Wilson, Woodrow, 235
Winds, 11, 171; monsoon, 171–172
Witchcraft, 93, 102
Witch doctors, 39

Wolof, *m* 7, 27 (box)
Women, role of, 164, *p* 297; education of, 298. *See also* Matrilineal society
World War I, 235, 240
World War II, 240, 242, 243–245, 248; African contributions to Allied victory in, 243–244, *p* 245
Writing, systems of, 43, 56, 172; missionary contributions to, 214

Xosa, *m* 7

Yaav Naweej I, 161. *See also* Mwato Yamvo
Yam, 27 (box), 96, 110, 122
Yasin, Abdullah ibn, 74, 75, 89
Yatenga, 105 (box)
Yemen, *m* 84
Yoruba, *m* 7, *m* 84, 110, 112, 114, 256

Zaire, 5, 8, 14, 31, 59, 125, 153 *f*, 162, *m* 255, 263, 278, 284, 303, 305. *See also* Belgian Congo; Congo (Kinshasa)
Zaire River, 278. *See also* Congo River
Zambezi River, *m* 6, 40, 119, 140, 141, 146, 148, 165, 177, 204, 219, *m* 232, 239
Zambezi River Valley, 122, 126, 141
Zambia, 8, 13, 14, 249, 282, 284, 300; languages of, 28, 119, 141, 145, 164, 207, 224, 249, 272; independence, 251, *m* 255, 266
Zambia African National Congress, 266
Zande people, *m* 7
Zanj, empire of, *m* 84, 127–129, *m* 149, 165
Zanzibar, 127, *p* 180, 184, 203, 212, 213, *m* 233; British protectorate over, 225, 231; joins with Tanganyika to form Tanzania (1964), 269
Zenata, 66, 78
Zimbabwe, 119, 140–146, 165, 176; first (Sotho) period, 146; second (Shona) period, 147–148; liberation movements, 282. *See also* Great Zimbabwe
Zinder, *m* 233
Zulu, *m* 7, 145, 146, 152, 165
Zululand, *m* 149